TINTAWN AND BINDER TWINE

Quality is a product of human endeavour which thrives best when the spirit is free.

Eric Rigby-Jones

TINTAWN AND BINDER TWINE

The STORY of ERIC RIGBY-JONES and IRISH ROPES

JOHN RIGBY-JONES

FONTHILL

Fonthill Media Language Policy

Fonthill Media publishes in the international English language market. One language edition is published worldwide. As there are minor differences in spelling and presentation, especially with regard to American English and British English, a policy is necessary to define which form of English to use. The Fonthill Policy is to use the form of English native to the author. John Rigby-Jones was born and educated in the United Kingdom; therefore British English has been adopted in this publication.

Fonthill Media Limited
Fonthill Media LLC
www.fonthillmedia.com
office@fonthillmedia.com

First published in the United Kingdom and the United States of America 2020

British Library Cataloguing in Publication Data:
A catalogue record for this book is available from the British Library

Copyright © John Rigby-Jones 2020

ISBN 978-1-78155-791-4

Typeset in 10.5 pt on 13pt Sabon
Printed and bound in England

Acknowledgements

This book started life as a final chapter for my earlier book, *Best Love to All*, about my grandfather's experiences as a young officer on the Western Front. However, as I researched more of his extraordinary life after the war, it gradually grew to become a book in its own right. For that, I am indebted to many people and organisations who have helped me uncover a story that has not been told before.

I am grateful to all those archives, museums, and data repositories that I have visited or that have made their documents available online—in particular, the National Archives, the National Archives of Ireland, and the Liddell Hart Centre for Military Archives at King's College, London. Their staff have been invariably polite and helpful, and the best part of this adventure has been to see and touch original documents and to find out new and exciting things. I must also thank all those other national and governmental organisations, including the UK Parliament and the Houses of the Oireachtas, which have granted an open licence for the use of their information. I have made good use of online newspaper archives, especially those of *The Times* and *Irish Times*, and I have been given particular help on Guy Rigby-Jones's wartime service by two American archives, the National Archives and Records Administration in Washington, DC, and the Mahn Center for Archives and Special Collections at Ohio University Libraries.

My thanks also go to the following individuals who have provided valuable information and photographs: Benny Maxwell, Deaglan de Paor, Mary Ryan O'Shea, and, especially, the redoubtable Pat Tinsley from Newbridge, as well as the many others who retain close personal and family ties with Irish Ropes; Eoin McVey and the *Irish Times*; Vivian Landon, the former chairman of Wigglesworths, who provided much needed help and direction at an early stage of this project and allowed me to get an invaluable insight into the life of Alfred

Wigglesworth and his company; Ian Murray for his 'Feat of Arms' website and comprehensive research into Operation Ladbroke; Capt. Michiel Tattersall for sparing his time to show me round the Graeme Warrack building at the barracks of the Royal Netherlands Marechaussee in Apeldoorn; Alistair Proctor for sharing the story of his father's escape from the Curragh and Irene Robertson at the Alyth Family History Project for putting me in touch with him; Geoffrey Holland for permission to use the drawing of the Tafelberg Hotel by his uncle, Reg Curtis; and Allan Esler Smith for permission to use a still from the film, *Theirs is the Glory*, which was directed by his uncle, Brian Desmond Hurst. I would also like to thank Christy Moore for allowing me to use lines from his song 'Lily', from his 2016 album of the same name, which evokes his clear memories of growing up in Newbridge.

Among members of my family, I must thank my father, Peter, who died in 2006, for his painstaking work on our family tree and for preserving an indispensable collection of family letters, photographs, and documents, and my aunt, Ann, for sharing her memories of Ireland and growing up at Morristown. Tim Rigby-Jones and Daniel Forshaw also merit a mention in dispatches. Above all, I am eternally grateful to my wife, Fran, who has been a constant support throughout my time researching and writing this book. Without her, I would be lost.

Many other people have also helped me—and I apologise for not mentioning them by name—but, as is customary on the occasions, I must make it clear that the responsibility for any factual inaccuracies and errors in the text are mine and mine alone.

This book is further evidence that relations between the two islands of the British Isles have rarely been easy in the hundred years since Irish independence. Sadly, I am writing at a time when borders and tariffs, and in particular those between Ireland and the UK, are again grabbing headlines and when British and European politicians have yet to resolve the complexities of the UK's unfortunate exit from the European Union and the so-called Irish backstop. When it is all over, I would like to think that the island of Ireland will still be at peace and that I will still be proud to call myself a citizen of both the UK and Europe.

CONTENTS

Acknowledgements   5

  1   Ormskirk, 1919–1930   9
  2   Ireland, 1919–1933   21
  3   The Founding of Irish Ropes, 1930–1934   36
  4   Sisal   54
  5   Newbridge, 1935–1939   73
  6   Knuckling Down, 1939   96
  7   Preparing to Fight, 1940   108
  8   Feeling the Pinch, 1941   126
  9   Facing Disaster, 1942   148
 10   A Family at War, 1942–1943   170
 11   Pulling Through, 1943–1945   194
 12   A Family at War, 1944–1945   210
 13   A Problem of Succession   227
 14   The Lifting of the Clouds, 1945–1948   249
 15   A Triumph of Brain and Effort, 1949–1952   268
 16   Michael, 1952–1972   288
 17   The End of the Ropes   317

Appendix: The Twelve Irish Business Leaders who died in
        the Staines Air Crash, 18 June 1972   328
Endnotes   331
Bibliography   347

1
Ormskirk, 1919–1930

Messrs H. and J. Jones and Company Ltd, the twine and cordage manufacturers, today complete a century in business in Liverpool. We congratulate the firm on their long and worthy record of a hundred years and especially the present management for their sound enterprise in attaining a position in the trade hitherto unprecedented in the history of the company. May their prosperity be long continued.[1]

Twenty-one-year-old Acting Captain Eric Rigby-Jones left Belgium for home on 30 January 1919. The following day, after three years' military service, he was formally discharged from the Territorial Force at Prees Heath Camp in Shropshire. His pay was stopped immediately, but he was allowed to wear his uniform for another week. He was lucky to be one of the first officers in his battalion to be demobilised. A week earlier, his father had sent him the required employment certificate that confirmed that he had a job waiting for him in his family's rope business in Liverpool and Ormskirk. He had been appointed a director of H. and J. Jones on his birthday two months before the Armistice, a week before he was presented with his Military Cross (MC) and bar by the king at Buckingham Palace. Once back home in Ormskirk, he would be able to start his life again. He had left school at the age of sixteen in 1914, a week before the outbreak of war, and he had then served an apprenticeship in Liverpool for a year before deciding that he had to join up. He was still six weeks short of his eighteenth birthday when he received his commission as a second lieutenant in the Liverpool Rifles, 6th Battalion, King's Liverpool Regiment.

Eric was returning to a country that was undergoing significant social change. It would take time for it to come to terms with the war and adjust to normal life again. The economy was in a precarious state; industry had to revert to peacetime production; almost 3 million people had worked in the munitions industry during the war; and almost 4 million were still serving in the armed forces at the time of the Armistice—they would have to be brought home and found employment in a 'land fit for heroes'. For the many thousands who had severe physical or psychological injuries, it would be almost impossible to find a job. A quarter of the population would be laid low by the influenza pandemic in 1918 and 1919, and more than 200,000 would die. Meanwhile, women had become more confident and independent. During the four years of war, they had done many of the jobs that had previously been reserved for men. Those over thirty had been able to vote for the first time in the general election at the end of 1918. The courts would be unable to cope when the divorce rate trebled in the year after the Armistice. The death toll from the war meant that by 1921, women outnumbered men by eleven to ten. The resulting 1.7 million 'surplus' women—a generation of spinsters for whom there were not enough husbands to go around—had to make their own way in the world. The old Edwardian class system in which everyone knew their place was crumbling. A disproportionate number of young officers had been killed, the shared experience of officers and men in the trenches had proved a great leveller, and the prospect of a life of service in a grand house no longer seemed attractive to the working man and woman even when its owner could still afford servants. In the 1918 General Election, the Labour party, which championed workers' rights and sought to nationalise the coal mines and other essential industries, increased its share of the vote from 7 to 22 per cent; in 1922, it would increase it again, to 30 per cent; and in 1924, Ramsay MacDonald would become the first Labour prime minister, albeit at the head of a minority government that was in power for less than a year. Those who looked overseas saw communism in Russia, a breakdown of law and order in Ireland, and the prospect of social and economic collapse in Germany even before the Allies' imposition of punitive reparations under the Treaty of Versailles.

Although the returning soldiers could never forget what they had been through, they usually preferred to stay silent about the horrors that they thought could only be understood by those who had experienced them for themselves. Coming to terms with why they had been spared when so many of their comrades had been killed or maimed was a burden that many would take to their graves. Nor was there any easy closure for those who had lost loved ones. So many had died and in such horrendous circumstances that it was impossible to find and identify, let alone repatriate, all their bodies for burial. It was decided that they should remain where they fell. The Commonwealth War Graves Commission was established in 1917 and still looks after the graves and memorials of more than a million British and imperial servicemen who gave their lives in the war. Only half of them have identified graves, a sixth have unidentified graves, and a third have no graves at all.

It would take time to establish the national rites of remembrance. At 11 a.m. on 11 November 1919, the country observed two minutes' silence for the first time to remember the dead. Everything came to a standstill for the Great Silence.

Trading on the stock exchange was suspended, trains were halted, and cars and horses were pulled up in the street as everyone stood to attention after the firing of maroons. It would be another year before the body of the unknown soldier was buried in Westminster Abbey and Edwin Lutyen's stone cenotaph in Whitehall replaced the wood and plaster prototype that had been erected for the national peace celebrations in July 1919. In 1921, the poppy was adopted as the symbol of remembrance. The Royal British Legion's poppy factory in Richmond, which was staffed by disabled ex-servicemen, started production the following year. It would be some years before every town and village in the country had its own war memorial.

Although Eric had warned his parents that he would need time to readjust to civilian life, he started work at H. and J. Jones at the beginning of March. The Joneses, as they then were, had been flax dressers in North Wales before moving to Liverpool at the start of the nineteenth century. By 1862, Eric's great-grandfather had made enough money to move his business to Dale Street, one of Liverpool's main thoroughfares, where he set himself up as a twine merchant opposite the city's magnificent new Municipal Buildings. However, it was his son, John, who deserved most of the credit for the family's current prosperity. As a sixteen-year-old, he had been left to supervise the move to Dale Street while his father went off to take a cure at the spa at Buxton. Not long afterwards, he and his elder brother, Henry, pushed their father into an early retirement before setting about the rapid expansion of the business. As one of the great *entrepôts* of the world, Liverpool's maritime economy was booming. In 1870, the two brothers bought and then mechanised an old rope works in Ormskirk, 10 miles to the north of the city, which already had an established export business. The combination of the two sides of their business would prove a great success. They renamed it H. and J. Jones, a name that stuck even after John changed his name to Rigby-Jones in 1881 and Henry died in 1898. Its registered address for telegrams was simply 'Twines, Liverpool'.

Seventy-three-year-old John was still its chairman when Eric started working there in the spring of 1919. He lived beside the ropeworks in a large house on Ruff Lane called Claremont. However, while he still attended the occasional meeting in Liverpool, he had long since handed over the day-to-day running of the business to his eldest son and Eric's father, Harry. Harry and his wife, Alice, lived with their three children half a mile further along Ruff Lane at the Ruff, the house that they had built beside Ormskirk's Ruff Wood in 1902. Harry spent most of his time in Liverpool, catching the train each day to Exchange Street Station before walking the short distance to Dale Street. After his father's death, he often called in at Claremont on his way home to check on his mother, Lillie, and his youngest sister, Frieda, who looked after her. One of his four brothers, Jack, was also a director of H. and J. Jones and based at Dale Street. It had already been decided that Eric would be based initially at the ropeworks. Having already proved his organisational skills during the war, it would not be long before he was given full responsibility for its operation.

Ormskirk, 1924. H. & J. Jones's chimney and ropewalk are in the centre and Claremont in the trees to their left. (© *Historic England*)

After the wealth of letters, diaries, and other documents that cover Eric's time on the Western Front, there are now comparatively few records of his life in the decade after the war. No family letters survive. However, prompted perhaps by his engagement in 1920, Eric began keeping a written record of the significant events in his life, he opened a ledger for his personal income and expenditure, and he and his wife, Dorothy, started a cuttings book after their marriage in 1922. His father, Harry, also later wrote a brief four-page history of H. and J. Jones while his eldest son, Peter, wrote in his retirement about his memories of growing up in Ormskirk in the 1920s.

These records suggest that H. and J. Jones continued to prosper in the first half of the 1920s as it had at the height of Liverpool's prosperity in the decade before the war. In 1921, the directors made the decision to move from Dale Street to larger premises in Victoria Street, which, in 1934, would give ten-year-old Peter a grandstand view of the opening of the Mersey Tunnel. It must have been a poignant moment for John who had supervised the move to Dale Street almost sixty years earlier. By then, Eric was playing an increasingly important role in the business. He had already reorganised and enlarged the ropeworks and installed the latest equipment. Peter remembered the two highly polished steam engines that were named Alice and Lillie after his grandmother and great-grandmother.

In two years, Eric's annual salary was doubled from £150 to £300 and then, six months later, was increased to £500. As a director and shareholder, he was also entitled to directors' fees and dividends, which averaged out at more than £200 a year. By the time that he was aged twenty-four, he was comfortably off. When he bought a new house for his wife and himself in Ormskirk in 1922, it cost him less than two years' income.

In the first half of the decade, Eric settled down to marriage and family life. In 1920, he asked Dorothy Davies to marry him. She was a year younger than him and had just completed three years at Liverpool's College of Domestic Science with his sister, Judy. She was the youngest of nine children and came from Rhosllanerchrugog, or Rhos for short, a large mining village near Wrexham, where her father, John Charles Davies, was the local doctor and his wife, Annie, worked as his pharmacist. They would only ever be known in the family as Taid and Nain, the Welsh for grandfather and grandmother. Taid was a Welsh-speaking Methodist who returned to Rhos in 1882 after qualifying as a doctor in London and then practiced there for sixty years until a few weeks before his death in 1942. He was a respected local figure. When the *Rhos Herald* ran a series of light-hearted articles on notable local people in 1938, he was their automatic first selection: '… a selected tribunal would probably place him as the greatest of all the sons of Rhos: he was sober, kind, little in stature but great in deeds, and last, but greatest, a public benefactor'.[2] He was known locally just as the doctor. Forty years after his death, Beech Avenue, the street where he had lived and worked, was given an additional name, Stryt Y Doctor, because that was how it had always been known.

His wife, Annie, had been brought up mainly by her mother and grandparents. Her father, William 'Chinese' Allan, spent most of her childhood abroad, first as an engineer with the European-Chinese Naval Force, which was sent to China in 1863 to suppress coastal piracy, and then as the first professor of marine engineering at the new Imperial Arsenal and Dockyard in Foochow. For the latter service, he was made an honorary blue-button mandarin. He returned to England in 1874 when Annie was aged fifteen and so was able to attend his father's funeral later that year. His father, also William Allan, was one of the leading figures in the British trade union movement in the nineteenth century. After founding the Amalgamated Society of Engineers in 1851, he was elected unopposed as its secretary for the next twenty-three years until his death; in 1871, he became treasurer of the Trades Union Congress. It meant that young Annie met many of the leading union and public figures of the day and was said to have sat on Garibaldi's knee during his visit to London in 1864. Sadly, her father died only four years after his return from China, when he was only forty years old. She met Taid shortly afterwards when he was renting a room at her mother's house in Bow while he was studying medicine at the London Hospital.

Eric and Dorothy were married in Rhos on 5 June 1922. Eric disliked wearing morning dress and so wore his Territorial Army uniform instead, as did Dorothy's father and her youngest brother, Harold, who was Eric's best man. After a

Eric and Dorothy's wedding at Rhos, 5 June 1922.

brief honeymoon in Devon, they settled down at Parkside, their new home in Ormskirk. Their first child, Peter, was born two years later on the day after their wedding anniversary.

Dorothy had had a difficult and distressing pregnancy. She suffered a haemorrhage shortly after conceiving and was admitted to hospital a month later with suspected tuberculosis. By then, her weight was down to less than 6½ stone. Eric must have feared the worst. Today, tuberculosis is still the greatest infectious killer of women of reproductive age; in the 1920s, it was also one of the greatest killers of children. Although the BCG vaccine had been used in France for the first time three years earlier, it would be another twenty-five years before it won widespread acceptance. The standard treatment at the time was long-term isolation in one of the many specialist sanatoria that sprang up across Europe. Even then, a contemporary statistic suggested that half of those who were admitted to them died within five years. Pregnant women with tuberculosis also ran the risk of miscarriage, and their specialists often recommended an abortion.

Taid helped find his daughter the best available treatment. For the next four months, she was under the care of the pioneering thoracic surgeon, Hugh Morriston-Davies, at his Vale of Clwyd sanatorium in Ruthin, some 16 miles from Rhos. Eric was distraught. As a lover of opera and musical theatre, he must have been reminded of Mimi and Violetta, the tragic heroines of La Bohème and La Traviata, who both died of the disease. He moved out of Parkside (which, according to his ledger, he rented out for £10 a month with an additional charge of 5s for the hire of linen) and moved back to the Ruff. Even if he had been allowed to visit Dorothy, it would have been difficult for him to get there from the other side of Liverpool. Christmas in 1923 must have been an anxious time. The medical bills, which ate up more than half of his salary, were the least of his worries.

Dorothy was finally discharged from the sanatorium at the beginning of February. She was now five months into her pregnancy. After spending a week with her parents to recover her strength, she returned to Ormskirk where she and Eric were persuaded to stay on at the Ruff. Peter would be born there in June. They were all still there two months later when a family photograph was taken in the garden of the baby with his parents, grandparents, and great-grandparents, John and Lillie. It is the only surviving photograph of the first four generations of the Rigby-Jones family.

Dorothy gave birth to a second son, Michael, two years later and a daughter, Ann, four years after that. She was born on Easter Day in 1930. It had been

Family photograph at the Ruff shortly after Peter's birth, 1924. *Front row*: Lillie, Eric, Dorothy, Peter, and John. *Back row*: Taid, Nain, Harry, and Alice.

another traumatic time for the family as Eric recorded in his register of significant events in February:

> Five-year-old Peter, having fallen from a tree branch two days ago, became seriously ill and was operated on for acute appendicitis. There followed many anxious days while his life hung in the balance but by God's great mercy he recovered gradually. His convalescence was retarded by his contracting scarlet fever in the hospital. In this he was nursed at the Ruff by his beloved Granny.

Peter was still in bed at the Ruff when his sister was born. Eric carried her up a ladder to show her to him through his bedroom window.

Just like his parents, who always tried to do more for the local community than their time and energy allowed, Eric juggled many other commitments alongside his business and family life. Although he never talked about his wartime experiences, he did not forget them or the men with whom he had fought. In 1919, he started writing up a diary of his time on the Western Front before finding that he no longer had the time to finish it; in July that year, he marched at the head of Ormskirk's peace parade; and in 1921, he was present at the unveiling of the town's war memorial by Lord Derby and the bishop of Liverpool. The names of the 112 local men who had died were read out at the ceremony and, if it was not Eric who did it then, he would do it at later Remembrance Day services. He was also a one-time vice-president of the Ormskirk branch of the British Legion and in 1929 hosted a meeting at Parkside to discuss the establishment of a local branch of Toc H.[3]

Until his marriage, Eric's main commitment outside work remained the Army. Although disbanded at the end of the war, the Territorial Force was reformed at the beginning of 1920 and renamed the Territorial Army. Eric applied to join and in August was finally promoted to a permanent captaincy, a rank that had eluded him throughout his wartime service. One of his first duties was to command the guard of honour when the Prince of Wales visited Liverpool in 1921 to open the Hall of Remembrance at the town hall. It would be a lasting memorial to the city's 13,000 war dead, most of whom, like Eric, had served in the King's Liverpool Regiment. Eric went on to attend annual training camps in North Wales before asking to be removed from the active list to the Territorial Reserve of Officers a year after his marriage. However, he continued to compete in his battalion's annual shooting competitions and was a one-time chairman of the Liverpool Rifles' Officers' Association. He would be called back to full-time service on two occasions, in 1921 and 1926.

In March 1921, when the government passed back their wartime control of the coal mines, an economic slump and a collapse in export prices prompted the mine-owners to seek an immediate and substantial reduction in miners' pay. When the miners responded by threatening strike action, they were locked out of the pits. The government declared a state of emergency. Army reservists were called up and troops brought back from Ireland, which had seen two years of escalating violence

The Prince of Wales inspecting the guard of honour at the opening of Liverpool's Hall of Remembrance, 1921. Eric is only partly in shot on the left.

and guerrilla warfare. At the beginning of April, Eric was appointed a temporary captain in the 6th Defence Force Battalion, the King's Liverpool Regiment. The certificate in his army service file, which is still held by the Ministry of Defence, confirms that he served throughout the emergency before being discharged in July.

The threat to the government and the country had passed quickly after the miners were abandoned by their colleagues in the rail and transport unions. Nevertheless, the strike dragged on until the end of June. The miners were eventually forced to accept pay cuts of 20 per cent. The deputy cabinet secretary, Thomas Jones, who was married to Harry Rigby-Jones's cousin, Eirene, was party to all the discussions within government. It was one of the few occasions when he disapproved strongly of the approach taken by Lloyd George. Since his appointment to the cabinet secretariat in 1917, he had always been a valuable sounding board for the prime minister. The two of them often discussed matters in private in their native Welsh and usually ended up in agreement. This time, Thomas was afraid that a simultaneous strike by all three major unions might prove catastrophic. However, Lloyd George realised that they did not share the same goals and so successfully called their bluff.

Nevertheless, the problems in the coal industry did not go away. Four years later, the new prime minister, Stanley Baldwin, appointed Sir Herbert Samuel to head a royal commission to investigate the problems in the industry. Although the Samuel report, which was published in March 1926, rejected nationalisation as a solution, it did propose a sweeping reorganisation of the industry, including the withdrawal of government subsidies and further reductions in miners' pay. The mine-owners again reacted by threatening to lock out the miners if they rejected their proposed pay reductions. This time, the trade unions' response was more robust. On 1 May, the Trade Unions Congress announced a general strike. The strike—the UK's only general strike to date—started two days later and would last ten days. The country was brought to a standstill. The port of Liverpool ground to a halt when shipyard workers and engineers joined the strike. Thomas Jones, who had carried on in post after the change of government, was again an active participant in its handling of the crisis. One of his duties was to read out the government's formal announcement that the strike was over.

This time, instead of calling up army reservists to maintain order, the government established a militia of special constables. Eric applied to join. It is not clear what, if anything, he was required to do. In the earlier strike, he had been paid £123 and a bounty of £5 for his three months' service. This time there is no record of his being paid. He did, however, carry on as a special constable and eventually received a long-service medal 'for faithful service in the special constabulary'.

Before the war, Eric had been one of the first to join the Ormskirk Boy Scouts troop. In 1929, he resumed his involvement with the scouting movement when Arrowe Park on the Wirral peninsula was selected as the site for the 3rd World Scout Jamboree, which would celebrate the movement's first twenty-one years. It would be a grand affair and organised along almost military lines. Eight canvas camps were pitched over 450 acres of the park to accommodate the 50,000 scouts who attended from around the world. The Prince of Wales was among the 300,000 visitors, and he wore his scout's uniform to invest the movement's founder, Robert Baden-Powell, with a peerage.

Eric volunteered to help and was given the job of guiding groups of scouts around Liverpool's magnificent new cathedral. It was the largest in Britain. Work on it had started before the war but had yet to be completed. More than 10,000 scouts were shown round over five days in parties of 200 every hour. Although Eric's parents had been involved in good works in the diocese throughout their married life—in 1922, the retiring bishop of Liverpool, Francis Chavasse, had presented them with a silver rose bowl for their silver wedding in recognition of their services—by 1929, Eric had his own connection with the cathedral through his friendship with one of the cathedral's canons, Frederick Dwelly. Sixteen years older than Eric, Fred was also a keen scout and organised the services in the cathedral for the jamboree. The following year, Eric asked him to be godfather to his daughter and to conduct her baptism in the cathedral. She would be the first person to be baptised in the cathedral itself rather than in the lady chapel, which had been used while the cathedral was under construction.

Fred and Eric found that they had much in common. Both were determined men who were keen to innovate, and although they insisted that things were done properly and with due pomp and ceremony, they also wanted them done their own way and were often intolerant of interference. It was a trait that won Dwelly friends and enemies in equal measure. His personality was stamped most obviously on the grand services of celebration held at the cathedral, which he organised meticulously and for which he rightly became famous. He organised the first of these, the consecration of the cathedral in 1924, when he was still a vicar in Southport. It led to his being appointed a canon of the cathedral the following year.

Although it is not clear how and when Eric and Fred first met, there are some intriguing entries in Eric's ledger. They show that he started making regular payments of 10s a month to 'F. W. D.' as early as 1922, before Fred had any involvement with the cathedral. Although he provided no explanation for the payments, he entered them in his charity account that he used for everything from charitable donations to Christmas presents and annual dues and subscriptions. We can only guess that, given Dwelly's own generosity in his financial support of others, they were probably to help with one of his many projects rather than to supplement his meagre salary.

Eric's friendship with Dwelly may have contributed to his being appointed to the cathedral's College of Stewards in 1928. Two years later, shortly after Ann's baptism, he was one of many who helped Dwelly organise a spectacular service at the cathedral to celebrate the diocese's fiftieth anniversary. It coincided with the Church of England's Lambeth Conference, which was held every ten years, and meant that more than 200 Anglican bishops and archbishops from around the world were able to attend. A special train was laid on to bring them up from London. The following year, Dwelly became the first dean of Liverpool. John Masefield, the Poet Laureate, wrote a special poem for his service of installation.

At some point, Eric was also appointed warden of the Liverpool Cathedral Commoners. Although the Commoners are now defunct and largely forgotten, they were sufficiently important at the time to have a commemorative medallion designed for them by Edward Carter Preston. Liverpool-born Carter Preston was responsible for designing not only the cathedral's interior, including its sculptural scheme and illustrated literature, but also a number of important medals, including the Distinguished Flying Cross (DFC) and the memorial plaques, known as 'death medals', which were presented to the next of kin of all those killed in the First World War. The membership of the Commoners and their precise role in the affairs of the cathedral are no longer clear and perhaps may never have been so. The almost masonic secrecy with which they seem to have conducted their affairs almost certainly reflected Dwelly's influence and fascination with ritual. It was this perhaps that prompted Eric to put his name to an undated pamphlet, *Replies to Questions Concerning the Liverpool Cathedral Commoners.* Of all my grandfather's letters and documents, it is the one that I find most difficult to reconcile with his character and attitudes. Perhaps it was Dwelly who wrote it for him:

> *Who are the Cathedral Commoners?*
> Neighbour makers united in spirit to Liverpool Cathedral under the watchwords, obedience and liberty to grow.
> *Where can you find them?*

In all parts of the world.
What is the Test of Membership?
Readiness to serve the purpose of the Cathedral.
What can you tell me about Commoners?
Only on exceptional occasions is publicity encouraged.
How has your number grown so large?
The fascination of the cathedral and its purpose stimulates the desire to serve it. When you have done something worthy of your vocation in line with the purpose of the cathedral you may be given the distinction if you so desire it.
What is the distinction? Is it a symbol?
Yes, a mounting eagle bearing the Arms of the Cathedral
Is there any membership fee?
No, but Commoners inevitably stimulate the passion to complete the Cathedral in every way, in stone and art and music, in tradition and in spirit—and you can give whatever you will in money to the Building Fund.
How do you recognise one another?
By our purpose.
What have Commoners done?
They have never failed to answer the Commoners' call, they have worked to make the Cathedral what it is. If you like what it is tell us what you would like to do for it.

Eric Rigby-Jones, Warden
Trevor Holden, Secretary

In addition to his involvement with the Army, the scouts, and the cathedral, Eric also worked to develop his business profile. In 1925, he was elected an associate member of Liverpool's Rotary Club during his father's year in office as its president. All in all, it would appear that by the end of the 1920s, he was leading a happy, successful, and purposeful life. He was now aged thirty-two and had been making a significant contribution to the family business for more than a decade, he was happily married with two young children and a third on the way, and, like his parents and grandparents before him, he had immersed himself in good works. He was well on the way to becoming a pillar of the local community. It is therefore all the more surprising to find him, at beginning of the 1930s, leaving his wife and young children behind in England while he set about establishing a new rope factory in Ireland. We cannot be certain now how and when he and his father arrived at this difficult decision. However, Dwelly's service of celebration for the cathedral's fiftieth anniversary in July 1930 would be Eric's last entry in his register of significant events. He also stopped writing up his ledger sometime that year. From now on, it would appear, he was spending much of his time in Ireland.

2
Ireland, 1919–1933

Some years prior to the war the company developed a considerable business with southern Ireland to take the place of the export business that it had lost chiefly because of the United States' capture of the West Indian trade. When the Eire government erected a tariff against British manufacturers, first of 20 per cent and later of 40 per cent, business with southern Ireland became impossible and Eric Rigby-Jones crossed to Dublin to investigate the possibility of forming an Irish company and to inspect likely sites for manufacturing. The result was the incorporation of Irish Ropes Ltd on 3 July 1933.[1]

In his brief history of H. and J. Jones Eric's father mentions only four events in the twenty-one years between the two world wars—his son joining the business in 1919, the move to Victoria Street in 1921, his father's death in 1926, and the incorporation of Irish Ropes in 1933. It is frustrating that he tells us so little and that on the last and most significant of these, he may have been confused on the timing of Ireland's imposition of tariffs and so have misrepresented the rationale for the establishment of Irish Ropes.

However, 1926 was clearly a turning point in the fortunes of the family business. Unfortunately, it was also the year that the directors chose to celebrate its centenary on the somewhat flimsy grounds that Eric's great-grandfather had opened his first bank account in Liverpool in 1826. Everything seemed rosy at the start of the year. The local papers, when they reported the centenary, claimed that the business was more successful than ever and that three generations of the family were providing continuity and sound management. An illustrated magazine article, which the directors reprinted for distribution to their customers, described it as an export specialist with well-established overseas markets that it had inherited in part with the acquisition of the ropeworks back in 1870. In spite

Inside the ropewalk at H. and J. Jones, 1925.

The warehouse and delivery bay at H. and J. Jones, 1925.

of Harry's later assertions, the article claimed that it still had strong trading links with the West Indies even though its main export business—of fishing lines, cords, and twines—was now with Australia, New Zealand, Canada, and the west coast of Africa. However, no mention was made of Ireland.

Things quickly deteriorated with the death of Harry's father in April, the general strike in May, and Eric's first visit to Ireland in June. Eighty-year-old John died at Claremont on Easter Sunday. When the three remaining directors—Harry, Jack, and Eric Rigby-Jones—wrote to their customers on black-edged paper three days later, they proudly claimed that their 'beloved chief' had been involved with the business for sixty-six years and its head for almost sixty. After a funeral service in Ormskirk, John was buried in Liverpool's Toxteth Park Cemetery in the same family plot where he had buried his eighth and youngest child, nine-year-old Richie, twenty-four years earlier. He had a quotation from the New Testament engraved on his tombstone: 'Not slothful in business; fervent in spirit; serving the Lord'.[2]

The following month, the general strike brought Liverpool to a standstill. Then, once he had completed his service as a special constable, Eric set off for Ireland. His father, it seems, had given him the task of reviewing their strategic options. Even at this early stage, his main purpose was probably to investigate potential sites for a new factory. He crossed from Liverpool to Cork and spent the next two weeks travelling round the south and west of Ireland with the company's Irish agent, Joseph Fennell, before returning via Dublin to Holyhead. While he was there, the Dáil, the parliament of the Irish Free State, debated a bill that would become law the following month as the Tariff Commission Act. The role of the commission would be to consider and report to the government on proposals for import tariffs to protect domestic manufacturers.

That autumn, Dorothy gave birth to a second son, Michael. Eric was then away again for six weeks at the beginning of 1927 on a whirlwind trip to the United States. He sailed from Liverpool in the middle of February and, on arrival in New York nine days later, moved on to Boston. From there, he spent three weeks touring seven states—Massachusetts, Rhode Island, New Jersey, Philadelphia, Pennsylvania, Washington, DC, and Virginia—before returning to Plymouth via New York at the end of March. Judging by the number of colour postcards that he collected of all the places that he visited he found it an eye-opening experience. However, the precise purpose of the trip is unclear and nothing, it seems, ever came of it. Ireland was a much better prospect. It was only a short distance across the Irish Sea, it lacked an industrial base and any real domestic competition, and H. and J. Jones already had an established market there. It had registered the trademark for its branded Red Setter twine there in November 1922, a month before the Irish Free State came into being. However, it was not the safest place at the time for a decorated former British Army officer to set up a new business, and especially one who still held a commission in the Territorial Army and whose extended family included someone who had played a major role in the negotiation of the Anglo-Irish treaty in 1921.

The pressure for self-determination in Ireland, which had grown throughout the nineteenth century, had finally erupted in 1916. The war was going badly for Britain at the time, and for Irish nationalists, Britain's difficulties were always seen as Ireland's opportunities. That Easter, more than 1,000 rebels took over strong points in the centre of Dublin and occupied the General Post Office in O'Connell Street. Seventeen of them were later executed, including seven who had put their names to a proclamation of an independent Irish republic. However, while the rising may not have had the level of support that its symbolic national status now suggests, the vigour of its suppression galvanised Irish opinion against what was seen as an armed and brutal British occupation. Two years later, when Lloyd George called a general election immediately after the armistice, 90 per cent of the seats for southern Ireland in the British parliament were won by the Irish nationalist party, Sinn Féin.

The new Irish MPs refused to take their seats at Westminster, choosing instead to establish their own parliament in Dublin under the leadership of Éamon de Valera. De Valera, like so many of independent Ireland's first generation of political leaders, had taken part in the Easter Rising and had been sentenced to death afterwards only for his sentence to be commuted to penal servitude for life. Released under an amnesty in 1917, he was imprisoned again in 1918. He was still in Lincoln jail when he won his seat in the 1918 election before making good his escape early the following year. When it met for the first time in January 1919, the Dáil ratified the 1916 proclamation of a republic, called on other nations to recognise its independence at the post-war conference in Versailles, and demanded an end to British military occupation of the island.

Law and order quickly broke down. The next two years saw escalating guerrilla warfare and violent reprisals on both sides. It was only after King George V made a plea for reconciliation that the so-called War of Independence was ended by truce in July 1921. The subsequent negotiations between the British and Irish governments led to the signing of the Anglo-Irish treaty in December and the creation of the Irish Free State a year later. Fresh from the collapse of the miners' strike, Thomas Jones played a crucial role in the negotiations as secretary to a British delegation that was led by Prime Minister Lloyd George and included Lord Chancellor Lord Birkenhead, Lord Privy Seal Austen Chamberlain, and the Secretary of State for the Colonies Winston Churchill. The Irish delegation was headed by Arthur Griffith, who had founded Sinn Féin in 1905 and was now minister for foreign affairs, and Michael Collins, who was both minister for finance and the Irish Republican Army's director of intelligence. De Valera chose to remain in Dublin where he expected to be able to exercise final control over any decisions taken by the delegation in London. Thomas Jones's opposite number as secretary to the Irish delegation was Erskine Childers, the author in 1903 of one of the first and greatest spy thrillers, *The Riddle of the Sands*. He would vehemently oppose the final terms of the treaty. Shortly before the Irish Free State came into being, he was arrested for possession of a pistol, tried, and executed by firing squad in Dublin.

Negotiations over independence—for one country's divorce from another—are by their nature difficult. The fraught history of Ireland's relations with Great Britain only made them more so. Among the matters that had to be settled, and about which the British government had most concerns, were trade, defence, finance, and the appropriate allocation of commitments and liabilities after the divorce. For Thomas Jones, however, there were two over-arching issues that needed to be resolved. The first was the degree of independence that was to be granted to Ireland and, specifically, whether it would be granted the full independence that the Irish demanded or only the semi-independent dominion status, which was as far as the British government was prepared to go. Second was whether the Protestant majority in the north would be forced to become part of an island-wide independent state or would be allowed to secede and remain within the United Kingdom. If it chose the latter, then a boundary would have to be drawn between the two states. It would become Britain's only land border.

As usual, Thomas worked tirelessly behind the scenes in his preferred role as fixer and *éminence grise*. He sought to restrain Lloyd George when he thought it necessary and, as a fellow Celt, he was able to develop a close relationship with Arthur Griffith and Michael Collins that would prove instrumental in getting the treaty signed, albeit only after de Valera had been effectively side-lined by Lloyd George's last-minute brinkmanship. When the chancellor of the Exchequer, Sir Robert Horne, wrote to congratulate Thomas after the treaty was signed on 6 December, he said that he had done more to bring it about than anyone except the prime minister. When Arthur Griffith died of heart failure the following summer, Lloyd George asked Thomas to represent him at the funeral in Dublin.

What was generally seen in Britain as a satisfactory and lasting solution to the Irish problem met with no such consensus back in Ireland. Although the treaty went much further than earlier proposals for home rule, any hopes for the full and immediate independence of the whole island were not fulfilled. Under the terms of the treaty, the newly-named Irish Free State would, on 6 December 1922, join Australia, New Zealand, Canada, Newfoundland, and South Africa as one of the autonomous dominions of the British Empire; the British king would remain the country's head of state as king in Ireland and would be represented in Dublin by a governor-general; and members of the new Irish parliament would still be required to swear an oath of allegiance to the monarch. De Valera protested that neither he nor his cabinet had been properly consulted before the treaty was signed. The parliament of Northern Ireland, which represented six of the nine counties of Ulster, was allowed to decide whether to stay within the UK and, by exercising this right, created the divided island that remains to this day. Michael Collins was in no doubt that the treaty would be seen by some of his countrymen as an unacceptable compromise. On their return to Dublin, he and Griffith had to defend their decision to sign it in the Dáil. He famously declared there that while the treaty gave Ireland its freedom, it was 'not the ultimate freedom that

Thomas Jones standing behind Lloyd George's daughter, Megan, and wife, Margaret.

all nations aspire and develop to, but the freedom to achieve it'.[3] Although the Dáil voted to approve it by sixty-four votes to fifty-seven, Collins had been heard to comment, when he signed the treaty in London, that he was also signing his death warrant.

In the general election that was held six months later to elect the Irish Free State's first members of parliament, 72 per cent of seats were won by those who supported the treaty. Within Sinn Féin itself, Collins's pro-treaty candidates received almost twice as many votes as those who supported de Valera and remained vehemently opposed to it. However, even so large a majority could not prevent a year of civil war. Collins, who was appointed to head the provisional government with Griffith in the run-up to independence, was, as he had predicted, killed in an ambush by the anti-treaty IRA just six days after he had carried the coffin at Griffith's funeral. William Cosgrave, who was another of those jailed for their part in the Easter Rising and who had served in de Valera's cabinet since winning a seat in the 1918 election, was appointed to head the provisional government in their place. In December 1922, he took office as the president of the Executive Council, the first prime minister of the Irish Free State. The following August, when those opposed to the treaty had finally conceded defeat in the civil war, he called the new state's first general election. His party, Cumann na nGaedheal, won sixty-three (or 41 per cent) of the 153 seats in the Dáil.

Although support for de Valera remained undiminished—his Republican party won forty-four (or 29 per cent) of the seats—he and his colleagues refused to swear the oath of allegiance to the king and so were unable to take their places in parliament. Cosgrave went on to serve as Ireland's prime minister for ten years, winning two much closer elections in 1927.

Although Griffith, when he founded Sinn Féin in 1905, had set out an idealistic vision for Ireland of tariff-backed self-sufficiency, Cosgrave, once in government, chose to pursue a cautious and pragmatic economic policy based on free trade. Realistically, he had little room for manoeuvre. The Free State was still an almost exclusively agricultural economy. It lacked a manufacturing base, most of the island's industry having been lost when Northern Ireland chose to remain within the UK, and it relied on imports for all of its energy supplies except peat. Furthermore, the Irish currency was still pegged to sterling and the civil service that Cosgrave had inherited, and in particular the all-powerful department of finance, supported free trade and low government spending. Above all else, however, was the simple fact that the new state remained economically dependent on its stronger neighbour and former master. In 1924, the UK bought 98 per cent of the Free State's exports, nearly all of which were of agricultural products or food and drink. It was a figure that would fall only slightly by the end of the decade, at which time the UK was also supplying 80 per cent of Ireland's imports.

In time, Cosgrave's rejection of Griffith's policy of tariffs to protect and encourage Irish industry set him against not only the business and farming communities but also the rank and file in his party and the nation at large. The scale of the opposition, together with the deterioration in world trade and economic outlook in the second half of the 1920s, forced him into a reconsideration. It is difficult now to assess the precise extent and impact, not least on Eric and his father, of Cosgrave's flirtation with tariffs. Although he had established a Fiscal Inquiry Committee shortly after taking office, he filled it with academics who supported free trade and reported back that the widespread introduction of tariffs would be detrimental. Nevertheless, tariffs were introduced on a trial basis in 1924 on a limited number of items that included footwear, soap, confectionery, and glass bottles. When the list was extended a year later to include clothing, blankets, and furniture, the minister for finance, Ernest Blythe, made it clear that no further items would be added before the general election in 1927.

Cosgrave's decision to establish a Tariff Commission, which he announced at his party conference in May 1926, a month before Eric's first visit to Ireland, was primarily a defensive measure to protect existing industries and to ensure that protectionism did not become an issue at the forthcoming general election. The commission, which was chaired by the secretary to the department of finance, James McElligott, had a limited remit to consider applications from interested parties for the protection of specific products. Its work would be laboured and ineffective. The first application that it considered, in January 1927, was from a small manufacturer of rosary beads and resulted in the imposition of a 33 per cent tariff for five years to protect it against competing cottage industries in France and

Germany. By the general election in 1932, the commission had completed only thirteen reviews for products that ranged from flour and butter to woollen and worsted cloths and fish barrels but did not include, it seems, rope and twine. The lack of a domestic industry meant that Ireland had no choice but to import most of its cordage.

After five years of independence, the general election in June 1927 was too close to produce a decisive result. It revealed, even if it did not reopen, the deep divisions within the country. Cosgrave's Cumann na nGaedheal lost sixteen seats, and although it was still the largest party in the Dáil with forty-seven seats, it now had only three more seats than de Valera's new Fianna Fáil party, support for which had remained steady at forty-four seats. The balance of power was held by a number of smaller parties and independent candidates who held sixty-two seats between them. Cosgrave would have lost his working majority even if Fianna Fáil had not now chosen to take its seats in the Dáil on the grounds that that the swearing of the oath was no more than an empty formula. The country risked becoming ungovernable. A month after the election, Kevin O'Higgins, Cosgrave's deputy and the minister for justice, was assassinated on his way to Sunday mass by members of the now illegal IRA. By August, when a vote of no confidence in the Dáil failed only after the speaker had cast his deciding vote in favour of the government, Cosgrave realised that he had little choice but to call a second election. With the crisis squeezing out the smaller parties, the two main parties were able to increase the number of their seats significantly—Cumann na nGaedheal by fifteen to sixty-two and Fianna Fáil by thirteen to fifty-seven. Cosgrave managed to secure a working majority with the support of the Farmers' Party, which won six seats, and a number of independent candidates.

His government pursued a more expansive industrial policy in its second full term, completing a number of important national infrastructure projects and taking its first steps to encourage new industry. The Shannon hydroelectricity scheme, which was completed in 1929, marked the start of the electrification of the country and would supply all of its electricity for some years to come, while 1932 saw both the establishment of the Electricity Supply Board to control its distribution and the consolidation and protection of the country's vital dairy industry.

However, Cosgrave's government was living on borrowed time. In its second term, the world careered from economic slump to long-term recession. The Wall Street Crash in 1929 marked the end of the era of free trade. Faced with financial disaster, governments across the world erected trade barriers and tariffs, not least to prevent foreign manufacturers dumping their surplus production at discounted prices. They only made things worse. Ireland was already facing an unemployment crisis by the middle of the decade. Falling emigration, caused largely by fewer job opportunities and tighter immigration controls in America, only exacerbated it. In Britain, Ramsay McDonald's minority Labour government found itself ill-equipped to respond. As export markets collapsed, the effect on Britain's industrial heartland was both immediate and devastating. By 1930, exports had halved and unemployment had doubled to 20 per cent of the workforce. By 1933, 30 per cent of workers in Glasgow were unemployed.

For a company like H. and J. Jones, whose success had been built on its export markets, the collapse in world trade was almost certainly of more immediate concern than any threat of Irish tariffs. It was a crisis that Eric and his father now had to face on their own after the death of Harry's brother, Jack, in 1928. He was only forty-three. Harry's financial responsibilities probably already included his widowed mother, Lillie, and his sister, Frieda, who looked after her. Now they may have extended to Jack's widow, Evelyn, who had no children to support her. Meanwhile, Eric's wife, Dorothy, was already pregnant with their third child at the time of the Wall Street Crash. They would soon have to think seriously about saving for their children's education. It quickly became clear to Eric and his father that H. and J. Jones was no longer likely to make enough money to support the whole family.

A change of government in Ireland would bring them no relief. The election of Fianna Fáil's first government in February 1932 marked a sea-change in Irish politics and the country's development as an independent state. Although de Valera fell just short of an overall majority—his party won seventy-two of the 153 seats in the Dáil against Cosgrave's fifty-six—an agreement with William Norton, whose Labour party had seven seats, enabled him to form a government.

Family photograph taken shortly after Ann's birth, 1930: Eric, Peter, Dorothy, Ann, and Michael.

He immediately set Ireland on a collision course with the UK. The Statute of Westminster in 1931 had already removed the British parliament's powers of legislation over the empire's six dominions. Britain's presence in the south of Ireland was now effectively limited to its continued occupation of the three 'treaty' ports—the Royal Navy's bases at Berehaven, Queenstown, and Lough Swilly—which it had insisted on keeping under the terms of the 1921 treaty. As de Valera had made clear during the election campaign, his goal now was to sever all remaining political and economic ties with Britain and to restore Griffith's nationalist vision of a self-sufficient and independent Ireland. His plans were encapsulated in two principal election pledges—the removal of the oath of allegiance and the withholding of the land annuities paid by Irish farmers.

Two months after the election, when he opened the debate on the Constitution (Removal of Oath) Bill, de Valera referred back to Michael Collins's speech in 1921:

> When the treaty was being put before the old Dáil one of the arguments put forward in favour of it was that it gave freedom to achieve freedom. Are those who acted on that policy now going to say that there is to be a barrier—and a perpetual barrier to advancement? Let the British say that if they choose. Why should any Irishman say it, particularly when it is not true?[4]

While this first battle was one of nationalist principal, to secure the final freedom that Ireland demanded, the second would have immediate and far-reaching economic consequences for both Britain and Ireland.

The land annuities were essentially mortgage repayments that were still being made by Irish farmers to pay off the money that they had borrowed when they were finally allowed to buy their land under various Land Acts between 1891 and 1909. It was an arrangement in which the British and Irish governments acted as intermediaries between the farmers and the British and Irish bondholders who had lent them the money. The Irish Land Commissioners collected the farmers' money, the Irish government passed it on to the British government, and the British government, which had also agreed to guarantee the payments, then made the final settlement to the bondholders. Although the 1921 treaty had made no reference to the annuities, the Cosgrave government had subsequently agreed with the British Treasury to continue to collect and hand them over in full. The arrangement was confirmed in the Ultimate Financial Settlement signed by the two countries in 1926, and although de Valera rightly claimed that this had never been properly presented to or approved by the Dáil, it was a commitment that was honoured in its performance. As a result, the British government, although advised by the Treasury that the legal position was not clear-cut, had some justification in viewing de Valera's threat to withhold the annuities as a unilateral and unacceptable rejection of both the financial settlement and the treaty.

During the election campaign, Cumann na nGaedheal had accused Fianna Fáil of a 'you pay, we keep' policy. It claimed that, if the farmers' repayments were no longer due to those who had lent them the money, then they were not due to anyone. However, de Valera never suggested that the farmers should be forgiven their debts, only that their payments should be kept by and within the Free State. He not only argued that there was no legal basis for their onward transmission to Britain but also questioned the morality of a country being required to buy back its own land, and especially when it had been taken from it by force by English military adventurers. At more than £3 million a year—or £5 million when other similarly disputed payments were taken into account—the sums involved were significant. Issues of nationalist principle and financial survival became inextricably tangled at a time of global financial crisis.

When the new minister for finance, Sean MacEntee, presented his first annual statement in the Dáil in May 1932, he revealed a budget deficit of more than £5 million. Projected tax and other revenues of £23.3 million fell short of the government's planned expenditure of £26.9 million even before any account was taken of the £1.6 million that it had earmarked for emergency measures to relieve unemployment. The withholding of the land annuities was a windfall that would allow the books to be balanced. In his statement, MacEntee highlighted the scale of Ireland's financial commitment. Although £51 million had been paid back to Britain since 1922 there was still another £76 million outstanding:

> It is clear that the continued payment of this sum is a burden which is far beyond the capacity of our people. As the Dáil knows, the whole question of this continuance is being reopened. The Government, because it feels that the issue is now one of life or death for the country, is determined to maintain our rights in that regard.… If it succeeds, and with the united support of the people there is every reason to believe that it will succeed, our budgetary position next year will be an easy one.[5]

Both governments made their positions clear in an exchange of dispatches shortly after de Valera became prime minister. Although there was then a series of meetings in London and Dublin between de Valera and J. H. Thomas, the British secretary of state for dominion affairs, they were unable to find any common ground. Realising that it would almost certainly be to his disadvantage de Valera refused Thomas's offer of arbitration after he had insisted that, in accordance with imperial policy, the arbitrator should be a citizen of the British Empire. By now, the date for the next six-monthly payment of the annuities was fast approaching. The Irish government had usually forwarded the funds to the British government in the second half of June so that it had time to forward them to bondholders on 1 July. On 17 June, with only a fortnight to go before the payment date, de Valera and Thomas addressed their respective parliaments. De Valera told the Dáil that, having sought advice from several prominent lawyers, his decision to withhold the onward transmission of the annuities was sound in both law and natural justice. On the other hand, Thomas argued in Westminster that the Irish government had a legal and moral obligation to make the payment. However, he suggested that there was an even greater issue at stake, and one which he acknowledged that the Irish prime minister had never tried to disguise: '… the Irish people must make up their minds. They are either part of the Commonwealth accepting its responsibilities and duties or they are not'.[6] He made it clear that he would stop at nothing to protect Britain's interests and that he would have no further dealings with the Irish government until the status quo was restored.

When the deadline passed without payment, the British government, as guarantor, had no choice but to pay the bondholders from its own funds. Within a fortnight, however, it had brought forward legislation to recover by other means the sums that the Irish had withheld. It introduced a 20 per cent tariff—subsequently increased to 40 per cent—on most imports from Ireland and in particular on cattle and agricultural produce. Rather than being a long-term solution, it was seen as a short, sharp shock that would have an immediate and disastrous effect on the Irish economy and quickly bring the country to its senses. Better still, it might threaten de Valera's position at the head of a minority government and hasten the return of Cosgrave. The Irish government, however, chose to retaliate with its own tariffs. Its Emergency Imposition of Duties Act was debated in the Dáil on the day that the new British tariffs came into force. It gave the Irish government the power to impose and amend customs duties as it saw fit as long as they were ratified by the Dáil within eight months.

It is hard to imagine a worse time for a young and economically dependent country to take on its more powerful neighbour. However, the British government had its own challenges to face. Its exports were in freefall and it had the worst balance of payments since 1919. At the beginning of the year, it had signalled the end to the era of free trade by introducing the Import Duties Act, which imposed a 10 per cent tariff on all imports except foodstuffs and raw materials. For the time being, the dominions were excluded from its application pending the outcome of the Imperial Economic Conference, which would take place in Ottawa at the end of July. The escalation in the Anglo-Irish stand-off was played out as the final preparations for the conference got under way. It did not help that this was the greater prize on which all eyes were now focused and that some of the leading players in the dispute were already preparing to make their way there. Attended by delegations from Great Britain, its six dominions (including the Irish Free State), and India, it was planned as a forum to discuss the global economic crisis and to formulate a co-ordinated, co-operative, and mutually beneficial response. Its particular purpose, under the policy of 'imperial preference' or 'Empire free trade', was to stimulate trade within the empire by means of trade agreements and preferential quotas and tariffs. At the end of the conference, Britain would sign agreements with all of the participating countries except the Irish Free State, which found itself excluded from the benefits of imperial preference.

Britain's team of seventy delegates and advisors was headed by former Prime Minister Stanley Baldwin and included among its ministerial members the chancellor of the Exchequer, the president of the Board of Trade, and the dominions secretary, J. H. Thomas. They sailed from Southampton on 13 July, a week after Thomas had opened the debate in the House of Commons on the second reading of the Irish Free State (Special Duties) Bill. The smaller Irish delegation, which had sailed from Belfast five days earlier, was led by de Valera's deputy, Sean O'Kelly, and included the minister for industry and commerce, Sean Lemass, the minister for agriculture, James Ryan, and Ireland's high commissioner in London, John Dulanty, who had been the conduit for the original exchange of dispatches between the British and Irish governments in March. To avoid a repeat of the debacle in 1921, the delegation was given strict instructions not to make any final decisions without first referring them back to Dublin for approval.

O'Kelly recognised the difficulty of Ireland's position in his opening speech to the conference on 21 July, two days before his government's new tariff powers were due to come into force. Having reminded the audience that his country's economic development was still in its infancy, he went on to say that 'special difficulties have recently arisen which affect 85 per cent of our external trade and which may involve substantial changes in the form and direction of that trade as well as in the internal economic structure of our country'.[7] He ended pessimistically by commenting that, while he hoped that the conference would be a success, he was unsure whether 'the people of the Irish Free State can share in the ultimate benefits to the same full extent as the peoples of the other nations whose representatives are gathered here'.

It was the start of a five-year Anglo-Irish trade war that almost certainly harmed Ireland the most. Its exports fell from £44 million in 1930 to a low of £19 million in 1933 before starting a steady recovery to £26 million in 1939. Its historic reliance on Britain as almost its only customer made it virtually impossible to find other customers and outlets for its goods and produce. The effect on its imports, which fell from £56 million in 1930 to £35 million in 1933 before recovering to £43 million in 1939, was equally dramatic. In Britain, the area around Liverpool was particularly badly hit by the trade war. The ports of Liverpool, Holyhead, and Birkenhead all lost shipping trade while the mines of Lancashire and North Wales suffered when Irish imports of British coal fell from 2.4 million tons in 1931 to 1 million tons in 1934.

By the end of 1932, the Dáil had passed its fourth and most comprehensive Finance (Customs Duties) Act in the nine months of de Valera's premiership. It introduced tariffs at various rates, both standard and preferential, on a long list of items that ranged from spectacles and coffins through worked metal and wooden objects (including cufflinks, corkscrews, church brass work, and beehives) to furniture and food. This last category included everything from meat, eggs, and fresh and dried vegetables to custard powder, which was charged at £60 a ton, and Christmas stockings and Easter eggs, which were charged at 3d each. By then, there was already a tariff on cordage at standard and preferential rates of 15 and 10 per cent. It was one of forty-three tariffs introduced by McEntee in May to help plug the projected budget deficit. He told the Dáil that he had discussed them with the ministry for industry and commerce and that they were 'necessary for the fulfilment of our industrial programme, since we are capable of producing here everything to which they are applied.'[8] Significantly, the new act in December, which doubled the rates on cordage to 30 and 20 per cent, specifically excluded binder twine, coir yarn, and plaited and cable-laid sash cords, presumably because they could not yet being manufactured in sufficient quantities at home. The act also gave the minister for finance the authority, after consultation with the minister for industry and commerce, to exempt specific importers of certain items from duties as long as they accepted any conditions that he might choose to apply. Cordage was one such item. It would be another year before the duty on it was increased to the 40 per cent mentioned by Eric's father in his short history of H. and J. Jones and another year again before the list was extended to include 'binder twine or yarns of manila, sisal, or any kindred hard fibre other than coir'.[9] By then, Eric had already set up his rope factory in Ireland and the purpose of the amendments was more to protect new industries such as his own than to penalise foreign manufacturers.

British policy towards Ireland had been driven in part by the mistaken belief that de Valera's minority government would not be able to last long. Early in the new year, after less than a year in office, de Valera called another general election to confirm popular support for his more radical brand of nationalism. His Fianna Fáil party gained four seats while Cosgrave's Cumann na nGaedheal lost another eight. He was now just one seat short of an overall majority. Having thus strengthened his position, he would go on to lead his country for the next fifteen years. Throughout that time, he retained the portfolio for external affairs for himself and, while he continued to focus on constitutional issues and the goal of achieving full independence, he left his young minister for industry and commerce, Sean Lemass, to build an independent and self-sufficient industrial economy.

Lemass, who was first elected to the Dáil in a by-election in 1924, was another who had taken part in the Easter Rising. Although he had avoided prison then because of his age—he was only seventeen—he was later jailed twice for his part in the Troubles before and after the signing of the treaty. In a reversal of Britain's long-standing policy, which had stifled Ireland's industrial development and reinforced its economic dependence on Britain, he now set about reducing his country's historic reliance on agriculture and creating for the first time a solid industrial and manufacturing base in the south of the island. Using tariffs as much to nurture new industries as to protect existing ones, his department quickly usurped the previously all-powerful department of finance as the driving force behind the country's economic development. He would use three main tools to reach his goal of a mixed economy—the creation of essential state-owned utilities and enterprises, the encouragement of new and foreign industries, and the provision of finance for industrial development. Within a year of taking office, he had nationalised the production of sugar beet and established the Turf Development Board to control the country's supply of peat for fuel. Three years later, he launched the state airline, Aer Lingus. He established the Industrial Development Branch to develop new and existing industries and the Industrial Credit Corporation (ICC) to provide finance for their development. Although the ICC's lack of capital would mean that it provided little long-term funding itself—by the end of 1936, it had made only twelve loans totalling £324,000—it played an important role as the underwriter of more than 60 per cent of share issues between 1934 and 1939.

Lemass was a pragmatist when it came to developing domestic industry. Although he was keen to promote Irish ownership, he recognised that, in the short-term at least, he needed foreign capital and expertise. Major enterprises such as Dunlop (tyres and rubber), Ever-Ready (batteries), and Pye (electronics) were all actively encouraged to invest in Ireland, often over the heads of local industries and entrepreneurs. So too were smaller businesses like H. and J. Jones, which faced the loss of their export markets. They were attracted in part by the availability of credit and the government's willingness to provide protective tariffs. In 1934, the tariff on imported boots was increased to 40 per cent specifically to encourage one British company to start manufacturing in Ireland. By 1936, there were almost 2,000 tariffs in operation.

In 1934, Lemass was also given the authority to introduce import quotas and declare any product a reserved commodity. He would use the latter sanction only once—for sewing cotton—preferring instead to agree confidential but non-binding guarantees of exclusive production with specific manufacturers. Such carrots allowed him to wield the stick of location. He was keen to attract the new industries to the smaller Irish towns to relieve local unemployment and to reduce the country's historic reliance on agriculture outside the major cities. Although he proved remarkably successful in this the small size of domestic markets meant that in time many of the new enterprises became virtual monopolies and so stifled competition.

It was against this background of global economic depression and protectionism, exacerbated by the fallout from de Valera's election and the start of the Anglo-Irish trade war, that Eric Rigby-Jones moved ahead with his final plans to establish a rope factory in the Irish Free State. Unfortunately, although the depression hit Ireland relatively late and relatively lightly, 1933 would be its worst year.[10]

3

The Founding of Irish Ropes, 1930–1934

On a sunny day in June 1933 the little town of Newbridge was quiet. To those who knew it well it was strangely quiet. The clatter of horses' hooves from the great cavalry barracks, built by the British more than 100 years before to defend the realm against Napoleon, no longer sounded. They had died away with the formation of the Irish Free State, and there were some who thought then that the town might never again see the prosperity which the garrison had meant to it for so long. It was to this Newbridge that a stranger came on that June morning.[1]

Irish Ropes Limited was incorporated as a company in Dublin on 3 July 1933. A fortnight earlier, the office of public works had recommended to the Irish government that Eric's new venture be granted a ninety-nine-year lease for part of the old British cavalry barracks in Newbridge, Co. Kildare. The rent was set at £60 a year. The barracks had been left derelict and unoccupied for more than a decade. Under the terms of his lease, Eric had a year to bring them back up to scratch and would then be responsible for keeping them properly maintained.

Irish Ropes held its first board meeting the following week.[2] The first item on the agenda was to complete all the administrative formalities that are required whenever a new company is set up. Eric Rigby-Jones and Patrick Doyle—who is described in the documents as a commercial agent and was probably already H. and J. Jones's representative in Ireland—were appointed to the board and confirmed in their positions as managing director and sales manager. They were then allotted one share each for which they both paid £1 in cash. Also present at the meeting were Eric's legal and financial advisors, Arthur Cox and Vincent Crowley, who were duly appointed the company's solicitor and auditor. Once the formalities were completed, Eric updated the others on progress with the final terms of the lease, the procurement of equipment, and the securing of a bank loan through the Trade Loan Guarantee Committee. He then left for England to put his affairs in order. He would return a fortnight later. This time, he was planning to stay. Irish Ropes officially commenced trading on Tuesday 1 August.

It is no longer clear how exactly Eric had spent his time since 1930, when he stopped writing up his ledger and register of significant events, and how and when he was introduced to Arthur Cox, Vincent Crowley, and Patrick Doyle. By all accounts, he was away from home for much of the time. Among the few surviving family documents from this time are some letters written by his son, Peter. He was seven when he wrote to his father from the Ruff just before Christmas in 1931.

> My dear Daddy
> We are having the train out today and have made three tunnels and Uncle Guy [Eric's twenty-year old younger brother who was studying medicine at Christ's College, Cambridge] has mended the little horse and cart and we are going to give it to Father Christmas and we've put a tail on and its legs and head and Michael is doing the Royal Scot jigsaw puzzle and I am writing to you and Mummy has gone to Rimmers to have her hair cut and I hope you will soon come home again and we have been in the wood. Michael is sending a letter too.
> The End
> Lots of love from Peter, Mummy, Michael (5), Ann (1)

However, it seems unlikely that Eric was able to enter into any serious discussions with the Irish government until after Fianna Fáil's election victory in the spring of 1932. The negotiations were then made more urgent not only by the introduction of tariffs on rope and cordage in May but also by the Control of Manufactures Act, which was approved by the Dáil in October and would come into force at the beginning of March. The act was a key element in the government's plans to develop a domestic industrial base and required all businesses based in Ireland to be more than half-owned by Irish nationals or otherwise to obtain a licence from the minister for industry and commerce. It prompted the brewer, Arthur Guinness, whose shares had been traded on the London Stock Exchange since 1886, to transfer its headquarters from Dublin to London as it could never be certain at any given time of the nationality of its shareholders. For Eric and Harry, it meant one final but significant hurdle to clear as they could no longer proceed with their plans on their own and without outside help. It explains why Patrick Doyle owned half the shares in the company at the start and corrects a popular misconception that Irish Ropes was originally a family business under the sole control of the Rigby-Jones family. It also gives added significance to Eric's choice of name. As well as defining its location and purpose, it was also a statement of national intent. Eric's goal was to make Ireland self-sufficient in the manufacture of rope and twine as quickly as possible.

However, the company was not established without opposition. The Federation of Irish Industries, which had been set up at the end of 1932 to protect the interests of domestic manufacturers, wrote in protest to Lemass a fortnight before the company's incorporation to demand that Irish nationals be given the first right to establish any new industry.[3] Four years later, it was still refusing to admit Irish Ropes as a member because of its perceived ownership.

Eric was either very shrewd or very lucky in his choice of advisor. It seems likely that he was steered towards them. Arthur Cox and Vincent Crowley became famous for finding and exploiting loopholes in the Control of Manufactures Act.[4] Arthur in particular was a remarkable man and remained involved with Irish Ropes for the rest of his career, serving as its chairman for twenty-five years from 1936 to 1961. Six years older than Eric, he had been a brilliant student at University College Dublin before the war where he mixed with many of the men who would become the political and intellectual backbone of the new Irish state. Among them were some of the younger members of the Cosgrave government, including John Costello, the attorney-general and later prime minister, and Kevin O'Higgins, the deputy prime minister and minister for justice who was murdered by the IRA in 1927. In 1920, after qualifying as a solicitor, Arthur established the Dublin law firm, which still bears his name and remains one of Ireland's leading commercial law practices. Although he later counted George Bernard Shaw and Winston Churchill among his personal clients, his lasting legacy was the role that he played in the development of Irish industry where he represented both government and business. In the early years of the Irish Free State, he used his connections to establish himself as the government's leading legal advisor. It seems likely that he advised on some aspects of the Anglo-Irish treaty in 1921 as he told a friend that he had to make eight trips to London during the course of the negotiations; he acted for the contractors, Siemens, on the building of the Shannon hydroelectric scheme before being appointed legal advisor to the Electricity Supply Board in 1927; and that same year, he advised the government on the reorganisation of the dairy industry. It led Terence de Vere White to comment in his obituary of Arthur in 1965 that 'nobody knew how many secrets were locked up inside that cautious head. He must have known the inner history of the early days of the State and of all its actors'.[5]

Although he was appointed legal advisor to the Turf Development Board in 1933, Arthur's government work dried up after de Valera's election victory. He turned instead to the private sector and in particular to advising foreign businesses on how to avoid the restrictions on control and ownership placed on them by the Control of Manufactures Act. As the act only restricted the overall proportion of shares that could be held by foreign nationals, it was relatively simple for him to devise a range of artificial share structures—using different classes of ordinary, preference, and voting and non-voting shares—to limit its impact. It meant that, while Irish nationals might technically hold a majority of the shares, they might not either have voting control or be entitled to a full share of the profits. Lemass was enough of a pragmatist to turn a blind eye to such schemes as long as they were legal and achieved his primary purpose of introducing foreign capital and expertise.

By the 1950s, Arthur was a director, and in many cases chairman, of at least fifteen major Irish companies. However, the two companies with which he was always most closely associated were P. J. Carroll, the family tobacco company that manufactured Sweet Afton cigarettes, and Irish Ropes.[6] Gaunt and often dishevelled, he gained a reputation as an eccentric genius. His shoes, when he was not wearing slippers, were often untied or tied only with string while a badly-buttoned waistcoat became known in Dublin as an 'Arthur Cox'. Yet, although his office was stacked haphazardly with files from floor to ceiling, he could always find what he was looking for; although shy, he gained an early reputation as a public speaker; although abstemious with food and drink, he loved chocolate and was a messy eater; and although passionate about literature, he was an equally avid reader of detective fiction. A Texan lawyer, when meeting him for the first time, famously described him as a Rolls-Royce engine mounted on a Ford chassis.[7] It was an image that Arthur probably cultivated to some degree and one that belied a man who was always in full control. Eric's son, Peter, remembered him as a frequent visitor at weekends who always looked forward to being served honeycomb for tea. He was a bachelor for almost fifty years until, in 1940, he surprised everyone by suddenly marrying Brigid O'Higgins, the widow of his former friend and murdered minister for justice. He told nobody beforehand and, to avoid any fuss being made, arranged for the wedding to take place at 6.30 a.m. on a bank holiday Monday.

One can only wonder how Eric, who was by all accounts a neat, meticulous, and methodical man, could work so closely and for so long with his apparent antithesis. However, theirs was clearly a relationship based on mutual trust and respect—Eric would tell the Dublin Rotary Club in 1940 that he served a board 'whose chairman is not taken in by anything but sound reasoning'—and one that was cemented by simple shared pleasures such as cigarettes, long walks, and literature. Although of different denominations, they both had a Christian devotion to hard work, which made it difficult to find time to meet during the week. Instead, Eric went up to Dublin on a Saturday or Arthur called in for tea at Newbridge on Sunday. Eric described two such occasions in 1938 in his weekly letters to his children at school in England:

17 July: I went to see Mr Cox on Saturday and after dinner we sat in his office until after ten o'clock working at papers together. Then we decided to have a break so we went to the pictures to see *Snow White and the Seven Dwarfs*. The show was getting towards the end and the box office was closed but we managed to get in and saw half the picture. Then we continued our discussions walking along the emptying Dublin streets for it was a beautiful night. Soon after midnight we adjourned and I came home—so I did not get up very early.

11 December: we went to the play, *Victoria Regina*, last night and much enjoyed it. Actually we went in after lunch as I had arranged to see Mr Cox. While the others were amusing themselves at the pictures in the afternoon we talked business and then took a bus to Dun Laoghaire to have a cup of tea at the Royal

Yacht Club. Then we started to walk back to Dublin—six miles along the shore but the rain became so heavy that we were nearly drowned.

The site chosen for Irish Ropes's new factory, and to which Eric had almost certainly been directed by the government, was Newbridge (or Droichead Nua in Gaelic), a small town on the River Liffey some 25 miles south-west of Dublin. It was well-placed for business meetings in the capital, for the delivery of raw materials from the docks, and for Eric to return to Liverpool whenever he needed. It also more than met the government's criteria for the regeneration and industrial development of small towns.

The town lay on the north-eastern edge of the Curragh, a flat grassy plain of some 8 square miles that is home to Ireland's premier racecourse and largest military base. It had been used as a muster-point since early times before the British built a permanent camp there in the middle of the nineteenth century. Local employment and farming had relied historically on horse-racing and servicing the needs of the British Army. As well as the racecourse, there were many stud farms and training stables in the area. Newbridge itself had grown up around the imposing British cavalry barracks built at the start of the nineteenth century, which occupied all of the southern side of the town and from which the horses were led down each morning to the watering gates on the river. By the end of the century, the barracks housed around 800 men and 500 horses, and Newbridge was a thriving garrison community. However, when British troops were withdrawn from Ireland after the signing of the Anglo-Irish treaty, the town, and Kildare in general, fell into an economic depression that lasted for more than a decade. The barracks themselves were used briefly as an internment camp during the civil war but were left in such a bad state afterwards that the new Irish Army refused to take them over. Many of the buildings were demolished when the site was taken over by the office of public works in 1925.

Serious efforts were made in the second half of the 1920s to relieve the area's growing poverty and deprivation. They were led by local head teacher, William Cummins, who sat in the Seanad, the Irish parliament's second chamber, and chaired the local council, the Newbridge Town Commissioners. In 1925, he arranged for the commissioners to take over the former married quarters at the barracks, which covered some 10 acres, as emergency housing and started a campaign to find an industrial use for the remaining 38 acres. Although it generated some interest from the press and a group of British industrialists, nothing came of it. By the end of the decade, unemployment was on the rise throughout the country. In his first St Patrick's Day broadcast to America shortly after becoming prime minister, de Valera made it clear that finding a solution to what he called this gravest of evils was the most pressing problem that he faced. Kildare was particularly badly hit. By the summer of 1933, there were vociferous cross-party calls for action from all three of the county's Teachta Dála (TDs, or members of the Dáil)—Fianna Fáil's Thomas Harris, Cumann na nGaedheal's Sydney Minch, and Labour's William Norton.

Newbridge, 1933. The river Liffey and the bridge are in the foreground with Main Street and the eastern end of the barracks behind. Morristown is hidden in the trees, top left. (© *Historic England*)

Newbridge cavalry barracks, *c.* 1910. (*Image courtesy of the National Library of Ireland*)

Minch raised the issue at the end of June in a debate on local government and public health:

> There is no county, I should think, that is worse off or more in need of industry than the County Kildare. You have Newbridge, Naas, Monasterevan, Celbridge, Athy and several large villages in which unemployment and depressed conditions are eating into every house and home.[8]

When Norton took it up a week later in a debate on relief schemes, he was clearly unaware that Irish Ropes had been incorporated four days earlier:

> It seems to me that the towns have been rather neglected from the point of view of the application of relief schemes, or the grant of moneys, in the past. I know a town in my own particular district that is absolutely reeking with unemployment. The whole constituency is bearing a population absolutely outside its capacity to sustain, under the existing circumstances. The whole County Kildare, at one time, lived on the fact that it was the area for the accommodation of large numbers of British troops. These troops are now gone … I suggested a number of schemes to the Department. I come back to one scheme that I think will be dear to the hearts of the people who believe in economic schemes, and

Looking east along Main Street, *c.* 1916, towards the bridge with the Bank of Ireland building on the left and the barracks on the right. (*Image courtesy of the National Library of Ireland*)

that is that something should be done with the derelict site of the Newbridge Military Barracks.[9]

Irish Ropes's lease was for only the south-west corner of the barracks, which housed the indoor riding school, two other riding schools, the hospital, and various stores. Although no mention was made of it at the time, it was a bold statement of Ireland's new nationalist confidence that it was prepared to hand over so potent a symbol of the recent British occupation to a decorated former British officer who still held a commission in the Territorial reserve. Eric would never be treated with anything but friendship and respect in the country that he would make his home. However, he made it clear from the start that he preferred to be addressed as mister rather than Captain Rigby-Jones. His own attitude is summed up in a letter that he wrote to his children shortly after the end of the Anglo-Irish trade war in 1938:

Everybody seems to be very delighted at the new agreement between Great Britain and Eire. The old, old quarrel is over and the countries are now going to be friends. Of course the people in the two countries have always been friends and it is only the big groups of people who have been at loggerheads. We are going to have another election in a few weeks' time but everybody expects that Mr de Valera will get in again.

Eric arrived back in Dublin early on the morning of Thursday 27 July. He was planning to get down to work immediately. It would mean missing the summer holidays back in England with Dorothy and the children. Dorothy Baxter, who worked in H. and J. Jones's offices in Liverpool and had agreed to move to Ireland as his administrative assistant and general factotum, arrived before him. He followed on with his car and thirteen packing cases—for luck, he said—which he had sent on to Newbridge by lorry. Although his suitcases were cleared within five minutes after a rudimentary check of one bag—'Good morning, Sir, is it a long stay you're making?' the customs officer asked him—it would take three hours of mounting frustration to get his car through customs. There were offices to visit, forms to fill in, statements to swear, and tariffs to pay on everything from the chassis to the spark plugs. After two hours, he was beginning to think that it might just be easier to sell it.[10]

He finally got away at noon. After stopping at the printers, he went on to see Arthur Cox in Dublin and did not reach Newbridge until teatime. Although he had found temporary lodgings for Miss Baxter and somewhere to get his meals, he chose to sleep in the barracks on the old camp bed that he had used on the Western Front. It would be the first of many uncomfortable nights. There was no light or electricity, the water and sanitary arrangements were not yet in working order, the pipes had burst, donkeys brayed nearby throughout the night, and a flock of sheep arrived each evening to eat the grass in front of his office. Nevertheless, he managed to collect some wood the following morning

Part of the south-west corner of the barracks leased to Irish Ropes in 1933. Back left is the former hospital where Eric originally lived and back right is the indoor riding school.

to heat water, and by 7.30 a.m., he was sitting outside in his old army canvas bath—like Buddha, he said—watching the clouds drift over the mountains to the south. He was disturbed only by the sheep, which tried to use his bath as a trough.

After picking up Miss Baxter and buying some essential supplies—pens, ink, a cash box, buckets, a pick and a spade, nails, putty, and sugar and biscuits— he spent the rest of the day at the office of public works in Dublin finalising arrangements to take formal possession of the barracks on Monday morning even though the lease had not yet been signed. He was keen to make a start on concreting the earth floor of the indoor riding school and replacing the 150 panes of glass in the hospital, not least to keep out the birds that roosted above his bed and disturbed his sleep. He was already attracting attention. People turned up at all hours of the day and night to see what was going on. He found that the only way to keep them out was by barking like a dog whenever they came close and shouting that they needed written authority to enter. On Saturday, he told them about his plans to recruit a local workforce and then spent the rest of the day in hard manual labour. On Sunday, he allowed himself a well-deserved lie-in until 8.30 a.m. and then helped Miss Baxter prepare the 1,500 letters that were to go out the following morning.

The letter was printed on the company's new headed stationery and featured the already familiar logo of H. and J. Jones's Red Setter twine. Eric and Patrick Doyle, who signed it as the company's two directors, announced 'with considerable pleasure' that Irish Ropes was now up and running and would in future be supplying the full range of ropes and twine that had previously been supplied by H. and J. Jones, whose business and goodwill in Ireland it had acquired. Customers were asked to place all new orders with Newbridge rather than Liverpool and to settle their outstanding accounts with Irish Ropes rather than H. and J. Jones. They were also told that, although the factory had yet to start production, the machinery was already on order and would be installed as soon as possible. Meantime, its rope and twine would continue to be sourced from England. Eric and Patrick closed by reassuring them that they were keen 'to maintain and develop the very friendly relations which have existed between the undersigned and their business friends within the Free State'.[11]

At the end of the week, they met for a second board meeting at Arthur Cox's offices in Dublin to review their progress. The priorities now were to prepare the premises for occupation, install the machinery, which Eric said would be more advanced than any then in use in British rope factories, recruit a workforce, and ensure that the company was built on solid legal and financial foundations. Production began on a single machine seven weeks later, on Saturday 23 September. By then, all the rubbish and turf mould had been cleared from the buildings, the floor of the indoor riding school had been concreted, the windows had been reglazed, a telephone system and a supply of electricity from the Shannon hydroelectricity scheme had been connected, and machinery and raw materials delivered from England with the help of Eric's father. It was a considerable achievement and testimony not only to the hard work of all those involved but also to the meticulous planning and organisation for which Eric had earnt a reputation as a young officer in the war.

In addition to Dorothy Baxter, Eric brought over a small and tightly-knit group of key staff who would be joined later by Horace Davies. A marine engineer by profession, he had previously worked on Liverpool Cathedral and for Associated Tin Mines in Nigeria. As well as being Eric's right-hand man, he would be responsible for the factory's plant and equipment. It was the start of a great adventure and one that they pursued with the enthusiasm and pioneering spirit of boy scouts. They turned the hospital into a hostel for themselves and said prayers together each morning before they started work. Some of them would still be living there, albeit in better surroundings, at the end of the war. The original workforce was completed with the recruitment of six local men who helped to clear the site before they were trained to operate the new machinery. Four of them—James Coogan, Patrick Geraghty, George Halford, and Joseph Whitely— would still be working there when Irish Ropes celebrated its silver jubilee in 1958. Sadly, the other two, John Doran and James Luker, died before then.[12]

In what he called a great experiment, Eric introduced new working practices by which he sought to redefine the traditional relationship between employer and worker and which he continued to develop throughout his life. He had inherited the liberal values of his father and grandfather, which had earned H. and J. Jones a reputation as a progressive employer—staff there were given a week's holiday pay and a small cash gift at Christmas long before it became the norm—and, as a young officer on the Western Front, he had always looked after his men's needs before considering his own.[13] Now, in a break with the established practice within the textile industry of employing cheaper female and child labour, he recruited a mainly adult male workforce in order to have the most impact in relieving local unemployment and improving living standards. As he told the Dublin Rotary Club later, he was determined to eliminate both 'casual or insecure labour with its haunting fear of unemployment' and 'blind alley juvenile employment with its even more destructive consequences'. Women, when they were employed, received the same pay as men and juveniles were only taken on as apprentices and were not allowed to make up more than an eighth of the workforce. More radically, he introduced a six-hour working day and a shorter working week while paying wages that compared favourably with those who had to work longer hours. When he first told the townspeople about his plans, he was told that there was likely to be 'throuble' and that the traditional way of settling labour disputes was for the employer to pick out the biggest man and lay him out. 'I'm prepared for this,' he wrote in his diary, 'but suspect it won't happen.'

A few days before the start of production, Eric, who gave H. and J. Jones's offices in Liverpool as his address, signed his own contract of employment.[14] It is a remarkably modern document. He would be employed for an initial term of one year from 1 August 1933 and then on three months' notice. He could be removed by the board at any time if he became incapacitated or was deemed unfit to continue as managing director and, if he left under any circumstances, he would not be allowed to set up another business in Ireland for a year. In addition to a starting salary of £650, he was entitled to a generous annual bonus of a third of the company's profits after its payment of tax and dividends.

The lease for the barracks was not finally signed until December. As a government contract, it had to be 'laid upon the Table of the House' for the requisite time so that members of the Dáil and Seanad could inspect it. By then, the company had completed its initial round of funding. The 1,590 preference shares issued at the beginning of August—800 to Patrick Doyle and 790 to H. and J. Jones—not only provided the necessary working capital but also meant that it was now fully compliant with the requirements of the Control of Manufactures Act. Patrick, an Irish national, now owned 50.3 per cent of the 1,592 shares in issue. That said, his majority stake and his role as a founding director and shareholder were probably always seen as a short-term solution to an immediate problem. It is unlikely that he had either deep enough pockets to continue to fund the company's growth or the skills and commitment to justify a permanent role as Eric's equal partner. The following month, another 5,408 shares were issued to bring the company's share capital up to £7,000. The issue, which was split between ordinary, preference, and preferred ordinary shares, each of which carried different voting rights, would be the last for two years. The company used most of the money raised to settle its outstanding commitments to H. and J. Jones, paying it £1,000 for the goodwill of its Irish business and £3,245 for its outstanding Irish accounts, which its customers would now settle directly with Irish Ropes.

It has often been asked how foreign firms like Irish Ropes could set up in Ireland at this time without first obtaining a manufacturer's licence from the government. It has been seen as evidence of the ease with which they could dodge the requirements of the Control of Manufactures Act but stay in control of their businesses. In the case of Irish Ropes, the Rigby-Jones family—whose overall stake comprised the shares held by Eric, his father, and H. and J. Jones—bought 49 per cent of the shares in 1933 and ended the year with 49 per cent of each class of share and hence 49 per cent of voting rights. Technically, they never held a majority of the shares and so never exercised outright control of the company. Arthur Cox's solution to the problem of control had been simple if somewhat unorthodox. He became a shareholder himself. With the 1,000 ordinary shares in the company now carrying ten votes each while the 3,000 preference shares and 3,000 preferred ordinary shares carried only one vote and half a vote each respectively, his purchase of 509 ordinary shares in September meant that he held not only 50.9 per cent of the ordinary shares but also 35 per cent of voting rights.

There is nothing to suggest that Arthur was ever, in any formal or legal way, simply a nominee for the Rigby-Jones family. However, as one of the company's advisors, it is difficult to see in what circumstances he could ever have voted against Eric and his father who controlled 75 per cent of the remaining votes. Today, when the rules of corporate governance are much stricter, it would be seen as a conflict of interest, and almost certainly illegal, for a company's solicitor to be one of its major shareholders, let alone, as would be the case with Arthur two years later, to be appointed its chairman. It was probably in recognition of the unusual nature of the arrangement that the company's articles of association, or constitution, were amended to make it explicit that:

A director may hold any office or place of profit under the company except that of auditor. The solicitor or solicitors for the company shall be entitled to receive full fees and remuneration for all work done by him or them for the company as

	Shares issued in 1933				Shares and voting rights at end of 1933				
	July	August	Sept.	Total	Ord.	Pref.	Pref. ord.	Total	Votes
Votes per share					Ten	One	Half		
Shares									
Rigby-Jones	1	790	2,639	3,430	490	1,470	1,470	3,430	7,105
Doyle	1	800	2,260	3,061	1	1,530	1,530	3,061	2,305
Cox	-	-	509	509	509	-	-	509	5,090
	2	1,590	5,408	7,000	1,000	3,000	3,000	7,000	14,500
% of shares									
Rigby-Jones	50	50	49	49	49	49	49	49	49
Doyle	50	50	42	44	-	51	51	44	16
Cox	-	-	9	7	51	-	-	7	35
	100	100	100	100	100	100	100	100	100

Shares issued by Irish Ropes in 1933 and shareholders' voting rights at the end of the year (the Rigby-Jones' shares comprise those held by Eric, Harry, and H. and J. Jones).

such solicitor or solicitors, notwithstanding that he or any one or more of them shall be a director or directors of the company.

The person who appears to have lost the most from Arthur's scheme was Patrick Doyle. He had bought 44 per cent of the shares but now had only 16 per cent of the votes to show for them. Apart from his single original ordinary share, he now held only preference and preferred ordinary shares. Arthur on the other hand had contributed only 7 per cent of shareholders' funds but now had 35 per cent of the votes. Furthermore, when Harry Rigby-Jones was appointed a director in September, Eric gained control of the three-man board. However, Patrick seems to have been happy with his lot. He might have thought himself lucky to be in the right place at the right time. It was a reward perhaps for his loyalty that he stayed on the board for the next thirty-seven years until 1970 when he was finally shepherded into retirement at the age of seventy-three.

At the beginning of December, and a few days after the lease for the barracks was finally agreed, the company secured a £5,000 bank loan with the help of a guarantee from Lemass as minister for industry and commerce. One of the conditions for this and future guarantees was that, in spite of the lesser requirements of the Control of Manufactures Act, a majority of every class of the company's shares had to be held by Irish nationals. With the company now established on a firm financial footing, the directors could concentrate on developing the business. Apart from a brief meeting in January to approve the minutes of previous meetings, the board would not meet again until August. Eric signed the final lease documents on 23 December and then left to spend Christmas with his family in Ormskirk. He would return six days later. Although he was exhausted, he must have been pleased with what Irish Ropes had been able to achieve in its first six months.

When Kennedy Crowley & Co. produced the first accounts for the company for the eight months from incorporation to the end of February, they showed that it had come close to breaking even. They reported a small loss of £131 on sales of £7,545, most of which were of imported manufactured goods that had been subjected to tariffs of £673. However, once the factory began making twine as well as rope in March, it was able to turn the loss into a small profit of £188 when its first annual accounts were produced for the fourteen months to August 1934. When the board met in October to review and approve them, Eric formally read out the directors' first annual report to shareholders:

It was inevitable that losses should be sustained during the company's earliest days but these have been more than offset by the profits made during the later months. During the year much time has been taken up with the reconditioning of the company's premises, installation of machinery, and in training operatives. By proceeding at a deliberate pace the directors have avoided the heavy losses which an impulsive policy might have occasioned and they are confident that reasonable profits will not be long delayed. Before the end of the present calendar year the company's spinning plant will be in operation. Not only will this relieve the company of their dependence on English and continental spinners but it will make possible a greater percentage of profit upon all their hard fibre products as well as increase the number of men employed.

The directors ended their report by thanking the workforce for their loyal and willing service, Arthur Cox and Vincent Crowley for their invaluable help and advice, and Sean Lemass for the support and interest that he and his department had shown. Eric would always be grateful for the protection that he offered fledgling industries, and not least in that first year when many commentators had predicted that Irish Ropes would fail. Although he and Lemass came from very different backgrounds, they were similar in age and ambition and, even if they could never be said to have become friends, they developed a firm respect for each other. Lemass would be a fierce supporter of Irish Ropes throughout his political career. One of his final duties, two days before stepping down as prime minister in 1966, was to receive a deputation of Irish businessmen led by Eric's son, Michael, who was at the time chairman of the Irish Management Institute. An early example of his commitment came in June 1934 when Eric wrote to him after reading a report in the press that the Belfast Rope Works, which was then the world's largest rope manufacturer, was planning to open a new factory less than 20 miles from Newbridge. He claimed that there was not enough demand in the Free State to keep two modern factories busy and, furthermore, that his competitor would almost certainly seek to use cheaper female and juvenile labour as it did in Belfast. For whatever reason, the new factory was never built.

The following month, Lemass was invited to be guest of honour when Irish Ropes celebrated its first anniversary. On his arrival, he and the other guests, who included Thomas Harris, Sydney Minch, and Williams Cummins, were given a guided tour of the factory by the directors. By now, all their machines were working at full capacity and more were in the process of being installed; the workforce was up to thirty-six and was expected to increase significantly at the end of the year when the new spinning mill was completed; and Eric was confident that he would soon be in a position to fulfil his promise of making Ireland self-sufficient in cordage production. It would be a vindication of Lemass's industrial policy. A year earlier, when Irish Ropes had yet to start production, Lemass had told the Dáil that, rather than generating significant revenues, his new tariff on cordage would soon be generating none at all as a domestic industry was being developed rapidly and would create much-needed employment for Irish workers.[15]

Eric provided all his guests with a leaflet when they arrived—a twelve-point manifesto (or gospel, as one person described it) that laid out the directors' ideals for the management of a commercial enterprise and covered such issues as the relationship between owners, managers, and employees, working hours, continuity of employment, and the restriction of female and child labour. It claimed that for them there were more important things than the blind pursuit of profit. They thought it vital for the well-being of their workers that the working day should be neither monotonous nor noisy and overlong, that they should be the masters, and not the slaves, of their machines, that they should be encouraged to acquire the highest levels of craftsmanship, and that this was more easily gained with the help of technical assistance rather than close supervision:

> It is not the purpose of industry merely to serve the interests of persons who have no relationship to it except that of some form of ownership. Nor indeed is it sufficient to provide for needs in terms of money, convertible alone into purchasable commodities or services. We shall fail utterly if all we secure is money-value achieved at the cost of monotonous toil and an inability to enjoy and rightly use the leisure which is the heritage of this generation.... The first and last duty of any particular director is so to organise his industry that both workers and investors may secure the fullest benefit with due regard to those less directly concerned—suppliers, users, and the rest.[16]

Over lunch, two of Irish Ropes's employees, John Doran and Peter Smullen, delivered a prepared address in Lemass's honour:

Lemass' visit to Newbridge on Irish Ropes's first anniversary, 30 July 1934. Those identified include, front row (from left to right): Thomas Harris, Sydney Minch, Sean Lemass, Eric Rigby-Jones, and William Cummins; back row: Major de Courcy-Wheeler, Harry Rigby-Jones (third left), Patrick Doyle (fifth), and Peter Smullen (eighth).

On behalf of the employees of this factory we bid you welcome. Your visit to us is yet another of many indications of your ambition to raise up the Irish workman; to provide him with a livelihood; to better his condition. You have seen today some of your patriotic labours. You may reflect with justice and with pride that your conception of a policy of industrial progress in our country is proving itself both practicable and sound. It will bring you still greater happiness to think into how many families employment has brought new hope, in how many homes there is now sufficiency where want so long enforced its presence.

The Irish workman is not devoid of perception and still less is he wanting in gratitude. The men in this factory know who is their benefactor and to whom their thanks must be given. On their behalf, and with the sincerity they feel, we express their acknowledgement of their debt to you and their wish that your genuinely Christian labours for them and your countrymen may be rewarded.

Your visit today must have the further interest that it provides you with an opportunity of informing yourself of the development of the progressive social ideals that are being reduced to practice in this factory. No one should know better than the employee what is the value of these ideals. You will accept as proof of their worth the contentment and activity you have seen about you.

The author of these ideals is our respected managing director, Mr Rigby-Jones. It is in no perfunctory sense that we avail ourselves of this public occasion to pay a sincere and grateful tribute, on behalf of our comrades, to an employer who makes it his practice to establish the most just conditions of employment, to exploit the possibilities of the most advanced social ideals, to invest the workman with the full dignity and responsibility of his employment. We feel that the names of Minister and manager may be coupled in this respect.[17]

Lemass, in his response, referred to the factory's national significance and the new concept in industrial relations that he and his fellow guests had just seen. He had not failed to notice, he said, the keen interest that every worker took in his job. He suggested that what he called 'this most interesting experiment' might provide a solution to all industrial unrest and that this Englishman's methods should be an example for all native manufacturers. He then thanked Eric and the company on behalf of the government and assured them of his continued support.

By the end of the year, Irish Ropes had secured a second loan—this time for £6,000—to fit out and equip its new spinning mill. The completion of the mill was announced in the press on 1 January 1935. According to the advertisement, the factory would now be producing higher qualities of rope, using not only traditional manila hemp for its new Liffey and Kildare brands but also a brand-new fibre, sisal, which it claimed was a match for manila but of better appearance.

By all accounts, Eric had overcome the many obstacles placed in his path. He had survived the imposition of tariffs, the passing of the Control of Manufactures Act, and the stand-off between the British and Irish governments that had turned into a damaging trade war. In almost no time, he had turned a derelict barracks

SPINNING MILL COMPLETED

IRISH ROPES LTD.

ANNOUNCE NEW QUALITIES—

●

'LIFFEY MANILA' High grade rope for steamship and heavy lifting purposes and for fishing ropes.

'KILDARE' MANILA. A new general purpose rope from pure fibre—for use where hard wear rather than high initial breaking strain is needed.

SISAL ROPE and CORDS. A beautifully white fibre—equal to Manila and of better appearance.

●

ALL 100% IRISH MANUFACTURE

Made under ideal conditions by
: ADULT MALE LABOUR :

IRISH ROPES Ltd., NEWBRIDGE, CO. KILDARE

Irish Ropes's advertisement announcing the completion of its spinning mill and its introduction of sisal rope and cord, 1 January 1935. (*With thanks to Irish Newspaper Archives and the Irish Press*) into a working factory, installed the latest equipment, recruited and trained a workforce, and introduced a new concept in industrial relations, which made clear the responsibility of the employer to look after the physical and spiritual well-being of his workforce. He had turned around the fortunes of a whole town but in doing so had sacrificed the chance of a comfortable life back home in England with his wife and young children. He had proved himself to be a successful taker of risks even when some of those risks were born of desperation. Now he was about to take on perhaps the greatest risk of all. He would stake the success of his new venture on a raw material that had yet to win widespread acceptance from makers and users of rope—sisal, the so-called white gold of East Africa.

4

Sisal

The story of Irish Ropes is largely the story of sisal.[1]

As Eric would tell the Dublin Rotary Club in 1941 in a talk on industrial fibres, there are two main types of vegetable fibre—soft fibres, like flax, hemp, and cotton, which come from the stems and seed hairs of annual crops that are grown from seed; and hard fibres, like manila and sisal, which are stripped from the leaves and leaf-stems of larger tropical plants that are grown from suckers and may take several years to mature before being harvested. It was not until the second half of the nineteenth century that hard fibres began to take over from soft when manila replaced hemp as the material of choice for making rope. Before the advent of synthetic fibres in the twentieth century, these vegetable fibres, together with animal fibres such as wool and silk, were the raw materials for nearly all cordage and cloth. Eric ranked them second only to foodstuffs in their importance to civilised man.

Manila hemp, or abaca, comes from a species of banana plant, *Musa textilis*, which is grown mainly in the Philippines. Sisal, *Agave sisalana*, is a native of Mexico and Central America and takes its name from the port of Sisal on the Yucatan peninsula. Although Agaves had long been grown in Mexico—not least to distil tequila from the blue Agave, *Agave tequilana*—their large-scale commercial cultivation began only in the second half of the nineteenth century when the development of mechanical reapers and binders in the US led to a massive increase in demand for agricultural twine. The Agave most commonly used for this was the lower-quality sisal variant, henequen, or *Agave fourcroydes*. Nearly all of this was sold by Mexico to the US through a government co-operative and so excluded from world markets. Sisal itself was rarely used. It would not be planted in East Africa until 1893. However, in less than fifty years, it became the region's most important export and the cornerstone of its colonial prosperity. By the end of the 1950s, it was the world's leading hard fibre and accounted for 67 per cent of global production against manila's 17 per cent and henequen's 16 per cent. With the British colonies of Kenya and Tanganyika producing 45 per cent of it and their neighbours another 17 per cent, it meant that East Africa was producing more than 40 per cent of the world's hard fibres.

Yet, a hundred years earlier, in the third quarter of the nineteenth century, explorers and missionaries were still the only permanent European presence on the mainland of central Africa. In 1858, John Speke became the first white man to see Lake Victoria when he was on an expedition with Richard Burton to discover the source of the Nile. Thirteen years later, when Henry Morton Stanley finally caught up with David Livingstone on the shores of Lake Tanganyika, local power was still in the hands of the Khedive of Egypt and the Sultan of Zanzibar, who controlled the routes into the African interior from the north and east. Even after the closing of Zanzibar's slave market in 1873, the local trade in slaves remained a lynchpin of the native economy.

The European powers' so-called 'scramble for Africa' was a phenomenon of the last quarter of the century. It began with a free-for-all in which individual adventurers—usually with the acquiescence, if not the active connivance, of their governments—secured land and trading rights after signing treaties of questionable legality with local chiefs and slave traders. Germany, which was only unified in 1871 and so came late to the colonial game, pursued it more vigorously than most. Great Britain remained an unwilling expansionist. Although the British government was keen that no one else should fill the vacuum, its priority was to keep control of its existing possessions in Africa and thereby ensure that it had continued access to its most prized imperial possession, India. This concern had a 'house of cards' quality that attached particular importance to the river Nile. It was feared that a failure to control its head waters in Uganda might threaten Egypt's water supply and so, in turn, the security of the country generally and the Suez Canal in particular, which had provided the quickest route to India since its opening in 1869.

The first attempt to bring some sort of order to the scramble was the Berlin conference held over the winter of 1884–5. Chaired by German Chancellor Bismarck and attended by all the major European powers, as well as representatives from the Ottoman Empire and the US, it was played out against the background of the final British debacle at Khartoum at the confluence of the Blue and White Niles. General Gordon had been sent there earlier in the year to investigate and report on how best to evacuate its British garrison after the insurrection of the Mahdi. He was hung out to dry. The forces sent to rescue him arrived too late, and he was killed in January 1885 when the Mahdi attacked the city.

The real significance of the Berlin conference is still a matter for debate. Although it concluded with the signing of a general treaty that set some basic ground rules on free trade and the suppression of the slave trade and required any power seeking to take over land on the African coast to notify the other signatories so that they had the chance to make good their own claims, it did not itself partition the continent or create the 'spheres of influence' that would shape many of the countries that we still know today. Indeed, the conference itself had prompted a last-minute round of land grabs and treaty-signing, most notably by Carl Peters, who had established the Society for German Colonisation at the beginning of the year. In the autumn, he visited East Africa in secret and without his government's backing and, after hurriedly signing a number of treaties with local chiefs, was back in Germany before the end of the conference. Until then, Germany had showed little interest in the region, its presence there being limited to a handful of German companies that employed agents in Zanzibar. It was a shock therefore for the delegates when Bismarck announced at the end of the conference that he had signed an imperial charter granting Peters's society the right to establish a protectorate in East Africa. Until then, Britain would have happily stayed out of the region and left it under the control of the Sultan of Zanzibar. Peters's actions, and his attempts to repeat them in British-controlled Uganda, now made that impossible. The following year, Britain and Germany reached their first agreement on their respective spheres of influence in East Africa by drawing a boundary between them from the coast of the Indian Ocean to Lake Victoria. However, it would be another four years before a new map of Central Africa was finalised with the creation of the colonies of British and German East Africa. The former essentially comprised present-day Kenya and Uganda and the latter mainland Tanzania. To their north was Italian Somaliland (present-day Somalia), to their west the Belgian Congo (now the Democratic Republic of the Congo), and to their south Portuguese East Africa (Mozambique).

At first, the British and German governments tried to administer their new territories by granting concessions to private companies along the lines of the East India Company. However, it quickly became clear that these companies lacked the capital and resources required for so great an undertaking. In 1891, Peters's German East Africa Company was bought out by the German government after he had been forced to call on the German armed forces to help suppress a rebellion. German East Africa was declared a German protectorate. Three years later, the British government had first to bankroll and then to buy out the Imperial British East Africa Company after near bankruptcy had forced it to consider pulling out of Uganda. The timing of these failures gave Germany a head start. It was an advantage that was compounded by the persistent British belief that Uganda, in its strategic position at the headwaters of the White Nile, was the greater prize in British East Africa. Kenya, with its 300 miles of desert shrub to negotiate on the first stage of the journey inland from the coast, was seen as little more than the means of getting there and not yet as a country rich in its own natural resources that were waiting to be exploited.

Britain's first major project in East Africa—to facilitate the transport of troops and supplies to Uganda—was the construction of a 600-mile railway line from the port of Mombasa to Lake Victoria. With there being no immediate prospect of it making money, it was clearly a project for government rather than private enterprise. It was dubbed the Lunatic Line by its opponents and ended up costing more than £5 million, or 4 per cent of the British government's total expenditure in 1899. It was nevertheless an extraordinary feat of engineering, as well as a bold statement of imperial confidence. George Whitehouse, who was given the job of building it, arrived in Mombasa at the end of 1895. He then had to find labour, clear scrub, dig cuttings, and build embankments and bridges, as well as find a way to overcome the sheer escarpments of the Rift Valley. He imported more than 32,000 workers from India. At Tsavo, after less than a quarter of the way, work almost came to a standstill when man-eating lions killed twenty-eight workers. It would be 1901 before the line reached Lake Victoria and another two years before a permanent line with stations and the necessary infrastructure was completed.

As the Foreign Office chose not to address the question of European settlement until after completion of the line, it was 1902 before prospective settlers were allowed to make their first applications for land. The subsequent disputes over its distribution and the protection of native reserves led to the resignation of the protectorate's first commissioner, Sir Charles Eliot. In his 1905 book, *The East Africa Protectorate*, he accused the government of dragging its feet in encouraging colonisation. Even after responsibility for the protectorate was transferred from the Foreign Office to the Colonial Office, the bureaucracy and lack of resources

Mile 363 on the Uganda railway—just past Nairobi and before the escarpment of the Rift Valley. (*The National Archives*, CO 1069/185(9a))

of the local land and survey department meant that, right up to the outbreak of the First World War, settlers often had to camp out in Nairobi for a year or more before they were allocated any land. Many could not afford to wait so long and had to give up. Meanwhile, as Eliot complained, Germany had forged ahead with the development of its coastal regions, which were well served with harbours:

> Whereas we have devoted our time and attention chiefly to the construction of the Uganda Railway and shown extreme parsimony and indifference in other respects the Germans have done little in the way of railway construction but have devoted themselves to the methodical development of the colony with a systematic thoroughness characteristic of the race, and a lavishness due to the determination to establish a colonial empire at any price.[2]

The idea of growing sisal in the colony originated with Richard Hindorf, a young agronomist with the German East Africa Company who was trying to find a plant that could be cultivated commercially on its dry coastal plains. In 1892, after reading an article on sisal in the monthly Bulletin of Miscellaneous Information published by the Royal Botanic Gardens at Kew, he tried unsuccessfully to source some plants from Mexico. The Mexican government had by then banned their export in an attempt to retain its own monopoly on the fibre. However, he managed to track down 1,000 plants in Florida, where an attempt to cultivate sisal had been made in the 1830s, and had them sent to him via Hamburg. Only 200 of them were still alive when they reached Germany and only sixty-two of them eventually made it to East Africa in 1893 where they had to be smuggled through customs in an umbrella to avoid quarantine regulations. Although more would later be imported from Mexico and the West Indies, these few plants, so the story goes, were the foundation of the East African sisal industry. They proved resilient to drought and easy to cultivate in the tropical climate and in soil that was too poor for crops like coffee. Within five years, the sixty-two plants had multiplied a thousand-fold. By the turn of the century, there were more than 500,000 sisal plants growing in German East Africa.

Building a market for the fibre would take time. Once an estate was cleared and planted, it was three or four years before the plants could be harvested for the first time. By then, their short, thick stems were throwing out rings of fleshy leaves up to 6 feet long and 7 inches wide, which could be cropped every three months. Then, after about four years of producing leaves, the plant would throw up a tall flowering stem, or pole, and die. The seed pods on this stem, known as bulbils, could then be used for replanting to start the cycle again.

Although sisal was suited to large-scale cultivation, it required significant capital investment. Narrow-gauge railways had to be laid on the estates to transport the cut leaves and factories built to process them. The processed fibre then had to be transported by train to the coast for shipping. The main processes involved at the estate-based factories were the decortication, or stripping, of the

Mature sisal after its first cutting. The poles and bulbils of older plants can be seen behind. (*The National Archives*, CO 0169/140 (7))

inner fibre from the leaves and the removal of any residual pulp by high-pressure water; the drying of the fibre, either on racks in the sun or later by machine; its brushing, to straighten it out and remove any unusable short fibres; and, finally, its compression and baling for transport to the coast. The resulting fibre accounted for less than 4 per cent by weight of the original leaves. Practically, this meant that around 30,000 leaves had to be harvested to produce a ton of fibre; and the processing of the leaves left huge amounts of leaf waste and contaminated water for which no sustainable commercial use was ever found. Eric reckoned that every ton of fibre gave employment to one man for a year, and although the cheapness of native labour made it economical to produce, large workforces had to recruited, housed, and fed. One of the ways that European farmers found to raise some quick capital when they returned to East Africa after the First World War was to act as recruiting agents for the sisal estates. Even then it was difficult to persuade the native tribesmen to adapt to the European practice of working regular hours. In 1899, the development of the first mechanical decorticator, the German-made Krupps Corona, radically improved the economics of production. Capable of processing 100,000 leaves a day, it was fifteen times faster than the hand-cranked raspadors still being used in Mexico. Away from the estates, however, the development of the ports, railways, and warehouses that were needed to support

Cut leaves being transported to the estate factory for processing. (*The National Archives, CO 0169/140 (13)*)

a growing export market was slow and would not be completed until just before the outbreak of the First World War.

The first sisal crop was harvested in German East Africa in 1898 and the first fibre exported two years later. By 1913, the colony had 60,000 acres under cultivation and was exporting 21,000 tons of fibre a year, all of it to Germany where there was growing demand for it in the manufacture of rope and marine cordage. In British East Africa, it was not until after the completion of the Uganda railway that it was realised that the interior offered exceptional agricultural opportunities. The Kenyan highlands around Nairobi, which became known as 'white man's country', benefitted from a temperate climate, rich soil, and good rivers and rainfall, as well as being largely undeveloped and unpopulated by the indigenous tribes. They would prove excellent for growing not only coffee, tea, tobacco, and other 'hot' country produce but also English vegetables as well as for dairy farming and animal husbandry. Once the railway had opened up the hinterland British and European settlers, excited by the challenge of making or recovering their fortunes in virgin territory, began to arrive in growing numbers. Hugh Cholmondeley, 3rd Baron Delamere, was one of the first. Dubbed the Cecil Rhodes of Kenya, he would become the unofficial figurehead of the colony's European community. Although he had first visited the country on a big-game safari in 1897, he did not buy a farm there until 1907. The territory was still largely unsettled by Europeans when five-year-old Elspeth Huxley arrived there with her parents in 1913. She would describe her experiences forty years later in *The Flame Trees of Thika*. That same year, Karen Blixen, the author of *Out of Africa*, arrived from Denmark with her husband with plans to start a coffee plantation.

Hindorf's gamble had given German East Africa a ten-year head start over its neighbour. Sisal was not planted in British East Africa until 1907. Two Irishmen, Thomas Randall Swift and Ernest Rutherford, are credited with having planted the first 1,000 acres there in the uplands north-east of Nairobi, some 275 miles inland from the port of Mombasa. Swift later explained to Elspeth Huxley how he and his partner had managed to secure the last consignment of 375,000 bulbils from German East Africa on the day before their export was banned.[3] The delay meant that British East Africa's sisal industry was still in its infancy at the outbreak of the First World War. In 1914, when it exported its first 42 tons of fibre, it had only 7,000 acres under cultivation.

Alfred Wigglesworth, who would later play a major role in the development of the sisal industry, visited the colony for the first time in 1913. The son of a partner in a flax-weaving factory in Belfast, he established his own fibre merchants' business in London in 1895 when he was thirty. Today, Wigglesworth and Co. is still a market leader in the production and selling of sisal and other fibres. Vivian Landon, who was chairman of the company from 1977 to 1999 and has been its unofficial archivist since his retirement, showed me a letter that Alfred wrote from Nairobi's Norfolk Hotel during his visit. It is a first-hand account of a country that was still largely undeveloped but already attracting speculators and adventurers. Although Mombasa boasted a golf course, Wigglesworth thought that the imposing facade of its Grand Hotel was deceitful 'as its comforts are nil and its chaos highly developed'. Nobody, he thought, would choose to stay in Mombasa for pleasure, and like many others, he preferred to sleep under canvas when he travelled around the country. From the coast, he took the train to Nairobi, which had started life as a depot on the Uganda railway and which had only been selected as the capital six years earlier. 'Here,' he wrote, 'I find a town in a rapid state of development, land being worth over £1,000 an acre which a few years ago could be had for 20 shillings [£1]. Fortunes are being made but dear money is checking the speculation slightly. Everything is very crude and the sanitation of the town and the hotel as bad as could be conceived—but such things are incidental.'

The following summer, Wigglesworth was asked to present a paper on the fibre industry in British East Africa at the third congress of the International Association for Tropical Agriculture held at the Imperial Institute in London. The association's two previous meetings had been in Paris in 1905 and Brussels in 1910. Although he expressed his own confidence in the future of sisal it was not a view that that was shared by Dr Bruck, the professor of tropical agriculture at the University of Giessen, who spoke before him on fibre cultivation in the German

Stripped fibre leaving the decorticator. (*The National Archives*, CO 0169/140 (16))

Fibre being laid out to dry on frames in the sun. (*The National Archives*, CO 0169/140 (28))

colonies. Bruck suggested, perhaps disingenuously, that sisal was a difficult crop that required large-scale cultivation to be economical and was unlikely ever to be an important global commodity.[4] Although the two men could not have been aware of its significance at the time, they were speaking on the day after the assassination of Austria's Archduke Franz Ferdinand in Sarajevo. Their countries would be at war less than six weeks later.

The First World War came close to strangling the infant commodity at birth. Many of the early settlers in East Africa were adventurers as much as businessmen. They left their farms to fight in Europe or Africa, leaving their wives behind to carry on as best they could. The war in East Africa would be one of the conflict's more fascinating side-shows. Germany lost much of its territory, its farmers were interned, and, by the end of the war, many of the sisal estates had been abandoned and were derelict. It would take time afterwards to determine German East Africa's future, possession of which Germany did not formally renounce until the signing of the Treaty of Versailles in June 1919. Although Britain had appointed Sir Horace Byatt to administer it as early as 1916 the new League of Nations did not formally place it under British mandate until 1922. From now on, it would be known as Tanganyika Territory while British East Africa would be known as Kenya.

Weighing and loading the dried and brushed fibre into a baling box. (*The National Archives*, *CO 0169/140 (23)*)

Although no time limit was placed on the British mandate, it was never intended to be a permanent solution. Britain was charged with administering the territory for the benefit of the native population and for making it self-governing as quickly as possible. The German settlers were required to surrender their land and leave. The secretary of state for the colonies appointed a custodian of enemy property to supervise the disposal of their assets. The first notices advertising their sale by public auction in Dar es Salaam under the Enemy Property (Disposal) Proclamation of 1920 appeared in the press in 1921. Thereafter, they appeared at regular intervals. The first rubber, kapok, coconut, and sisal plantations were auctioned in June. By early 1923, more than 850 properties had been sold. Although the smaller sisal estates were often bought by Greek and Dutch farmers the larger ones usually ended up in British or Indian hands. When German settlers were finally allowed to return to the territory in 1925 some of them tried to buy back their old estates. It gave their new owners the opportunity to make significant windfall profits. According to a report on Tanganyika's prospects in *The Times* in 1926, one owner had recently turned down an offer of £60,000 for an estate that he had bought four years earlier for £1,200 and on which he had spent no money.[5]

The author of the report, the paper's Dar es Salaam correspondent, reckoned that the revitalisation of the sisal estates had made the biggest contribution to the territory's return to prosperity. The first Englishman to buy one was Colonel Tommy Boscawen, the youngest son of the 7th Viscount Falmouth, who would go on to become the largest private estate owner in the territory. Alfred Wigglesworth was another early buyer. At the prompting of the colonial secretary, he formed a syndicate with two Zurich businessmen, Johann Franz and Walter Schoeller, to purchase a number of estates. As Amboni Estates they would become the model for all large sisal estates. Alfred reckoned that their acquisition marked the start of the modern sisal industry.

Britain's control of both Kenya and Tanganyika meant that it was now well-placed to develop the market for sisal at a time when there was growing demand for a new and economical fibre. Although manila remained the fibre of choice for most makers and users of rope, half of its trade had left London's commodity markets in 1898 after Spain ceded the Philippines to the US. America's subsequent imposition of export duties on its sale to any country other than itself further damaged its competitiveness. Other fibres also became harder to source after the war. Production of native fibres in the developed world, such as flax in Northern Ireland and *Phormium tenax* in New Zealand, fell sharply as growers found it increasingly difficult to compete against the cheapness of third world labour. Russia also withdrew from world markets after the 1917 revolution. It had been the world's largest producer of hemp before the war. Now it stopped its export. It also cut back its production of flax before eventually holding all of it back for domestic use. As Eric would tell the Dublin Rotary Club in 1941, 'self-sufficiency is a creed which over-rides everything there and today Russia ties her sheaves of corn with material which might be made into fine linen'.

Alfred Wigglesworth.

At the same time, Great Britain had to take on greater imperial responsibilities, especially in the Middle East and Africa, after the defeat of Germany and the collapse of the Ottoman Empire. Its empire now comprised almost sixty countries and covered a quarter of the world's landmass. The war, however, had stripped the country of its human and financial resources just when they were needed the most. Every territory, colony and protectorate would have to be developed as quickly as possible so that they were no longer a drain on the British economy. The stimulation of economic growth and self-sufficiency throughout the empire would be a fundamental element of British imperial policy throughout the 1920s.

It was still the era of free trade, and the British electorate remained strongly opposed to protectionism in the belief that it would lead to higher prices. The Conservative party lost eighty-six seats when Stanley Baldwin made the mistake of fighting the 1923 general election on an anti-free trade platform of tariff reform. The resulting hung parliament enabled Ramsey MacDonald to form the country's first Labour government. It survived for less than a year before a suitably chastened Baldwin was returned in a landslide victory. Shortly before his defeat, Baldwin had chaired an imperial economic conference in London, which resulted in the creation of the Imperial Economic Committee. Although the committee's original remit was limited to improving the marketing of the empire's food products to the British consumer this was gradually extended, first to include raw materials and manufactured goods and then to perform more general reviews of imperial trades and industries. By the time that it met for the first time, after

Baldwin's return to power, more than 17 million people had been to see the great British Empire Exhibition at Wembley in 1924. Another 10 million would go the following year. It was the largest exhibition that the world had ever seen.

The idea for such an exhibition had first been suggested before the war as an appropriate way to celebrate the Prince of Wales's twenty-first birthday in 1915. The plans were resurrected after the Armistice with the additional purpose now to celebrate the empire's achievements during the war and to encourage closer ties between its peoples. At an inaugural meeting at the Mansion House in June 1920, the letter that the prince had written to the lord mayor of London in support of the plans was read out:

> It is unnecessary, my Lord Mayor, for me to emphasize the importance of such an exhibition as a means of developing the resources and trade of the British Empire. For four years the resources of the Empire and the inventive and manufacturing energy of its peoples have been utilized almost exclusively in the terrible work of destruction. The effort in which they united has saved civilization from the deadliest menace with which it has ever been threatened, and you will, I am sure, agree that there can be no more fitting way of commemorating the triumph of our cause than by uniting again to develop for constructive work the vast potential resources and the manufacturing power of the Empire.[6]

The exhibition's organising committee met for the first time later that month, a 200-acre site in Wembley was purchased the following year, and the exhibition was finally opened by King George V on St George's Day, 23 April 1924. Every country in the empire was represented there except the Gambia, Gibraltar, and the new Irish Free State, which claimed the urgent need to make economies and the difficulty of making proper preparations in its current circumstances.[7] As well as an Elgar march, a twelve-volume survey of the Empire, and the Royal Mail's first set of commemorative stamps, the exhibition also saw the building of the original Wembley Stadium, which hosted the FA Cup final for the first time in 1923. The exhibition, which Eric visited shortly after it opened and just a fortnight before the birth of his first child, also provided a perfect opportunity for the industries of the empire to meet to plan their futures. One such gathering was the Empire Textile Conference organised by the Textile Institute, which took place over three days in June. Alfred Wigglesworth, who chaired the institute's London committee as well as the local committee of Kenya's Empire Exhibition Council, was one of the speakers and delivered a paper on the empire's production of flax and hemp fibres.

A year after the exhibition closed the Imperial Economic Committee established the Empire Marketing Board as a vehicle to promote imperial trade. Over the next seven years, the EMB used posters, films, and other media to create some of the most stylish, innovative, and influential marketing campaigns that Britain has ever seen. With a budget of £1 million a year, its original remit was to publicise and promote empire goods to British consumers. Its first poster, Highways of Empire, showed a map of the world marking the empire's main shipping routes with Great

Britain at its centre and its imperial possessions coloured in red. Below it was the simple message, 'Buy British Goods from Home and Overseas'. Its later posters encouraged consumers to buy sultanas from Australia, honey from New Zealand, dried fruits from South Africa, cigarettes from Cyprus, tea from India, and bacon from both Canada and the Irish Free State. With their images of kangaroos, kiwis, springboks, wild goats, elephants, bison, and Irish wolfhounds, and later the crops and landscapes of the empire, their purpose was as much to educate as to promote.

However, instead of the 15 per cent originally planned, the board ended up spending 65 per cent of its budget on research to improve imperial production. Its attitudes may seem jingoistic today—one of its posters in 1927, which revealed that tropical Africa's exports to Britain had just overtaken its imports for the first time, carried the headline, 'Jungles today are gold mines tomorrow'—but it played a vital role in developing the market for commodities such as sisal. A strikingly vivid colour poster, which depicted the harvesting of the fibre in East Africa, was issued the same year as part of a series called 'Empire Trade is Growing'. Two years later, British Instructional Films, which collaborated with the Imperial Institute, produced a silent black and white film, *Sisal Grass Industry of East Africa*, as part of a series on textiles that showed all the stages involved in the harvesting and processing of the fibre. However, the board's most significant contribution to developing the market for sisal was its funding of research into its potential uses. The results were published in the pamphlet *Empire Grown Sisal and its Importance to the Cordage Manufacturer* in 1928. As EMB 10, it was only the board's tenth publication in its first two years and the first to address the marketing of a specific commodity rather than general or regional agricultural research. It shows how vital sisal was believed to be in the development of economic self-sufficiency in East Africa. The pamphlet's authors, the Imperial Institute's Advisory Committee on Vegetable Fibres, had a vested interest in making it a success. The committee was chaired by Wigglesworth and included representatives from the Admiralty, the Board of Trade, the Ministry of Agriculture, and the Department of Overseas Trade, as well as from Britain's leading rope manufacturers and their trade associations. The pamphlet opened with a statement confirming the growing availability of East African sisal and its recently proven suitability for marine cordage and ended with an equally direct and patriotic exhortation:

Manufacturers are therefore advised to turn their attention to East African sisal which they will find superior in many respects to other cordage fibres. British firms, both at home and overseas, will doubtless endeavour to increase their utilisation of the fibre for the added reason that by doing so they will assist the sisal-growing industries of British East Africa and other parts of the Empire, and thus promote inter-colonial trade and the development and well-being of the Empire as a whole. For the furtherance of such Empire trade the Empire Marketing Board was set up by the Government in 1926 and appeals to all citizens of the British Empire to give their preference, wherever possible, to Empire products.[8]

One of the major challenges faced by sisal producers and merchants was that manufacturers and users of marine cordage had yet to be convinced of its ability to withstand exposure to saltwater. The EMB turned for help to the Imperial Institute (later the Commonwealth Institute), which had been set up in 1887 to fund scientific research into the industrial and commercial development of the empire. Its research included dumping crates of sisal rope off Southend Pier and leaving them there for periods of three, six, and twelve months to test its durability. However, although Sweden and Germany were already using sisal for marine cordage and the institute's experiments, which continued well into the 1930s, showed that sisal compared favourably against traditional manila rope, it would take time for the new fibre to win acceptance in Britain, where demand for it remained stable in the mid-1920s at around 8,000 tons a year or 12 per cent of the country's hard fibre imports against manila's 75 per cent. Demand then fell to 5,000 tons at the beginning of the 1930s before leaping to 37,000 tons by 1935.

Wigglesworth, who was now a sisal grower as well as a fibre merchant, clearly had good reasons to promote the fibre. However, his firm also traded in other fibres and his prescient and almost evangelical commitment to sisal seems to have gone beyond purely commercial considerations. He was a man of strong opinions and was never afraid to share them. Throughout his life, he was a prolific public speaker and pamphleteer as well as a regular correspondent to *The Times*. He even found time in 1931 to co-author an economic study of the current recession with his brother, Frederick. Britain, he wrote in the introduction to *The Gold Tangle and the Way Out: Meaning and Causes of the Great Industrial Collapse*, was facing its greatest crisis since the war:

> We British people stand stricken, distressed, impoverished, losing our grip of Empire, our confidence gone, our credit depreciated, our industries paralysed, our people bewildered, our rulers distraught.... We stand at the cross-roads. Which way shall we choose?[9]

In order to win acceptance for sisal and extend its range of uses, Wigglesworth believed that it was essential to improve its competitiveness in terms of quality, price, and availability. Before the war, all the fibre exported from German East Africa had been shipped to Hamburg in small ungraded consignments and then sold on the London commodity markets on the basis of description and samples alone. Mexican henequen was similarly ungraded and the wide variance in its quality led to manufacturing problems, equipment breakdowns, and general frustration for American spinners. Wigglesworth therefore made the decision to standardise bale sizes and to grade all the fibre produced on his own estates and on the other estates in East Africa that his firm represented. He would later be proud to boast to a meeting of the Mozambique Sisal Producers Association in 1949 that it had never been necessary to resort to arbitration on the quality of Amboni sisal. This reassurance on quality, consistency, and continuity of supply gave European manufacturers the confidence to buy in bulk prior to shipment, which in turn enabled Wigglesworth to persuade the East African shipping lines, most of which were still German-owned, to ship the fibre directly to the ports nearest his customers. At the same time, while the harvesting and processing of other tropical fibres such as jute and manila were still largely manual processes in the hands of native labour, Wigglesworth was determined to mechanise every possible stage in the production of sisal, from decortication through drying and brushing to baling. In a brief history of his firm's first forty years in 1935, he claimed that 'of all fibres, the production of sisal may be considered to be the best organised, its modern factories being a model of up-to-date mechanical appliance'.[10]

The political and administrative problems that had to be addressed in Tanganyika after the war meant that its sisal exports did not recover to their pre-war level until 1926. However, when they were aggregated with Kenya's growing exports, they would show seventeen years of uninterrupted growth from 1921 to 1938. Their combined exports more than doubled in the second half of the 1920s, from 28,000 tons in 1925 to 66,000 tons in 1930, and then almost doubled again in the 1930s, in spite of the global recession, to reach 129,000 tons by 1938.[11] In the process, sisal doubled its share of the world's hard fibre markets. As with any crop prices reflected annual variations in the yield and quality of the harvest. However, the growing acreage under cultivation, mechanisation, the economies of scale that could be achieved by the larger estates, and improvements in transportation to and from the African ports all had a downward effect on the costs of production. Prices remained relatively stable throughout the 1920s, rising from an annual average of £33 a ton in 1920 to £37 in 1925 before falling back again to £33 in 1929, but then, to the shock of the growers, suddenly plummeted at the start of the 1930s.

The global recession hit East Africa as hard as anywhere. In 1931, after eighteen years in Africa, Karen Blixen had to sell her coffee estate and return to Denmark when she ran out of money and finally had to accept that she would never be able to make it work. Lord Delamere died the same year. It was the end of an era. By 1931, the price of sisal had fallen by 61 per cent to £13 a ton and would not recover for five years. Prices for other commodities and fibres also collapsed but not quite so steeply—manila by 57 per cent, jute by 49 per cent, cotton by 46 per cent, and flax by 32 per cent. Worse still, as Wigglesworth recognised, these annual averages hid a short-term volatility that made life almost impossible for the growers:

After reaching the slaughter price of £12 per ton in August and September 1931 the market improved to £18 and has been hovering around £16 and £18 during the past ten months except for a temporary dip to £15 in December. This price offers no encouragement to further production: indeed it precludes any satisfactory profit being earned. It may safely be stated that the price should

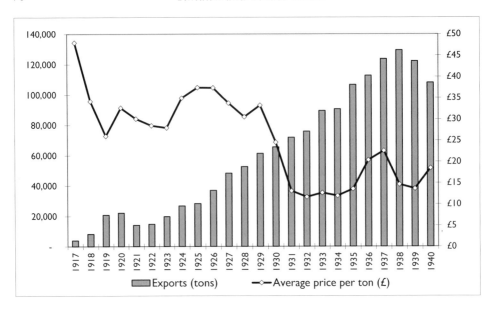

Quantity and average price of annual sisal exports from Kenya and Tanganyika, 1917–1940 (from figures in Lock, *Sisal,* Appendix I).

exceed £20 a ton to justify the heavy capital outlay incurred in sisal production. Meanwhile little increase in production may be expected. If the world requires a larger output of sisal than that which is being produced today the price must be adjusted accordingly.[12]

While the fall in price was welcome news for manufacturers in Europe, and especially for a new enterprise like Irish Ropes, it was catastrophic for the sisal estates. Many owners of the smaller estates had limited resources and were forced out of business. Even the larger ones faced difficulties. At the time, there were only two East African sisal companies listed on the London stock exchange. The first, East African Sisal Plantations, paid no dividends between 1921 and 1935 and the second, Bird & Co. (Africa), paid dividends only in 1924 and 1925. Their mounting losses forced both to reorganise their share capital in 1935.[13] Sisal did not look an attractive investment, and the growing acreage under cultivation risked over-production, which would only force prices lower. Unlike other commodities, it was not easy to cut back production. While rubber could be left untapped in the tree sisal, after its long gestation period between planting and first harvesting, had to be cut several times a year to encourage leaf growth and maintain the plant's productive life. The war had shown that the estates would quickly revert to jungle if they were left abandoned for even a year or two. Moreover, many of the growers had financed the purchase, development, and mechanisation of their estates with bank loans. They could not get out now without crystallising substantial losses.

Fortunately, demand for sisal kept pace with its increasing supply. Growers and merchants never had to resort to stockpiling to manipulate price or demand. They could not, however, withstand the financial pressures for long and within them lay the seeds of a conflict that would flare up again both during and after the Second World War. In 1943, a widely distributed Colonial Office memorandum on sisal production in British East Africa described how growers had often suffered at the hands of merchants in the 1930s:

> Sisal was not in over supply, but supplies and demands were very nearly balanced and, since many producers were weak financially and could not wait for their money, the market consisted of many weak sellers against comparatively few strong buyers. Prices suffered accordingly, and the weaker sections of the East African industry lived from hand to mouth. Much of the industry has consequently never been adequately and efficiently equipped nor able to afford first class technical staff. This is of great consequence at the present time.... Too large a proportion of the East African industry consists of small men, without previous training or experience, buying their knowledge dearly.[14]

The growers accused the fibre merchants of being complicit in the collapse in price. Some even tried to cut them out completely by planning to build their own rope factory at Tanga on the coast of Tanganyika. They were forced to stop when the Colonial Office threatened to put a tariff on imported rope to protect the 20,000 jobs in the British cordage industry. Meanwhile, Wigglesworth remained convinced that the future of the industry lay with the larger, more efficient estates like his own that were professionally run and able to produce fibre of the highest quality at an economical price. He responded harshly to his critics by accusing them of naivety, pointing out that the henequen industry in Mexico had been held back by the monopolistic practices of its government co-operative. The price of sisal, like other commodities, had been hit by factors outside the merchants' control. Indeed, they deserved praise rather than criticism for ensuring that there was a ready market for the fibre. Any future growth in demand, he argued, depended on its competitiveness against other fibres, the discovery and development of new uses for it, and the merchants' own intimate understanding of their customers' requirements. In turn, he put much of the blame on the smaller Greek and Asian growers who championed the idea of a co-operative because their sisal tended to be of poorer quality and whose lack of working capital regularly forced them to sell their stock at knock-down prices.

Although markets began to recover in the middle of the 1930s—the price of sisal increased from £12 a ton in 1934 to £23 in 1937—Wigglesworth had yet to win the case for sisal over manila. He was convinced that high-quality graded fibre of good colour was essential for the development of the new products on which he believed that any future growth in demand depended. New machinery was now coming on to the market, which enabled such sisal to be spun into fine yarn that might then compete with soft fibres like Italian hemp. He also actively promoted the extension of its use beyond agricultural twines and marine cordage to matting, underlay, and sacking and suggested that the short fibres that had previously been thrown away as a waste product could be used to make plasterboard and to stuff mattresses and upholstery.

To further these ambitions, he helped establish a sisal research station at Ngomeni in Tanganyika in 1934. Its main goal was to develop new and hardier plant hybrids and to improve methods of cultivation and processing. The following year, the Tanganyikan and Kenyan Sisal Growers Associations, with help from their colonial governments, also started to fund research at the Linen Institute Research Association (LIRA) at Lisburn in Northern Ireland. It had enough space to set up a dedicated sisal section with its own laboratories and with facilities for testing new spinning and rope-making machinery. It was also conveniently close to Mackies in Belfast, which was, at the time, the world's leading manufacturer of textile machinery. Wigglesworth kept in regular contact with LIRA's director, William Gibson, and provided him with statistics when he presented a paper on sisal and flax production in East Africa to the Dominions and Colonies section of the Royal Society of Arts in 1938. It meant that there was now a growing group of like-minded growers, merchants, machinery manufacturers, ropemakers, and research scientists who were keen to work together to realise sisal's full potential.

We do not know now how and when Eric Rigby-Jones and Alfred Wigglesworth first met. It is quite possible that H. and J. Jones had been a customer of Wigglesworths for some time before Irish Ropes was established. Although Alfred was older than Eric's father the two men developed a close working and personal relationship. It was almost certainly Alfred who encouraged Eric to adopt sisal as Irish Ropes's primary raw material. He also went out of his way to support the company in its early years, offering it attractive credit terms that drew complaints of preferential treatment from British spinners. The two of them shared a vision for the future of sisal and were determined to realise its potential. Wigglesworth's belief that merchants needed to have an intimate understanding of their customers' needs was warmly embraced by Eric who gained a reputation as one of Wigglesworths's most demanding clients. Like Alfred, he was certain that fine spinning was the key to the development of new products and that this required fibre of the highest quality. As well as helping to fund research in East Africa, he began his own practical experiments in Newbridge; he was close enough to Northern Ireland to make regular visits to both LIRA and Mackies to find out what they were doing and to pass on his own ideas; and, after the war, he would be the first ropemaker to visit East Africa to see for himself how things were done there and how quality might be improved.

5

Newbridge, 1935–1939

Droichead Nua is a town reborn. For ten long years it knew the darkest depression with its attendant spectres of loss of trade, unemployment, and want. Now all that is passed and its face is turned towards prosperity. New life has been infused into the town. Traders are doing better business, unemployment is less than normal and the prospect for the future is bright indeed. The town is growing fast.[1]

Eric's gamble with sisal paid off. Five months after the opening of its spinning mill, Seamus Moore, a TD for Wicklow, spoke of farmers' positive reaction when Irish Ropes's sisal twine was introduced to the public at the Royal Dublin Society's annual spring show. He went on to suggest that those who were critical of Lemass's industrial policy should visit those towns like Newbridge that had benefited from it:

So far from finding fault with the development we ought to be very glad that we have seen the period arrive in our country when, instead of going on at the rate of one little miserable attempt at a new industry in five years, we see now new industries being established one after another through the country, and happily being so decentralised that almost every town of importance in the country is sharing in its advantage.[2]

The establishment of Irish Ropes marked the start of Newbridge's recovery. By the end of its first year, the factory employed thirty-six staff, a figure that went up to seventy-five the following year and topped 200 in 1936. Although Eric was the first to arrive, he was not the only so-called 'tariff-hopper' to set up in Newbridge. Soon there were two more factories at the barracks. According to its advertisements, Newbridge Cutlery, which opened there in 1935 under the management of William Haigh from Sheffield, made the finest cutlery on the latest machinery, 'made in Ireland by Irish workers'. Discussions between William Cummins and other local politicians and British cutlers had led to five English craftsmen moving to Newbridge. The firm, now known as Newbridge Silverware, is still based in the town. A smaller concern, the Irish Last Works, made wooden lasts for shoemakers and was run by a Mr Whitten from Northampton. He brought three men over with him and employed a staff of thirty. It remained in Newbridge until 1960 when it relocated to Co. Cavan. It was no coincidence that all three firms were run by Englishmen who came from the traditional heartlands of their respective industries and who were all threatened by Ireland's imposition of tariffs. However, locally owned businesses like Counihan's dairy and the Ballysax Brick and Tile Works also found a new lease of life and contributed to the town's recovery.

The most visible and symbolic sign of the town's revival was the completion of a new bridge over the Liffey in 1936. The bridge gave the town its name and identity and was the first structure seen by any visitor arriving from Dublin. There had been repeated calls for it to be rebuilt in the 1920s, not least to relieve local unemployment, but the money had never been found. Now at last it was finished, and beside it stood an equally impressive new public library.

In spite of the growing success of his new venture, Eric did not immediately cut his ties with home. He was still warden of the Liverpool Cathedral Commoners at the beginning of 1934 when he found himself caught up in an unfortunate diocesan dispute for which his friend, Fred Dwelly, was responsible and which rapidly escalated into a national controversy. Dwelly, who had been appointed Liverpool's first dean after his organisation of the celebrations to mark the diocese's fiftieth anniversary, had courted controversy by inviting non-conformist ministers to preach at some of the cathedral's minor services. It was perhaps characteristic of his unshakeable belief in the righteousness of his own cause that he did not seek the bishop's permission beforehand. However, once he realised how much of an upset he had caused, he apologised unreservedly and undertook not to do it again. For some, it was too little and too late. Lord Hugh Cecil, the conservative MP for Oxford University and a prominent high Anglican, effectively accused him of encouraging heretical opinions and cited the bishop to his superior, the archbishop of York, for offences against ecclesiastical law. The affair dragged on for several months even after the bishop had refused to take any further action against Dwelly and had himself suffered the humiliation of being formally rebuked at a meeting of his fellow bishops.

Eric was forced to return from Ireland only a few days after spending his first Christmas at home after the foundation of Irish Ropes to chair a special meeting of the Cathedral Commoners at which he made a spirited defence of his friend. The meeting, which was held when the scandal was at its height, was reported in *The Times* where Eric was quoted as saying that, as the watchwords of the Commoners were obedience and liberty to grow, 'the conviction was strong among them that the cathedral must be an ever-open door to God', and that 'when the offices of the regular services had all been fulfilled, the open door of the cathedral provided a unique opportunity'. 'The issue was not just a trivial local matter,' he went on, 'issues vital to every Christian were concerned and to compromise would not merely be to restrict the liberty of Liverpool Cathedral and damage its usefulness; it would be to surrender their faith.'³ Eric's intervention was never going to be the end of the matter. Peter Kennerly even suggested in his 2004 biography of Dwelly that the split between the cathedral, represented by the dean, and the diocese, represented by the bishop, had yet to be healed.⁴ However, although Eric stayed in touch with his friend, it seems that he had no further association with the cathedral after this episode.

It would be another two years before Eric finally resigned his commission in the Territorial Army. On 11 November 1935, the seventeenth anniversary of the Armistice, he wrote to advise the military authorities that, as he was now living and working full-time in Ireland, he was no longer able to fulfil his obligations as an officer. It is the final document in his army personnel file that is still held by the Ministry of Defence. Two months later, the directors of Irish Ropes voted to increase his salary from £650 to £750. They thought it was important to document it formally in the minutes not only because it was his first pay increase but also, and more significantly, because he had not originally thought that he would be working full-time in Ireland. It is the first clear sign that Eric was now confident of Irish Ropes's survival and eventual success. However, it would be another year before he found somewhere permanent to live and was finally reunited with his family.

Meanwhile, he was a regular passenger on the ferry across the Irish Sea. Dorothy and the children visited Ireland for the first time at Easter in 1934 and spent three weeks in the works hostel. Peter remembered that his father still had to fill buckets of water for their baths. It must have been distressing for Eric to be separated from his wife for so long and to miss the chance of seeing his children grow up. It also placed a great strain on his parents who were now in their mid-sixties. Once Eric had established himself in Ireland, Dorothy and the children moved out of the family home at Parkside and moved in with Harry and Alice at the Ruff where, in order to preserve some degree of independence, she was given a sitting room of her own. Peter had just turned nine when Irish Ropes was founded, Michael was six, and Ann three. Although they spent some of their school holidays with Dorothy's parents at Rhos, they were brought up mainly by Harry and Alice. In due course, they would be away at boarding school for much of the year. After some time at Ormskirk Grammar School, Peter was sent away to the Craig, a preparatory school in the Lake District, in 1935. Three years later, he moved on to Rossall, a tough school on the bleak Fylde coast north of Blackpool where his father and uncle had both been educated. Michael followed in his footsteps two years later and Ann was eventually sent away to board at Liverpool College for Girls.

Peter felt the lack of a family life acutely. Many years later, when he wrote his memoirs in his retirement, it was his grandparents that he remembered with particular affection. Alice, he believed, had been the main influence for any good in his life. His parents on the other hand rarely showed any emotion and he never felt close to them. He always thought that they preferred Michael and would never feel at home in Ireland.

Dorothy encouraged the children to write regularly to their father. Ann's earliest 'letter' in 1934, before she had learnt to write, was just a series of scribbles. She later sent drawings of herself with brief but poignant messages asking when she would see him again. Eric wrote comments like 'Ann's first letter' on their envelopes and then locked them away in his desk. Dorothy only found them again after his death. In later life, he could often appear to be austere and somewhat remote without any obvious sense of humour. It was an impression that owed much to a rather severe photograph of him that was taken for an Irish Ropes brochure at the end of the 1940s, which some have suggested shows him haunted by his memories of the First World War. However, Ann told me more than fifty years after his death that he was really quite a sentimental man.

In October 1935, a month before Eric resigned from the Territorial Army, the board of Irish Ropes met to review the company's performance in its second year. Only Eric and Patrick Doyle were present for what was essentially a formality at the auditors' offices in Dublin. Eric again read out the directors' annual report to shareholders, which highlighted further substantial progress. The opening of the new spinning mill at the start of the year had enabled the factory to

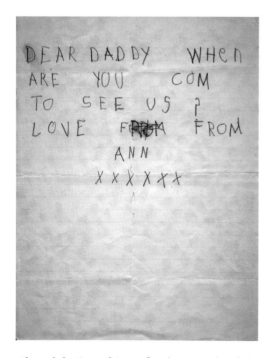

Above left: One of Ann's first letters to her father.

Above right: One of Ann's drawings.

produce its first 100 tons of binder twine in time for the 1935 harvest. Although this represented only an eighth of the country's needs, Eric was confident that a full year's production, combined with his latest plans to double the factory's capacity, would mean that no twine would have to be imported in 1936. By now, the company was already benefitting from the protection of tariffs. Shortly after the introduction of Irish Ropes's twine at the Royal Dublin Show, the Irish government extended its 40 per cent tariff on ropes and cordage to include binder twine. It was one of twenty-nine new duties introduced specifically to protect fledgling industries. When they were debated in the Dáil in May, Lemass insisted that, although he had had to grant a temporary import licence for twine that year because domestic production had started too late to meet demand in full, year-round production would in future eliminate the need for any imports.[5] Furthermore, domestic manufacturers, instead of importing the yarn that they needed to make it, would soon be required to spin their own. It was something that only Irish Ropes could do at the time. When he was challenged over whether there were enough yarn spinners in Ireland the minister of finance, Sean MacEntee, could not resist answering that the opposition benches were full of them.

Two months later, Lemass was able to reassure the powerful farmers lobby, which had asked some legitimate questions about the quality, price, and availability of Irish Ropes's new twine, by confirming that the company had guaranteed not to charge higher prices than those traditionally set at the start of each year by English manufacturers. He also said that he was confident that, as the company was using the latest machinery and processes, it would have no difficulty competing on quality. It was a significant political statement—and welcome evidence that his plans to develop domestic industry could be achieved without any disadvantage to the Irish consumer. 'Here, at all events, for the first time,' conceded Professor O'Sullivan, the opposition TD for Kerry North and Cosgrave's former minister for education, 'there is a guarantee given that the tariffed article is not going to be dearer. In other cases we had nothing of that kind; we had some prophecies.'[6]

However, the directors' satisfaction with Irish Ropes's trading performance was tempered by continuing legal and financial concerns. Not only were they several months behind schedule in securing the funds needed for the company's next stage of development, but they were also not yet compliant with a second and much stricter Control of Manufactures Act. The act had been passed a year earlier to close the loopholes in the first act that men like Arthur Cox and Vincent Crowley had been able to exploit without any difficulty. Whereas the first act had required only that Irish nationals held a majority of shares in any Irish company, the second act ensured that they exercised effective control by requiring that they also held two-thirds of voting rights and formed a majority on the board of directors. Although Eric and his father now held only 49 per cent of the shares in Irish Ropes they still controlled 49 per cent of the voting rights and formed a majority on the three-man board. If the company was to continue to grow, it needed to attract new Irish investors and directors, and preferably those who were prepared to give Eric some leeway to continue to run it himself under Arthur Cox's supervision. It was the start of a busy and stressful few months. In the first eleven months of 1935, the board met only five times—and three of those meetings were almost certainly by proxy to approve the use of the company's seal on important corporate documents. In the next four months, it would meet nine times as it finalised the company's new capital structure and board membership.

The immediate problem of legal compliance was resolved by the end of February 1936 after the company's share capital was increased in stages by £10,000 from £7,000 to £17,000. Eric and Harry invested another £4,800, while Arthur Cox invested £3,000 and bought 1,000 shares from Patrick Doyle. The remaining 2,200 shares were purchased by two new investors, John O'Neill and Major Hugh Henry, who also joined the board. At the same time, the share structure was simplified. The classes of preference and preferred ordinary shares were eliminated and the resulting 17,000 ordinary shares were split simply between 6,000 voting shares and 11,000 non-voting shares. The restructuring left Eric and his father, the only foreign nationals, with 48 per cent of the shares but only a third of the voting rights and just two seats on the five-man board, thus meeting the requirements of the new act. However, Arthur Cox now held 27 per cent of the shares and 38 per cent of the voting rights and, when his stake was added to theirs, they held 75 per cent of the shares and 72 per cent of voting rights between them even though they appeared, for the time being at least, to have lost control of the board.

The strengthening of the board was also a reflection of the company's growing stature. John O'Neill was one of Dublin's leading industrialists, having turned his original bicycle repair business into a major motor dealership and the largest manufacturer of bicycle parts in the British Isles. A one-time senator and an early supporter of the country's industrialisation, he had helped found the Dublin Industrial Development Association and had been an advisor to the government before, during, and after the creation of the Free State. Having chaired the All-Ireland Munitions Commission during the war, he was asked by the first Dáil to head the Commission of Inquiry into the Resources and Industries of Ireland

	Shares			**Share split**		**% of total**	
	Before	New	After	Voting	Non-voting	*Shares*	*Votes*
Rigby-Jones	3,430	4,800	8,230	2,000	6,230	*48*	*33*
Doyle	3,061	(1,000)	2,061	500	1,561	*12*	*8*
Cox	509	4,000	4,509	2,300	2,209	*27*	*38*
O'Neill	-	2,000	2,000	1,000	1,000	*12*	*17*
Henry	-	200	200	200	-	*1*	*3*
	7,000	10,000	17,000	6,000	11,000	*100*	*100*

Irish Ropes' share issues, December 1935–February 1936, and shareholders' voting rights (minus figures are shown in brackets).

from 1919 to 1921. He went on to serve on the Economic Relations Commission in 1921 and, at the time of his appointment to Irish Ropes's board, was a member of the 1934 Banking Commission. His experience there would be particularly valuable as the commission's remit included reviewing the government's use of credit and guarantees to help develop the country's agriculture, industry, and social services. Major Hugh Henry was another influential businessman if not perhaps of quite the same stature. A director of the Bank of Ireland and deputy chairman of Great Southern Railways, where his father-in-law was chairman, he had the advantage of living in Newbridge in what is now the Keadeen Hotel. Arthur Cox was also persuaded to join the board and was appointed chairman. It meant that, although four of the six directors were now Irish nationals, Eric and his father could not be outvoted as long as Arthur voted with them and cast his deciding vote in their favour.

The board's original plans for the next round of the company's financing were never completed. At Arthur's first meeting as chairman in February, the directors agreed, somewhat surprisingly, to proceed with a share offer to the public as soon as the accounts for the six months to the end of February were available. Although these were prepared at great speed and presented to the board in the middle of March, they were not needed. Major Henry, who had already offered to sound out who might be interested in underwriting the share offer, now volunteered to speak to James Beddy, the secretary of the Industrial Credit Corporation, which Lemass had set up in 1933 to provide long-term finance for industry whether as an underwriter, a lender, or a shareholder. Four months later, the ICC invested £20,005 in Irish Ropes's shares. Its investment allowed the company's share structure to be simplified further. All the shares were now converted into a single class of ordinary share, each of which was entitled to one vote. In order to bring the company's share capital up to £40,000, which would leave the ICC with a majority stake of 50.01 per cent, another 2,995 shares were issued over the next few months. Most of them (2,500) were bought by Bernard Roche who joined the board as sales director at the start of 1937. He had set up his own rope factory in Cork three years earlier and had been buying his yarn from Irish Ropes. He now closed this down and moved his machinery to Newbridge where it would become known as 'The Cork Set'. Eric's right-hand man, Horace Davies, also bought 150 shares while the rest were bought by Eric and his father.

At the start of the process, Irish Ropes had had £18,000 of funds for investment, made up of £7,000 of share capital and the two bank loans of £5,000 and £6,000 that had been guaranteed by the Minister for Industry and Commerce. Now, a year later, it had £59,000 of which £39,000 (or 66 per cent) had been provided or guaranteed by a government body. In addition to its £40,000 of share capital, it had £19,000 of bank loans, a third loan for £10,000 having been secured early in 1936 and £2,000 of the earlier loans having been repaid on schedule. The company also had a strong seven-man board, five of whom were Irish nationals, and was fully compliant with the second Control of Manufactures Act. All was set

| | Shares | | | % of |
	Before	New	After	total
Rigby-Jones	8,230	345	8,575	21
Doyle	2,061	-	2,061	5
Cox	4,509	-	4,509	11
O'Neill	2,000	-	2,000	5
Henry	200	-	200	1
Davies	-	150	150	0
Roche	-	2,500	2,500	6
ICC	-	20,005	20,005	50
	17,000	23,000	40,000	100

Irish Ropes's share issues to the Industrial Credit Corporation (ICC) and others, September 1936–February 1937.

fair for the future. Apart from some minor changes forced by circumstances the directors and shareholders remained unchanged for the next ten years and would see the company through the Second World War.

Two simple sets of figures illustrate Irish Ropes's progress in its first four years. The first shows that its annual profits improved steadily from £355 in its first year to August 1934 to £2,268 in 1935, £9,097 in 1936, and £12,533 in 1937.[7] The second, which is based on answers provided to questions in the Dáil in 1938, shows that domestic cordage production increased from 912 tons in 1933 to 2,079 tons in 1936 before settling back to 1,975 tons in 1937. Over the same period, imports fell from 1,290 tons to 367 tons.[8] When added together, they show that overall consumption grew by 6 per cent while the domestic share of production more than doubled, from 41 per cent to 84 per cent.

Sometime in 1937, with the Anglo-Irish trade war still unresolved, the British cigarette manufacturers, W. D. and H. O. Wills, issued a series of fifty cigarette cards on Irish industries. Whatever their motives for doing so, the notes on the back of each card delivered a clear and powerful message about the extent of Ireland's recent industrial progress. Unsurprisingly, the first card in the series was on agriculture and depicted a horse-drawn mechanical binder and some ears of corn. The notes on the back highlighted the recent increase in acreage under wheat, from 94,000 acres in 1934 to 255,000 in 1936. Although this was still well short of the 800,000 acres needed to make the country self-sufficient, it was encouraging news for the manufacturer of binder twine. Later cards featured well-known Irish products like whiskey, Guinness, and Jacobs' biscuits, as well as significant new industries such as the Shannon hydroelectric scheme, boot and shoe making (where factory numbers had tripled in five years), car assembly (with the notes claiming that every popular make of car was now being assembled in the Free State), and neon signs (which were currently being manufactured by three firms, all of which were less than three years old). The thirty-ninth card featured the manufacture of rope and twine. The notes on the back explained that there were now nine ropemakers in Ireland, the oldest of which dated back to the nineteenth century, but that the manufacture of binder twine had only begun in 1935.

The year 1937 would be an important one for Eric and Irish Ropes as well as for Ireland itself. In July, de Valera's new constitution was approved by 57 per cent of voters in a national referendum. When it came into force at the end of the year, Ireland would effectively be independent. The British monarch would be removed as head of state, the office of governor-general replaced by an elected president, the Irish Free State would be renamed Ireland (or Eire in Gaelic), and the green, white, and orange tricolour would be adopted as the national flag. From now on, the prime minister would be known as the Taoiseach and his deputy as the Tánaiste. Although the new constitution claimed jurisdiction over the whole of the island this was firmly rejected by the British government, which made it clear that Northern Ireland remained a willing part of the UK. Otherwise it accepted it with minimal protest in the belief that it did not fundamentally alter Ireland's membership of the British Commonwealth. In the general election that was held on the same day as the referendum, De Valera was returned as Taoiseach, his Fianna Fáil party winning sixty-nine, or exactly half, of the 138 seats in the Dáil against Fianna Gael's forty-eight.[9]

Until now, Eric had continued to live in the hostel at the barracks. However, with Irish Ropes now firmly established and the world finally coming out of recession, he recognised (with some prompting from Dorothy) that it was time to find a permanent home in Ireland for himself and his family. The house that he found—Morristownbiller House, or Morristown for short—was a substantial but neglected Georgian mansion on the north-western edge of Newbridge where the Taylor family had lived until the death of William Taylor in 1935. A lot of work needed to be done inside and out to make it comfortable. Twelve-year-old Peter came over at Easter to help him get it ready for occupation. Inside it was cold and damp and lacked any central heating; the bath was branded 'Fin de Siècle' and the lavatory 'The Deluge'; and, until Eric installed an electric pump, water had to be pumped by hand to the storage tanks in the roof. Eric and Dorothy would rent it for the rest of their married life. Two sisters were recruited as live-in maids to help Dorothy with the cooking and housework while Power, the gardener, lived above the garage without any running water or electricity. The children quickly renamed his lair Powerscourt after the Wingfield family's magnificent mansion in County Wicklow. Other nicknames followed that reminded them of England and home. The greenhouse became known as the Crystal Palace, the drive as Ruff Lane, the path to the stables as Rotten Row, the lawn as Green Park and the path around it as Brooklands, the summer house as Maesgwyn, and the rubbish heap as Mount Pleasant.[10] In time, the road that ran past the house became known locally as

Morristownbiller House.

Jones Lane. Eric made a workshop for himself in the basement, which he also used as a dark room to develop his photographs. Outside, he and Dorothy had an acre of kitchen garden with an abundance of fruit trees and raspberry canes. Once cleared and replanted, it would become a vital source of fruit and vegetables during the war.

Eric and Dorothy moved in a few days after the referendum. It must have been a relief to be together again and to have the children with them for the summer holidays. They now also had the space to entertain friends and business acquaintances and to accommodate the many members of their families who wanted to visit. Horace Davies and Dorothy Baxter, who were still living at the hostel, visited regularly at the weekend to play tennis and usually stayed for supper while Arthur Cox and John O'Neill often called in to discuss business over afternoon tea. Eric's parents were among the first to visit and would return many times. Eric's brother, Guy, came with them along with Dorothy's sister, Lottie, and her family. Harry, who was increasingly worried about his weight, wrote in the guest book that he gained 4 pounds, Alice that she enjoyed reseating and cleaning six old chairs, and Lottie that her son, James, learnt to ride a bicycle.[11] Sadly, Dorothy's mother, Nain, had died a year earlier and Taid, who was now seventy-eight, could only visit once before war and old age intervened. Otherwise, it would be an idyllic two years. Eric and Dorothy's guest book shows that they played host to business acquaintances from around the world, including Denmark, Switzerland, Holland, Hong Kong, Canada, and the Philippines, as well as to sisal growers and government officials from East Africa.

By now, Irish Ropes was employing 200 staff and manufacturing 500 types of rope and twine. It would quickly become a world leader in the fine spinning of sisal. The new machinery now coming on to the market meant that it could spin 2,700 feet of yarn from a single pound of fibre. Its branded twines—Green Seal packing twine, Red Seal binder twine, and, most famously, Red Setter baler twine—were already firmly established and would remain household names in Ireland for many years to come. Eric was now keen to build on his success by developing new uses for sisal, which, unlike agricultural twine, were not reliant on seasonal demand. He installed a laboratory at the factory and began collaborating with Alec Nisbet, a chemistry graduate from Queen's University Belfast who was a member of LIRA's sisal research team at Lisburn. His decision to diversify into the manufacture of sisal matting and floor coverings would be one of the most significant in Irish Ropes's history. Large-scale carpet production, which was made possible by the fine spinning of sisal, would be a major step forward from weaving smaller floor mats and products like shopping bags and table mats. Irish Ropes's sisal carpets, which were sold under the brand name of Tintawn, an anglicised version of *tintean*, the Gaelic for a hearth stone, would become an iconic global brand in the 1950s and 1960s. Although production began in the spring of 1937, it was not until the following year that Tintawn was registered as a trademark and introduced to the public.

It would be another important year for Irish Ropes and Ireland—and one for which we now have more detailed family records. Although Eric almost certainly wrote regularly to his family before he and Dorothy moved into Morristown, none of his letters from that time survive. However, once they were settled in, he got into a routine on Sunday evenings during term-time of typing a weekly round-robin letter to his children at their various schools in England. A hundred of these survive for the period from March 1938 to July 1942. They provide an intriguing insight into his life in Ireland immediately before and after the start of the Second World War. He always tried to fill one side of foolscap but never went on to a second page, and although he added other members of the family to the circulation list from time to time, he usually tried to telephone the Ruff the same evening so that he could talk to everyone there. Although Dorothy, Harry, and Alice also wrote regularly to the children—Ann remembers being grateful that she always could count on getting four letters a week when she was away at school—none of their letters survive.

One of Eric's first letters, which was written on 13 March 1938, the day after Nazi Germany annexed Austria, is a good example of their usual mixture of information, education, and gossip. It also suggests that the family's halcyon days at Morristown might be over almost before they had begun.

Dear Children and especially Ann,

Perhaps in another hundred years the boys and girls at school will be learning yet another date—1938. Today it seemed unbelievable that in so many parts of the world people should be at war with each other when it has been another wonderful spring day here—quiet, still except for the birds, and sunny. Last night we went to the Abbey Theatre to see a play called Moses' Rock. It was about Ireland in the time of Parnell when for once it seemed that all Irishmen were so united as to seem as strong as a rock: then Moses split the rock, the rock of Ireland was split and men were falling out with each other again.

Today we have had a lazy day—I'm afraid I did not get up until nearly eleven o'clock. Yesterday afternoon I did some more clearing in the wood and lit a huge bonfire: today it still burned but is now all gone. I have cleared a great space among the trees and Mummy has swept out under one of the bay trees so that inside is like a goblin house, all twisted branches. Already there are a lot of flies about and it would appear that we are going to have swarms of them this summer.

This week I have overhauled Power's Flying Machine—his lawn mower—and, having put it all together again, was glad to have it start off at the first go. Diana Davies [Horace's daughter] has been here for tea with her father and mother and spent her time in the garden scratching for worms and carrying them about. Did you hear a loud squeal this week? Mummy picked up a frog by mistake! We have a holiday on Thursday—Saint Patrick's Day—when the works are closed.

Have you heard of the Exhibition to be held in Glasgow this year? There will be a pavilion for Eire and we have just been asked if we can make the carpet for the floor but I don't know whether our Tintawn will do.

Peter starts his first term at Rossall on Tuesday, 3 May, which means that he will have four and a half weeks for holidays. It is the second day of the Dublin Show but I will try to go over to Rossall with him if it can be managed. He will have to wear stiff collars and, like me, I'm sure he will be glad to get back to a soft collar in the holidays. We have not heard when Michael begins again. His school number is 220. We heard this week that Brian Davies [the son of Dorothy's brother, Harold] has been rushed off to hospital with appendicitis but, when we rang up, we heard that he was going on all right. We had a line from Mr Hewitson to say that he thought Peter was doing well in his exam. Will you please keep your papers, Peter, and bring them home for us all to see? I don't suppose anybody has been to see you boys this weekend. You have so many visiting Sundays and half-terms: we only had the one half-term and were lucky to see somebody then.

I have just been reading a book by Sir Leonard Woolley about archaeology—the digging up of old cities. He has done a great deal of work at Ur in Mesopotamia and has been able to show that Moses lived in a house—and not always in a tent as we thought. He has found houses that existed before the Flood which descended on Mesopotamia which was almost all the civilized world then. We learn that thousands of years ago people had houses with drains and yet today there are many houses which are much worse than they used to be.

I am at the end of my news and have only just managed to make it reach the bottom of the paper. Our biggest news at present is the good weather—it is so surprising that we cannot help talking about it.

Good night and lots of love, your ever-loving Daddy.

As well as the introduction of Tintawn, 1938 also saw the end of the Anglo-Irish trade war. The first sign of rapprochement had come with the Coal-Cattle Pact in 1934 when the British government had relaxed its quotas on Irish cattle imports in return for the Irish government's agreement to buy all of its coal from Britain. A series of events from 1935 onwards—including Edward VIII's abdication in 1936 and the Irish constitutional referendum in 1937—only increased the mutual desire for a resolution and made the British government realise the futility of prolonging the dispute. Stanley Baldwin had become prime minister in 1935 after deteriorating health had forced Ramsay MacDonald to step down. Later that year, MacDonald's son, Malcolm, succeeded J. H. Thomas as secretary of state for dominion affairs. At thirty-four, he was the youngest member of the cabinet and would be instrumental in changing the government's attitude towards Ireland and in bringing about a settlement to what he considered at the time to be the most serious disagreement within the empire. The following summer, as de Valera finalised the terms of his new constitution, he presented a detailed report to the cabinet on relations with Ireland. One of his twelve recommendations was that the two governments should open negotiations. Britain, he believed, had a moral obligation to seek a resolution.

The subsequent negotiations were neither quick nor easy. De Valera played a leading role and, as usual, was an intransigent negotiator from whom it was difficult to prise any concessions. A settlement was finally agreed in April 1938—and then on terms that looked distinctly one-sided in Ireland's favour. Firstly, Britain would receive £10 million in full and final settlement of the outstanding land annuities—it was substantially less than the £76 million that Sean MacEntee had said was outstanding in 1932. Secondly, it would withdraw from the three 'treaty' ports at Berehaven, Queenstown, and Lough Swilly that it had continued to occupy since 1922 on the grounds that they were vital for its own defence—although de Valera saw their continued occupation as a slight to Irish independence, it was a concession that was bitterly opposed by Winston Churchill and many others in Britain. And, lastly, both countries would end their tariff war. For the British government, which had introduced its tariffs in 1932 to make good its losses from the withholding of the land annuities, it was a logical consequence of the settlement of that issue. However, Ireland would be allowed to retain some of its tariffs in order to protect its new industries. The Finance (Agreement with United Kingdom) Act of May 1938 reduced the rates of duty on rope and twine imported from Britain and Canada from 40 per cent to 33½ per cent but increased those on imports from elsewhere to 60 per cent and 50 per cent respectively. The following month, de Valera called his second general election within a year where his Fianna Fáil party won seventy-seven of the 138 seats and so regained its overall majority.

A week after the signing of the agreement, Eric again used the Royal Dublin Society's spring show as the vehicle to launch his latest product. Irish Ropes's advertisement for Tintawn was a prominent feature of the full-page advertorial for the show in the papers. Its new floor covering, it claimed, was hard-wearing as it was made from the toughest vegetable fibre known to man; economical as it did not require any underlay and could be turned over and relaid when one side became worn; and hygienic and easy to maintain as dirt did not get caught in the fibres but fell through to the floor where it could easily be swept up. It was suitable, it said, not only for private houses and seaside cottages but also for ships and large public buildings like cinemas, hotels, and churches. The advertisement also announced that Tintawn had been chosen as the floor covering for Ireland's pavilion at the British Empire Exhibition in Glasgow, which was due to open on the day after the opening of the Dublin show. It was also the day on which Peter was due to start his first term at Rossall. At first, Eric did not know how he could fit everything in. He eventually decided to go over to England with Peter and then rush back for the final days of the Dublin show.

The Glasgow exhibition, which ran from May to December 1938, was the first British Empire exhibition since that at Wembley in 1924. It seems astonishing now that independent Ireland should chose to be represented there only a few months after the introduction of its new constitution and just a week after the resolution of the Anglo-Irish trade war. However, the idea for the exhibition had been suggested more than a year earlier and Ireland had received and accepted an early invitation to attend and to design and build its own pavilion. Its trade with and economic dependence on its neighbour made it important for it to be represented there. It was also a perfect opportunity to put the country on display and to show how much progress had been made in just a short time. It would be the first time that Ireland was represented at an international exhibition in its own right.

By then, there was a certain ambivalence about both the British Empire and Ireland's place within it. The official guide to the exhibition referred to both the empire, with its dominions and colonies, and the British Commonwealth of Nations. Four years earlier, the Irish Free State had competed in its own right at the second Empire Games held in London. Before then, at the inaugural games in Ontario in 1930, a team of five athletes had been selected to represent the whole of the island, three of whom were never able to compete because of the late arrival of their ship. Ireland then chose, partly for reasons of cost, not to attend the third games, which were held in Sydney just three months before the opening of the Glasgow exhibition.[12] However, Ireland's pavilion now stood proudly, and perhaps defiantly, on Dominion Avenue between the pavilions of Australia, Canada, South Africa and New Zealand. Facing it on Colonial Avenue was the pavilion shared by Southern Rhodesia and East Africa that included exhibits on growing coffee and sisal and played films about the plantations and native life as well as holiday opportunities.

According to the official guide, Ireland's pavilion was the country's most ambitious venture in national publicity to date. The advertisement placed in it by Ireland's high commissioner in London, John Dulanty, claimed that it showed what could achieved in a decade and a half of effort under a 'native' government.[13] It was a strange choice of words. Inside, a large illuminated wall map at one end showed where all of its new industries had been established. Each of the

Irish Ropes's advertisement in the advertorial for the Royal Dublin Society's spring show, 6 May 1938. (*With thanks to Irish Newspaper Archives and the Irish Press*)

Ireland's pavilion on Dominions Avenue at the Glasgow Empire Exhibition, 1938. (©
Newsquest (Herald and Times))

seven bays into which its sides were divided displayed different aspects of Irish
industry or life. As well as agriculture, horse racing, and brewing and distilling,
they included the Shannon hydroelectricity scheme, traditional Gaelic sports, and
modern Irish art. At the other end, a second map showed Ireland's key position
on the new transatlantic air route, which the governments of the US, Canada,
Great Britain, and Ireland had agreed to establish three years earlier. In 1939,
Pan American Airways would begin regular mail and passenger flights across the
Atlantic. The limited range of aircraft at the time meant that they would have
to make intermediate stops between the US and Britain at their first landfalls in
Newfoundland and Ireland. Geography gave Ireland a seat at the high table. It
established its first European terminal at Foynes on the Shannon estuary where
it was possible to land flying boats. However, work had already begun on a new
airport at Rineanna on the other side of the estuary, a model of which was on
display in the pavilion.

Mainie Jellett, one of Ireland's leading modern artists, was commissioned to
design the murals for the pavilion, and at the beginning of 1938, Eric was asked
whether he could provide Tintawn for its floor. Although he realised that it was a
great honour, he thought that it might be premature. The first Tintawn was made

of undyed sisal and the looms on which it was woven meant that it could only be manufactured in rolls a yard wide. While this made it suitable for staircases and corridors larger areas could only be covered if a series of rolls was stitched together. Nevertheless, Eric quickly overcame any doubts that he had about its suitability and the short time that he had left to produce it. Within a fortnight of being asked, he had started production.

That June, after stopping off to address the Rotary Club in Liverpool, he picked up his parents and Guy in Ormskirk and drove them up to Glasgow to see the exhibition. As well as the Irish pavilion, they wanted to visit the Coal Hall in the British pavilion where Eric's brother-in-law, John Forshaw, had helped create a working model of a coal mine. According to the guide, it was one of the five best exhibits in the pavilion, which focused on Britain's three great national industries of coal mining, shipbuilding, and iron and steel. *The Times* described it as the finest scale model of a coal mine ever built.[14]

A native of Ormskirk, John Forshaw had served with distinction in the Royal Engineers during the war before graduating with a degree in architecture from the University of Liverpool in 1922. In 1926, shortly after marrying Eric's sister, Judy, whom he had met when they were captains of Ormskirk's men's and women's hockey teams, he was appointed architect to the Miners' Welfare Commission

The interior of Ireland's pavilion showing the mural of the transatlantic air route. (*RIBApix*)

in the aftermath of the general strike and the Samuel Commission's report on miners' welfare. He was as keen as his brother-in-law to improve the lot of the working man. Over the next thirteen years, he supervised an extensive building programme throughout the coalfields to improve miners' bathing facilities and provide them with other welfare and recreational amenities. One commentator later claimed that, of all architects working in Britain between the wars, no one matched his level of design and technical competence over so large a body of work.[15]

As he wandered around the exhibition, Eric may have noticed an element of competition from Northern Ireland. The province's exhibits were spread over a number of pavilions with, for example, the agriculture, fisheries, and forestry building including a section on the flax research being carried out at LIRA. However, its official display, which focused on industry and tourism, was in the shipping and travel building. One of the stands there was for the Belfast Ropework Company, then the largest ropeworks in the world, which had been making rope for 200 years and currently employed 3,000 staff on its 40-acre site in the city. It had also taken out an advertisement in the official guide to promote its speciality, Bluebell binder twine. The building's floor was covered with an enormous carpet that the guide said had been specially woven by Ulster Carpet Mills to withstand a lifetime of wear concentrated into six months of heavy use by the millions of visitors to the exhibition from around the world. Perhaps Tintawn's early sisal matting suffered by comparison. When the World Fair was held in New York the following year, Michael Scott's shamrock-shaped Irish pavilion won the prize for the best building. Mainie Jellett had again been asked to design its murals but its floor was left uncarpeted.

Alfred Wigglesworth also visited the exhibition to give a talk on sisal. Although he focused on the cultivation and processing of the fibre, and made no reference to Tintawn or its use in the Irish pavilion, he ended by predicting that 'sisal, far from being unknown, may soon become a household word'.[16] He and his wife then moved on to Ireland where they were entertained by Eric and Dorothy at Morristown. Although they still had obstacles to overcome, he and Eric had good reason to celebrate. East African sisal had come a long way in the fourteen years since the Wembley exhibition during which time exports from Kenya and Tanganyika had increased almost fivefold, from 27,000 to 129,000 tons a year. For Alfred, the long-term future of the industry now depended on growers being able to earn a satisfactory return on their investment. The first, albeit premature, signs of recovery had appeared two years earlier, in 1936, when average annual prices increased from £14 to £20 a ton. When prices reached £28 a ton the following autumn, Wigglesworth started to feel bullish about a prolonged period of prosperity.[17] Suddenly, everything changed with prices falling back to £15 in 1938 and £14 in 1939. He put the blame squarely on the US, which, with Canada, was now buying half of the world's agricultural twine. It suffered an economic aftershock in 1937 and 1938, which, when combined with a poor harvest in 1937, left agricultural twine unsold and stockpiled.

Irish Ropes was unable to avoid the fall-out. Sisal was now accounting for 90 percent of the raw fibre that it used. After strong profit growth in its first four years, the company suffered a loss of £7,250 in 1938. As the manufacturer of a product that was of vital national importance but made from imported raw materials Eric had already established a policy of holding large stocks of both raw materials and finished goods in order to ensure continuity of supply and production and to limit the impact of any sudden movements in commodity prices. While the policy would stand Eric in good stead at the start of the war, when he could no longer be assured of the continuity of supplies, this current collapse in sisal prices meant that he had to book a substantial write-down in the value of his stocks. They were no longer worth what he had paid for them. As he reminded Arthur Cox ten years later when the company faced a similar situation but on a much larger scale, 'we bit the dust in 1938 by creating a stockpile at £28 a ton only to find the price fall to £16.'[18] Fortunately, it was only an isolated shock and the company returned to profitability the following year.

By then, Tintawn was turning out to be a major success. So much interest had been shown at the spring show that Irish Ropes had to move its stand afterwards to a window display on St Stephen's Green. The orders began to roll in. Killarney Cathedral and a church in Belfast ordered rolls of red Tintawn to be ready in time for Christmas. The Irish navy also placed an order for the fleet. However, as Eric conceded in what he called his 'Christmas number' to his children, the navy at the time owned only one ship, SS *Muirchú* (the 'hound of the sea' in Gaelic), a fisheries patrol vessel whose main role was to monitor rogue French fishermen

	Source	Tons
Raw fibres		
Sisal	East Africa & Java	2,000
Manila	Philippines & Borneo	200
Yarns		
Cotton	Lancashire Spinners	140
Jute	Goodbody's of Clara	100
Hemp	Italy, Belgium, & Hungary	60
Other		
Oil (for process work)	USA (oil companies)	250
Sizing flours	Holland & Sarawak	30
Dyes, chemicals	Various	20

Supplies used annually by Irish Ropes immediately before the war.

and keep them away from Irish waters. All too often she was unsuccessful. 'When the Frenchmen see the *Muirchú* sailing away westward,' Eric wrote, 'they know they will be safe for a few weeks until they see her smoke again in the east. She does not go round the world—only round Ireland.' By the spring of 1939, Irish Ropes had opened an office and showroom in Dublin and employed an agent in London's Cheapside. Although he would not have known it at the time, Eric had just six months to establish an export market for Tintawn before the outbreak of war.

Immediately after its launch, Eric set about ways to improve it. He and Horace Davies went over to Barnsley to buy a larger loom so that they could double its width to 2 yards. He also started to experiment with dyes and ways of extending his range of designs and weaves. When he came across problems with the dyes, he spent a lot of time in the laboratory trying to find the cause. It was some time before he thought that he had the answer. The water from the Liffey was too peaty—it was good for making Guinness but not for dying carpets.

In spite of Tintawn's success, Eric was facing growing criticism from the agricultural lobby over the cost and quality of his twine, which still accounted for half of the factory's production. The farmers' case was argued by Joseph Johnston, who would shortly be appointed professor of applied economics at Trinity College Dublin, in two articles in which he emphasised the continuing and predominant importance of agriculture and agricultural exports to the Irish economy. Farming, he pointed out, still accounted for half of the country's employment and made up almost all of its exports apart from stout, biscuits, and some textiles.[19] He questioned the value of the new and, in his view, artificially stimulated manufacturing industries. In too many cases, he claimed that they had merely substituted imported raw materials for imported finished goods. The raw materials themselves were still subject to tariffs and the small scale of manufacturing needed to meet the demands of the domestic market meant that the finished goods were expensive to produce and buy. Why, he asked, did the government force farmers to buy Irish binder twine when it was cheaper to import it? It only added to farmers' costs and made their exports less competitive. He suggested that the country could only truly become self-sufficient if it used home-grown flax instead of imported fibres.

Such arguments had been heard in the Dáil since 1936 when the first significant increase in the price of sisal since the foundation of Irish Ropes had had a knock-on effect on the price of twine. With harvest approaching, farmers were furious when they heard that the price of twine had increased from £35 to £55 a ton. Accusations of profiteering were bandied about. James Dillon, a Fine Gael TD for Donegal and a future minister for agriculture, sought reassurance that 'farmers who must use this binder twine are not being exploited by certain individuals who have a monopoly of the trade'.[20] However, the government rejected the opposition's request for a referral to the Price Commission on the grounds that the increase could be explained simply by the increased cost of raw materials. In 1939, when the price of twine had fallen to £44 a ton, the argument was taken up again by James Hughes, a farmer and local Fine Gael TD for Carlow and Kildare. He complained that the government's current economic policy was skewed in favour of industry and that the new industries seriously held back agricultural production.[21] Like Johnston, he argued that those industries that manufactured essential agricultural products should, wherever possible, use raw materials grown by Irish farmers. There was some mileage in this argument. Self-sufficiency had always been the goal of Irish nationalism and imports might be disrupted in time of war. The case for Ireland's only native fibre, flax, would be made again then. Sir John Maffey, who would be appointed the UK's representative in Dublin at the outbreak of war, was clearly aware of it when he provided the Dominions Office with a general update on the situation in Ireland shortly before the German invasion of France in 1940:

> Obviously the real wealth of this country lies in the agricultural industry. But Mr de Valera has dealt the farmer heavy blows. In the first place he entered light-heartedly and quite unnecessarily into an economic war with the United Kingdom in order to get political kudos by repudiating the Land Annuities. With Eire in a state of economic siege the farmers had to slaughter their stock and curtail all developments. From these trials they emerged weak and broken. Today they are ill-equipped to take the chances which the war offers them. Further Mr de Valera in his Gaelic enthusiasm embarked on a policy of economic self-sufficiency. If he had built factories to deal mainly with raw materials which this country could produce he would not have gone far wrong, but he established a whole range of manufacturing industries depending upon raw materials imported from abroad, and now the world is at war.[22]

Eric remained convinced that such arguments had no basis in commercial reality. The quality of Africa's soil and climate, the cheapness of native labour, and high levels of mechanisation all made sisal much less expensive to produce than flax. However, as he admitted in a speech to the Dublin Rotary Club shortly after the outbreak of war, it had been difficult to overcome farmers' prejudices:

> In an ancient industry like that of rope making there is a tendency to assume that the methods in use are essential when in fact they may be obsolete. Especially dangerous is the practice of putting new wine into old bottles even if encouraged to do so by the conservatism of the distributive trades and of the consumer himself. The biggest thing that has happened to the cordage industry of recent years has been the introduction of sisal fibre on a large scale. For five years we have been fighting to establish its use here as the most economical material for quite the majority of cordage and we have just about won through but only just in time. Today, owing to the war, fibres of many kinds are scarce but sisal gives reasonable promise of being in abundant supply. We must of course beware of over-doing our championship of sisal as so many other fibres, with different characteristics, are better suited to many purposes. Perhaps this is particularly

necessary in a country where it is becoming the practice to fight battles that are already won.

Meanwhile, he found himself busier than ever at the end of 1938. He spent much of his time travelling, and descriptions of his journeys became a staple part of his weekly letters to his children. He made regular visits to Dublin each week for both business and pleasure and sometimes found himself having to go in every day. He drove 15,000 miles in a year after he bought a powerful Ford V8 and claimed a record of 159 minutes, or almost 50 miles an hour, for the 130-mile journey on narrow roads from Newbridge to Cork. In October and November, he made visits to Goodbody's new jute mill in Waterford as well as to Cork and Ballina in County Mayo; he drove to Northern Ireland with Horace Davies to spend time at LIRA; and he crossed over to Liverpool for visits to Preston and Manchester where Irish Ropes was now supplying British carpet makers with coloured yarns. He thought that he might also have to go to London and was wondering whether to fly, and he was summoned to appear before a government commission in Dublin where, as he jokingly told the children, he was required to present yards of information about binder twine. He also started to make plans for the Christmas holidays and wrote to the children in October with some preliminary ideas. They were now all apart. Peter was in his second term at Rossall, Michael was still at the Craig preparatory school in Windermere, and eight-year-old Ann was living with her grandparents and going to school in Ormskirk:

> Granny and Grandpa want us all to spend Christmas at the Ruff so we are planning dates and have provisionally decided as follows:
>
> | | |
> |---|---|
> | Friday, 4 November | I will cross to Liverpool. |
> | Saturday, 5 November | Michael comes to Ormskirk for half-term. |
> | Sunday, 6 November | Michael and I go to Rossall for an exeat with Peter. |
> | Friday, 25 November | Mummy will cross to Liverpool to do her Christmas shopping. |
> | Wednesday, 30 November | Mummy (and perhaps Granny and Grandpa) will go to Rossall for Peter's confirmation. Mummy will return on the next day. |
> | Tuesday, 20 December | Mummy will cross to Liverpool. |
> | Saturday, 24 December | I will cross. |
> | Tuesday, 27 December | We all return here. |

The children would then spend the New Year and the rest of their holidays at Morristown. Although everything eventually went according to plan, they must have been disappointed to receive their father's letter of 11 December in which he told them that 'we are wondering if you would all mind staying at school for another week or two because we are not ready for Christmas. We have counted up the days several times and find that there is only a fortnight when we thought it was still a month away.' However, Dorothy managed to get over as planned and was able to drive the children to Rhos to spend a day with her widowed father. Eric caught the overnight ferry from Dublin on Christmas Eve and arrived in Liverpool the following morning. He had breakfast with Fred Dwelly and then caught the train to Ormskirk where he met up with his family at church for morning service.

It would be their last Christmas together before the war. Eric took Peter and Ann back to England in the middle of January. As twelve-year-old Michael did not have to return so quickly, he stayed on for another week before going back on his own. In February, Eric added a handwritten note to the bottom of his weekly letter: 'I know Granny and Grandpa will be glad to have you back again but I miss you very much'.

6

Knuckling Down, 1939

Then came catastrophe...[1]

The war clouds had been gathering in Europe throughout Irish Ropes's first six years. Hitler became German chancellor in 1933, five months before the company's incorporation, and Führer the following year, a few days after Lemass visited Newbridge to celebrate its first anniversary. In the autumn of 1935, as the directors were about to review its second year performance, Mussolini invaded Abyssinia, threatening Kenya's northern border and forcing Emperor Haile Selassie to flee. The following spring, as the town's new bridge was nearing completion, the German army crossed the Rhine in violation of the Treaty of Versailles and marched into the demilitarised zone between France and Germany. It was Hitler's first act of external aggression. In the autumn, shortly after the Olympic Games were held in Berlin and just as the ICC was finalising its investment in Irish Ropes, Thomas Jones accompanied Lloyd George on a three-week fact-finding trip to Germany where they were entertained to lunch by Hitler at his holiday retreat in the Bavarian Alps. Lloyd George, it seems, was naïve enough to believe that he did not pose a military threat and wanted to remain on friendly terms with the UK. That said, he was mindful enough of the offence that it was likely to cause back home to turn down the Führer's invitation to attend the annual Nazi party rally at Nuremberg the following week. Thomas went in his place and confessed to being terrified by the spectacle.

In March 1938, two months before Tintawn was launched at the RDS spring show, Hitler annexed Austria. In September, after securing the acquiescence of the other European powers at Munich, he annexed the Sudetenland in Czechoslovakia. By then, Eric knew that the future was bleak. In June, when he addressed the Liverpool Rotary Club before going up to Glasgow, he had chosen not to give one of his usual talks on rope-making or the practical aspects of running a business. Instead, he delivered an uncharacteristically sombre and almost philosophical discourse on honesty and morality in business against the background of the worsening international situation. 'We have not merely lost our direction in this year 1938,' he told his audience, 'but have no direction at all.' What was needed now was not 'the preservation of a mind so open as to be empty' but one which was 'made up upon issues so reduced to fundamentals that there can be no compromise'.

Eric wrote to his children with his preliminary plans for Christmas two days after Chamberlain's return from Munich with his message of 'peace for our time'. He himself had just returned from Liverpool where he had found that the boats were already crammed with people returning to Ireland to get away from what he called the 'war dangers in crowded cities'. 'Nearly all quarrels are the result of misunderstandings,' he told the children, 'and, if it is difficult for two people to understand each other, it is a million times more difficult for nations to do so.' Everyone in Ireland was already talking about the prospect of war. George Duncan, the professor of political economy at Trinity College Dublin, later offered a simple catalogue of events:

> European war became a possibility in January 1933, a high probability in March 1935, a moral certainty in July 1936, and inevitable in September 1938.[2]

On 16 July 1939, Eric wrote his last weekly letter before the summer holidays. By the time that he wrote again, on 8 October, Europe was at war. The family was still at Morristown when Germany invaded Poland on 1 September and the UK and France retaliated by declaring war on Germany. Eric's sister, Judy, was also staying with them with her husband, John Forshaw, and their two children, Oliver and Eleanor. They must have thought about their parents in Ormskirk who had been in the same situation a generation earlier. Then Eric had been sixteen and Judy fourteen. Eric and John had both gone on to fight and be awarded the MC for their bravery. Now Peter was fifteen, Michael thirteen, and Oliver twelve. Their schooldays might be over before the war ended. Then they too would have to fight like their fathers.

Some things changed quickly. Eric's father, Harry, who was now sixty-six, decided to sell the ropeworks in Ormskirk—thus bringing to an end several centuries of rope making in the town—but to continue to run H. and J. Jones's wholesale business in Liverpool. For the time being, nine-year-old Ann was kept at home in Ireland and taught by her mother. When her brothers returned to Rossall at the end of the month for what would be Michael's first term they found that they had been evacuated 100 miles north to Carlisle to make room at the school for the ministry of pensions. For the next year, their home would be Naworth Castle, the ancestral home of the earls of Carlisle. The castle had no sports facilities, army-style latrines had to be dug in the grounds, and wooden huts hastily erected to serve as classrooms. Peter was lucky to find that the countess's

Family photograph from the mid-1930s. Back row: Eric, Guy, and John Forshaw; middle row: Dorothy, Alice, Harry, and Judy; front row: Michael, Ann, Peter, Eleanor, and Oliver.

bedroom was now his dormitory. Eric took them over and, on his way back from Holyhead, experienced the first of many night-time crossings of the Irish Sea during the war. 'We did not sail until nearly five o'clock,' he told them in his next letter, 'and then came across like mad—faster than ever and zig-zagging as usual—almost skidding round the corners.'

In the middle of October, HMS *Royal Oak* became the first British battleship to be sunk when she was torpedoed by a U-boat at Scapa Flow with the loss of more than 800 lives. Eric passed on the news in his letter the next day:

The tragedy of the *Royal Oak*, which we all know so well, has cast a cloud over us this weekend. You will remember that we boarded this ship in Liverpool and Mummy saw her again at Plymouth. Perhaps you also remember that we had with us here for several months a Mr Calonius who came from a very big company in Finland. Its works, which gave employment to thousands, was in Tammerfors, one of the towns which has now been evacuated for safety's sake.

We have been so interested to have your letters and to hear something of Naworth. It is hard to visualise you at work, at play, and at your leisure if you get any. I often wonder what you are doing and have to be content with wondering. When you were at Rossall I had a good idea all the time but I am sure Naworth is very different in all sorts of ways. I am equally sure that you are able to put up with all these wartime changes and keep a cheery heart and that you will gradually settle down to a reasonable comfort as we did in the last war when a really dry hole in the mud became the place one longed for after returning from a patrol in no man's land.

'Sorry we have been unable to get through tonight,' he added in a postscript to the copy that he sent his parents, 'there is so little news on the wireless today that one wonders what is happening. I am afraid that we shall have a lot of such waiting.'

In Ireland, the government was quick to react to the invasion of Poland. The Department of Industry and Commerce had already established an Emergency Supplies Branch in 1938 to ensure that the country had enough food and essential supplies in the event of what it described as a major emergency. It also encouraged businesses to stockpile as much as they could even though it held back from offering them any financial assistance. On the day that the UK and France declared war, the Dáil rushed through the Emergency Powers Act, which gave the government wide-ranging and unbridled executive powers. Within a week, de Valera had moved Lemass to the new Department of Supplies where he was charged with ensuring the continued procurement of essential supplies and their fair pricing and distribution to the domestic consumer. John Leydon moved with him as the departmental secretary while most of the staff were transferred from either the Emergency Supplies Branch or the Prices Commission, which had been set up in 1937. The government also introduced compulsory tillage as a first step towards self-sufficiency. All farmers with more than 10 acres were required to turn over 12½ per cent of their land to the cultivation of crops. For Irish Ropes, it would mean working around the clock after Easter to meet the expected increase in demand for agricultural twine. Coupons were introduced to ration petrol but the allowances were too generous to have any real impact. A compulsory blackout of the areas around the Curragh and the coast was announced but then quickly withdrawn—but only after Eric had made all the necessary arrangements at the factory. Permits were now required for all travel between Britain and Ireland, flights were suspended temporarily, and telephone connections between Morristown and Ormskirk became difficult. Cement was suddenly in short supply. Otherwise life largely went on as normal and Irish Ropes Sports Club went ahead with its plans for its first annual dance that would be held at the end of September.

De Valera had always made it clear that Ireland would remain neutral in the event of a European war. The Second World War would be known in Ireland simply as the Emergency. Although the country had come a long way in two decades, from nationalist insurrection to stable and independent democracy, neutrality was pragmatically the government's only option. Ireland was still a small, young, and weak state that lacked the military apparatus to defend itself against either Great Britain or Germany. Its army had only 13,000 men and was short of weapons; its air force had only sixteen planes, all of which were obsolete; and the navy its single fisheries patrol vessel, SS *Muirchú*. However, neutrality was not only a yardstick of Ireland's new independence but also a defiant statement of the democratic right of small nations to stay out of the politics and wars of the great powers. Furthermore, the wounds from the country's recent past were still too raw. Frank Aiken, the new minister for the co-ordination of defensive measures and one of de Valera's closest allies, was pragmatist enough to suggest that, if Ireland ever did decide to join the war, it would first have to fight another civil war to decide on whose side it should fight. One outcome of any alliance with Britain would almost certainly be the unacceptable sight of British soldiers once more on Irish soil, and although the new Irish constitution claimed jurisdiction over the whole island, it was still divided. Partition remained an open sore for de Valera, and one that he would use again and again to justify his refusal to abandon neutrality.

Yet Ireland was far from being the only country to choose to remain neutral at the start of the war. So, too, did Portugal, Spain, Sweden, Switzerland, Hungary, Yugoslavia, Romania, Bulgaria, and Italy, as well as Norway, Denmark, Belgium, Holland, and Luxembourg, all of which would be occupied by Germany in 1940. Neutrality would be no guarantee that small nations could either stand aside from the fighting or avoid the disruption and privation of a European war. What made Ireland different was its proximity to, its recent history with, and its economic dependence on its more powerful neighbour. In British eyes, Ireland was not only an invaluable 'nearby larder', but also a shield with which to protect the Atlantic shipping routes on which both countries would come to rely. It was still only a year since Britain had surrendered the three 'treaty' ports, a decision that still rankled with Churchill, who had now become first lord of the Admiralty once more. Without them, the Royal Navy's range in the Atlantic would be limited. The partition of the island also meant that the UK and Ireland shared their only land border with each other. With many still crossing from the south each day to work in Londonderry and elsewhere, it would be almost impossible to enforce strict border controls. The British government's sensitivity towards the catholic minority in Northern Ireland also meant that it would be the only part of the UK where conscription was not introduced, and while neutral Ireland continued to rely on belligerent Britain to sustain its export trade and to supply it with fuel and other essential commodities, Britain equally relied on Ireland for food and on Irish men and women to serve in its armed forces and supplement its industrial workforce. Up to 150,000 Irish citizens are reckoned to have served in Britain's armed forces during the war and another 200,000 in its wartime industries. It was a significant number for a country of only 3 million people and another reason why a ban on travel between the two countries was never practical.

There is no doubt that, in opting for neutrality, de Valera had the overwhelming support of the Irish electorate and, at least at first, the understanding of many in Britain and elsewhere. However, war quickly brought into focus the potential threat that Ireland posed to Britain's security, however benevolent its government might claim to be. In the three years since the post of governor-general had been abolished in 1936, the British government had been without any diplomatic representation in Dublin. It now found itself desperately short of intelligence. Other countries had established legations after the abdication of Edward VIII and the adoption of the new constitution in 1937. Dr Eduard Hempel was appointed German minister that summer and would remain in Dublin with his legation throughout the war. Ireland had also had a high commission in London since the creation of the Free State, and British-born John Dulanty, who was high commissioner from 1930 to 1949, would play a significant role during the war as a conduit between the two governments. To rectify the situation, sixty-two-year-old Sir John Maffey was hastily brought out of retirement and despatched to Dublin in October 1939 as the UK's representative to Ireland. His title was a compromise that avoided the use of sensitive words like ambassador and minister. A distinguished imperial administrator, he had spent most of his career in the Indian civil service before serving a seven-year term as governor-general of the Sudan. For his final four years before retiring in 1937, he had been the permanent under-secretary of state, or leading civil servant, at the Colonial Office.

In Ireland, there were fears that the British might try to recover the treaty ports by force, not least because Ireland was now seen as an obvious target for any rearguard or diversionary attack on Britain. German agents were parachuted into the country from the earliest stages of the war and, as in the previous war, there were rumours that the German navy was being allowed to use Ireland's west coast to shelter, fuel, and supply her U-boats. Although these were largely unfounded, U-boats were frequently sighted off the coasts of both northern and southern Ireland. To calm British and Irish fears, Maffey was joined in Dublin in November by a naval *attaché*, Captain Alexander Greig, whose first task was to organise a system of coast watching.

Eric had kept abreast of events as the crisis deepened in 1939. Back in March, he had told the children that 'we listen anxiously to the news these days and Mummy alarmed me last night by telling me that parliament had been summoned for last night—she meant the Cabinet.' He was already a keen fan of the radio. In 1924, only two years after the BBC's first broadcast, he had bought what he described as 'a receiving set for broadcast wireless telephony' for his new house in Ormskirk. It cost £15, or almost a fortnight's salary. Now he listened avidly each night to the BBC news, which could not be censored by the Irish government.

With Irish Ropes relying on imports for nearly all of its raw materials, all of which had to be trans-shipped via Britain, Eric's first priority after the outbreak of war was to ensure the continuity of his supplies. With the Irish government pressing for a substantial increase in agricultural production, he needed to gear up both his production and storage capacity. By the beginning of November, he was under pressure from Lemass's new ministry. 'To-morrow I have to go to Dublin and pay one of my now frequent visits to the Ministry of Supply,' he told the children, 'they are anxious for us to get in plenty of raw materials for next year's harvest. We already have the warehouse nearly full but we are also using very much more.' He was also facing renewed criticism in the Dáil. Following up his attack from the spring, James Hughes claimed that Dutch twine was both cheaper and better.[3] Six months later, Germany's occupation of Holland would cut off this source.

Unlike many Irish manufacturers, who were not prepared to build up their stocks without some sort of protection or financial assistance from the government, Eric had long since started to plan ahead. In spite of the shortage of cement, he pressed ahead with plans to extend the factory. Although the first new building was completed in December, work on new offices and another laboratory was then held up for three months because of the weather. Meanwhile, machinery was already being moved into the new rope mill that was due to commence production in April. The factory's largest machine to date was scheduled for delivery in February. 'We are busier than ever,' Eric told the children in October, 'and the big problem is to get materials enough to keep going. So far we are managing very well but lots of factories are having a hard time already.' Intriguingly, he also told them that 'we are making some experiments at the works to produce camouflage material and were working with a few special men yesterday afternoon to rush through a trial lot of stuff. We just got it through in time to catch a train which was waiting.' Whatever it was that he had been asked to make, he never mentioned it again.

At first, a high level of co-operation at both government and industrial level meant that Ireland's trade with Britain was barely disrupted. Even Ireland's lack of a merchant fleet and its reliance on foreign shipping was not seen as a problem. A survey by the Emergency Supplies Branch in 1938 had revealed that Irish vessels accounted for only 5 per cent of the tonnage entering Irish ports while British vessels accounted for 64 per cent and other countries for 31 per cent. For the time being at least, the British were happy to add any Irish requests for cargo space to their own. In October, senior civil servants from the departments of Supplies and Agriculture went over to London for constructive discussions with their British counterparts. As well as reaching an immediate agreement for Britain to purchase all of Ireland's flax harvest in 1939 and 1940, they continued to meet into 1940 and laid the groundwork for a meeting of ministers in April to conclude a formal trade agreement.

Meanwhile, Eric had the simple plan of trying to get hold of as much fibre as he could. Wigglesworths almost certainly helped him find whatever cargo space was available. With much of the East African trade having been carried by German shipping lines before the war, cargo space was now at a premium. Stocks of sisal quickly built up at the docks in Mombasa and Dar es Salaam. However, it was the threat to merchant shipping, even in home waters, that was Eric's greatest concern. At any time, he might have up to ten ships carrying consignments of

A delivery arriving at Irish Ropes on a Great Southern Railways cart, 1938.

fibre from Africa and the Far East. He tuned in to the shipping news each evening and, in a spirit of wartime economy and 'just to show Uncle Guy that he is not the only pebble on the beach', tried his hand at knitting while he listened. He could not keep it up for long. In early November, he told the children that 'we listen carefully in the news each day for any information about steamers in which we are interested and are at present interested in these: *Matiana, Magician, City of Evansville, Mito Maru, Denbighshire,* and two more I cannot remember at the moment.'

In October, the *City of Mandalay*, which was bound for England from Singapore with 15,000 bales of manila, 100 of which were scheduled for onward shipment to Irish Ropes, sank after being torpedoed by a U-boat 500 miles off the French coast. The following month, Eric heard of the loss of the *Adolph Woermann* on which he had a cargo of sisal. The liner, which was owned by the German East Africa Line, had been detained since the outbreak of war by the neutral Portuguese authorities in Lobito in Portuguese West Africa (now Angola) while on her way back from Mombasa to Hamburg. On 16 November, she slipped out of port disguised as a Portuguese ship and made for South America at full speed. HMS *Neptune* set off in pursuit and, as she closed in, the *Woermann's* captain, Otto Burfeind, scuttled her near Ascension Island in accordance with his standing orders. Her forty-one passengers and 121 crew were picked up and taken to England to be interned.[4] Eric, however, lost vital raw materials, and although he was entitled to compensation, the payment would be delayed when the case was referred to the House of Lords.

The *City of Hereford* and *Agapenor*, which were carrying 500 tons (or about three months' supply) of sisal for Irish Ropes, managed to reach Liverpool safely before Christmas. However, early in the new year, Eric had to fly over to inspect a damaged shipment of hemp from Java. Luckily, Dublin's new airport at Collinstown had just opened and its first flights were to Liverpool. However, snow delayed his return flight for several days and he eventually had to catch the boat back from Holyhead. Although air travel was still at the mercy of the weather, at least it was safer than going by sea. The ferries and mail boats that crossed the Irish Sea were always at risk of being sunk by an enemy mine. It was a fate that befell the *Munster* the week after Eric returned, the *Lady Connaught* later in the year (she had previously struck a submerged wreck, and perhaps the *Munster* herself, in February), and the *Innisfallen* in December. All were hit close to land—in Liverpool Bay, off the Mersey lightship, and close to the Wirral shore.

By the end of October, Eric's thoughts had turned again to Christmas. This year, he and Dorothy were expecting to stay in Ireland but hoped to be able to get over to Ormskirk at some point. He asked each of the children to write him 'an extremely confidential letter' to tell him what they thought was best and what they themselves would like to do. As well as the dangers, the higher cost of travel meant that it would not be possible for them all to come back to Morristown. It was eventually decided that Ann would stay at the Ruff as she had been in Ireland most recently, and that although Eric had originally suggested the drawing of lots, Michael should come home rather than Peter as he had been forced to stay on at school for an extra week after a bout of German measles. Peter would get his chance at Easter. Eric hoped that they would then all be reunited for the summer holidays.

When Michael returned to England after the holidays, Eric and Dorothy described feeling as if they had been condemned to another three months of solitary confinement. They missed their children badly and felt helpless when each in turn caught flu in the spring. At least Peter managed to get home for the Easter holidays. By then, all contact between Britain and Ireland had become difficult. Letters took longer to get through and were subject to rigorous censorship. Peter had one letter home returned by the Irish censor after he included banned printed material in it in the form of a single label, and Ann, who was a gifted pianist, remembers not being allowed to take home any sheet music to practice the pieces that she had been learning at school. Later in the war, she found herself on the same flight as the renowned pianist, Solomon, who was due to play a series of concerts in Dublin. He too had his music confiscated and so was unable to practice.

Eric had more immediate problems to face in the new year. In February, a strike at Dublin's docks held up those supplies of raw materials that did get through just as the factory was gearing up to work longer hours. By the beginning of March, it had spread to municipal workers. The streets of Dublin were left unswept and the government had to make plans for an emergency fire service. At the same time,

An Irish Agricultural Wholesale Society lorry laden with 10 tons of Irish Ropes's twine.

the arguments about twine in the Dáil had moved on from price and quality to availability. When Lemass was challenged that distributors were already being rationed and could not get hold of enough twine to fulfil their customers' orders, he had to reassure the house that there would be adequate supplies by harvest time and that they would be distributed fairly.[5]

On 9 April, the Phoney War that had prevailed since September came to an abrupt end with Germany's invasion of Denmark and Norway. Although the French and British reacted quickly by landing forces at Narvik, they were there for less than a fortnight before being evacuated. Exactly a month later, Germany marched into Luxembourg as the first stage of its invasion of the Low Countries and France. Earlier that day, the British prime minister, Neville Chamberlain, had lost a vote of confidence in the House of Commons after a two-day debate on the failure of the Norwegian campaign. He resigned the following day and was replaced by Winston Churchill. In his first speech as prime minister three days later, Churchill famously declared that he had nothing to offer but blood, toil, tears, and sweat. By then, the British Expeditionary Force, which had been deployed in northern France since October, was already retreating in the face of the German *blitzkrieg*. Its evacuation from the beaches of Dunkirk would begin on 27 May and continue until 4 June, by which time almost 350,000 British servicemen had been rescued.

Back in Ireland, Eric's brother, Guy, and his wife had arrived at Morristown at the end of April for a fortnight's holiday. Eric had saved up 'a few pints of petrol' for their visit and had told his brother to buy a cheap lightweight suitcase as his luggage would be limited to 33 pounds. Guy, who would be thirty in May, was fourteen years younger than his brother. After Rossall and Cambridge, he had spent three years as a medical student at St Thomas's Hospital in London during which time he had lodged with John and Judy Forshaw in Epsom. He had met his wife, Peggy Pearmain, when they were working together as house surgeons at the Royal Cancer Hospital (now the Royal Marsden Hospital). They were married by special licence in Hampstead a week after the outbreak of war. Harry and Alice met their daughter-in-law for the first time at the wedding. Their stay at Morristown was now cut short when they were recalled to London on the day after the invasion of France. Harry and Alice had also come over by plane for the first time the day before for a week's holiday and had brought Ann with them. That evening, they all gathered round the radio to listen to the news.

Eric continued to follow events closely throughout May. Although he was worried, he reassured the children that he was as confident of eventual victory as he had been during his darkest days on the Western Front:

> The news has been flashing to us over the wireless at a speed which makes a mockery of time and last night I ran a line to take the loud-speaker upstairs. The war news now occupies all our thoughts and the names of many of the places to which the Germans have penetrated are familiar to me although they have not yet reached the places where we fought. It seems terrible to think of the lovely fields of Picardy being turned into ruin again—but all that is nothing compared to the destruction of lives because of a mad lot of gangsters. We are wondering when the turn of the tide will come but are as sure that it will turn as we are of the tide in the sea.

Eric remained glued to the radio throughout the evacuation of Dunkirk. As he told the children, 'we have been listening to every news bulletin but have now to be patient and be content with little or no real news.' Although Ireland's strict new censorship rules controlled what could be reported in the Irish press and banned the import of British papers, nothing could stop him tuning in to the radio. On 24 May, he and Dorothy were thrilled to be able to listen to King George VI's Empire Day broadcast on the BBC:

> The decisive struggle is now upon us. I am going to speak plainly to you for, in this hour of trial, I know you would not have me do otherwise. Let no one be

mistaken: it is no mere territorial conquest that our enemies are seeking. It is the overthrow, complete and final, of this Empire and of everything for which it stands: and, after that, the conquest of the world. And, if their will prevails, they will bring to its accomplishment all the hatred and cruelty which they have already displayed. It was not easy for us to believe that designs so evil could find a place in the human mind. But the time for doubt is long past. To all of us in this Empire, to all men of wisdom and goodwill throughout the world, the issue is now plain: it is life or death for all.[6]

7

Preparing to Fight, 1940

Sorry I have not much news this week—Mr Hitler is taking it all for the moment but we shall have plenty of time when his mad effort is over.[1]

Eric was in better heart the following week when the evacuation of Dunkirk was almost complete. The British Isles would almost certainly be Germany's next target. As well as the threat to Britain itself, Germany's newly-acquired access to the Atlantic seaboard from Norway down to the Pyrenees, its reportedly successful use of fifth columnists and *agents provocateurs* in Norway and France, its contempt for the neutrality of small nations, and the speed of its military movements all brought home the threat of Ireland to Britain's western flank. As well as being weak and neutral, it harboured anti-British activists in the form of the now illegal IRA. It would be a perfect base for a German invasion of Britain by the backdoor or for a diversionary attack to stretch its defences, and once it was occupied, German naval and air bases could harass Allied shipping in the western approaches, cut off Britain's supplies from Ireland and America, attack targets on the British mainland, and threaten Northern Ireland's production of the aircraft, ships, and armaments that were vital to the British war effort. Britain simply could not afford to let Ireland be occupied.

On the day that France was invaded, Sir John Maffey called on de Valera to gauge his immediate reaction and to find out in particular whether Germany's violation of Dutch and Belgian neutrality had prompted him to reconsider Ireland's position. He reported back to the War Cabinet that the Taoiseach had chosen only to repeat his well-rehearsed arguments for neutrality and to invoke once more what he called 'the old bogey of partition'. However, both men acknowledged that, in the current crisis, there would be some advantage in their countries sharing information and developing some sort of co-operation.

Contact between their two intelligence services had been established in 1938 when concerns about increased German activity in Ireland had prompted the Department of External Affairs—a portfolio that de Valera retained for himself throughout his premiership—to ask for British help in setting up a security service. The discussions were headed by the department's secretary, Joseph Walshe, and led to the appointment of Colonel Liam Archer as head of the Irish intelligence service, G2. At the same time, Guy Liddell, who ran MI5's counter-espionage branch, asked his brother, Cecil, to head up a new Irish section to monitor the German legation in Dublin and all communications going in and out of it. Although this so-called 'Dublin link' resulted in regular and friendly contact throughout the war, its role was effectively limited to counter-espionage and the monitoring of German residents and agents in Ireland.

On 15 May 1940, six days after Germany's occupation of Luxembourg, Archer flew over to meet the Liddell brothers at Droitwich. According to his cover story, he was there to take a cure at the spa. Although the purpose of their meeting was to improve illicit wireless interception, Archer was quick to emphasise his government's anxieties about a German invasion and its lack of the resources and weapons needed to meet it. Maffey received the same message that day from de Valera himself. As a result, and at the instigation of the Taoiseach, Walshe and Archer were sent over to London eight days later for a meeting with the under-secretary of state for dominion affairs, Sir Eric Machtig, and representatives from the Dominions Office and British armed services to discuss military co-operation in the event of an invasion, which, it was thought, would probably be spearheaded by a parachute landing.

Machtig opened the meeting by summarising his understanding of the Irish position. It was one that would remain unchanged throughout the Emergency:

> Eire would fight if attacked by Germany and would call in the assistance of the United Kingdom the moment it became necessary. The political situation in Eire, however, was such that there could be no question of the Eire Government inviting in United Kingdom troops before an actual German descent, and before fighting between the German and Eire forces had begun. If the United Kingdom forces arrived before such fighting had taken place Mr de Valera could not be responsible for the political consequences. If, on the other hand, fighting was in progress between Eire and German forces and the United Kingdom forces came in to help, Eire opinion would give whole-hearted support to British forces.[2]

By the time that the talks reconvened the following morning, both parties had recognised that, rather than continuing to exchange generalities, the situation demanded that they take immediate and decisive action and, in particular, establish effective channels of communication between the British and Irish armed forces. It was vital that there was an agreed procedure for calling on British help and that it was made as quick and simple as possible. Machtig had accordingly asked some 'experts' to join the meeting. One of them was Lieutenant-Colonel Dudley

Clarke, who would go on to be a leading figure in British intelligence during the war. With any British rapid reaction force likely to be dispatched from Northern Ireland, it was agreed that Clarke should fly to Belfast that afternoon with Walshe and Archer to meet General Huddleston, the commander of British Troops in Northern Ireland (BTNI). They would then fly on to Dublin the following day, a Saturday, with two of Huddleston's staff officers to meet the Irish chief of staff, General Dan McKenna.

That long weekend, from Friday 24 May to Tuesday 28 May, would be a crucial time for the UK's future as a free and independent state. It has been explored in detail in John Lukacs's 1999 book, *Five Days in London, May 1940*, and more recently in Joe Wright's 2017 film, *Darkest Hour*. The War Cabinet met several times each day as the fall of France became ever more inevitable. It had to decide whether to seek an accommodation with Nazi Germany or to carry on fighting to the bitter end. When it reconvened for the third and final time on Sunday after the departure of the French prime minister, it had before it a paper from the chiefs of staff on options in the event of a French capitulation. One of the paper's fourteen recommendations for immediate action was that 'every possible measure should be directed to obtaining the active support of Eire, particularly with a view to the immediate use of Berehaven'.[3] As the most westerly of the three treaty ports, it was best placed to extend the range of the Atlantic convoys and to counter the threat of German U-boats in the western approaches. Chamberlain, who was now lord president of the council, undertook to instruct Maffey to explain to de Valera the seriousness of the situation and to emphasise the importance of an immediate British occupation of the port. Late that evening, final orders were issued for the evacuation of Dunkirk.

The die was now cast. Belgium had surrendered by the time that Dudley Clarke returned from Dublin on Tuesday. Later that day, Churchill told the House of Commons that, while its members should prepare themselves for bad news, the UK would fight on through grief and disaster to the final defeat of its enemies. The following day, his chief staff officer, General 'Pug' Ismay, passed him the minutes of the recent Anglo-Irish meetings. He explained in a covering note that 'information from secret sources points to the fact that the Germans have concerted detailed plans with the IRA and that everything is now ready for an immediate descent upon the country'.[4]

When Clarke briefed Machtig about his trip, he confirmed that the Irish political and military authorities had been wholly open and co-operative. He and Walshe had already agreed that Britain should send military and air *attachés* to Dublin to liaise with the Irish armed forces and BTNI and that a senior British officer should be appointed to head a military mission to Ireland and to assume command as and when any British intervention was requested. While the Irish had again stressed their overriding need for military equipment and supplies, they had, like Maffey, played down both the threat of the IRA and the likelihood of a German invasion. However, they had not been able to convince the British delegation whose concerns about Germany's potential use of quislings and fifth columnists can only have been confirmed when Archer and Liddell passed on details of the recent arrest of Stephen Held in Dublin.

It was an unfortunate coincidence that, on the morning of Walshe and Archer's first meeting in London, G2 had raided the home of Michael Held, a naturalised Irish businessman of German descent, during a search for a German parachutist and had arrested his stepson, Stephen. It was claimed that a month earlier, while on a business trip to Belgium, Stephen had crossed into Germany to buy guns for the IRA and to pass on plans for a joint German and IRA attack on Northern Ireland. G2's search of the house uncovered a German parachute, $20,000 in cash, a wireless set, coded messages, and a set of questionnaires seeking information on places of military importance in Northern Ireland. They were the basis for what became known as Plan Kathleen. However, the full facts would not be pieced together until the arrest of Dr Hermann Görtz in Dublin at the end of 1941. Having already been jailed in Britain for espionage in 1936 and deported in 1939, Görtz had been parachuted into Ireland early in May 1940 to help Held. Ismay had clearly been made aware of the case when he passed Churchill the minutes of the Anglo-Irish meetings six days after the raid. Held was charged under the Emergency Powers Act and in June was sentenced to five years' penal servitude by a special court in Dublin.

The perceived threat of the IRA made the British government extremely wary of supplying any weapons to Ireland. In any case, it needed every available weapon for its own armed forces, especially after the loss of materiel at Dunkirk, and there was little mood to accede to the request as long as Ireland remained neutral. The weapons might be lost during a German invasion, or stolen by the IRA, or even turned against its own armed forces if the Irish chose to resist a pre-emptive British attack. There were some grounds for these fears even if, like the rumours of German U-boats using the west coast, they were mostly inaccurate and sometimes bordered on obsession. The Irish spy in the pay of Germany would become a regular character in British war films, as in the invented character of Patrick O'Reilly in the 1956 film, *The Man Who Never Was*. However, while the IRA did make approaches to Germany both before and after the outbreak of war, republican feeling in Ireland tended to be more anti-British than pro-German.

The IRA had declared war on Britain at the start of 1939 after issuing an ultimatum demanding the withdrawal of British troops from Northern Ireland. They followed this up with a sustained bombing campaign on the British mainland under the old nationalist slogan of 'England's difficulty is Ireland's opportunity'. Almost 130 attacks were carried out over the next six months. Although they caused considerable damage, only one person was killed and fifty-five injured. The campaign was then stepped up at the end of August, only a week before the outbreak of war, when a bomb in Coventry killed five people and wounded more than fifty. Three men and two women were arrested. After a three-day trial in December, three were found not guilty but the other two, James Richards and Peter Barnes, were sentenced to death and hanged at Birmingham Prison in February.

De Valera's appeal for clemency went unheard. However, the Irish government had already taken its own steps to eliminate the IRA threat by issuing warrants for the internment of seventy of its members as soon as the Emergency was declared. Nearly all of them had been arrested by the beginning of December when the courts ruled that their detainment was illegal and ordered their immediate release. Then, on Christmas Eve, the IRA launched an audacious and highly embarrassing raid on the army's magazine fort in Phoenix Park in Dublin. They used thirteen lorries to carry off almost all of its small arms and more than a million rounds of ammunition, weighing some 27 tons. Although most of the weapons were recovered after a tight cordon was placed around Dublin, it was a rude awakening and was later described as Ireland's Pearl Harbor. Early in the new year, an emergency meeting of the Dáil passed legislation reintroducing internment. By July, the government was confident that most of the IRA's leaders had been arrested. Most of them would spend the rest of the Emergency interned at the Curragh Camp.

Within a week of Clarke's return to London, Major Meyric ap Rhys Pryce and Wing Commander Ralph Lywood had been sent to Dublin as British military and air *attachés*. The speed of British reactions throughout the summer of 1940 shows just how seriously they took the threat of a German invasion of Ireland. Pryce was plucked from a staff posting at Sandhurst; MO8, the branch of the War Office to which he sent his reports, had only been set up in April to oversee the Norway campaign but was then made responsible for Ireland; and Major General 'Jimmy' Harrison, who was appointed head of Military Mission 18 in July and given overall responsibility for liaison with the Irish armed forces, came straight from the governorship of Jersey, which he had evacuated only a fortnight before ahead of the German occupation of the Channel Islands.

Pryce and Lywood settled in quickly at Dublin's Shelbourne Hotel and made contact with Walshe and Archer. The office that they shared next door to Maffey's became known as the Cloak and Dagger Department. While Pryce's orders made it clear that he reported to Maffey rather than the War Office the main elements of his job, which he likened to that of a go-between, were to pass back information on the Irish army and Department of Defence, to find out all that he could about German movements and plans, to liaise with BTNI, and to send regular reports of his findings back to the War Office. Although a military *attaché*, he was forbidden to wear uniform or to use his rank. Instead he was to work incognito and keep secret the true nature of his role.[5] He would spend most of his time swapping information with Archer, usually in clandestine meetings after dark, writing up reports, and travelling around the country to find out all he could about Ireland's geography, military strength, and preparations. Detailed descriptions of his routes, and their suitability for troop movements, became a staple part of his reports, which were sent back to London in the diplomatic bag after they had been scrutinised by Maffey.

The Irish were also making their own preparations for a possible invasion. On 25 May, as Clarke and his companions flew on from Belfast to Dublin, de

Valera ordered the destruction of hundreds of government files. He established the Local Security Force three days later. Although it was originally intended to be an auxiliary police service, it was split in two a month later and half of its strength was transferred to the army as the Local Defence Force. Almost 45,000 men signed up within the first fortnight. By the end of August, numbers were up to almost 150,000. In July, Irish Ropes was one of thirty-two businesses that paid for a full-page advertisement in the national press that called on Irishmen to defend their country in its hour of need by joining one of the defence forces—either the regular army as a permanent career or for the duration of the Emergency, or the volunteer force for three months' immediate service followed by three years as a reservist, or the Local Security Force for aerial observation and coast watching and to monitor potential breaches of neutrality.

Irish Ropes's factory was now busier than ever. Eric told the children at the beginning of June that they were in a race against time and weather to make enough twine for the harvest. However, he still found time to join the Local Security Force along with most of his workforce and many in the Protestant community. In spite of the lack of weapons, he was asked to teach musketry, just as he had as a teenage officer in the King's Liverpool Regiment during the First World War. At first, it did not seem to matter that he was British. Later, when all recruits were required to swear an oath to obey orders, he was almost certainly one of those who chose to stand down rather than risk being given an order to fire on British troops. Meanwhile, he told the children: 'I am giving my energies to my own work and to trying to stiffen people up in this country and getting them to move. I expect eventually to find myself doing some other job so our arrangements can only be made for a short time ahead and we are not thinking about holidays at present'. It is another of his intriguing snippets of information. We can only guess what this other job might have been as he does not mention it again. Meanwhile, Dorothy started attending Red Cross lectures several times a week with Dorothy Baxter.

Basic defensive measures were put in place in Ireland at an early stage. Harbours were mined and railway sleepers were planted vertically in Phoenix Park to prevent it being used as an airfield. In time, all golf courses would be similarly staked. Pryce disclosed in one of his reports that the rather superior Portmarnock Golf Club north of Dublin had been raided and closed down after its members had assumed that the order did not apply to them. The Automobile Association's Irish representative, C. H. Murphy, supervised the removal of all the association's road signs that had previously made Ireland one of the best-signposted countries in the world. He knew more about Ireland's roads than anyone and would later be approached by Pryce to provide valuable information. Meanwhile, many Irishmen were relishing the prospect of another guerrilla war. They were sure that they could make life difficult for any invader, whether German or British. In June, Pryce passed on to the War Office a seemingly genuine request from General McKenna for instructions on how to make a Molotov cocktail. In due course, he received back a typed recipe, as he called it, for both simple and improved versions where whiskey bottles were filled with equal parts of petrol, naphtha, and creosote. Before sending it, someone in London had thought to add a useful handwritten note to clarify that 'in the unlikely event of there being a shortage of whiskey bottles in your country beer bottles may be used'.[6]

Their lack of weapons and equipment remained the main concern of the Irish government and armed forces. 'I've got the manpower,' Archer protested to Pryce in June, 'but what I want is the firepower.'[7] De Valera gave Maffey the same message when he asked to see him urgently that evening. He specifically asked that he pass it on to Neville Chamberlain and Malcolm MacDonald whom he believed were his closest allies in the British government. Although desperate times called for desperate measures, and Britain was certainly desperate in the summer of 1940, Pryce was already being told privately by the War Office that the request was likely to be denied.

When the War Cabinet had met four days earlier on Sunday 16 June, it was given a decrypted telegram from Jan Smuts, the South African prime minister and former member of the War Cabinet in the First World War, in which he emphasised the threat of a German invasion of Ireland and the consequent risk to Britain's vital supplies from America. It was his view that 'there should be no delay in countering this move and in securing the Irish position. If Ireland will not see or admit the terrible dangers, the question should be seriously considered whether the Irish ports on the Atlantic should not be secured in spite of Irish remonstrances. This precaution may well be the turning point in victory or defeat'.[8]

Chamberlain also reported that he had received alarming reports about German activities in Ireland from Sir Charles Tegart who had visited the country several times that year at the request of the intelligence services. At the time, he was probably the government's leading expert on terrorism, security, and policing. Born and educated in Northern Ireland and then at Trinity College Dublin, he had been a senior police officer in India for thirty years before advising the government on security and policing in Palestine during the Arab revolt of the late 1930s. Chamberlain told the cabinet that he considered the Irish threat to be so serious that he had already invited de Valera over to London. However, as it would be almost impossible for either of them to travel incognito, the cabinet decided instead to send Malcolm MacDonald, who was now minister of health, over to Dublin the next day to brief de Valera about the War Cabinet's conviction that a German invasion of Ireland was imminent.

The War Office was still telling Pryce informally at the end of the month that 'if anything is a certainty it's a German attack on Eire in the very near future'.[9] Maffey remained unconvinced. However, when he suggested to Machtig that what was needed was a reasoned assessment of the dangers of an invasion and clear direction on what was expected from the Irish government, he was told bluntly that the British government's position had changed completely since the fall of France. Until then, its priority had been to keep the Atlantic shipping routes open and to counteract the threat of German U-boats. Now, as Machtig told him, 'he danger of an invasion of Eire is regarded as so serious, not merely from the Eire point of view but also from our own, that the Government here were prepared to go to the lengths which they have in order to try to create a situation in which they could be reasonably confident of resisting or overcoming any such attempt'.[10]

By then, MacDonald had been through ten days of shuttle diplomacy between London and Dublin, which had ultimately ended in failure. The British government was convinced, with some justification, that the continued partition of the island remained the chief stumbling block to any Irish renunciation of neutrality. De Valera had said as much in the days after the fall of France in both public speeches and private conversations with Maffey. In a speech to a Fianna Fáil convention in Galway on 12 May, which prompted a protest from the German legation, he had claimed that, while British and Irish interests were aligned in many ways, there was still one major cause of disagreement between them. Partition was, as Maffey had reminded the Dominions Office in April, a great and genuine Irish grievance. He likened de Valera's repeated references to it to an old gramophone record that had got stuck. The future poet laureate, John Betjeman, came to the same conclusion when his employer, the ministry of information, sent him on a fact-finding mission to Ireland in June. In his report, he stressed the urgent need for an end to partition, which he said was seen as more important than anything in Ireland. As well as speaking to an unusual cross-section of people, he managed to get interviews with both Joseph Walshe, the secretary at external affairs, and Sean MacEntee, Lemass's replacement as minister for industry and commerce. Both assured him that the government 'will come out into the open on the Defence question and will co-operate with British Forces in Ireland to resist enemy invasion once some unification of the Six Counties and Eire is achieved. But they say that no useful military co-operation is possible on the lines of defence alone, some sort of symbolical union of Ireland must be established first.'[11]

It was not a view that was shared by all in government. Frank Aiken, a republican to the core, reportedly told a senator sometime that summer that there were absolutely no terms on which Ireland would abandon its neutrality.[12]

Meanwhile, MacDonald had returned to Dublin for a second round of talks on 21 June. This time discussions focused on a range of options for a united Ireland, whether neutral or belligerent, and the immediate British occupation of the treaty ports and other strategic sites in Ireland. It proved impossible to find any common ground. The British government, which had not yet made the government of Northern Ireland aware of the talks, could offer no more than the declaration of a united Ireland in principle but must have known that even this would be almost certainly unacceptable to the loyalist majority in the north. However, this did not go nearly far enough for de Valera at a time when Germany was in the ascendant, Ireland was undefended, and any abandonment of neutrality would only increase the probability of invasion. In turn, he held out for a united but neutral Ireland. As this would leave Britain even more exposed, it never stood any chance of being accepted.

When Chamberlain reported back to the War Cabinet about the stalemate on 25 June, he proposed that MacDonald be sent back to Dublin for a third time with a final British proposal. Although there was little chance of success, he was keen to try everything. The main elements of this final proposal were, first, that the British government would make a public declaration of a united Ireland in principle and then facilitate talks between the Irish and Northern Ireland governments to agree the details; second, that Ireland would abandon its neutrality and agree to the establishment of an Anglo-Irish defence council that would allow the immediate deployment of British forces to Ireland and enable the supply of much-needed military equipment to the Irish; and, third, that all enemy aliens and suspected fifth columnists in Ireland would be interned.

MacDonald spent two and a half hours with de Valera on the evening of 26 June. He had to read out the British proposal himself because de Valera had by now almost lost his sight. It made subsequent comments in the British press about the blindness of the Irish position all the more spiteful. Once he got back to the British embassy, he sent off a telegram that reached London at 3.50 a.m. He was not optimistic. Although the situation was not yet hopeless, the chances of success were slim. At least de Valera had agreed to discuss the proposal with his colleagues before making a final response. As a fall-back, MacDonald was proposing to back down on the demand for Ireland to abandon its neutrality as long as it allowed the Royal Navy access to its ports and let the Army and RAF establish bases in the country. He must have known that this would never be acceptable to either Ireland or Germany.

Given the subsequent history of Northern Ireland, Irish acceptance of the British offer would almost certainly have changed history. It might have avoided or just accelerated the Troubles. Depending on one's perspective, it was either the ultimate concession or the ultimate betrayal. When Northern Ireland's prime minister, Lord Craigavon, heard about it, he condemned it as an act of treachery and called it a shabby reward for the province's loyalty. In any case, the Irish government rejected it. It did not go far enough.

Relations between the two countries deteriorated in the immediate aftermath of the rejection. There was now a growing belief within both the Irish government and the country at large that Britain, by launching a pre-emptive strike, was now the more likely aggressor. Unbeknown to the British, the Irish government received a welcome, if disingenuous, assurance from the German Foreign Ministry in Berlin at the beginning of July that it had no intention of violating Irish neutrality. Less than a fortnight later, however, it seems that Hitler commissioned plans for the invasion of Britain and Ireland. In September, the German high command's mapping and surveying service published a secret dossier of military and geographical information on Ireland similar to one it produced about Britain. It pulled together all the information that was readily to hand and included maps, town plans, photographs, and postcards of key sites in Ireland and Northern Ireland.[13]

Among the factors that contributed to the breakdown in Anglo-Irish relations were Britain's continuing reluctance to provide military equipment, the withholding of which it was now more difficult to justify as it had been willingly offered if

Ireland for Ever!

'Ireland for Ever!', *Daily Mirror* cartoon of de Valera, 9 July 1940. (*Mirrorpix*)

Ireland abandoned its neutrality; hostile comments and cartoons in the British and American press, which the Irish believed were actively encouraged by the British government; casual remarks by Pryce and Lywood to their Irish counterparts that it would be unrealistic for them to expect Britain to give an unequivocal guarantee not to take pre-emptive action; and continuing distrust of Churchill, who was never seen as Ireland's friend. Indeed, he had told the War Cabinet on 16 June that he would not hesitate to use force as a last resort and hinted as much publicly in the House of Commons a fortnight later:

> We are making every preparation in our power to repel the assaults of the enemy, whether they be directed upon Great Britain, or upon Ireland, which all Irishmen, without distinction of creed or party, should realise is in imminent danger.... These preparations are constantly occupying our toil from morn till night, and far into the night. But, although we have clear views, it would not, I think, be profitable for us to discuss them in public.[14]

It seems almost certain that, while continuing to work with their Irish counterparts to develop joint plans in line with the conditions laid down by de Valera, the British military chiefs were also working on their own plans for a pre-emptive strike. The likely speed of a German attack and the weakness of the Irish forces to meet it would have made it foolhardy not to do so. It was quite possible that any Irish call for assistance would come too late.

In this already charged atmosphere, the Irish were further upset by what they saw as unexplained and provocative British troop movements near the Northern Ireland border in the first half of July. Although Maffey put it down to Irish overreaction, claiming that the only British movement was the occupation of new barracks at the border town of Strabane, it was hardly a triumph for open liaison. BTNI, it would appear, was either unaware of or chose to ignore the nuances in the relationship between the British and Irish intelligence services in Dublin. Given that they were co-operating fully through official channels, the Irish understandably took a dim view of any unilateral or independent British action, especially if it involved Irish citizens or was done without due discretion.

Then, on 15 July, a BTNI staff officer, Major E. Y. Byass, was arrested by the Irish police at Mullingar, 45 miles west of Dublin, after he had been repeatedly sighted studying a map. He and his wife claimed that they were on holiday. It was an unauthorised, embarrassing, and amateurish bungle that only antagonised the Irish further. Pryce had warned in one of his reports only a few days earlier that it was almost impossible for anyone to move or work in Ireland without being detected. Byass was eventually released after being held in Arbour Hill Detention Barracks for three days—but only after Pryce had been required by Archer to accompany him there to establish his identity.

Archer subsequently confirmed that he had no objection to Pryce and Lywood continuing to travel wherever they wanted in Ireland as long they used their real names and did not attract undue attention. In spite of their being required to work under cover, their existence had quickly become known. Pryce reported back regularly to London on the former army officers who were keen to offer him their services. Among them were Lord Monteagle, Lieutenant Colonel Grattan-Bellew, Colonel Shane Magan, and Major McCormick, MC of Blackrock. When fifty-one-year-old McCormick was turned down by a medical board in Belfast because of his deformed hand, he complained bitterly to Pryce that it had not stopped him serving as a machine-gun officer for fifteen years. He was desperate to ensure that his friends at his London clubs could not accuse him of taking refuge behind his disability in Ireland. When Colonel Jury, the director of the Shelbourne Hotel, approached Pryce in September, he forwarded his details to the War Office with a covering note saying that he was keen to serve and worth employing. In reply, he was told that there were hundreds of men like him turning up at the War Office and asking to be re-employed.

Eric was one of them. He too had volunteered his services at the outbreak of war only to be told by an elderly general that, at the age of forty-two, he was too old even though he had only resigned his territorial commission four years earlier.

He tried again at the beginning of July, a month after he had told his children that he was expecting to get another job. This time he flew over to London on Friday 5 July, and then went straight up to Manchester for a meeting before taking the weekend off to visit Peter and Michael at Naworth and to take Ann to see her new school. He told them that he had to be back in London on Monday before flying home on Tuesday. On Monday evening, MO8's Walter Skrine sent off a secret report to Pryce with details of Eric's unscheduled visit to the War Office earlier in the day.[15] Eric had apparently told him that he lived near the Curragh, that his business took him all over Ireland, and that he was in regular contact with the departments of Industry and Commerce and Agriculture and on friendly terms with its officials. He was keen to be of any service that he could and was prepared to pass on any information that he picked up on his travels. He claimed to know all about Pryce and suggested that he might like to spend a night at Morristown so that they had time to discuss things at leisure and in private. Skrine advised Pryce to discuss it with Maffey and then fix a time and place for meeting.

Eric's visit to the War Office coincided with the arrival in Northern Ireland of General Harrison as head of Military Mission 18. He would be based at first at BTNI's headquarters in Lisburn and spend the rest of the month setting up and staffing his mission before going down to Dublin to meet de Valera and the other key figures on the Irish side.

Eric and Pryce met for the first time over lunch at the Shelbourne Hotel on Sunday 28 July. Pryce reported back to the War Office the following day that, although Eric thought that relations between the two countries were improving again, he was adamant that any British attempt to enter Irish territory before being invited would be bitterly resented. The following Wednesday, Pryce drove up to Northern Ireland to pick up General Harrison and bring him back for the first of what would become regular monthly meetings with his Irish counterparts. Harrison was expecting to move his headquarters shortly to an 'advance base area' south-west of Dublin, presumably at or near the Curragh. Over two days, he was introduced to de Valera, who pressed him once more for the urgent supply of weapons, and had meetings with Frank Aiken, the minister for the co-ordination of defensive measures, and Oscar Traynor, the minister for defence. Pryce then took two days driving him back to Northern Ireland, going by an indirect route that took in the north-west coast at Sligo and the border country between Bundoran and Enniskillen. He then drove himself back down again on Tuesday, 6 August. As usual, he made detailed notes of his route and sent copies to the War Office and BTNI. This time, instead of driving straight back to Dublin along the coast road, he cut off inland after the border at Dundalk and drove through Kells and Trim to Enfield, some 30 miles west of Dublin. It was the first stage of one of three routes from Northern Ireland to Limerick that BTNI had specifically asked him to investigate. Although his notes stopped at Enfield, he almost certainly went on to stay the night with Eric. The following morning, he signed the visitors' book as 'M. H. Pryce, Attaché, Office of UK Representative'.

Pryce's visit coincided with the start of the children's holidays. After their disappointments at Christmas and Easter, Eric and Dorothy had originally hoped that they would all be able to get home for the summer. It was looking increasingly unlikely when Eric wrote to them during the evacuation of Dunkirk:

> You have probably seen the news that there are to be serious restrictions on travel between England and Ireland and that no one will be allowed to travel unless on important national business. This makes it look very improbable that you will be able to come over for your summer holidays but we hope that matters will be easier by then. If you cannot come I hope you two boys will be able to give some help on the farms. I am sure that Uncle Jos or Uncle Colley or Edfryn Jones will be very glad to have you and I'm sure you would much enjoy the work and the opportunity of making an important contribution to the national need.[16]

Alice's uncle, Jack Shorter, also wrote from Australia offering to look after the children for the duration of the war.[17] For Eric and Dorothy, it was a step too far. Their three children eventually managed to get home for the summer. Although Eric had originally booked berths for them on the ferry, they ended up coming home by air on the day that he met Pryce for lunch at the Shelbourne. His letter of 21 July would be his last for three months.

The Irish armed forces were in a significantly stronger position by the time that the first version of Plan W, the joint plan for the defence of Ireland in the event of a German invasion, was issued in September. In October, General McKenna highlighted what he had been able to achieve in the previous five months in a formal report to the minister for defence. Although the army was still short of the government's target of 42,000, its strength had increased almost threefold from 13,000 to 37,000 men; twelve barracks had been reoccupied, eighty civilian properties had been taken over, and almost 300 huts had been built or were under construction; training had commenced to ensure the earliest possible intervention by Irish troops against any hostile act; mobile columns had been organized into four geographical commands; and a detailed system of road blocks and demolitions had been planned for coastal areas.[18] It was a substantial achievement. The finalisation of Plan W and the thaw in Anglo-Irish relations meant that the arms and ammunition, which de Valera had been demanding, were finally being released. By early September, the army had already been sent 100 Bren guns, twenty-six Bren gun carriers, and more than 100 tons of high explosive by Britain and was expecting the arrival of 20,000 rifles from the US.

Events, however, had moved on. The chances of a German invasion receded with the passing of summer. In September, Maffey wrote to the Dominions Office asking for clarification on what he called an important question of policy. In his view, if the official view in London was that there was no longer any immediate threat of invasion, then there were good reasons for withholding any further supplies of arms and equipment.

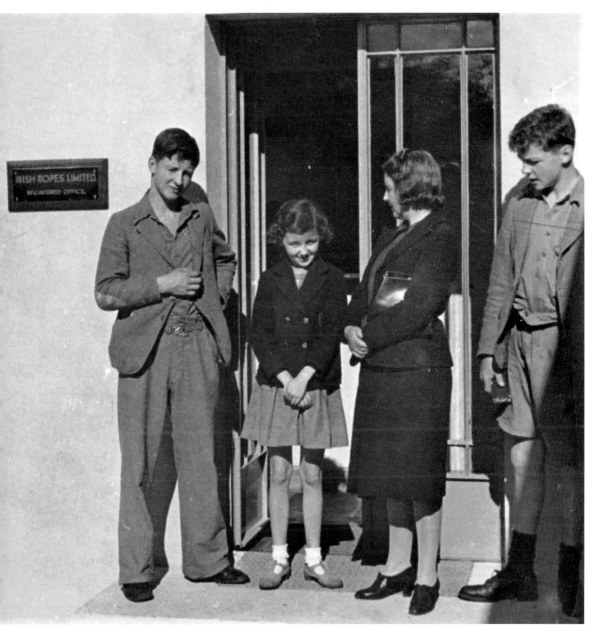

Michael, Ann, Dorothy, and Peter outside Irish Ropes's new offices, summer 1940.

Since August, the RAF had been fighting the Battle of Britain in the skies over Southern England. Attention was also focused once more on the Atlantic and the heavy cost of the U-boat war. Between June and October, 270 Allied ships were lost. The crews of the U-boats, which were now hunting in wolf packs, called it *Die Glückliche Zeit*, or happy time. Ireland's neutrality, and its refusal to allow the Royal Navy access to the treaty ports, came to be portrayed in Britain as a brutal betrayal of its moral responsibilities and natural allies. The development of Londonderry as a naval base at the end of the year limited the impact of the loss of the ports but did nothing to lessen British animosity. Then, in September, the Luftwaffe began its sustained bombardment of British cities. The eight-month Blitz targeted major ports and industrial centres throughout the British Isles including both Belfast and, perhaps by accident, Dublin. London was bombed on seventy-six consecutive nights. More than a million homes in the capital were damaged or destroyed with Londoners accounting for half of the 43,000 civilians killed in the country. Of more immediate concern to Eric, both commercially and personally, was the bombing of Liverpool. As a major port and base for the Atlantic convoys, it was an obvious target. Only London had it worse. The Blitz began in earnest there in the early hours of 9 August, a fortnight after Peter, Michael, and Ann had returned to Ireland for their summer holidays. By the end of the year, almost 1,500 people had been killed and more than 1,600 seriously injured. More than 70,000 homes were damaged or destroyed. When he returned to England, Peter remembered being able to see the bombing from his bedroom at the Ruff.

Although Eric and Pryce continued to meet regularly in Dublin, Pryce's role had become less important by the autumn. He had originally expected his posting there to last only a couple of months and so, unlike Lywood, had decided not to bring his wife over. By September, he was feeling fed up. As he told Lt-Col. Conyers-Baker, his boss at MO8, 'this life is no fun alone, especially as one has to be a semi-ghost all the time and can never come out into the open and talk freely and make friends in one's real capacity'.[19] He wanted to get back to proper soldiering. 'I know there is a war on!' he protested, 'but NOT here.' He would eventually fall out with Maffey at the end of the year. On the evening of 19 December, he was told by a reliable source that, as a result of a rumour that a BTNI force was preparing to move south, all leave had been cancelled in the Irish army and units were being rushed to the border. He was keen to avoid an incident, especially as Archer had warned him back in August that 'there's a lot of tinder lying about on each side of the border and there are a number of people on each side of the border who would be only too pleased to set it alight. Your job and mine is to prevent it being lit.'[20] In order to get the information to BTNI as quickly as possible, he bypassed the usual channels and sent an urgent telegram direct to the War Office without first getting it approved by Maffey. He then went out to enjoy a Christmas dinner at the US Club. Two days later, Maffey gave him a dressing down over a glass of sherry. He made it clear that Pryce's orders were to act through him and that he could not allow himself to get involved in any intelligence work. The incident was final proof that it was impossible to expect Pryce to report to Maffey while at the same time satisfying the demands of the War Office, BTNI, and Colonel Archer at G2. Although Conyers-Baker sided with Pryce—and especially after he discovered that Maffey had already been made aware of the Irish army's movements but had chosen not to share the information with Pryce or London—he refused his request for a transfer. Instead, Pryce would replace General Harrison as head of Military Mission 18 in April and remain in Ireland until the end of 1941.

Meanwhile, as the summer holidays and the harvest came and went, Eric found himself busier than ever. He was still able to visit Northern Ireland regularly even if the censor took exception to one of his letters in October:

> On Tuesday I went to Belfast with Mr Davies. Luckily there was a good moon so the black-out was not as much trouble as it was when Michael and I were there. We spent all [cut out] where they are doing all kinds of war work. It was all very interesting but I cannot tell you much about it in a letter except that I was amazed at the amount of work which goes into the making of our biggest [cut out]. I thought we might have had some delay in getting over the border but there was none whatever.

In spite of the worsening situation and the threat to its raw material supplies, Irish Ropes had still been able to produce 700 tons of binder twine in time for the harvest. Farmers did not have to go short. In October, the minister for agriculture, James Ryan, visited the factory to thank the workforce for its efforts and to find out whether the company's plans for the following year's harvest were on track. Disaster struck a fortnight later.

On Thursday 31 October, Eric took Dorothy up to Dublin for the evening to celebrate her forty-second birthday. He was planning to go over to England the next day to visit Peter and Michael who had now returned to Rossall from Naworth Castle. He had to cancel his plans. Shortly after midday on Friday, a fire broke out in the raw material store that housed the factory's reserve stocks of sisal. Reports of the blaze made the front pages of the national papers the following morning. The men who were working the hoist that lifted the bales of sisal to the roof of the store reported seeing a spark about 20 feet off the ground. It was too high for the factory's fire extinguishers to be of any use before the flames took hold of the dry and combustible fibre. In spite of the combined efforts of the workforce, the Local Security Force, the military fire brigade from the Curragh Camp, and the crews of the Dublin Fire Brigade, which had been dispatched at the urgent request of Arthur Cox, the only thing that they could do was to ensure that the fire did not spread to the rest of the factory and the other businesses at the barracks. It took them two hours to contain it and another four to put it out. Fire-damaged bales of sisal were still being moved out into the open the following morning and doused with water. By then, the roof of the store had collapsed and 800 tons of fibre, it was reckoned, had been lost. It was more than

The Irish Press

Vol. X., No. 263.   SATURDAY, NOVEMBER 2, 1940.   The Truth in the News   PRICE THREE-HALFPENCE

BRITISH CROWDS WATCH SEA WAR

Damage Caused By Kildare Blaze

Spare Rome, Save Athens, Italy Says

The Pope Calls World To Prayer

Ships Shelled: Berlin Claims 13 Sunk

BRITISH ships in the Straits of Dover were heavily shelled by German guns mounted on the French coast yesterday, states the Press Association correspondent at Dover. A squadron of dive-bombers followed up the attack, circling low over the ships, and each dropping three bombs, says a Press Association message.

Thousands of people gathered on the Kent cliffs to watch the bombardment. More than a hundred shells were fired in three quarters of an hour and each caused huge columns of water to shoot up from the sea.

The Press Association report states that the aircraft after a second attack were driven off by shell fire and that after an hour's bombardment none of the ships appeared to have been hit.

A German statement says that direct hits were scored on a destroyer and three merchant ships in a strongly protected British convoy.

Thirteen ships, totalling 47,000 tons, were sunk and nine, totalling 35,000 tons, badly damaged in attacks on three convoys off the British coast during the day, the German radio states.

The Droichead Nua fire. Top picture shows the burnt-out building, and the lower picture, firemen at work.

Big Rope Works Fire In Kildare

(IRISH PRESS Reporter)
DROICHEAD NUA, Friday night.

EIGHT hundred tons of sisal fibre, the property of Irish Ropes, Ltd., was still burning in the factory at the Old Military Barracks here to-night, many hours after it had caught fire.

Award For Galway Doctor's Research

RAIDS on Naples and on Tirana and other

Albanian ports by British airmen, and on Athens, Corfu, Larissa and Salonika by the Italian air force were reported yesterday.

The city of Athens, though raiders were over it four times, was not bombed. A semi-official British statement last night said that it had been announced in Rome that Athens would not be bombed so long as the British do not bomb Rome.

Both Sides Use Crack Troops

3,000 Miles To Bomb Naples

Four Air Raids On Athens

SUNDAY, November 24,

has been ordered by His Holiness the Pope to be observed as a day of prayer throughout the world. Masses and public prayers have been directed on that day for the pressing needs of human society.

TURKS NOT TO ENTER WAR NOW, SAYS PRESIDENT

French Cabinet Approves Talks With Germany

The meeting between Herr Hitler and Marshal Pétain on the border of occupied and unoccupied France—a radio picture from New York.

(Continued on Page 7)

GERMANS CLAIM DIRECT HITS

WHOLE CHANNEL COAST SHAKEN

BRITISH BOMB CARGO SHIP

WEEK-END TIDES

BRITISH SHIPPING LOSSES

BOMBAY MARKETS CLOSED

Front page of the *Irish Press*, 2 November 1940, reporting the factory fire. (*With thanks to Irish Newspaper Archives and the Irish Press*)

Some of the workers who helped fight the fire. According to Newbridge Down Memory Lane they are Stephen Dunne, Bill Geraghty, Christy White, Joe Jones, and Tom Geraghty.

had been needed for that year's harvest. It had cost the company £32,000 to buy but Eric knew that, with the current disruption to supplies, it would probably cost four times as much to replace.

Luckily only the store was damaged and production was halted for less than an hour. However, hundreds of bales of sisal now lay soaked and smouldering outside over an area of more than an acre. No one was sure whether they could be salvaged. Although the fibre beneath the charred exterior of the bales looked sound, it might be too short to spin, and if it was left where it was over the winter, it would rot. Eric gave himself six weeks to find a solution.

8

Feeling the Pinch, 1941

... and soon the company lost access to much of its raw material supplies.[1]

Although Eric was insured, there was little chance of his getting any compensation quickly. In any case, it would not be enough to replace what he had lost. Threatened with the ruin of his business and the potential loss of Ireland's harvest in 1941, he determined to make a fight of it.

To reassure his customers, he placed a large notice in the papers on Sunday and Monday:

> In view of the serious nature of the fire which on Friday destroyed one of our hemp stores, we feel that a frank statement is due to our customers and to those who use cordage for so many essential needs. The loss is confined to a large reserve of sisal fibre kept in a separate store, accumulated in consequence of present world conditions, and is to be deplored especially on that account. We still have an ample stock of sisal to permit maximum production to be continued, and all possible endeavours are being made to safeguard the more distant position. No part of our factory other than the store mentioned is damaged or affected; no other stocks have been touched; full employment will continue, and our usual delivery services will be maintained.[2]

He then left Horace Davies behind in Newbridge to supervise the demolition and rebuilding of the ruined store; he sent Alec Nisbet, who had by then joined Irish Ropes as works chemist after the suspension of LIRA's sisal research at Lisburn, to Belfast to find out from the experts at Queens University whether flax could be used as a substitute for sisal; and he took himself off to England for a week to get advice from Wigglesworths and to buy salvage equipment. After visits to manufacturers in London, Lancashire, and Yorkshire, he placed an order with Tomlinson's in Rochdale for a drying machine similar to those used in East Africa to dry sisal after decortication. It would have to be specially built and installed at a cost of around £3,000. Within a week of his return the store's new roof was almost finished and a site had been found and made ready for the drying machine. To protect himself against another disaster, Eric leased an off-site warehouse at Chapelizod on the outskirts of Dublin, installed an overhead travelling crane to replace the hoist in the sisal store, and bought a bright red Merryweather fire trailer on which the factory's fire brigade would now practice their drills every Saturday morning. 'It will throw a jet over a hundred feet into the air and will work either from the mains or from a river or pond,' he told the children, promising to give them a demonstration in the holidays.

In December, he returned to Tomlinson's to check on progress before collecting the children from Ormskirk for the Christmas holidays. His persistence paid off. The drying machine was delivered in the second half of January while he was away taking them back to school. The following week, he told them all the latest news in his first Sunday letter of the term:

It took me two days to get back. I spent all Saturday going to and returning from Barton [Manchester's airport] from which no plane could fly because of the weather. On Sunday I ought to have had plenty of time for my train from

Irish Ropes's Merryweather fire trailer.

Lime Street [in Liverpool] but we were held up by the snow at Aughton for fifty minutes and, although I raced through deep snow to Lime Street, I had no chance. However I was lucky to catch a train to Chester from Rock Ferry and then met the Lime Street train coming in after it had been held up for a long time near Warrington. Then I had to wait hours for the Irish Mail. We eventually slipped out of Holyhead just before dusk. It was very rough indeed but with a following sea which was not as bad as it would have been if it had been head on or abeam. Mummy and Brannigan [the family's nickname for Dorothy Baxter] had been waiting at the Hibernian since three o'clock and we did not reach home until eleven o'clock.

The next morning we had the worst blizzard I have known and the roads were soon blocked. Many wires were down and we had to stop the works twice for over twelve hours each time. Our road was completely blocked and there is still over two feet of snow across one side though the snow has gone everywhere else except in these drifts. The back road was reasonably clear except for a drift near the station. Mr Davies was almost cut off and had to walk all the way, climbing over hedges and into the fields where the drifts were worst. He lunched each day at the hostel and started home early each evening. Up to yesterday he could not get his cycle through all the way but has been leaving it at Counihans.

The drying machine is being put together now. It is a very complicated box of tricks and we expect to take about three weeks erecting it. An expert has now arrived to take charge but to begin with he was delayed and Mr Davies and I started on our own and enjoyed the puzzle. It is rather a wonderful affair for it has nine fans which send the hot air through the machine in a spiral.

I have been very lazy today, making up for last weekend though I have spent some time on the wireless this afternoon, moving it away from the window and soldering all the joints. It has much improved the reception. Tomorrow I am going to Dublin and then on that night to Belfast for the following day.

I want to take some photos from the look-out and then build up a panorama with all the landmarks marked for reference.[3] I keep promising myself to make another copy of the garden pictures which Granny wants but I don't look like having much spare time for the next few weeks.

I went down to the village for the papers on my Spitfire before supper. It seems to be running much better now that it has had a good running in by you folk. I keep it in the greenhouse now and she starts at once. I don't know what I should do without it now as we are getting no petrol at all. There are hardly any cars on the road though the buses are running as usual.

This is all my news for tonight. I hope Ann is happy in her new house and that you boys are alright for tuck. Did you find yourselves able to get what you need at school? You must shout out when your pocket money begins to run low.

Lots of love from us both, your ever-loving Daddy.

Although Eric had reckoned that it would take three weeks to assemble the drying machine, Horace Davies had the shed ready to house it by the beginning

Peter McConnon loading sisal into the Tomlinson drying machine.

of February and the machine itself installed and ready for testing a few days later. Staff then worked around the clock for the rest of the week to complete their preparations. The first 2 tons of fibre were salvaged successfully on Saturday 8 February, fourteen weeks after the fire. Eric and Horace then spent Sunday working with a small team to make last-minute adjustments before the salvage operation began in earnest at 6 a.m. the following morning. 'We don't expect to stop for as many weeks as we may have before the warm weather arrives,' he told the children, 'we shall have a hundred men taking a turn of three hours a week at the week-ends to keep it going on Saturdays and Sundays.'

Meanwhile, the outlook for Ireland, and in particular its trade relations with the UK, had deteriorated significantly in the three months in which Eric had had little time to think of anything but his salvage operation. The talks between the two countries, which had started so positively at the start of the war, had led to the British suggestion that they should try to reach a comprehensive trade agreement. It would clearly be of benefit to both countries. The Irish government needed to keep Britain as effectively its only customer and its only source of essential imports, while the British government realised the advantage of having Ireland as its 'nearby larder'—and especially after it introduced rationing (originally for bacon, butter, and sugar) at the beginning of 1940. However, it also had to be seen to be acting fairly. Irish farmers could not be allowed to get a better deal than their

An example of Horace Davies's ingenuity: Eric's photograph of what he described as an 'independently driven but coupled high-speed scouring and washing machine attached to Mackie polisher—built at Newbridge, designed by H. E. Davies'.

British and dominion counterparts, and under the principle of equal hardship, Irish consumers had to suffer at least as much as British when commodities were in short supply.

Lemass and Ryan, as the ministers for Supplies and Agriculture, were given the responsibility of taking the negotiations forward at ministerial level. Although substantial progress was made at a first meeting in London at the end of April 1940, difficulties arose at the second three days later when the British delegation requested storage and trans-shipment facilities in Irish ports in order to relieve the congestion in their own. It was something that the Irish delegation could not concede if it was to preserve Ireland's neutrality. In its turn, it asked for Irish farmers to be paid the same price for what they exported to Britain that British farmers received. Although this had already been agreed in respect of the Irish flax harvests in 1939 and 1940, the British were adamant that for all other products they should be paid no more than other dominion producers.

The talks could not have become deadlocked at a worse time. The German invasion of France and the Low Countries a week later meant that the negotiations could not be resumed until August when the British issued a first draft of a proposed agreement. By then, a lot of water had gone under the bridge—the Phoney War was over, Britain had a new and less amenable prime minister, and relations between the two countries were at a low ebb. However, the earlier sticking points had yet to be resolved. The British draft agreement included terms for storage and trans-shipment facilities in Irish ports that the Irish would never find acceptable—not least because Germany, which would shortly announce a total air and sea blockade of Britain, had already made it clear that acceptance would fundamentally alter its view of Irish neutrality. Although the British refused to back down on this, they did try to compromise on prices while making sure that they could not be seen to be putting the other dominions at a disadvantage. In spite of his distaste for what he saw as the subsidy of a disloyal dominion, Churchill reluctantly agreed to offer a lump sum of £500,000, albeit for one year only, to make good the shortfall in prices.

In September, with the talks stalled once more, a group of Ireland's leading civil servants wrote a last-minute memorandum to de Valera's secretary, Maurice Moynihan, to underline the importance of reaching an agreement:

> The continuance of a supply of industrial materials is almost as vital to the economic life of the country as is the assurance of a market for domestic exports as almost every branch of industrial production is absolutely dependent to a major degree on a continuance of imports.... On purely economic grounds there is, therefore, an unanswerable case for making every effort possible to accept such terms of any draft agreement as are reasonable and do not endanger this country's neutrality.[4]

Of course, this was exactly what the British proposal did endanger. When the Irish cabinet met to consider it a few days later, it confirmed that it was unable to entertain any agreement on storage or trans-shipment. It meant that a trade agreement would never be signed.

It is always difficult to assign blame when negotiations collapse, and in this case to Britain for making demands that it must have known were unacceptable or to Ireland for overplaying a weak hand. The consequences for Ireland now were that, if it lost access to any commodity imported from Britain, it would have only four options left—to find another source, to find a substitute, to negotiate a new agreement with Britain at whatever the cost, or to stop using it altogether. Eric himself had to consider all four options at some point during the Emergency. Meanwhile, the impasse was another example of an abiding element in Anglo-Irish relations: the Irish doubted British good faith while the British were frustrated by Irish intransigence.

A fortnight before Germany's announcement of its air and sea blockade of Britain the British government introduced its own measures to control neutral shipping and prevent trading with the enemy. They were announced in the House of Commons at the end of July by Ronald Cross, the minister of shipping, and Hugh Dalton, the minister of economic warfare. From now on, any neutral ship that did not have a British ship's warrant would be refused fuelling and other facilities in British and Allied ports, and any ship that had not obtained a valid 'navicert' for every voyage to or from a European port would be assumed to be carrying 'goods of enemy origin or interest' and might be intercepted by the Royal Navy and taken into port for examination. At best, this would mean considerable delay and at worst the confiscation of both the vessel and its cargo. However, Dalton stated categorically that, rather than trying to extend the blockade to neutral countries, these new rules would help those engaged in honest neutral trade and allow them to import adequate supplies for domestic consumption.[5] In time, Ireland would find out that they could be used as an offensive as well as a defensive weapon of economic warfare.

Churchill's attitude to Ireland and its refusal to allow the Royal Navy access to the treaty ports was as uncompromising as ever when he updated parliament on the war situation at the beginning of November:

> More serious than the air raids has been the recent recrudescence of U-boat sinkings in the Atlantic approaches to our islands. The fact that we cannot use the south and west coasts of Ireland to refuel our flotillas and aircraft and thus protect the trade by which Ireland as well as Great Britain lives, is a most heavy and grievous burden and one which should never have been placed on our shoulders, broad though they be.[6]

However, it was an Irish republican who was the catalyst for a hardening of British policy towards Ireland. Shortly after Churchill made his speech, Maffey received a damning memorandum on de Valera and his government from a man whom he chose not to name but whom he described as 'a 100 per cent Irishman, who was himself a rebel and certainly believes what he says as I know from conversations with him.'[7] It began as follows:

Since de Valera has been in power the British government have consistently made the mistake of expecting from him a generous response to a generous gesture. Generosity is not in his nature. He is cold, calculating, and egotistical. His first interest is himself—that he should be the leader and monopolise the limelight.

Given the gravity of the U-boat threat, the memorandum went on to suggest that no British cargo space should be made available for any supplies bound for Ireland; that all traffic across the Irish Sea should be suspended with the exception only of the mail boat between Holyhead and Dublin; that all ships bound directly for Ireland should be disrupted and 'put through all the delays and troubles of contraband control at a British port well out of their normal route'; and that all imports from Ireland should either be halted or have their prices so reduced as to make it uneconomical for Ireland to export them. Such measures, the author of the memorandum believed, would quickly close Irish factories and increase unemployment and so cause a fatal loss of support for de Valera, who would be 'swept from power for good in a wave of indignation'.

The anonymous memorandum quickly made the rounds. Maffey sent it to Machtig, who sent it on to Viscount Cranborne, who had recently taken over as secretary of state for the dominions, who in turn forwarded it to Churchill. Churchill immediately asked the minister of food, Lord Woolton, to let him know what the impact would be of cutting off food imports from Ireland for, say, six months. In reply, Woolton suggested that Britain was already subsidising Irish beef and bacon production to the tune of £3.5 million a year. It only fuelled Churchill's indignation. Once all the other relevant government departments had been given the chance to comment the memorandum was tabled at a meeting of the War Cabinet on 6 December. The prime minister was never likely to back down from this new hard line, which was expected to be short-term and bear immediate dividends. When the new measures were eventually introduced, he asked to be updated regularly on their effect. From his perspective, they were clearly meant to be punitive—to pierce the bubble of Irish complacency—even if they were presented as an economic necessity. He found it necessary to remind Cranborne and the chancellor of the Exchequer of this in a personal minute in February:

> I hope we shall not fall into the error of becoming too tender-footed in this policy. The intention was to make Southern Ireland realise how great a wrong they were doing to the cause of freedom by their denial of the ports. We must expect they will make some complaints from time to time. A stern mood should prevail in view of the ordeals to which the British nation is exposed.[8]

A new policy of restricting exports to Ireland was approved by the cabinet on 2 January and implemented the following week by means of a Board of Trade order that came into force on 20 January. It was communicated to the Irish government on the same day in an *aide-memoire* to John Dulanty, the Irish high commissioner in London, which explained that the policy had been made necessary by the need to conserve supplies and to limit the export of any goods in short supply. The Board of Trade order simply removed the exemptions that Ireland had previously enjoyed and, by requiring it to obtain licences for the import of certain listed items, placed it in the same category as all the other dominions. It was therefore difficult to criticise on the grounds of equity. In practice, no licences would be granted for any items that were in short supply in Britain—a list that included agricultural machinery, chemical and electrical goods, and paper and cardboard, as well as fibres, yarns, hemps of all kinds and binder and reaper twine—and, as and when any licenses were granted, quantities would usually be restricted to half of what had been supplied in 1940. Food would be supplied on the principle of 'equal sacrifice' while ensuring that Irish consumers always fared slightly worse than British. Trans-shipment of goods to Ireland would be held up by ensuring that there was no available space on British and neutral ships or, if that did not work, by requisitioning or otherwise holding those goods in Britain. The risk of increased smuggling along the border with Northern Ireland would be monitored, while Viscount Cranborne's planned visit to Dublin, which de Valera had suggested to Maffey in December, was put on hold.

It was a simple but elegant finesse by the British government. By portraying its policy as being dictated solely by necessity, it could apply pressure on the Irish government without losing the goodwill of the population at large. The latter would be grateful for its considerate treatment in difficult times, while the former would be left in no doubt that it was being punished for its intransigence.

The British change of policy came at a bad time for Ireland. De Valera was recovering from an operation on his one remaining good eye, and while there had been previous isolated incidents of German bombs in August and December, the first bombing of Dublin and the surrounding counties of Meath, Kildare, Wicklow, and Carlow came early in the new year when Eric's children were still at home for the holidays. The military fire brigade at the Curragh Camp had to be called out when the area around Newbridge and the Curragh was hit by thirty to forty high explosive and incendiary bombs. It was helped by Newbridge's volunteer firefighters and Irish Ropes's new fire service.

Some effects of the hardening of the British attitude were felt in Ireland even before the end of the year. Although the country still had adequate stocks of most commodities, the British Ministry of Shipping had, by December, released no ships for a month for cargoes of wheat, maize, and animal feed.[9] Then, on Christmas Eve, the country suddenly and without warning ran out of petrol. It would be a week before deliveries were resumed on a limited basis. It was a brutal wake-up call to the realities of war and a sudden end to what Professor Duncan described as fifteen months of a fool's paradise. As in Britain, petrol had been rationed in Ireland since the outbreak of war. However, while the British ration was robust enough to be effective—restricting cars to 100 or 200 miles a month and London cabs to 2 gallons, or around 34 miles, a day—in Ireland, the ration was too generous either to preserve stocks or to cause any serious disruption to motorists. Although the reasons for the sudden shortage were never fully explained, the immediate cause appears to have been the sinking of two tankers carrying petrol bound for Ireland. However, the writing was already on the wall. In his report to the minister for defence in October, General McKenna had said that, although the country still had 5.3 million gallons of petrol at the end of September, stocks had fallen by 2.3 million gallons in a month. By December, Lemass was aware that, while the country still had six months' supply of wheat, its stocks of petrol were down to less than nine weeks.

The crisis prompted the former prime minister and leader of the opposition, William Cosgrave, to demand an emergency debate in the Dáil to discuss essential supplies and their equitable distribution in the event of an acute shortage. By the time that the Dáil met on 16 January for the first time since Christmas, Dulanty had already been informed of Britain's new hard-line policy. The debate lasted throughout that afternoon and evening and was not adjourned until after midnight on the following day. Lemass put his cards on the table when he spoke immediately after Cosgrave had introduced his motion:

[People] are beginning to realise the fact that war is a very unpleasant business, not merely for those countries who are directly engaged in it but for a great many other countries as well. It is quite impossible for the Government to take measures which would prevent the effects of the war being felt, and being felt very severely in some directions, in this country. Apart from the question of the marketing of our surplus production, it is a fact that before the war our economic structure depended upon imports in the case of a very large number of important commodities. These will not be available in the future in the quantities in which we were accustomed to get them; some of them, in fact, may not be available at all. The public in this country must count themselves lucky that, for the past fifteen months, they have not felt the effects of the war more severely, and the country may also count itself lucky that it is possible, by our own efforts, to produce sufficient food to save our own people from starvation.[10]

It was a message that de Valera reiterated when he spoke towards the end of the next day:

We are very fortunate to have gone so far without suffering greater hardships. We cannot expect to get on for the future as well as we have done in the past. This war is really only beginning, so far as anybody looking out on it can judge. The hardships that are going to be inflicted on every country are going to increase from now on and if this community is going to survive and come through it—and I hope, with God's help, we shall—we will have to take a number of these problems much more seriously than we have taken them up to the present.

Worse was to come. Little attention was probably paid at the time to a government notice that appeared in the papers on the second day of the debate announcing an outbreak of foot and mouth disease just north of the border in Co. Londonderry. An immediate ban on the cross-border movement of livestock was not enough to prevent it spreading south of the border. Within a week, the first case had been reported in Donegal. It would develop into Ireland's worst outbreak of the disease to date and a national crisis for an agricultural economy that was still heavily dependent on its cattle exports. By the end of January, all shipments of livestock to Britain had been halted. With slaughter seen as the only way to control the spread of the disease, the government offered farmers full compensation if they reported outbreaks promptly and properly. By the beginning of March, more than fifty cases had been reported and more than 3,800 animals destroyed. All fairs, markets, and public sales of livestock were banned. By May, the value of monthly exports of livestock was down to £32,000 from the previous year's £1,023,000. All race meetings and sporting events involving horses or dogs were suspended. Outbreaks continued to be reported throughout the summer. By July, when Dublin's cattle market was reopened and the export of cattle from specific areas was resumed on a small scale, there had been almost 450 reported cases and more than 27,000 animals had been destroyed, including 19,400 cattle and 5,600 sheep. Although only two of the twenty-six counties were still affected by the beginning of August, export restrictions would not finally be lifted until the end of October.

Meanwhile, the new British trade embargo was having an immediate effect. The Irish government had to introduce rationing for commodities in short supply, starting with coal at the end of January and then extending the list to include fuel oil, flour, tea, sugar, peat, and many other basic commodities. As Eric told his children at the beginning of February:

> We are beginning to know that we shall soon feel the pinch of things. Tea is rationed down to two ounces each and butter supplies are cut in two. But the worst is the shortage of petrol. I have enough in my Spitfire to last me most of the month but don't know when we shall be given more coupons. We have enough to run the truck at the works for many weeks and some reserve for the fire engine but we dare not dip into our stocks for anything else.

Eric agreed to garage two of his colleagues' cars in the outbuildings at Morristown. He kept his own Ford V8 at the factory for emergencies only, either to pull the fire trailer or for use as an ambulance to ferry local people to hospital. He relied instead on his baby Austin, which he kept going in the forlorn hope that he might occasionally get hold of some petrol. However, as he admitted, 'no coupons have been issued this month except a very small ration to a few essential people and the prospect for next month is no better'. For the short journey to the factory each morning, he used his Spitfire motorbike, donning an old raincoat, gum boots, leather helmet, and the leather jerkin that his parents had sent out him during his first bitingly cold winter on the Western Front in 1917. He now used trains and buses to get to Dublin. The reduction in services meant that they were always crowded. Travel elsewhere within the country became almost impossible. With Irish Ropes's board finding it difficult to meet formally, Eric was largely left to get on with things on his own. By autumn, there was just a single train to Dublin each day, and the mail was so slow that Eric reckoned that they were back in the days of the stagecoach.

In the first week of February, Erskine Childers, the son of the author of *The Riddle of the Sands* who was the secretary of the Federation of Irish Manufacturers as well as being a TD, wrote to tell Maffey that his members were already feeling the pinch and that their loss of access to raw materials would lead to an increasing number of business failures in 1941. A month later, Maffey reported back to Machtig in a similar vein:

> The cold blast of the economic measures—very skillfully introduced—is being increasingly felt here and things may be in a bad mess before long.... So far there is remarkably little general talk of the trade restrictions being imposed in retaliation for the non-surrender of the ports. In more knowledgeable circles the verdict is not so generous.... We can therefore assume that the de Valera government are well aware that there is a punitive ingredient in our measures.[11]

At the end of the month, Geoffrey Braddock, the British trade commissioner in Ireland, was asked to write a detailed report on the effect of the sanctions to date. They could hardly have been more successful:

> Industries are slowing down ... most of the factories are working short time while a number have closed their doors for a longer or shorter period. Within the past two months the position has become far more acute, and each week it becomes more so. Many of the factories are working on reserves and their stocks are diminishing.[12]

He went on to confirm that there had been an acute shortage of petrol since Christmas. Most private cars had already been taken off the road, while cars in Dublin were being fitted with gasbags to run on gas. Sales of new cars in Ireland would fall from 7,480 in 1939 to 240 in 1941. The government was already considering a total ban on the use of petrol cars—except under special licence by doctors, vets, midwives, priests, and certain key government officials who would receive an allowance of 8 gallons a month—but would hold off doing so for another year. Although food supplies were generally adequate, the tea ration was halved to an ounce per person per week in April and then halved again soon afterwards. Wheat shortages had already led to the introduction of the wartime brown loaf, while flour stocks were not expected to last beyond June. Cattle fodder was running out. In February, an emergency scientific research bureau was set up by professors from University College Dublin to investigate and promote the use of native substitutes for imported raw materials. Lemass asked industrialists for their help to keep production going for as long as possible. With imports of British coal reduced in both quantity and quality de Valera called for another 3 million tons of peat to be cut over the summer. Nevertheless, Eric reckoned that the country would be out of fuel by winter for both industrial and domestic use.

However, the core of the problem, as Braddock highlighted in his report, was Ireland's lack of a merchant fleet. It was unable to organise any alternative source of imports on its own. The government established Irish Shipping early in 1941 to try to make good the deficit but soon found that there were now few ships left to buy and that nearly all of those were in poor condition.[13] Even if they were made seaworthy, it would be difficult to find fuel for them or to protect them when at sea, and as Ireland had almost no export trade except with Britain, it risked adding substantially to its costs by bringing the ships in full and sending them out again empty.

It was against this worsening background that Eric decided to go and see things for himself. At the beginning of March, with the salvage of his sisal well under way and the British sanctions beginning to bite, he went over to Britain on a week's fact-finding trip to assess the prospects for Irish Ropes's current and future supplies.

By now, sisal was an essential wartime commodity with its price and production controlled by the British government.[14] At the outbreak of war, the increased demand for rope and twine and the threat to merchant shipping had prompted the government to reduce its reliance on manila from the Philippines and to secure instead adequate supplies of sisal from East Africa. It was the war that finally forced British manufacturers and users of rope to switch from manila to sisal. In November 1939, they agreed between themselves that, to conserve supplies of manila, all cordage—with the exception only of the highest grades where there might otherwise be a risk to lives or ships—should be made from at least 25 per cent sisal. At the same time, in order to secure adequate supplies, the government arranged with the colonial governments in East Africa to reserve for itself and France a preferential quota of 90,000 tons of sisal in 1940. Although exports from Kenya and Tanganyika had grown to almost 130,000 tons by 1938, most of it went to continental Europe, while only 30,000 tons of it was bought in the UK. The government determined its quota simply by doubling the country's previous usage to factor in the loss of manila and the anticipated increase in wartime demand and then earmarking another 30,000 tons for France. The growers in East Africa, whose markets in Europe were now either at risk or already lost, would be allowed to sell any surplus production over and above the quota to certain neutral countries as long as they did not undercut the price agreed with the British government. For the time being at least, it looked as if Irish Ropes would have no difficulty getting hold of enough sisal.

Like the Irish government, the British established a ministry of supply at the outbreak of war and seconded to it men with relevant experience to co-ordinate and control the purchase and distribution of a wide range of essential commodities that included flax, cotton, jute, iron and steel, non-ferrous metals, plastics, fertilisers, paper, timber, and wool. One of the sixteen controllers of raw materials appointed on the day of Britain's declaration of war was Alfred Landauer, a partner in one of London's leading firms of fibre merchants.[15] His remit as hemp controller would cover hemp in its widest sense.[16] He had reporting to him sections for every hard fibre, each under an assistant controller recruited from one of the major fibre merchants. As well as playing a key role in distributing supplies and co-ordinating the needs of the armed services with the directorate of cordage production, he would also be responsible for allocating orders to merchants and for fixing their rates of commission. In effect, he took over their role for the duration of the war. Many of the merchants would soon regret releasing him their 'duds', as Eric called them, rather than their best men.

At the same time, the colonial governments in East Africa appointed Sir William Lead as sisal controller in Dar es Salaam. It was an important job for an important man. In many respects, Sir William was to Tanganyika what Lord Delamere had been to Kenya. A pen portrait sent by the colonial government to the Colonial Office ahead of his first trip to London as sisal controller early in 1940 described him as 'the elder statesman par excellence in this Territory'.[17] As well as owning one of the largest sisal estates there and being a founder and former president of the Tanganyika Sisal Growers Association, he was also leader of the seven 'unofficial' representatives (being those who did not hold a government position) on the territory's twenty-strong legislative council. In 1937, he was selected as one of Tanganyika's two representatives to attend the coronation of King George VI. Now, working in collaboration with the hemp controller in Britain, his job as sisal controller would be to allocate the British quota fairly between the growers and to organise its transport, warehousing, and shipping to and from the ports in East Africa.

Eldred Hitchcock, who was manager of Bird and Co.'s sisal estates in East Africa and sat on the board of its British parent company, Sisal Estates Ltd, would also play an increasingly influential role. He found himself in the right place at the right time as the paid chairman of the Sisal Growers Association, which the local growers' associations in Kenya and Tanganyika had established in London at the end of 1938 to represent and promote their interests. Along with all the other major players in the industry Alfred Wigglesworth was one of the twenty-four men who sat on its council.

The invasion of the Low Countries and France in May 1940 forced the British government into a radical rethink of its sisal arrangements. With its markets in continental Europe now completely cut off, supplies of sisal far exceeded demand. Figures produced that June suggested that, if nothing was done, 30 per cent of the world's hard fibre production, or some 100,000 tons, would be unlikely to find a buyer. Sisal was now so important to the colonial economies of East Africa that it was feared that the loss of its markets might destabilise the region both economically and politically. At emergency talks in London with the Treasury, the Colonial Office, and the Ministry of Supply, Hitchcock and Landauer agreed that East African production would have to be cut by a quarter, from 130,000 to 100,000 tons a year, and that the government would almost certainly have to contract to buy it all. Prices would be held at 1939 levels for the time being with any future increases being based on average costs of production after making a small allowance for profit. Thrown a lifeline that would enable many of them to stay in business, the growers in East Africa unanimously supported the proposals. Although a final agreement would not be approved by the War Cabinet's Committee on Export Surpluses until the beginning of 1941, the reduction in output was implemented immediately. It was split proportionately between Kenya and Tanganyika and then allocated between the estates on the basis of their average production over the previous three years. In the short term at least, it could be achieved without too much hardship through a more judicious harvesting of the leaves and a prohibition on the planting of new bulbils to replace exhausted stock. The re-confiscation of the German-owned 'enemy' estates and the internment of their owners also helped. In the 1930s, the Germans' repurchase of their former estates, which had been encouraged by the Nazi policy of offering attractive financing arrangements so that they could regain a foothold in their *Deutsche Heimat in Afrika* (or German home in Africa), meant that by the outbreak of war, they were producing a quarter of the territory's sisal.[18] However, as their estates tended to produce sisal of higher quality, they were usually leased out to other growers by the Custodian of Enemy Property rather than allowed to revert to jungle.

From now on, the wartime market for East African sisal would be restricted and highly regulated. It would be of no help to Eric that it was all imported into Britain on the government's account. He no longer had any room for manoeuvre on the quality, price, and availability of his main raw material. When he traipsed round London, Manchester, Liverpool, and Glasgow on his trip in March, he also saw the impact of the British embargo on trade with Ireland. Once he got back, he sent off a bleak report to his fellow directors:

> This time I appreciated much more than before the impact of total war upon the commercial life of the country. So long as no one lacks essential food and other absolute necessities nothing else matters but the implements of war. Home consumption and the production of goods not actually vital is being depressed to an extent that would never be tolerated if the mass of the people did not feel themselves engaged in the greatest life and death struggle of all time.... Early in the war considerable emphasis was laid upon the need to conduct the extraordinary business of wartime through the usual trade channels. Cutting across this principle there now comes a ruthless re-direction of those normal channels as war industries gain momentum and are ready to absorb more and more of the country's manpower and equipment of all kinds. Not only individual factories but whole trades will be sacrificed to increase the direct war effort.

He reckoned that Dundee's jute industry was one of those at risk after the government's decision to transfer manufacturing to factories in India. It was not the only one. He had previously had no trouble buying cotton yarn, which Irish Ropes used to make parcel twine, as British mills had been encouraged to maintain production and exports. Now he thought it 'too painfully obvious' that supplies would dry up as British cotton mills were closed or converted to war work. Although he found no evidence of a curtailment of rope production—it was after all an essential wartime commodity—it was clear that some fibres, such as flax and European hemp, were already in such short supply that government departments were battling with each other to get hold of enough.

Eric's trip had been prompted in part by a hunch that the onward shipping of his sisal to Dublin was being disrupted once it reached British ports. His fears were confirmed as soon as he reached Glasgow and saw things at first hand. A large consignment of sisal had just arrived at the port, 500 tons of which were destined for Irish Ropes. Arranging their release and onward transportation was fraught with complications. They first had to be cleared through customs in a form acceptable to the Ministry of Economic Warfare, a task that was made all the more difficult because Eric's cargo was split into more than twenty parcels on five ships. The lack of warehouse space in Glasgow also meant that merchant ships often had to unload their cargoes in mid-channel at the mouth of the Clyde estuary where lighters then took them to smaller ports and jetties up to 30 miles away from the city. Eric discovered that some of his bales had even ended up by accident in Middlesbrough on the other side of the country. Exasperated, he told the directors:

> Apart from friends ready to help one anytime and apart from the efforts of our most excellent friends, Wigglesworths, nobody cares two straws about our little difficulties. I gave myself the pleasure of telling Hemp Control what I thought of them but one cannot quite fall out with one's only source of supply. The whole job was a prize example of official blundering though there was a set of difficult circumstances which would have tasked the resources of anybody.

Although lighterage and transit war risk charges added an unknown element to his costs, Eric was resigned to the fact that 'all that really matters is to get the sisal and hang the cost'. The port authorities were, in any case, so far behind with their invoicing that he was usually working blind when it came to costing. As a result, he was not yet able to tell the Ministry of Supplies what Irish farmers were likely to have to pay for their binder twine that year. Both he and his father, who had a reputation in the family for his mental arithmetic, believed that accurate costing was critical to the success of any manufacturing enterprise. It had certainly underpinned Eric's management of Irish Ropes in its early years. He had even bought an electronic comptometer just before the war to perform complicated costing analyses. 'It does all kinds of calculations, adds, subtracts, multiplies, and divides—and remembers what it has done too,' he told the children, 'I don't think Grandpa would have much use for it. All you have to do is to press a button and it runs for the second or so necessary to finish the calculation by electricity.' Now all that had to go by the board.

In sharp contrast to an earlier trip at the height of the IRA bombing campaign in 1939, Eric was surprised to find that there was little bad feeling towards Ireland. Instead, he found what he described as an acute and abiding disappointment over the treaty ports—'but only when people feel that lives are being lost because this aid is denied'—and a widespread belief that the Irish government was deliberately using censorship to conceal the moral issues of the war from its people. With respect to the main purpose of his trip, to assess the prospects for future supplies, he had to accept that, although the British government had refrained so far from doing anything that might be seen in Ireland as victimisation, 'now that everything is out of the way the curtailment of supplies is quick and rigorous'.

His visit coincided with the imposition of a total ban on the export and trans-shipment of hard fibres to Ireland. 'Now the door has been completely shut against us,' he told the directors; 'as from 1 March London brokers may not sell hemp outside the UK if such hemp has come into UK ports for trans-shipment.' His only surprise was that it had not happened sooner. With Irish Ropes being, so he thought, the only foreign purchaser of fibre from Britain and thus the only business to be affected by the ban, he would have to do everything himself if he wanted the decision overturned.

At least he was better off than many other Irish businesses as he had continued to stockpile all the raw materials on which he could lay his hands regardless of price. In spite of the fire in the sisal store, he reckoned that he still had more than six months' supply. It was more than he had ever had and certainly much more than the average manufacturer in Britain. He also had some still in transit and was hoping that it would be released even though it did not reach Britain before the ban was imposed. Thereafter, he could count on no more at a time when Ireland's demand for agricultural twine was growing dramatically. He investigated other sources of supply while he decided the best way to approach hemp control to relax the ban. He had already met with shipping companies in Dublin and had arranged for some shipments of sisal to be sent direct from Lisbon in neutral Portugal. He had also bought 100 tons that were scheduled to arrive in New York at the beginning of April and was deciding whether it was worth trying to buy any more. It was not an easy solution. The cost of buying and shipping it was much greater; it was difficult to find any cargo space to ship it across the Atlantic; and, although he could use sterling to buy the fibre itself, he had to find the foreign currency to settle the freight charges before it could be shipped.

As he started to eat into his stocks, Eric cut back on other production to ensure that there was enough fibre to meet that year's demand for agricultural twine. Although it was less profitable, he accepted that 'it is the national need which must rule our policy today'. He cut his product lines from 500 to less than sixty, sent out economy leaflets to all his customers, and rationed his supplies of non-agricultural twine by requiring all orders to be taken in part in other materials. Most customers accepted this approach. However, he encountered resistance from some retailers and their trade representatives, and most notably from the grandly-named Paper Bag, Wrapping Paper and Twine Manufacturers and Distributors Trade Guardian Association of Ireland, which complained of his dictatorial behaviour. He felt compelled to deliver a strong riposte shortly after he returned from his trip:

> We cannot forbear expressing our sense of very deep disappointment at the trade's reluctance to support our campaign for economy in the use of raw materials. We draw our raw materials from a very wide field and are very closely in touch with the supply position in the textile industry. We find that very few people indeed in this country have yet allowed themselves to become aware of what total war means in the economic field. It is only because we have devoted an enormous amount of energy and have taken most extravagant risks that we are today in the fortunate position of having substantial stocks. But we also know that on the present showing our supplies of raw materials are probably being cut off entirely already. We do not intend to let ourselves reach the stage which some other industries have already reached of facing a complete stoppage. It has been well impressed upon us that supplies of cordage of various kinds rank very high indeed in the list of absolute essentials to the commercial and agricultural life of this country. For this reason we are well prepared to take such steps as appear to us to be in the best interest of the consumer and to risk the displeasure of the distributive trade believing that in the end the merchant will commend our action.

Meanwhile, Eric's salvage of his fire-damaged sisal was going well. Only 600 tons, it now appeared, had been damaged. More men were taken on to keep the drying machine going around the clock. In a good week, they could treat up to 100 tons. Eric spent a lot of his time in the drying shed and took his turn at the dryer at the weekend. He often spent the night at the factory and, even when he did not, he returned after supper after he had listened to the BBC news. Although the bad weather that spring hampered progress, the severe frosts extended the life of the untreated fibre by limiting bacterial damage. The salvage work continued until the middle of May. Eric laid down a narrow-gauge railway track to carry the damaged bales to the drying shed but soon discovered that a donkey and cart were better. Trial and error also showed that the best tools for removing the burnt fibre from the outside of the damaged bales were two First World War Gurkha knives that he had picked up in an antique shop for next to nothing.

In June, Eric wrote a detailed report on the salvage operation in which he highlighted the lessons that had been learnt and paid tribute to the efforts of Horace Davies and Alec Nisbet. He was happy to send a copy to anyone who was interested. In October, two days after the drying machine was finally turned off, having given work to an extra twenty men for eight months, he spoke about the whole operation in a talk to the Dublin Rotary Club. As the fire had penetrated only the outer 3 inches of the closely packed bales, it had been possible to salvage almost half of his damaged stock, some 270 tons, and to spin it into binder twine. Another 150 tons had been baled and sent to the paper mills for making paper: given the shortage of newsprint, Eric had started to experiment with turning his waste products into pulp before the fire. Most of the remaining 180 tons were sold as material for gas filters or dyed and curled as padding for upholstery. Even the poorest fibre was mixed with peat and coal dust to make briquettes to eke out fuel supplies. Eric's concerns about the quality of the salvaged fibre meant that he did not at first allow it to be used to make the company's branded twines. It was sold instead as Standard Binder Twine. However, Alec Nisbet's tests in the laboratory showed that it was actually of higher quality. Soaking it had softened it in the same way as the retting of flax.

Eric was happy to admit that the operation had not been particularly profitable. However, he said that it had provided a certain glamour and excitement in bleak times and claimed that 'the real profit has been in the valuable experience gained, in the enthusiasm and initiative which the whole adventure evoked, and in the stimulus which it gave to every man in the place'. They had tried a number of experiments, most of which had failed. However, Irish Ropes was now recognised as an expert in fibre reclamation. Perhaps at the instigation of John Forshaw, who was now working for London County Council, Eric had already inspected some small lots of Blitz-damaged sisal on his trip to London in March. Now a visit to Newbridge in July by a four-man delegation from the British Ministry of Supply resulted in Irish Ropes's being asked to reclaim 165 tons of damaged sisal from bombed-out warehouses in Docklands. Hemp control agreed to release the fuel oil that was needed to process it and, in return, Irish Ropes was allowed to keep a quarter of all the fibre that it recovered. Unfortunately, it could salvage only 34 tons and so kept only 8 tons for itself. However, it showed that, in spite of the embargo, there was some scope for co-operation between the two countries.

Meanwhile, the military outlook had only got worse for Britain in the spring of 1941. Germany occupied Yugoslavia and mainland Greece in April and Crete at the end of May, while Rommel arrived in North Africa with the *Afrika Korps* in February and now threatened Egypt and the Suez Canal. Germany and its allies were now in control of nearly all of mainland Europe and the Mediterranean. As well as the foot and mouth outbreak, Ireland itself had to cope, at the end of May, with the worst bombing of Dublin of the war. Twenty-eight people were killed, forty-five wounded, and 400 left without homes. It coincided within an escalation in the Blitz across the British Isles. Liverpool, after four months of relatively low casualties, saw almost 1,750 killed and 1,150 seriously injured in a month. Belfast was bombed in the middle of April and again at the beginning of May. The death toll on the first night was almost 1,000, making it probably the heaviest wartime loss of life on a single night in any British city apart from London. The Luftwaffe may well have mistaken Dublin for Belfast. However, some thought that the bombing was deliberate retaliation for de Valera's earlier magnanimity when he had sent every available Irish fire engine north to help when Belfast was bombed. It would be 1958 before West Germany finally accepted responsibility and compensated the country for the damage to its capital.

The raids turned out to be the Luftwaffe's parting shots. On 22 June, Hitler surprised the world by invading Russia, with whom he had signed a non-aggression pact in 1939. It put paid to any immediate threat of a German invasion of Britain or Ireland. From now on, Britain's attention would be directed to theatres of war elsewhere. At the end of the war in Europe, Joseph Walshe at the Department of External Affairs wrote that there had been eleven crises for Irish neutrality during the Emergency. All but two of them, he claimed, had occurred before the invasion of Russia.[19] For the rest of the war, Ireland would be an increasingly isolated backwater. Life got much worse as the full effects of the British embargo were felt.

As well as rationing his customers, Eric did everything else that he could to keep the factory going and ensure that farmers did not run out of twine to gather the harvest. Throughout his life, he was determined to be the master of his own destiny and was usually ahead of the game, doing things for himself that others were only later encouraged or compelled to do. Before the war, he had cut up the empty barrels of grease used at the factory and sold them to local farmers as feeding troughs. As well as starting to experiment with turning waste fibre into paper pulp, he and Alec Nisbet had gone up to Dublin in May 1940 to meet Professor Dillon from University College Galway, who had spent six years researching the potential industrial, commercial, and agricultural uses of seaweed. With Irish Ropes's supplies from Holland now cut off, they wanted to find out whether seaweed could be used as a substitute for the sizing agents that were used in the manufacture of rope to soften the fibres and prevent them breaking during the spinning process. In response to de Valera's call for increased turf production, Eric also started his own peat-cutting project in the spring after renting a large stretch of local bog from the Newbridge Coal Fund Committee.[20] He would use it not only as a substitute for heating oil at the factory but also to help the townspeople over the winter. Digging it would provide full-time employment for twenty men at a time when the shortage of raw materials for the manufacture of anything except agricultural twine meant that he was planning to close the factory for a week at Easter and for two weeks in August rather than the usual one. He was confident that Horace Davies, with his previous experience in the Cornish tin-mining industry, would make a success of the project by mechanising every available process.

Cutting began in May. Eric bought a pump to keep the workings clear of water and a gas-powered truck to transport the peat from the bog. By October, when cutting ceased for the season, more than 500 tons had been cut, dried, and stored at the factory and more had still to be brought in. In the new year, Eric would congratulate himself that the 'people in the town are very glad to have our turf now that the weather is so cold: we are glad we kept it all until now'. After some unsuccessful trials, the peat was used to fire the boiler at the factory for the first time in May 1942. By then, enough had been cut to supply a paper mill in Dublin and a weaving factory in Naas as well as to sell 250 tons to the army at the Curragh Camp.

As usual, Eric was keen to exploit its full potential. In July 1941, he and Horace Davies visited Ardgillan Castle north of Dublin to look at the kiln that the castle's owner had recently installed there to make charcoal from timber. They wanted to see whether peat could be used in the same way. When they found that it could, they had their cars converted to run on the charcoal produced from their turf and from the trees that Eric had cut down at Morristown. Contraptions had to be fitted to the car boots to produce gas from the burning charcoal. Peter remembers them sending out streams of sparks that flew along in the wind whenever the cars were driven. Eric reckoned that he needed 30 pounds of charcoal for a return trip to Dublin in his Austin. Horace found that his smaller car had a range of only 20 miles and that he was restricted to 20 mph.

By the spring of 1941, Irish Ropes was turning out 40 tons, or 10,000 miles, of twine a week. It was still not enough to meet the expected demand for the harvest that year. In his report to the directors in March, Eric had claimed that his plans had been 'knocked silly' more by 'the extraordinary increase in the amount of binder twine required' than by his salvage operation. At its peak that year, Irish Ropes would be producing more than 15,000 miles of twine a week.

During the First World War, British and Irish farmers had been required to turn over 10 per cent of their land to tillage—to the growing of wheat, cereals, and other crops, including potatoes, fruit and vegetables, and flax, at the expense of dairy farming and animal husbandry. At the start of the Emergency, Irish farmers who had more than 10 acres had again been required to turn over a proportion of their land to tillage as part of the government's drive towards self-sufficiency. Failure to comply might result in a fine of up to £100, six months' imprisonment, or even the confiscation of their land. The proportion, which was set originally at 12.5 per cent, was increased to 16.7 per cent in October 1940 and 20 per cent in January 1941 before eventually being raised to 25 per cent in 1942 and 37.5 per cent in 1944, at which time its application was extended to all farms of more than 5 acres. It was a daunting prospect for farmers and one that was made all the more difficult by the shortage of fertilisers and farm machinery as a result of the British embargo. The doubling and eventual tripling of the acreage under tillage also meant that much more binder and baler twine would be needed.

In 1941, Irish Ropes increased its production from 700 to 1,700 tons. It meant that by the end of the harvest, it had almost no sisal left. Eric was expecting the delivery of another 1,000 bales shortly, but after that had no idea when and where he might get hold of anymore. That autumn, he began to experiment with making thinner twine. He told his father that, when he increased its length by 40 per cent, from 650 to 900 feet per pound of fibre, the results were 'very satisfactory when in the hands of capable farmers but not so good in other cases'. He finally settled on a maximum of 750 feet per pound.

Irish Ropes's new factory gates, February 1942.

Eric had already warned the directors back in March that 'if the 1941 harvest season looks secure the prospect for 1942 is black'. If anything, it only got blacker as the year progressed. He would find 1942 to be the most challenging year of the war. His erection of new factory gates at the start of the year was a very visible statement of his determination to survive. The company's name was now written in a large arc over the gates above a wrought-iron silhouette of Rusty, the dog that H. and J. Jones and Irish Ropes had always used as the trademark for their Red Setter twine. 'If we do come to an end,' Eric told the children in February in one of this last surviving letters, 'we shall at least go down with our colours flying.'

9

Facing Disaster, 1942

*Engineer became husbandman again when Irish Ropes turned to fibre production
and operated one of the largest and most successful flax-growing schemes in the
British Isles.*[1]

Everything changed on the morning of 7 December 1941 with the Japanese attack
on Pearl Harbor. The US declared war on Japan the following day. With Russia and
the US now fighting as allies of the UK, the future looked brighter. However, after
Japan moved on to occupy the Philippines and Indonesia, the Allies lost access
to 90 per cent of the world's supply of rubber and all of its supplies of manila.
The hemp controller, Alfred Landauer, immediately placed further restrictions on
the fibre's use. With the exception only of those ropes that had to be made from
manila, even the highest grades of rope would now have to be made from at least
25 per cent sisal while the lower grades would have to be made from between 50
and 100 per cent. The loss of all fibres from the Far East and the sudden increase
in demand for rope from the US Navy meant that sisal moved overnight from
being a distressed colonial commodity subject to restrictions on production to
being a priority commodity in short supply. As the Colonial Office's memorandum
on sisal production in September 1943 would make clear, 'any question of an
upper limit on the quantity to be purchased was naturally abandoned, and the
industry was called on to produce all it could'.[2]

Six days after Pearl Harbor, Winston Churchill left for Washington on board
HMS *Duke of York* to meet his new ally, President Roosevelt, and decide with
him how best now to prosecute the war. Their so-called Arcadia conference
led to the creation of a Combined Chiefs of Staff to oversee the Allies' military
strategy as well as three other combined boards to oversee munitions, shipping,
and raw materials respectively. Although Britain and America had already been

co-operating over supplies, the new Combined Raw Materials Board would give this work a formal structure and purpose. Its first task was to review those raw materials that were likely to be in short supply as a result of Japan's entry into the war.[3]

The two-man board comprised William L. Batt from the US Office of Production Management and Sir Clive Baillieu, the director-general of the British Purchasing Commission in Washington. Although they would not meet formally until February, their secretariats were hard at work from the turn of the year. In a note to Baillieu in the middle of January, his deputy, George Archer, who also acted as secretary to the British delegation, highlighted rubber, tin, manila, and sisal as the four commodities that required the Board's immediate attention. By then, Batt had already written to President Roosevelt to stress the importance of tin and sisal. Although the Board's report on manila and sisal was the second that it issued it was probably the first to be completed in draft form, its British and American staff having slaved together all one Sunday in a hotel room to produce it. The board then spent most of its third meeting on 3 March discussing hard fibres. Baillieu and Batt were keen to remove all restrictions on production, to push both British and Portuguese East Africa to produce as much sisal as they could, and to reach an agreement with the neutral Portuguese government to buy all of its fibre. They also used the meeting to make their first definitive allocation of raw materials. The US would release 6,700 tons of manila to Britain, and Britain, which would continue to be the sole purchaser of sisal from British East Africa, would retain 68,000 tons for itself but release 105,000 tons to the US and Canada. This overall production target of 173,000 tons of sisal represented an increase of almost 75 per cent over the 100,000 tons to which growers had previously been restricted. The fact that it was achieved in 1942, and at such short notice, was due in large part to the more judicious cutting of leaves in the previous two years. However, it was unsustainable. Production fell back to its pre-war level of 125,000 tons in 1943 and then recovered to remain stable at around 140,000 tons for the next three years. Meanwhile, the growers in East Africa had to adapt quickly to this radical change in outlook. Large native workforces, many of which had been let go when production was cut back, had to be recruited again; the estates' former professional and technical staff had to be tracked down and, in many cases, released from military service; and urgent repairs had to be carried out on machinery, and spare parts or replacements found—not least for the decorticators and the narrow gauge railways that were used to carry the leaves from the fields to the factory. As much of this equipment had originally been manufactured in Germany, it would prove to be an almost impossible task.

The growers' efforts were also handicapped by the death of Sir William Lead early in the new year. He had been unwell for some time and died in a Nairobi nursing home shortly after an exploratory operation had shown that he had untreatable cancer. He had already been taken ill on his trip to London in 1940, and it seems likely that one of the reasons why Eldred Hitchcock was sent out to East Africa in the summer of 1941 was to stand in for him as Sisal Controller.

The chairman of Sisal Estates, Colonel Charles Ponsonby, MP, hinted as much at the company's annual general meeting in London the following year when he congratulated Hitchcock on the valuable work that he had been doing there with both government and growers in all matters connected with the industry.[4] Although Hitchcock also oversaw the day-to-day management of Bird and Co.'s estates in Tanganyika and was still being paid as chairman of the Sisal Growers Association in London until well into 1942, his expenses in East Africa were split 2:1 between Sisal Control and the Tanganyika Sisal Growers' Association. However, when it was suggested that the Colonial Office should pick up the cost of his airfare, it declined to do so.

At the end of December, and three weeks after Pearl Harbor, Hitchcock advised the Colonial Office by telegram that, in light of the Combined Raw Materials Board's preliminary decision to go for all-out production of sisal, he was planning to stay on in East Africa for as long as he was needed. However, any hopes that he may have had of being appointed Sisal Controller after Lead's death were quickly dashed. Tanganyika's governor, Sir Wilfred Jackson, thought that Lead's greatest achievement had been his ability to hold together the many divergent elements and interests within the sisal industry. He had trusted him totally and had largely left him to get on with things on his own. Hitchcock, on the other hand, he considered a divisive rather than a unifying force. In the absence of any other outstanding candidate, he asked the territory's director of agriculture, R. W. R. Miller, to take over as sisal controller while carrying on with his existing duties.

In February, Hitchcock informed the Colonial Office that, as he had served his purpose, he was no longer required in East Africa. With his eye always on the main chance, he suggested that he should be sent to Washington where his skills might be better employed to free up log jams and cajole the Americans into providing the equipment and spares that the sisal estates so desperately needed. However, it would appear that, whatever Hitchcock's undoubted abilities as a negotiator, many of those with whom he worked thought him most useful when he was furthest away and least able to cause any disruption. He was a small man and, as many would find out for themselves, could often be pugnacious, abrasive, or just downright rude. Jackson and his government agreed that he was no longer needed in Africa; the Colonial Office and Ministry of Supply wanted to keep him away from Washington but reckoned that he would be less trouble there than back in London; and the Sisal Growers Association, which was proving itself quite capable of carrying on without him under the acting chairmanship of Nicholas Bosanquet, the chairman of Consolidated Sisal Estates of East Africa, thought that he could contribute most by staying where he was in to help maintain fibre quality and press for maximum production. He ended up staying in East Africa.

Late on the evening of Pearl Harbor, Churchill had sent de Valera a brief but cryptic personal telegram: 'Now is your chance. Now or never. "A nation once again." Am ready to meet you at any time'.[5] Whatever its precise meaning and the circumstances in which it was sent, it had no effect. Neutrality was now an article of faith for both the Irish government and the great majority of its citizens.

Within a week, de Valera had restated his position in a speech at a parade of the Irish Defence Force in Cork:

> People who do not understand our conditions have asked how America's entry into the war will affect our neutrality here. The policy of the state remains unchanged. We can only be friendly neutral. From the moment this war began, there was, for this state, only one policy possible, neutrality. Our circumstances, our history, the incompleteness of our national freedom through the partition of our country, made any other policy impossible. Any other policy would have divided our people and for a divided nation to fling itself into this war would have been to commit suicide.[6]

Brigadier Wodehouse, who had taken over from Pryce as head of Military Mission 18 three days earlier, was present at the parade with his second-in-command, Major Borrowdaile. In January, they appeared in a group photograph on the front page of the *Irish Times* when Maffey introduced them and the new British naval and air *attachés* to the minister for defence, Oscar Traynor, and General McKenna and Colonel Archer.[7] It was a far cry from the summer of 1940 when Pryce and Lywood had been required to work under cover. Although, like all who served in the British armed forces, they were not allowed to wear their uniforms in Ireland, their roles were now clear and they could use their military ranks. It was in de Valera's interest now to be seen to support the Allied cause and to promote Ireland as a friendly neutral.

Meanwhile, the British embargo on supplies to Ireland would only bite harder in 1942. When he reported back to the Dominions Office in February, Maffey likened de Valera's attitude, although no longer hostile or detrimental, to that of a hedgehog. He believed that Ireland would eventually be reduced to a state of friendless beggardom. With the country now suffering acutely from a shortage of supplies, he suggested that the embargo should only be relaxed in return for specific services where Britain might benefit from some sort of *quid pro quo* arrangement. It would be the basis of British trade policy towards Ireland for the rest of the war.

Detailed statistics on Ireland's imports would be reported to the British War Cabinet's Committee on Economic Policy towards Eire from 1942 onwards.[8] When the final figures for 1942 were presented to the committee in March 1943, they provided incontrovertible proof of the embargo's success. Imports of nearly every commodity were substantially down on their pre-war levels. If anything, the comparative figures, which were based on average imports for the three years to 1937, understated the scale of the decline as they covered the final years of the Anglo-Irish trade war and so did not reflect the resumption of normal trade in 1938 and 1939.

Ireland's imports of wheat, all of which was now sourced from the Americas, were down 60 per cent, having fallen from 374,000 tons to 151,000 tons. In addition, a poor domestic cereal harvest in 1941 led to a shortfall of 80,000 tons.

'000 tons	1935–7	1942	1943		1935–7	1942	1943
	average				average		
Food				**Fuel**			
Wheat	373.7	150.9	62.3	Coal and coke	2,476.3	1,070.4	1,044.3
Flour and meal	10.8	0.2	0.4	Gasoline for cars	121.3	37.8	33.2
Fruit & nuts	47.8	2.3	3.0	Kerosene	59.3	16.8	29.9
Sugar	27.6	1.4	18.0	Gas oil and fuel oil	30.6	14.9	24.3
Tea	10.4	3.8	2.4	Pitch and coal tar	12.1	54.1	49.1
Coffee	0.3	5.2	1.1	Lubricating oil	9.9	4.4	3.9
Farming				**Other**			
Oilseed cake and meal	29.4	0.6	0.6	Cement	352.6	0.7	0.7
Fertilisers (potassic)	27.9	0.9	n/a	Iron and steel	123.7	15.4	12.9
Fertilisers (phosphates)	25.6	0.1	12.6	Paper and cardboard	65.7	14.3	13.8
Seeds for sowing	17.0	3.1	2.5	Hemp & hemp yarn	1.5	0.3	1.0

Selected Irish imports (in '000 tons) in 1942 and 1943 with pre-war comparative for 1935–7 (compiled from figures in TNA, CAB 72/25).

In March, Lemass had to tell the Dáil that without rationing wheat stocks would run out by the end of May.[9] Malting was suspended and exports of beer and stout restricted so that the brewers' reserve stocks of barley could be diverted to making bread. Tea imports fell to almost a third of their pre-war level in 1942 but were offset, at least temporarily, by an increase in coffee. Imports of coal and coke not only fell by almost 60 per cent, from 2.5 to 1.1 million tons, but were now of much poorer quality, comprising mostly finely sized slurry and duff. Although more pitch and coal tar was imported to make briquettes as a substitute for coal, the impact was too small to be significant. By June, coal was no longer available for domestic use. To preserve fuel supplies, the government banned the sale of domestic cookers and heaters and restricted the domestic use of town gas, which was made from imported coal. The regulations were enforced by the Emergency's new bogeyman, the Glimmer Man. Supplies of petrol for cars fell by almost 70 per cent. By summer, private cars were a rare sight on the roads. 'Everybody has been refused permission to drive a car – so far as I can gather,' Eric told the children in May, 'they are determined to bring private motoring to a complete stop even before considering who really needs a car for nationally important business.' Irish farmers were particularly badly hit after imports of seeds, fertilisers, and oilseed cake and meal for animal fodder virtually dried up. Factories closed for want of raw materials and fuel and led to growing unemployment. By the end of the war, industrial production and employment had fallen by a quarter. However, there were some snippets of good news hidden among the figures. As well as growing more of its own cereals, Ireland was also producing more sugar beet and making all of its own cement.

The Emergency affected different sections of the population in different ways. Those in rural areas could grow and eat their own produce but, without access to petrol or public transport, were cut off from the outside world and unable to travel or sell their surpluses. The urban poor were deprived of their basic staples of life—not only essential foodstuffs like tea, sugar, jam and white bread (although there was never a shortage of butter) but also, because they often lacked any access to electricity, fuel and candles for heating, lighting, and cooking. Nevertheless, except for the poorest, life in Ireland during the Emergency was probably never as harsh as it was in Britain. The blackouts were lifted early on, and Allied troops stationed in Northern Ireland (including American servicemen from early in 1942) could make regular weekend jaunts to Dublin to enjoy a gaiety that they could no longer find elsewhere.[10] Welcoming the government's introduction of stricter rationing the editor of the *Irish Times*, Robert Smylie, summed up the situation in March in an article under the pen name, Nichevo:

> Neutral Ireland has suffered little.... When the citizen of Eire sits down to his breakfast, and enjoys a couple of eggs and three or four rashers of bacon, let him think of the Englishman, or inhabitant of Northern Ireland, who gets a single egg in a fortnight. When he is spreading good Irish butter on his bread—even if it be wholemeal bread—let him think of his neighbour whose weekly butter ration is measured in ounces. When he is consuming a succulent steak, let him think of those unfortunate people on the continent of Europe for whom meat of any kind is as rare as caviare. In a world of privation, Ireland is living in comparative luxury. The trouble is that we do not realise how well off we are.[11]

The relative price and availability of goods north and south of the border in Ireland led to a lucrative black market and an increase in cross-border smuggling. Meat, butter, bacon, and eggs found their way north, while candles, soap, white bread, sugar, tea, and flour came south. Eric's daughter, Ann, remembers that she was very popular at school in England when she returned at the start of each term with a 4-pound block of bright yellow Irish country butter. It was more than six months' rations for a British adult. A family friend in Ireland also gave her 144 penny bars of Cadbury's chocolate every Christmas as a way of thanking her father for his having paid for her hospital treatment. Ann found that the only way to stop them being confiscated by customs when she arrived back to Liverpool was to throw a tantrum.

Meanwhile, Morristown's kitchen garden, and the skills that Dorothy had learnt at Liverpool's college of domestic science during the First World War, were proving invaluable. By 1939, as she recorded meticulously in her house-keeping diary, she was making more than 200 pounds of jams and conserves a year from the fruit and vegetables grown in the garden. As well as strawberry, raspberry, and damson jams, and redcurrant, blackcurrant, and apple jellies, she bottled cucumbers, plums, dried apples, and tomatoes. Between 1940 and 1942, she increased her output to almost 250 pounds a year. We must presume that she gave a lot of it away as Ann claims that her father only ever ate meat and potatoes. She also preserved more than 600 eggs each year by dipping them in a mixture of warm water and isinglass, a collagen made from the dried swim bladder of fish,

Dorothy working in the kitchen garden at Morristown.

and then leaving them to dry. Although they then lasted for between six months and a year, they were better for baking than breakfast.

Eric's parents, who tried to visit Morristown at least once a year during the war, remembered their stays most fondly for the food. In May 1940, Harry wrote in the guest book 'a perfect seven days—gained six pounds'. Alice wrote the following year that she had relished 'a week of peace and plenty—gained four pounds' and in 1944 that she and her husband had 'enjoyed our meals like hungry children'. Eric's parents were small and wiry, and their preoccupation with their weight and health was already a standing joke within the family. Now it became a real worry. Both were still doing more than could reasonably be expected of them. Harry, who would turn seventy at the end of 1942, was still running H. and J. Jones in Liverpool. Alice was a year older. As well as looking after evacuees and members of the family at the Ruff and generally acting *in loco parentis* for their grandchildren, they were both still heavily involved in local good works. When both fell ill at the end of 1941, Eric tried without success to persuade them to move to Ireland. He was also unable to accompany his mother when she had to go to London to see a specialist. At the bottom of one of his letters in October, he wrote in frustration that 'we do wish we could be with you to help just now and do cuss the travel restrictions'.

In spite of the decision of the Combined Raw Materials Board to go for all-out production of sisal, Eric's chances of securing any for Irish Ropes were slim. In March 1942, shortly after the fall of Singapore, he wrote another detailed memorandum to the directors on the company's current situation and future prospects. As no others survive, it may well have been the first that he wrote since his trip to Britain the previous spring. In any case, it is lucky to have survived. The copy that he sent his father, who was the only director not living in Ireland, was intercepted by the British censor and copied before being released for delivery. It was sent on to the Raw Materials Department at the Ministry of Supply and then forwarded to the flax controller.[12]

The memorandum painted a bleak picture. Eric was convinced that manila would not be available again for several years; although his quota of cotton yarn had already been cut by 85 per cent, he thought that he was now unlikely to get even that due to the prioritisation of British demand; and, because of its shortage and the difficulty of finding cargo space, he reckoned that he would be unable to persuade the British authorities to release any more sisal. The only saving grace was that he had access to supplies of jute from Goodbody's in Clara. He was hoping that he might be able to use it as a substitute.

At the end of 1941, the Irish government lost the opportunity to secure 1,000 tons of twine from the International Harvester Company in America when no ships could be found to transport it across the Atlantic. However, the outlook for the harvest in 1942 was not as bad as it might have appeared at first sight. Although Irish Ropes had almost no raw fibre left, it still had more than 500 tons of manufactured twine in stock; the Irish Agricultural Wholesale Society had also managed to import 500 tons before the end of the year; and it was thought that wholesalers were holding on to another 300 to 500 tons but were waiting to see how the market moved before they released it. In all, it was not that far short of the 1,700 tons that had been needed in 1941. However, farmers had yet to see any of it and were reluctant to sow their crops in 1942 without first knowing that they would have the twine to harvest it. With spring wheat being sown between February and April and harvested in August and early September, the time for making some final decisions was fast approaching.

By then, the British government had already turned down a request from the Irish government to release more sisal. However, Eric still had 250 tons awaiting onward shipment from Lisbon—and the chance to secure another 250 tons on which he had yet to make a final commitment—and another 250 tons on order from Portuguese West Africa, which was to be shipped to New York, where it would have to be unloaded and sent by train to Canada before it could be shipped across the Atlantic by Irish Shipping Lines. If all three cargoes reached Newbridge safely, Irish Ropes would have enough sisal to get through the year. However, at £90 a ton, it was significantly more expensive than the £35 that Eric had been paying for sisal trans-shipped from Britain. He would have to decide how best to factor this into his pricing and whether it was really worth chasing these alternative sources of supply.

In any event, it is unlikely that he ever got any of it. Although the figures in the various British and Irish sources are inconsistent, their overall message is clear. A report by the British Ministry of Economic Warfare in August 1942 listing all the navicerts that had been granted or requested for Irish imports since the start of the year revealed that, although authorisation had been given for the shipping of 250 tons of sisal via the US, the cargo had been requisitioned by the American government upon its arrival. A second navicert, for the shipment of 500 tons of sisal from Portuguese West Africa, had yet to be approved. It was one of a number of cargoes—for tallow, palm oil and kernels, and oleo oil (used to manufacture margarine), as well as for sisal—that had been held up in Lisbon.[13] It was clear evidence of Britain's new hard-line approach. A month earlier, the Raw Materials Mission in Washington had been informed by the Ministry of Supply that Ireland already had enough sisal to last it the year and that there was therefore no reason to release any more. The Ministry of Economic Warfare also thought itself quite capable of deciding Ireland's needs without first discussing them with the Irish government. It could always change its mind later, it said, if the Irish complained or were prepared to offer some *quid pro quo*. Meanwhile, the Irish Department of Supplies was in no doubt that its attempts to source sisal and binder twine from other countries in 1942 were being frustrated by the British refusal to grant navicerts. They were now being used as a weapon not only to prevent supplies getting into enemy hands but also to control all commodities in short supply. A departmental memorandum claimed that, on one occasion, 1,000 tons of sisal had been seized in Canada while *en route* to Ireland from South America.[14]

According to the British figures, Ireland imported only 273 tons of hemp and hemp yarn (including sisal) in 1942, 256 tons of which came from Portugal and only 17 from the UK. However, when even this was added to the stocks already on hand, it was just possible that Ireland would have enough twine for that year's harvest. It would mean that disaster could be postponed for another year. After that, there would be no more.

In February 1942, shortly before Eric wrote his memorandum, the Irish Department of Supplies issued the first, and most important, of its only two emergency orders relating to binder twine. While other industries were subjected to a multitude of such orders under the Emergency Powers Act 1939, it was not required in the case of binder twine because Irish Ropes now manufactured of 90 per cent of the country's cordage and there were only seven major distributors in the country. It meant that both manufacture and distribution could be controlled on a voluntary rather than a statutory basis. The departments of agriculture and industry and commerce routinely met with the manufacturers at the start of each year to decide how much twine would be needed after factoring in the expected increase in the acreage under tillage. This first emergency order now limited the use of binder twine to mechanical binders (rather than for general farm use) and restricted its sale to a four-month window from July to October. The second order, which was issued six months later, gave the government powers of inspection to check that the regulations were being followed.

When Eric visited the department of agriculture that February, its director, Dr Adams, had again raised the question of whether home-grown flax might be used as a substitute for making binder twine. At first, Eric rejected the suggestion out of hand: he likened it to using silk to make coal sacks. Furthermore, with green (or unretted) flax costing up to £120 a ton, and retted flax even more, it was not only much more expensive than sisal sourced from Lisbon or America but also made poorer twine. Eric had always rejected the arguments made before the war, not least by Ireland's agricultural lobby, that industrialisation had only replaced the country's reliance on imported finished goods with one on imported raw materials and that the Irish cordage industry could only ever be considered truly self-sufficient once it started using home-grown fibres. For him, the economics of production and the cheapness of African labour meant that flax would never be able to compete with sisal. In January 1940, he had told the children of an earlier visit to the department when he had said 'goodbye to the idea of flax production by us in Newbridge. The matter may crop up again but not until somebody else shows signs of carrying some of the burden'. He had been forced to revisit his decision later that year after the fire when he had sent Alec Nisbet to Queens University Belfast to find out whether flax might be used as a substitute for sisal. However, just two months later, when he addressed the Dublin Rotary Club, he was still maintaining that flax, 'which commands an immensely higher price than other fibres, has yet been a barely profitable proposition here save in wartime'. Other vegetable fibres like cotton, jute, sisal and hemp all thrived, he said, in sub-tropical climates where they were harvested by native labour 'happy to work for wages so much lower than ours by the simplicity of their needs'. Flax was simply too expensive for anything other than the high-value linen products made in Northern Ireland. Furthermore, every spare acre of agricultural land in Ireland was now being used for wheat and other cereals, and the boggy land around Newbridge was totally unsuitable for growing flax. Now he told the directors in his memorandum that, with every other source of fibre cut off, he had been forced to reconsider flax.

Flax production was still a largely manual, small-scale, and somewhat haphazard process. There were three main stages involved. The crop was usually harvested, or 'pulled', by hand so as to preserve the full length of the fibre from root to flower. It took one man a week to pull an acre, while a mechanical puller towed by a tractor could pull 5 acres in a single day. Once harvested, the stalks were then steeped in water for up to a fortnight to rot, or 'ret', the gum that held the inner fibre to the outer woody stem. This was usually done in dammed depressions or prepared pools on the farmer's land but could also be done by packing the stalks in crates and leaving them in rivers or flowing water, by immersing them in tanks of warm water, or by laying them out in the dew or rain. They were then retrieved and spread out in the open to dry. A farmer needed both luck and judgement to decide whether there were still enough sunny days left for them to dry after retting. The decline in flax-growing between the wars meant that it was becoming a lost skill.

The dry stalks were then sent away to mills for 'scutching', the process whereby the woody stems were broken into pieces and separated from the fibre, and 'hackling', where the fibres were straightened and any broken ones removed.

Pulling and binding flax in Co. Antrim, by W. A. Green. (© *National Museums Northern Ireland, Ulster Folk and Transport Museum, HOYFM.WAG.1011*)

Steeping the flax in Toome, Co. Antrim, by W. A. Green. (© *National Museums Northern Ireland, Ulster Folk and Transport Museum, HOYFM.WAG.1013*)

Scutching flax, by Robert John Welch (1859–1936). (© *National Museums Northern Ireland, Ulster Museum, BELUM.Y.W.99.00.9*)

Although scutching was still usually done by hand, it could now also be done using turbine scutchers.

Before the war, William Gibson had directed much of the work of the Linen Institute Research Association at Lisburn to improving seed yields and investigating better methods of production. He was particularly keen to find out whether costs could be reduced significantly by doing away with retting and mechanising the scutching process. By the time that he left LIRA in 1939, he was confident that there was a bright future for green, or unretted, flax. He claimed to have shown in a full-scale demonstration that unretted fibre could be produced by a simple mechanical process that required no specialist knowledge or expertise on the farmer's part and that it could then be used for everything except those products requiring the finest fabric. He was being wildly optimistic. Time would show that green flax was still very much at an experimental stage at the outbreak of war. However, doing away with retting did have other advantages. It was no longer necessary to find a way of getting rid of the retting water, which was many times more toxic than ordinary sewage, or to hold back part of the crop to provide seeds for the following year. All the seeds could now be removed and retained prior to scutching.

Both Gibson and Wigglesworth had written to *The Times* in the spring of 1939 calling for an immediate increase in domestic flax cultivation. This had almost doubled in Northern Ireland during the First World War to 100,000 acres before collapsing to a low of 6,000 acres by 1932. With war certain to create another massive increase in demand, it was short-sighted, they said, to waste a year by delaying sowing to 1940. John Milne, who had been in charge of flax exports for the Ministry of Blockade during the previous war, felt the same. Describing flax as a fundamental and vital wartime commodity, he called for immediate steps to be taken to increase cultivation both at home and within the empire.[15] By then, Russia, the world's largest grower, was no longer exporting any of its fibre, while supplies from Belgium and the Baltic States, where Britain sourced 80 per cent of its fibre, would be cut off in the spring of 1940. With enormous quantities now required for a wide range of military and civilian uses, the British government had already placed orders for almost 3 million yards of linen and canvas in the second half of 1938. John Ferrier, who took over as flax controller for the latter stages of the war, would later give details of its use in a speech in Belfast in 1945. His list included 54 million square yards of aircraft fabric, 60 million yards of heavy duty and other canvas (which the Royal Navy used for tarpaulins and hatch covers), 75 million yards of linen covers for general purposes, 26,000 miles of hosepipe, and 20,000 miles of parachute harness.[16]

If the decline in flax cultivation between the wars meant that traditional skills might already have been lost then Gibson's research into green flax offered a potential solution. In May 1939, a report to the cabinet by the minister for co-ordination of defence made much of its potential, claiming that the Admiralty had already conducted experiments on its suitability and had concluded that its large-scale development would be crucial to securing sufficient wartime supplies. However, when war broke out four months later, there was still almost no flax being grown in Britain except at the small research station that Gibson had set up on the royal estate at Sandringham in 1931. The lack of local retting skills and the potential savings from mechanisation meant that all the flax grown in Britain during the war would be unretted. The early results were disappointing.

When the director of the Imperial Institute, Sir Harry Lindsay, was appointed flax controller at the outbreak of war, he immediately restricted its use to essential government contracts and, until 1942, to the manufacture of luxury linen goods for export so as to secure valuable foreign currency. The acreage under flax in Northern Ireland doubled each year in the first two years of the war—from 21,000 acres in 1939 to 46,500 acres in 1940 and on to 90,000 acres in 1941. Although it then fell back to 75,000 acres in 1942, mainly because of the previous year's bad harvest, it recovered to more than 100,000 acres by the end of the war. By then, it was accounting for an eighth of all the land under tillage in the province. It was still not enough to meet demand. As Milne had suggested, the empire's dominions and colonies were also encouraged to grow more. Imports from Canada increased from 36 tons in 1938 to 1,033 tons in 1941. By 1941, Australia, New Zealand, and Kenya, which had all started growing it from scratch, were supplying 679 tons between them. However, southern Ireland was a much more attractive prospect due to its proximity and history of flax growing, as well as the fact that its main flax-growing areas—in Donegal, Cavan, Monaghan, and Meath—were all close to the border and so could take advantage of the expertise and processing facilities to be found in Northern Ireland. In 1938, Britain had imported 712 tons of flax from southern Ireland. It accounted for 95 per cent of what it sourced from within the empire. In spite of the difficulties between the two countries, it was essential now for Britain to retain and increase its supplies of Irish flax.

At the outbreak of war, the British Ministry of Supply had made immediate arrangements with the Irish Department of Agriculture to buy all of Ireland's flax harvest in 1939 at the same price that it was paying farmers in Northern Ireland. By then, as in the north, the Irish flax industry had been in decline for a number of years. Although the Dáil passed a Flax Act in 1936, which sought to encourage its cultivation and regulate its production and sale, it had little effect. The country's acreage under flax fell from 5,118 acres in 1936 to 4,244 acres in 1937 and then to 3,914 acres in 1938. However, the price of £110 a ton for scutched flax that was now being offered by the British ministry was much more attractive to Irish farmers than the £80 that the Department of Agriculture had set for 1939 and 1940 under the terms of the Flax Act. By January 1940, the British Ministry had set the price for the following year's harvest. At £160 a ton, it was 45 per cent more than the previous year and twice what Irish farmers had expecting only a few months earlier. Nor was this any private or confidential arrangement between the two governments. The Department of Agriculture placed an official notice in the Irish papers in February giving details of the prices and making it clear that the British Ministry of Supply had agreed to buy all of that year's crop.[17] Anticipating a surge of interest from farmers, the department had already arranged for the British ministry to provide adequate supplies of seed. As a result, Ireland's acreage under flax more than doubled to 10,000 acres in 1940 and then increased again to 15,500 acres in 1941.

Flax was now an attractive proposition for Irish farmers. In 1941, they exported 1,736 tons of fibre to Britain. The British government was keen to get more. That summer, as its trade embargo began to bite and the Irish Department of Agriculture was focused on containing the outbreak of foot and mouth disease, it approached the Irish government with a request to increase its area under flax to 25,000 acres. Although John Dulanty responded positively on behalf of the government, there were a number of preliminary issues that had to be resolved. As well as being provided with adequate supplies of seed and fertiliser, Irish farmers wanted the reassurance of a long-term deal and a return to the price parity that they had originally enjoyed with farmers north of the border. Ireland also lacked the retting and scutching facilities that were needed to cope with so large an increase in cultivation. Although there were now ninety-three scutch mills in the country, eighty of which were in Donegal and Monaghan, they had only five turbine scutchers between them. They needed another ten. The mill owners were prepared to fund the necessary investment but needed a long-term contract to justify the risk, as well as the British government's agreement to release the equipment that they required. It was unlikely to be a major obstacle as the British government had already established the principle of 'assured markets' whereby it was prepared to enter into longer term contracts that lasted until one year after the end of the war. The greater problem was the £20 price differential that had arisen in autumn 1940 when prices were increased in Northern Ireland to compensate farmers for a statutory increase in agricultural wages but were not automatically passed on to their colleagues south of the border. Believing that they had agreed a general principle of price parity rather than simply a fixed price, Irish farmers felt aggrieved at this apparent breach of good faith even though they themselves had not had to fund an equivalent wage increase. For the time being, the differential was only an encouragement to greater smuggling.

The final terms of the new arrangement were the subject of considerable discussion and disagreement between the various government departments in both London and Dublin. Too many parties now had an interest but were not directly involved in the negotiations. It would be early 1942 before the British Ministry of Supply was finally in a position to agree terms. The Irish Department of Agriculture also had to see off a challenge from the Department of Finance. In September, the minister for agriculture, James Ryan, wrote to complain to Sean O'Kelly, the Tánaiste and minister for finance, that the latter's officials seemed to be fundamentally opposed to the scheme on the grounds that it was against the national interest because flax was neither a food crop nor grown for domestic consumption and Britain had not agreed to release anything in exchange. O'Kelly's response was that, as Ireland was now exporting more than it imported, it had a growing trade imbalance and so was building up sterling assets that might be at risk at some point in the future. However, on this occasion, his view that financial considerations should take precedence over agricultural did not prevail.[18]

In February, the Irish Department of Agriculture was finally able to announce that, in addition to agreeing a retrospective supplement of £20 a ton for the 1941 crop to make good the price differential and making available 400 tons of seed at market rates, the British Ministry of Supply had agreed to buy all of the Irish flax crop for the rest of the war and for one year thereafter at an average price of £192 a ton for retted and scutched fibre. The price would not stay fixed for long. In November, it was increased retrospectively to £204 a ton and the price for 1943 set at £220, with a further bonus on offer for increasing the acreage under cultivation. With the price of flax now almost three times what it had been at the start of the war, there was a chance for Irish farmers to make substantial profits.

For Eric, the prices can only have confirmed what he already knew, that it would be senseless to buy flax to make binder twine. Even if he could get hold of any, when it was all being sold to the British government, it was many times more expensive than the sisal that he had been buying from Britain before the embargo. Instead, as he told the directors in the spring of 1942, he was now planning to grow and process his own. It was this proposed retention of some of the Irish flax crop that first attracted the attention of the British Ministry of Supplies. However,

John Ferrier at Flax Control reckoned that they already had enough problems with their own green flax without wanting Eric's as well.

Eric always recognised that flax, which he described as a 'king among fibres', was never going to solve his raw materials problem. As he would tell the minister for industry and commerce in 1944 in a return on the post-war planning of industry, 'it is anomalous that we, as the one firm in the country whose products are right at the bottom of the textile scale, should have turned in the emergency to the production and potential use of the fibre which belongs exclusively to the top'. Flax came up short on every criterion—availability, suitability, and price—and, in any case, any flax that he grew in 1942 would only make a difference in 1943. He later told John Ferrier that the only reason for his starting his flax scheme in 1942 was because the British Ministry of Supply had cut off all his supplies of sisal and the Ministry of Economic Warfare was refusing to issue navicerts for any fibre that he managed to source from elsewhere. In desperation, he had turned to the only available substitute that could be grown and harvested within a year. Even at the time, he had known that it was totally unsuitable for binder twine and no more than 'a forlorn resort in dire emergency'. He admitted that he had even considered buying industrial laundry equipment to dry the fibre: '... altogether a very far-fetched notion but it is the way one was thinking in 1942'.[19]

Nevertheless, Eric was as determined as ever to be the master of his destiny. New challenges always excited him, and once he had decided on something, he followed it through quickly and vigorously. What would set him apart from other Irish flax growers during the war was that he recruited, trained, and co-ordinated an army of new and inexperienced growers, built and financed his own scutching mill, produced green rather than retted flax, and made twine from it rather than sold it.

Within a fortnight of writing his memorandum, he was telling the children that 'we are seriously thinking of growing flax ourselves but this part of Kildare is not a good area as all one side of us is taken up by bog or by the Curragh.' By then, Mackies had already taken him to visit a scutch mill in Drogheda where he was able to buy a few tons of raw flax so that he could start making some experiments with Alec Nisbet and Horace Davies. They soon found out that the fineness of the fibre made it difficult to process on their machinery, which had been designed for coarser fibres, and that cutting the resulting twine was like 'trying to cut fine silk with a pair of blunt scissors'. A mechanic would have to be trained up and sent round the farms after the 1942 harvest to adjust all the older reapers and binders before flax twine could be used on them the following year. Worse still, because the flax was unretted, the gummy residue left behind on the fibre caused the twine to rot. Unless it was boiled in a solution of copper sulphate, it would be covered in mould even before it left the factory. They also calculated that, even if all of Ireland's flax crop was to be diverted to making twine, it would still not be enough to meet demand. Nevertheless, they felt that they had no choice but to persevere.

As there was no suitable land around Newbridge, Eric began calling on farmers in the neighbouring county of Carlow to try to persuade them to grow flax for him under contract. At a first open meeting in Tullow, he offered to pay them up front for the cost of seed, fertiliser, and harvesting, and then pay a guaranteed minimum price per ton once the flax had been harvested. Although the farmers agreed to form a committee and sow a few trial acres, their progress would have been too slow had it not been for the enterprise of local auctioneer, Patrick Dawson, who went on to organise similar meetings in every town and village within working distance of the factory. By the beginning of May, when the first flax seeds were sown, Eric had already signed up 700 acres. It was substantially more than his original target of 500 acres and gave him the confidence to order a second turbine scutcher. Within another month, he had 1,000 acres under contract, 600 of which had already been sown. He was reckoning on a harvest of around 2,000 tons from which he might be able to extract some 300 tons of processed fibre. He also took on two flax experts from Donegal to advise him and to train the farmers who had no previous experience of growing flax. When the flax seeds were found to be too small for regular corn-drills, staff at the factory had to make fiddle-sowers, which scattered the seeds in a wide arc when the bow of the fiddle was pulled back and forth.[20] Throughout the summer, Patrick Dawson kept the farmers informed by placing regular notices in the local press on behalf of Irish Ropes.

As usual, Eric kept meticulous financial records. They show that Irish Ropes invested £17,500 in the scheme between 1942 and 1944.[21] It was a substantial sum for what one paper dismissed as the sponsoring of an experiment. Although it would be difficult to get hold of all the machinery that they needed, Eric was certain that Horace Davies would make the most of what they got. Once he had decided to build his own scutching mill at the factory, he bought two turbine scutchers from Mackies at a cost of £3,223 and in time bought a third. He also spent £3,258 on a building to house them, £752 on a barn to store the flax prior to processing, and £709 on machinery to remove and bag the seeds prior to scutching. He acquired a 6-acre site in Tullow for £484 where farmers would bring their flax to be weighed and spent £3,560 on a weighbridge and storage facilities there. Tractors, trailers, mechanical flax pullers, and a Dodge lorry to transport the flax from Tullow to Newbridge all followed in due course. The Tullow Flax Scheme, as it became known, was officially launched in October after the first harvest when Eric's parents were staying at Morristown to celebrate Harry's forthcoming seventieth birthday. Both Eric and his father had an interest in their family's history. It cannot have escaped their notice that, after almost a century, they were now flax dressers once more, as they had been in Wales and Liverpool for several generations.

Although Eric was determined to make his new venture a success, his first priority was to make sure that there was enough twine for that year's harvest. Although February's emergency order had prohibited the release of any twine before July, questions were being asked in the Dáil about its availability as early as April. Meanwhile, Eric continued his experiments with Alec Nisbet and Horace Davies to see if they could eke out their stocks by making thinner twine and introducing a proportion of jute. It was good news for Goodbody's, which had more fibre than it needed and enabled its workforce, which had been working

TIMES PICTORIAL

INCORPORATING THE WEEKLY IRISH TIMES

VOL. 68. NO. 3,630 (NEW SERIES)   SATURDAY, NOVEMBER 21, 1942   (OVERSEAS)   PRICE THREEPENCE

FLAX INTO TWINE

BINDER twine is essential for harvesting the big corn crops—and there was talk of a shortage. Now the country is producing the twine from its own fields. Flax grown in the Tullow district is being converted into binder twine on machinery specially devised for the purpose in a factory at Newbridge. These pictures show you some of the processes through which the flax must pass before it is ready to bind the sheaves when the next grain harvest is ready for the reapers.

Scutching the flax in turbines.

" What is the quality of the crop?"

Flax is de-seeded by a roller machine.

One of the growers—Laurence Murphy, Ardoyne.

Two processes in making the twine. 'Above: Flax fibre enters the combing machine. Below: To ensure uniformity the fibre gets another—and a finer—combing.

Microscopic examination of the fibre.

For next year—the seed is cleaned.

'Flax into Twine', a full-page spread on the Tullow Flax Scheme in the *Times Pictorial*, 21 November 1942. (*By kind permission of the Irish Times*)

half-time, to increase its hours by a third. Eric and his colleagues also rebuilt some of their spinning machines to see if they could spin new twine from salvaged twine. As he told his children:

> We had to make do with whatever material we had. Parts are a bit Heath Robinson but they do the job. We can make new ropes (of a sort) from old ones. At first we had a very bad result from them and it almost looked as though it might be a failure but our plans were proved right and only a few minor adjustments were needed. We started on Monday and by Friday had got the thing working. All that remains now is to improve.

His optimism was premature. In June, Lemass had to tell the Dáil that the attempts to salvage and re-spin old binder twine had not been successful.[22] However, Eric did not give up. In the autumn, he placed a series of advertisements in the papers encouraging farmers to salvage their twine. They would be a paid a penny for every pound of twine that they returned before the end of year. His initiative would be poorly supported. In the spring, Dr Ryan had to tell the Seanad that not enough had been returned to make even one good car rope.[23]

In June, Lemass made another important speech in the Dáil in which he explored the supplies position in some detail. He explained that, although things were worse than had been anticipated, Ireland was still suffering less than many countries, whether neutral or belligerent. With manila unobtainable since Pearl Harbor and sisal in short supply, he reckoned that there would now be only 1,650 tons of twine available that year against an estimated requirement of some 2,500 tons. It meant that not only had demand increased by almost 50 per cent in a year, but also that, were it not for the continuing drive towards tillage, there would not have been a shortfall. He went on to outline the measures that had already been taken to limit the impact of the shortfall, including the restriction of its use to mechanical binders, reductions in its weight and strength, and experiments with using green flax as a substitute. Nevertheless, he admitted that 'even if we can manage to meet the problem of binder twine in the current year, the problem next year will be almost insuperable'.[24]

Final decisions followed quickly after his speech. When the four-month window for the sale of twine opened a week later, Lemass told retailers that they would be receiving only 75 per cent of what they had bought the previous year. There was simply no more available.[25] At the same time, Irish Ropes placed a series of advertisements in the papers. Headed 'Binder Twine', they were said to have been issued 'in the interest of urgent national economy with the concurrence of the Department of Agriculture' and opened with the reassurance that 'with economy there should be sufficient binder twine for this year's harvest, but only just enough. It is therefore imperative that each farmer only purchases enough for his exact needs'. Below this there was a list of the price and strength of thirteen types of twine, which gave for each the area that could be covered in both standard and Irish acres.[26] Irish Ropes's branded Red Setter twine, at 500 feet per pound, cost £2 for a bale of six spools, while its thinnest Standard twine, at £2.35, was 17½ per cent more expensive but, at 750 feet per pound, would go 50 per cent further. The prices were the equivalent of £80 and £94 a ton. With the government now setting maximum retail prices for a wide range of products, from biscuits and bicycle tyres to binder twine, Eric could not afford to pay too much for his raw materials.

At the beginning of September, with two months of the window still open for the sale of twine, Irish Ropes announced that, as a result of the extreme shortage of raw materials, it would be distributing no more that year. Farmers and retailers would not be allowed an opportunity to speculate or stockpile. In October, Dr Ryan told the Dáil that, although there had been barely enough to go around, he had not heard any reports of farmers being 'left stranded absolutely for the want of binder twine'.[27] More surprisingly, he went on to state that, although he was not yet in a position to make a definitive statement, he was confident that there would be enough twine in 1943.

For Eric and Dorothy, this good news was tempered by significant family developments over the summer. Dorothy's widowed father, Taid, died in June at the age of eighty-three. As she and Eric had only just returned from their sons' prize-giving at Rossall, they did not have the time to arrange the necessary travel permits and so were unable to attend his funeral in Rhos. Harry and Alice went in their place and saw a procession almost three-quarters of a mile long follow his hearse to the church. It was a community's moving tribute to a man who had served as their doctor for more than sixty years and had led the men of the village in the First World War. Then, at the end of July, eighteen-year-old Peter arrived home with Michael after his last term at Rossall. Although his longer-term plan was to study chemistry at London University, he had signed on for the Royal Navy a year before leaving school. He now had only three weeks at home before he had to report to HMS *Raleigh* in Plymouth for his initial training. Like Harry and Alice a generation earlier, Eric and Dorothy now had another thing to worry about as the war entered its fourth year. Their eldest son was on active service.[28]

BINDER TWINE

With economy there should be sufficient Binder Twine for this year's harvest, but only just enough. It is, therefore, imperative that each farmer only purchases enough for his exact needs. This comparative table will enable him to calculate the amount he requires.

Per bale of 6 spools.

Brand.		Feet per lb.	Retail price	Statute Acres	Irish Acres
*BLUE JAY	...	500	40/-	10	6¼
BLUE SEAL	...	600	40/-	12	7½
EMERALD	...	500	40/-	10	6¼
*GREEN TOP	...	500	56/3	9	5½
PREMIER	...	600	40/-	12	7½
REAPERS PRIDE	...	500	40/-	10	6¼
REAPERS PRIDE		600	40/-	12	7½
RED SETTER	...	500	40/-	10	6¼
RED SEAL	...	650	45/-	13	8
*RED TOP	...	600	60/-	11	7
STANDARD	...	500	40/-	10	6¼
STANDARD	...	600	40/-	12	7½
STANDARD	...	750	47/-	15	9¼

*Imported.

SALVAGE ALL YOUR USED TWINE

It will pay you to salvage all your twine cut from sheaves at threshing.

(a) For tying sacks, etc.

(b) To substitute for hay-yarn and thatching yarn—now both unobtainable.

(c) For respinning. Dealers are authorised to pay you 1d. per lb. on our behalf for all salvaged Twine returned by the 31st December, 1942.

Issued in the interest or urgent national economy with the concurrence of the Department of Agriculture by

IRISH ROPES LIMITED

DROICEAD NUA, CO. KILDARE.

'With economy there should be sufficient binder twine for this year's harvest, but only just enough'—Irish Ropes announces its binder twine prices, 18 July 1942. (*With thanks to Irish Newspaper Archives and the Nationalist and Leinster Times*)

'Salvage your Binder Twine'—Irish Ropes's advertisement, 26 September 1942. (*With thanks to Irish Newspaper Archives and the Nationalist and Leinster Times*)

A Family at War, 1942–1943

Arm yourselves, and be ye men of valour, and be in readiness for the conflict.[1]

As a volunteer under the Y scheme, which recruited boys of potential officer material while they were still at school, Peter had first to undergo twelve weeks' basic training as an ordinary seaman. By November, he had completed this and was waiting to hear of his first posting. At the beginning of December, he was ordered to board a train to Dumbarton on the Clyde estuary where he was to join the newly-built anti-submarine sloop, HMS *Woodpecker*. Once she had completed her sea trials, she sailed for Tobermory in the Inner Hebrides. Peter and her crew would spend Christmas there before moving on to Londonderry where she was to join her first Atlantic convoy early in the new year. The move only hardened Peter's already ambivalent attitude towards Ireland, a country that he never grew to love or think of as home. 'One side of the river Foyle,' he wrote in his retirement, 'was in the Irish Republic, then neutral. From this shore boats would come out selling butter. No doubt there were German agents and sympathizers not far away.'

He would leave it to another Liverpudlian who served in the Atlantic convoys to write the most vitriolic and compelling denunciation of Irish neutrality during the Emergency. Nicholas Monsarrat was thirty when he joined the Royal Navy in 1940. He was promoted to lieutenant-commander three years later and went on to command corvettes and frigates before resigning his commission in 1946. In 1951, he wrote *The Cruel Sea*, his classic novel about a corvette on convoy duty in the Atlantic. In it, he delivered a bitter two-page tirade in which he likened Ireland to a woman who, rather than occasionally giving her partner the cold shoulder, persistently and knowingly betrayed him in the arms of another man. Although he conceded that Ireland had been within her rights to opt for neutrality,

HMS *Woodpecker*. (© *Imperial War Museum, FL 9733*)

he condemned its decision as morally reprehensible and taking indecency to a new level. He was certain that all those who served in the Atlantic would never be able to forgive their country's smiling and self-satisfied neighbour, which readily accepted its share of the vital supplies that the convoys carried but was not prepared to lift a finger to protect the men who were risking their lives to make sure that they got through.[2]

The Battle of the Atlantic was at its height when the *Woodpecker* joined convoy ON 164 and sailed for New York and Newfoundland at the beginning of February 1943. The previous year, U-boats had sunk an average of more than 500,000 tons of shipping a month. The sinkings had reached their peak at 729,000 tons in November before falling back over the winter months. Peter would be at sea for four weeks before returning to Liverpool in March, by which time sinkings would be back up to 627,000 tons. The weather was atrocious. The mountainous seas meant that the smaller corvettes disappeared from sight between each wave. The crews were issued with thick woollen long-johns, or 'Narvik drawers', to keep warm and had to scrape the ice from the superstructure of their ships every morning. However, it was almost certainly the weather that saved them. The U-boats were unable to hunt in packs. Although the *Woodpecker*'s crew was regularly called to action stations and often found themselves out of sight of the other ships at first light, it was a lucky convoy. According to Peter, not one ship was lost on either the outward or the return journey.

Once back in Liverpool, the *Woodpecker* was set to join Captain 'Johnnie' Walker's Second Escort group, which was then in the process of being formed. Walker would go on to become the most prolific destroyer of U-boats. The six boats in his group sank at least sixteen of them between May 1943 and July 1944. The *Woodpecker* was involved in seven of the sinkings before she herself was torpedoed early in 1944. Her crew was rescued, but she sank in a storm while being towed home. Exhausted and over-worked, Walker died of a cerebral thrombosis a few months later.[3] However, ON 164 would be Peter's only Atlantic convoy. As soon as he got back to Liverpool, he was ordered to leave the *Woodpecker* for officer training at HMS *King Alfred* on the south coast. He was given a week's leave at the Ruff before he started there as a cadet rating in the middle of April. It would be six months before he returned to active service. At least it was one less thing for his parents to worry about.

Peter received his commission shortly after his nineteenth birthday in June. He was now Temporary Acting Midshipman Rigby-Jones, RNVR. Although he was promoted to acting sub-lieutenant in December, his rank would not be confirmed until he was twenty the following summer. With promotion in the Royal Navy still dictated by age, he would not be eligible for promotion to lieutenant until his twenty-second birthday in 1946. From HMS *King Alfred*, he moved on to the Royal Naval College at Greenwich. He was now close enough to his uncle and aunt, John and Judy Forshaw, who lived in Cheam, to be able to spend weekends with them. For longer leaves, he could get back to his grandparents in Ormskirk, but there was little chance of getting home to Morristown.

After thirteen years at the Miners' Welfare Commission, John Forshaw had left in the summer of 1939 to take up an appointment as deputy architect for London County Council. It was a once-in-a-lifetime opportunity. With around 1,700 staff, the architect's department was probably the largest architectural office in the world at the time. As well as carrying out all the duties that might be expected of any municipal authority—from the design, building, and maintenance of local hospitals, schools, and houses to the preservation of historic buildings and the enforcement of planning, building, and fire regulations—it was already gearing itself up to take on new responsibilities in the event of war. John must have been aware of what he was letting himself in for. He must also have known that, if things went well, he would succeed Frederick Hiorns as architect when he retired in 1941. He would then have the most prestigious job in the public sector for a British architect—and at a time when the capital was facing its sternest challenges. In the month that he joined, the council began a programme of building 1,000 bomb shelters and took over the operation of the Heavy Rescue Service. While the capital's twenty-eight boroughs would continue to run the majority of civil defence functions, including the provision of basic first-aid, the council would manage a centralised rescue service across the capital to recover casualties and demolish or shore up damaged buildings. In November 1940, two months after the start of the Blitz, John was asked to take charge of this service. By then, he was already running the War Debris and Disposal Service that had been created

Michael, aged eighteen, as a naval
airman in the Fleet Air Arm, 1944.

Peter, aged nineteen, as a midshipman
in the Royal Navy, 1943.

to relieve the pressure on the rescue services by taking over responsibility for the clearance of bomb sites, the speedy removal of debris, and the salvage of all reusable materials. A vital part of its job was to ensure that the capital's transport and communication links were kept clear, its utilities and telephone lines restored as quickly as possible, and the morale of Londoners maintained.

John was in direct charge of these two services, which were the focus of the council's wartime activities and were later considered its greatest contribution to the war effort, for the rest of the Blitz until May 1941. At their peak, they were employing 30,000 men. Managing them proved an enormous challenge for the regular staff in the architect's department, whose numbers had been drastically cut at the outbreak of war. Most of the department's professional and technical staff had little, if any, experience of managing large workforces and, unlike the armed forces, had no established manuals or disciplinary regulations on which to fall back. The services also had to be set up from scratch at a time when men and equipment were in short supply. Depots had to be established, lorries and transport found, heavy equipment and timber purchased, and the workforce, which was recruited mainly from the building industry, trained, provided with uniforms and protective gear, and found accommodation for what would be a shift-based service around-the-clock.

The War Debris Survey working in Lower Thames Street after a V1 raid, 1944. (*COLLAGE: the London Picture Archive, 36699*, © London Metropolitan Archives, City of London)

In the nine months of the Blitz, the Heavy Rescue Service attended 20,000 incidents, saved 10,000 lives, and lost thirty-four of its own men. Over the same period, the War Debris and Disposal Service removed almost 2 million tons of rubbish, 30 million bricks, 630,000 cubic yards of hardcore, 79,000 tons of wood, 30,000 tons of metal, and 400,000 slates and tiles.[4] Wherever possible, any useful materials were salvaged and reused. The hardcore was used at first to make runways for the aerodromes that were springing up all around the country and later to build the huge concrete sections, each weighing between 2,000 and 6,000 tons that would form the Mulberry harbour at Arromanches on D-Day. Meanwhile, the basements of damaged buildings were turned into reservoirs so that the Fire Brigade always had a supply of water. More than 1,600 of these were built, holding enough water between them to fill 150 Olympic-size swimming pools.

The last major raid of the Blitz, before Germany turned its attention to Russia, was on 10 May 1941. There was then a three-year hiatus before the capital was targeted first by V-1 doodlebugs and then by V-2 rockets in the summer of 1944. However, John was given no time to recover his strength. By July, when he succeeded Hiorns as architect, he was responding to another significant challenge, and one that may properly be considered to be his lasting achievement. That spring, the minister of works, Lord Reith, had asked the council to prepare a provisional plan for the reconstruction and redevelopment of London after the war. As well as raising Londoners' morale, it would provide a unique opportunity to develop a wide-ranging and radical plan for the capital that was unconstrained by statutory regulations. Given its significance, the council decided that it should be undertaken by the architect in collaboration with a recognised expert. John would find himself working with Patrick Abercrombie, the professor of town planning at University College London, who sat on the board of the Miners' Welfare Commission and was, like John, a graduate of the University of Liverpool's school of architecture. The completion of their plan in wartime in just two years was testament to the hard work and dedication of all involved.

Forshaw and Abercrombie's *County of London Plan* was published in July 1943. The first edition sold out immediately and had to be reprinted twice. In all, 22,000 copies were sold. In his foreword, Lord Latham, the leader of London County Council, described its authors as practical visionaries. The book itself, with its many coloured maps, photographs, and diagrams, was a richly illustrated masterpiece of modern design. Its production would have been a remarkable achievement even in peacetime. Lord Lathom claimed that, while those who studied it might be critical, they could not be indifferent.[5]

According to the pamphlet that accompanied the exhibition at County Hall, Forshaw and Abercrombie wanted to create a decent place for Londoners to live and work and a worthy capital of the British Commonwealth.[6] Their aim was to come up with a comprehensive and structured plan that replaced Greater London's haphazard historical development, which had led to houses and factories being built beside each other, with discrete industrial zones and trading

Patrick Abercrombie (left) and John Forshaw (right) explaining their plan to the king and queen at County Hall, 20 July 1943. (*By courtesy of The University of Liverpool Library, D113/3/3/40*)

estates; that substituted new self-contained local communities and estates for old and overcrowded housing; that relieved traffic congestion by creating inner and outer ring roads with major arterial roads that led in and out of the city's centre; that improved public transport and diverted heavy traffic away from residential and shopping areas; and that provided parks and open spaces so that children no longer had to play in the streets. It was a far-sighted and far-reaching plan the effects of which, both positive and negative, are still being felt today. Docklands, the South Bank, high-rise and often brutalist council blocks, garden suburbs, the great roundabouts at Elephant and Castle and Hyde Park Corner, the multi-lane carriageways in and out of London, and the M25 orbital motorway can all, in part at least, trace their history back to the plan.

   In order to reach as wide an audience as possible, the exhibition that accompanied the plan was moved from County Hall to the Royal Academy at the end of its month's run.[7] By then, the king and queen had been among its 80,000 visitors. A week after their visit, John took Peter to see it before giving him lunch at the Reform Club where he was bought a glass of port by Malcolm MacDonald's brother, Alistair, who, like John, was one of a new generation of socially conscious architects and planners. It was an eye-opening experience for nineteen-year-old Peter. John would be the main reason why he eventually chose architecture as a career. He returned to Cheam for a final weekend before moving on to Devonport and then to Scotland to start his training on motor torpedo boats.

Eric's younger brother, Guy, was the other uncle to whom Peter always felt closest. At thirty-two, he was closer in age to Peter than he was to his brother and therefore saw himself as much an older brother to him as an uncle. Five days before John's exhibition opened at County Hall, he took part in Operation Ladbroke, the glider-borne assault that was the first stage of the Allies' invasion of Sicily. He would be the only medical officer to reach the island safely.

Unlike Germany, which had developed an airborne service before the war, it was not until the summer of 1940, when both Britain and Ireland faced invasion from the air, that Churchill ordered the creation of an airborne force of at least 5,000 men. Such a force, whether dropped by parachute or landed by glider, would require a new sort of medical support. As it would be impossible to evacuate casualties or send them back to medical facilities behind the lines, any airborne medical service would have to take in with it everything that it needed to set up and operate temporary aid posts and dressing stations—from transport in the form of jeeps, carts, stretchers, and collapsible bicycles to operating tables, instruments, and wicker panniers filled with drugs, bandages, and medical supplies.

Colonel Arthur Eagger was appointed assistant director of medical services, or the senior medical officer, of the 1st Airborne Division at the end of 1941. Although preliminary work on the formation of an airborne field ambulance started immediately, it would be spring before a unit was formally established and recruitment began. The 181st Airlanding Field Ambulance would be the Royal Army Medical Corps' first airborne unit. As an 'ambulance', it would comprise a complete and self-contained medical unit of around twelve officers and 200 men comprising five sections, two surgical teams, and a headquarters staff. Although as an airlanding unit, it would go into action by glider, it was as entitled as the parachute units to wear the maroon beret and Pegasus insignia of the Airborne Service.

Guy and his wife, Peggy, had returned to their medical careers in London after their recall from holiday in Ireland in May 1940. Peggy would stay on at the Royal Cancer Hospital and continue to work there throughout the war, while Guy moved on to become resident medical officer and then surgical registrar at the National Temperance Hospital near Euston Station. He completed his surgical training at the end of 1941 and was appointed a Fellow of the Royal College of Surgeons of Edinburgh at the same time that he received his commission as a lieutenant in the RAMC. He then spent the first half of 1942 working at the Army's Royal Victoria Hospital at Netley near Southampton before being transferred to the 181st at Bulford Camp on Salisbury Plain. It would be autumn before the ambulance received its first proper training on gliders, by which time Graeme Warrack had taken over as its commanding officer. As well as undergoing the same training as every other airborne soldier, the medics had to trial a whole range of new airborne medical equipment and learn how best to load and unload their gliders. Guy and the other surgeons also had to keep their surgical skills up to scratch on week-long secondments to the local military hospital. What made them different from the other units in the Airborne Service was that, in order to ensure their safety under the Geneva Convention, they were not allowed to be fully armed and were provided only with revolvers for self-defence.

The Airborne Division's first major deployment was to North Africa at the end of 1942. The first units arrived there shortly after Montgomery's victory at El Alamein and the Allies' successful occupation of Morocco and Algeria. Victory in North Africa, as well as boosting morale at home, paved the way for an Allied invasion of occupied Europe. Britain and America would finally be able to relieve the pressure on Russia where, in February, the German Sixth Army would be forced to surrender after the bloody five-month battle for Stalingrad.

The Allied invasion of Sicily would be the largest amphibious operation of the war, as well as the first time that a massed glider formation was used in a major operation. Evidence of the importance attached to its success is provided by the preliminary schemes of deceit and diversion that have subsequently been made famous in Ewen Montagu's *The Man Who Never Was* and Ben Macintyre's *Operation Mincemeat*. Sicily's proximity to both North Africa and mainland Europe meant that it was the obvious point of attack. It was therefore essential that the Germans were convinced that the target was more likely to be Crete, the south of France, or the islands of Corsica and Sardinia.

Operation Ladbroke required 2,000 men from the 1st Airlanding Brigade to go in by glider on the night before the main seaborne invasion to secure the Ponte Grande bridge south of Syracuse, the ancient Greek port 30 miles up the island's east coast from its south-eastern tip. Its capture would open the way for a rapid advance up the coast to Catania and Mount Etna and then on to the port of Messina at the island's north-eastern tip, where the straits that separated it from mainland Italy were only 2 miles wide. The operation meant that the brigade would have the honour of being the first major Allied force to land in occupied Europe.

The detailed plan called for two companies of the 2nd Battalion of the South Staffordshire Regiment to go in as a *coup de main* force two hours ahead of the rest of the brigade to secure the bridge before the enemy had a chance to blow it. The battalion's two other companies would join them there to hold it. Then, while Syracuse was subjected to a sustained bombing raid, the 1st Battalion of the Border Regiment would follow through to capture strategic points on the western edge of the city and to make what progress it could against the port itself. Supporting the two battalions would be a company of Royal Engineers and the 181st Airlanding Field Ambulance. Although the commander of the 1st Airborne, Major-General Hopkinson, described it as a straightforward operation by glider-borne troops, it would be no easy task for a small force at night against well-defended enemy positions.[8] Even today, the countryside is littered by Italian pillboxes.

The 181st sailed from Liverpool in the middle of May and arrived at the Algerian port of Oran at the end of the month, a fortnight after the Axis forces' final surrender in North Africa and a month after the body of Major William Martin, 'the man who never was', had been washed ashore on a Spanish beach carrying the forged documents that would convince the Germans that Sicily was not the Allies' target. On 10 June, they began three weeks' intensive training. The original plan had been for them to use British Horsa gliders. However, when it proved impossible to get enough of them to Africa in time, they were left with no choice but to use American Wacos, which were airlifted from the US in crates and had to be assembled on arrival. It meant that there was little time to learn how to load or fly them. Worse, they were only half the size of the Horsas and so could carry only fifteen rather than thirty men. It meant that two gliders would be needed for each platoon rather than one. Worst of all, the ambulance was allocated only six Wacos instead of the sixteen Horsas that it had been expecting. It meant that the size and shape of its force would have to be reduced by 80 per cent. The ambulance would now take in only five officers and seventy-one other ranks, including a single seven-man surgical team. Guy, who was now a captain, would command it as surgeon and senior officer and would be supported by his anaesthetist, Captain John Graham-Jones. Their role would be to perform essential surgery, first at an advance dressing station near the Ponte Grande bridge, the precise location of which would not be decided until Lieutenant-Colonel Warrack arrived with Brigade HQ, and then at a main dressing station in Syracuse. Each of the ambulance's six gliders would carry a blitz-buggy (or jeep), a folding bicycle, and a medical handcart to transport equipment and evacuate casualties. In addition, the surgical team would carry a stretcher trailer loaded with plasma, plaster, and other essential equipment. The complement of each glider was designed, so far as was possible, to function independently as a modified dressing station. However, with only one surgical team and the surgeon and anaesthetist on board separate gliders, it would only be possible to operate a full medical service if all the gliders landed safely and on target.

Guy, who turned thirty-two on the day that the 181st left Liverpool, wrote to Eric a week before the operation to thank him for his birthday wishes. It was now three years since he and Peggy had stayed at Morristown. 'I always think of that week we spent there in the spring of 1940 as my last real holiday,' he wrote. All in all, he said, he had settled down well in North Africa and had got used to the heat and dust. He had found the time to see some of the local sights, had managed a couple of swims in the sea, and was enjoying the local wine, which cost 10 francs a bottle. Like most of the men, he preferred to sleep out in the open under an olive tree. He had also rigged up his own shower and made an armchair for himself from an old German machine-gun mounting. Peggy had recently sent him a photograph of their eleven-month-old son, Tim, who was beginning to teeth and had told him that Peter was now an officer—'on the whole a very good war, as they go, at the moment,' he reckoned.

At the end of June, the 181st flew on to Tunisia for a final week of preparations and briefings. On the day before the operation, they were visited by General

Montgomery, who flew in to give them some final words of encouragement. The following evening, on 9 July, Guy's was one of 143 gliders to take off from six airfields around el Djem and Goubrine. Only fifty-four of them would reach landfall in Sicily and only twelve of those would land near their designated landing zone. Some ended up more than 50 miles away. Almost half of them, sixty-nine in all, had to ditch in the sea. Of the rest, eleven never left Africa and nine were never accounted for.[9] Almost everything had gone against them. The British glider pilots were flying by night without any navigational aids and after only limited training on the Wacos, which they thoroughly disliked. Once airborne, they were hampered by strong winds and poor visibility. Many lost contact with their tugs on take-off when their communication cables snapped as the towing cables were pulled taut. Worst of all, they were let down by the inexperience of the American tug pilots. Many took evasive action as soon as they were picked up by searchlights or caught in anti-aircraft fire and released their towing cables prematurely, even though this was the responsibility of the glider pilots except in an extreme emergency. It meant that the gliders were often too low or too far out to sea to stand any chance of reaching land. One of the most telling statistics in the subsequent reports of the operation is that, while all but four of the fifty gliders that were released, as planned, within 3,000 yards of the coast made it to land, sixty-four of the seventy-three that were released early had to ditch in the sea. Although many of the men managed to swim ashore or were picked up by the main seaborne force the following morning, between 250 and 300 of them were reckoned to have drowned.

Glider 26, which carried Guy, his five surgical orderlies and their equipment, three stretcher bearers, and (for some reason) a cook as well as the two glider pilots, was the only one of the ambulance's six gliders to reach land. The other five all ditched in the sea with the loss of one officer and sixteen other ranks. The whereabouts of the unit's anaesthetist, Captain Graham-Jones, remained unknown for two days after his glider ditched 5 miles out to sea to the east of the landing zone. Guy's own glider was cast off early when it was at only 2,000 feet and still 3,000 yards from shore. However, the pilot, Staff Sergeant Walter Naismith, managed to bring it down only 300 yards short of its landing zone, 3 miles south of the Ponte Grande bridge—but only after it had hit a tree, which slowed it down and ripped off its right wing and undercarriage, and come to a halt after hitting a stone wall.[10] Given the damage to the glider, it was a miracle that Guy and his men were able to escape with no more serious injuries than a single broken nose. Many of those whom Guy later treated for their injuries, and especially the glider pilots, had either broken their legs and ankles or had other lower limb injuries caused by the stone walls and uneven rocky ground on which they had been forced to land.

Some of the larger Horsa gliders had eventually been able to make it to North Africa a fortnight before the operation after being towed by air all the way from England. Eight of them would be used to transport the eight platoons of the *coup de main* force. Only five of them made it to land, and only one of those

Guy's glider after crash landing in Sicily: its number, '26', is just visible under the wing. (*By courtesy of the United States National Archives and Records Administration, photo no. 342-FH-3A27093-B26827ac*)

The damage sustained to the cockpit of Guy's glider. (*By courtesy of the United States National Archives and Records Administration, photo no. 342-FH-3A27093-B26828ac*)

landed safely on target near the Ponte Grande bridge. Another came under fire as it approached the landing zone, setting off the explosives carried on board and killing all but three of its passengers. Remarkably, the single platoon that landed safely managed to capture the bridge intact within half an hour and without any loss of life. Operation Ladbroke owed its success to them. Its commander, Lieutenant Lennard Withers, would later be awarded the MC. Others joined them there in dribs and drabs during the night. There were eighty-nine men holding the bridge by the following morning, but with the Italians still controlling the main road to its south, they were cut off from all support. They managed to hold on until the afternoon but were finally forced to surrender at 3.30 p.m.

Accounts of events on the night of the landing and over the course of following day are incomplete and inconsistent. They rely for the most part on the personal accounts of the few who landed safely, and these often became distorted on retelling. The chain of command was broken immediately. Among the gliders that had to ditch in the sea were those carrying the ambulance's senior officer, Colonel Warrack, the Airborne's senior medical officer, Brigadier Eagger, and the commanding officer of the 1st Airlanding Brigade, Brigadier 'Pip' Hicks. They would not reach the Ponte Grande bridge until the evening. Warrack's second-in-command, Captain Greeve, never made it. He was listed as missing and later declared dead. What does seem clear is that Guy and his men were some of the first to approach the bridge after the *coup de main* force. Although they came across only a few other men and gliders as they moved forward from the landing zone, it took some time for them to realise that they were on their own. The area was not yet cleared of the enemy and they were without most of the equipment and men that they needed to establish an advance dressing station. They would have to rely on their own initiative until the main seaborne force arrived.

By 3 a.m., they had established themselves at a farm a few hundred yards south of the bridge. Apart from setting up a temporary aid post and digging in, there was little more that they could do. As they were only lightly armed, they were prevented from getting any closer to the bridge by an Italian strongpoint on a road junction 200 yards to their west, which guarded the main road up from the south. They were joined at the farm by Major du Boulay and some men from the Borders' support company whose glider had landed in the same field as theirs. Lieutenant Welch, from the Brigade HQ defence platoon, came across them there as he led his men forward from where they had landed at the southern end of Syracuse bay. He left his signallers and their handcart with them before circling around the strongpoint with his remaining seven men and reaching the bridge at 4.30 a.m. They would be the first to make contact with Withers's platoon there.

Roderick Macdonald, the *Sydney Morning Herald*'s war correspondent, had also been a passenger on Welch's glider and would be the first journalist to write an eyewitness account of the operation. It was published a week later and syndicated around the world, a shortened version appearing in *The Times* on 16 July. He described how the gliders had landed over a wide area and how the men from each, under the command of intrepid junior officers, had made for the bridge in small parties, joining up with each other as they went. His own party, he said, had seen off some spineless Sicilian home guards before meeting up with a number of signallers and medics shortly after 2 a.m. It can only have been Guy's group. After getting some treatment for his raw knees, Macdonald moved on to the bridge with Welch and was taken prisoner in the afternoon.[11]

The following morning, the farm was attacked by around thirty Italians. The only surviving records of the incident are the medal citations for Guy and one of his orderlies, Private Victor Winter, which were presumably based on their own accounts. In spite of their being only lightly armed, Guy decided to counterattack and gave covering fire to a flanking party led by Private Winter before joining in the attack himself. They took twelve prisoners and killed or wounded several more. Winter, who had armed himself with a captured enemy carbine and a knife, laid down his weapons once the fighting was over and returned to his duties as an orderly. It was almost certainly this incident that prompted Warrack to recommend in his subsequent report that medical staff should henceforward be armed with offensive weapons as well as revolvers. Eagger turned it down.

Although the fighting remained confused that morning, the position began to improve at midday after the enemy strongpoint was captured. Guy and his men could now set about establishing an aid post and bringing in casualties. For transport, they commandeered five donkey carts loaded with melons, which they tucked into eagerly before they started. With the main seaborne force now ashore and moving up from the south, the Ponte Grande bridge was retaken by

The modern Ponte Grande bridge looking east across the bay towards Syracuse with an Italian pillbox on the left (author, 2015).

the Royal Scots Fusiliers within an hour of it being reached. They caught up with and released Withers and his men as they were being marched back to Syracuse.

By early evening, Guy and his team had established as much of an advanced dressing station at the farm as they could. They were still desperately short of men and equipment and could not use their surgical instruments and pressure lamps as they had been damaged on landing. Meanwhile, Withers organised parties to search for and bring in the casualties from the area around the bridge. Although unable to perform any surgery, Guy's dressing station was in action for the next twenty hours and treated almost fifty casualties, including twenty Italians, before sending them back to the 141st Field Ambulance's main dressing station at Cassibile, 6 miles down the coast. He and his men eventually followed the 141st into Syracuse where they took over two wards of the hospital and spent the next ten hours operating on the wounded.[12] As well as gunshot and shrapnel wounds, they had to treat sixteen simple and compound fractures, six of which had been sustained in glider crashes. Guy's anaesthetist, Captain Graham-Jones, finally turned up the following morning. He would be left behind when the rest of the ambulance were embarked on landing craft for the choppy crossing back to Tunisia. They had been away for only five days when they arrived back on 14 July. According to Guy's citation for the MC, he had throughout that time 'displayed tremendous energy, resource, and initiative and spread a tremendous feeling of confidence in his own small command and in the many wounded he treated'.[13]

Guy wrote again to Eric at the beginning of August before he went off for four days at a rest camp. By then, the Italian government had fallen and Mussolini had been deposed. 'I am sorry to hear you have had a return of the rheumatics,' Guy wrote, 'I am as fit as a flea and brown as a berry. I expect you heard about our jaunt to Sicily from the news. It was an interesting and exciting experience but I am afraid that details will have to wait until after the war is over.' Although he was still enjoying himself, he admitted that, having now seen more of Africa, 'anybody who wants it can have it'.

After working for a time at a hospital in Algiers, Guy was himself admitted to hospital with jaundice. It meant that, when the ambulance was moved to Taranto in September, four days after Italy's unconditional surrender, he had to stay behind with three officers and thirty other ranks to run the camp and guard its stores. The following month, he heard that he had been awarded the MC and promoted to major. He eventually made it home early in the new year. In February, Peter spent a night with him and Peggy in London on his way back from leave in Ireland. 'He looks quite a bit older,' he told his parents, 'his hair seems to have gone very straight.'

Meanwhile, Eric's own contribution to the British war effort remains a matter for speculation. His children were always led to believe that he was involved in some way with British intelligence, but as he chose never to speak about it himself, it is unclear whether this went beyond his contact with Major Pryce in the summer of 1940. One story, which I am sure that my father told me when I was young but which he later denied ever having heard, hints at another sort of involvement. According to the story, Peter secretly kept a motorbike in an outhouse at Morristown. Once, when he went to collect it, he was surprised to find some British airmen hiding there. That evening, his father took him aside before supper and said that he would not tell his mother about the motorbike as long as he promised not to tell her about the airmen. The story sounds too good to have been made up. However, although I vividly remember hearing it, I have never found anything to corroborate it aside from the fact that Eric kept his Spitfire motorbike in the greenhouse and allowed his children to ride it. Underlying it, however, is a tantalising kernel of truth.

British and German pilots did indeed crash in Ireland during the war or were forced to land when they lost their bearings, ran short of fuel, or had a mechanical failure. In strict compliance with international law, the Irish government chose to intern them rather than repatriate them. From the earliest days of the war, Tintown at the western end of the Curragh Camp had been used as an internment camp for members of the IRA. Not much later, a second and smaller camp, K-Lines No. 2, was built at its eastern end, nearest to Newbridge, to house the downed British and German airmen in adjacent compounds.

The first incident involving British airmen in Ireland occurred on the day that war was declared. Two seaplanes were forced to land in Dublin Bay after going off course in bad weather on a flight from Wales to Scotland. De Valera decided to treat them as distressed sailors rather than combatants and allowed them to go on their way. A few days later, another seaplane landed off the west coast but was able to take off again after its fuel pipe had been repaired at a local garage. Although there were more such incidents during the Phoney War, it became more difficult to adopt the same relaxed attitude after the fall of France. With Ireland now threatened with invasion by both Germany and Britain, it had to be seen to apply its neutrality in practice.

The first airmen to be interned, in August 1940, were the crew of a German Focke-Wulf that had set off from Bordeaux on a long-range reconnaissance of Ireland's west coast and crashed in bad weather on the Dingle peninsula.[14] The first RAF pilot, Paul Mayhew, arrived at the camp a month later.[15] When his fighter section had taken off from Bristol to intercept some German bombers, he had lost his bearings after going off on his own to pursue eight Heinkels near the Irish coast. With the light fading and his Hurricane running low on fuel, he was forced to make an emergency landing in County Wexford. As the first and, for the time being, only British internee at the Curragh, he was taken in charge by Sir John Maffey and his wife who paid him regular visits with their son and four dogs. Although he was no horseman, Mayhew was given honorary membership of the Kildare Hunt and allowed to enrol as an external student at Trinity College Dublin. When his father came over to visit him at Christmas, he stayed with the Maffeys. By then, Paul had been joined by five other British airmen and was the proud owner of a Cocker Spaniel puppy that had been given to him by a friend of Lady Maffey.

Although British servicemen had a duty to escape, wherever they were imprisoned, the regime at the Curragh was relaxed. Unlike the IRA internees,

One of the two surviving buildings from K-Lines No. 2, now in use as a private residence.

they were allowed to leave the camp as long as they gave their parole, or word of honour, that they would not try to escape while they were out. Maffey visited regularly with whisky and spirits to replenish their bar; they were allowed to attend race meetings at the Curragh and to visit public houses in Newbridge, which were allocated between the British and German internees to avoid brawls; they were invited to dinner by local sympathisers, for the most part Protestant Anglo-Irish landowners, and some went hunting with them; and some of those who were married were permitted to live outside camp with their wives, who moved to Ireland for the duration of their husband's internment. Peter remembered one uncomfortable trip to the cinema in Newbridge when he was home on leave from the Navy with a girlfriend. He found it packed with British and German airmen who were given seats on different sides of the stalls.

One of the British internees, Hugh Verity, described K-Lines as a concentration camp even though he admitted to being well treated.[16] He had been forced to land in a field near Dublin's Leopardstown racecourse in May 1941 when he hit bad weather and ran short of fuel while flying his Bristol Beaufighter back from Malta after a refit. Although he would be there for only five weeks before he escaped, he still found time to send butter, bacon, and marmalade back to his parents in England. It must have been one of the few occasions that a prisoner of war sent rather than received a food parcel. It was, of course, much easier for the British to escape than the Germans. They shared a language if not an accent, the land border with Northern Ireland was only 100 miles away, and there was still a regular train service between Dublin to Belfast. Konrad Neymeyr was the only German to escape. In January 1942, he suddenly seemed to disappear from the camp and, after making his way to Dublin, was able to stow away on a boat bound for Lisbon. He was arrested when the boat had to call in at Cardiff to comply with British shipping controls. Although the Irish authorities would later adopt a more lenient attitude towards British escapers, they had to be seen to apply the rules impartially as long as Germany was in the ascendant. It was an approach that the British accepted. On at least one occasion an Allied airman was returned to Ireland by the authorities after breaking the rules of parole to make good his escape. However, when Maffey suggested that all the internees should be released and repatriated, the Dominions Office rejected the idea on the grounds that the Germans were likely to have acquired more valuable information than the British.

Verity managed to escape with Mayhew and seven other airmen on the evening of 25 June 1941 in what was the first major successful breakout from the camp. Mayhew had previously made an attempt in January but was arrested on a bus the following morning, 9 miles from Dublin. However, this new attempt was more carefully planned. It was the day of the Irish Derby and the internees had been granted parole to join the crowds at the Curragh to watch it.[17] The escapers reckoned on the area still being crowded in the evening and the guards being in a relaxed and jovial mood.

Six of the nine made good their escape. Even many years later, Verity remained coy about how exactly he and Mayhew did it, claiming that the identities of the local people who had helped them were still under some sort of security wrap. Mayhew was equally reticent. However, the Irish authorities were quick to identify the hand of MI9, the branch of the British intelligence service that was responsible for helping agents and prisoners of war to evade capture and escape from foreign countries. One of its priorities at the time was to make good the shortage of pilots by repatriating as many of them as it could. The Irish believed that the wire-cutters used in the escape had been smuggled into the camp by an MI9 agent posing as a friend visiting an internee and that the details of the rendezvous and escape routes had been arranged in coded letters with MI9. The plan was for the six 'official' escapers, who included Mayhew and Verity, to be picked up by two cars at Athgarvan Cross, 2 miles south of Newbridge, and then whisked away to the border as quickly as possible. Close by the crossroads stood Arthgarvan House, the home of Captain Reeves, whom some of the internees later identified, when they were debriefed on their return to England, as one of the sympathisers who were prepared to help escapers and provide them with food and shelter. Although he was not specifically associated with this escape, he was said to have helped make the ladders that were used in another attempt the following February.[18] Many of those named in these debriefings were either former British Army officers or people connected to the horse racing world, including the successful trainer, Captain Darby Rogers, who lived close by the camp at Curragh

Grange and had provided food and clothing to Covington and Proctor when they tried to escape in January 1941, and Nesbit Waddington, who managed the stud farms of the Aga Khan. MI9's Irish operations were apparently run by two British officers named Welman and Goodbody who were based in Northern Ireland but made frequent visits south of the border. Their names are almost too good not to be aliases. However, Goodbody was a well-known name in Ireland, and in 1960, the same Major W. H. E. Welman was one of the founder members of Blessington Sailing Club at nearby Poulaphouca along with Eric's son, Michael.

Mayhew and Verity's pick-up did not go according to plan. The Irish army was already out in force by the time that they reached their rendezvous. The cars that were meant to pick them up had already left. They had to spend most of the next day hiding up trees before meeting up again in the evening. As they were now hungry, they decided to throw themselves on the mercy of some local people who they thought might help them. They were eventually smuggled out to Dublin where they were put on board the train to Belfast wearing disguises and with false identities. It must have been disconcerting to find themselves sitting beside a party of British officers who were returning quite legitimately from leave in Dublin and speculating loudly about what might have happened to the escaped airmen. Mayhew was back in London within ten days of escaping. He was married less than a week later. He returned to his squadron and was killed the following February when his engine stalled as he came in to land after a mission. He was too low to recover. Meanwhile, Verity took over command of 161 Squadron's 'A' Flight at Tangmere and flew twenty-nine missions to pick up agents and grounded aircrew in France, a story that he later told in his book, *We Landed by Moonlight*. When he returned to the Curragh many years later, he discovered that his wife's family, who lived locally, still thought of those who had helped them escape as traitors.

Their escape was never a secret. The *Daily Express* rang Mayhew's family for confirmation even before he got home and, in his last letter before the summer holidays, Eric told the children that 'it says in the *Daily Mail* that the first airman to be interned here is being married in England this week so he must be one who escaped'. However, it did prompt the strongest of Irish protests. MI9 had to agree not to organise any more escapes, although it would continue to help escapers once they were outside the camp. In any case, the internment of British and Allied pilots effectively came to an end when America entered the war at the end of the year. The Irish had no desire to increase the number of internees or the administrative headaches that came with them. By the summer of 1942, it usually turned a blind eye when Allied aircrews came down in Ireland. They were helped to take off again after they had given the prepared excuse that they were on instructional or non-operational flights. It was not an excuse that the Germans could use so easily. However, as long as Allied and German airmen were interned in the same camp, it would be difficult to release the former without risking a formal protest from the German ambassador in Dublin. In the autumn of 1943, the remaining thirty-two Allied internees were transferred to Gormanston camp, north of Dublin. Twenty of them were released almost immediately and debriefed when they arrived back in England in October. The rest could not claim to have been on non-operational flights. The last of them was not released until just before D-Day.

Before then, there had been several more attempts to escape. A failed attempt by eleven airmen in August 1942, shortly after Peter arrived at Torpoint, led to the arrest and trial of a Dublin doctor, Thomas Wilson. In a repeat of the previous year's Derby Day escape, the plan had been for him to drive one of the escapers, Flight Lieutenant Bruce Girdlestone, to the border with the help of another member of the so-called Escape Club, the elusive and unidentified Dicky Ruttledge. However, cars were now such a rare sight on the roads that they did not go unnoticed. Wilson could only still drive because, as a doctor, he was entitled to a special petrol ration. He was also naïve enough to flaunt his membership of the Escape Club and liked to show off his cigarette box, which he had had engraved 'Derby Day, 1941' to commemorate Mayhew and Verity's escape. However, although Maffey later described him as being intoxicated by the lure of the Scarlet Pimpernel, Wilson was no dull-witted or irresponsible thrill-seeker. Rather the reverse, he was something of a renaissance man. A keen sailor and artist, he had played rugby for Trinity College Dublin while studying medicine there. He would later write a textbook on paediatric diseases of the ear, nose, and throat and serve as president of the Royal College of Surgeons in Ireland from 1958 to 1961. *Victorian Doctor*, his acclaimed biography of Sir William Wilde, the Victorian polymath and father of Oscar Wilde, was published in 1942 and included sixty of his own illustrations. By a strange coincidence, it was reviewed in the *Irish Times* on the day after he and Girdlestone were stopped in his car and arrested by the police.

In October, a fortnight after Eric's official launch of the Tullow Flax Scheme, Wilson stood trial before a special court at Collins Barracks along with Norman Pearson, a financial agent from Dublin who had already been held in Mountjoy Prison for two months. The charge against them was that they had 'assisted a person liable to internment with intent to hinder arrest'.[19] Wilson was defended by the Fine Gael TD and former Attorney General John Costello, who in 1948 would succeed de Valera as Taoiseach. Maffey, who had known nothing about the case until he read the notice of the trial in the papers, wrote immediately to Machtig at the Dominions Office, infuriated by what he saw as a pointless exercise by the Irish government and seeing behind it the hand of Frank Aiken, the anti-British minister for the co-ordination of defensive measures. He then sent off a brusque letter to Joseph Walshe at External Affairs in which he predicted that, were the trial not to be stopped, it would cause 'a wild fire of resentment in press and on platform in the United Kingdom, the Commonwealth, and the USA'. 'The first symptoms of it,' he warned, 'are reaching me now in a steady crescendo.'[20]

Walshe responded by giving Maffey extracts from the government's dossier on Wilson's previous activities in the Escape Club. He would be even more shocked, he added, if he was ever allowed to see the complete dossier that had been provided to the court. It was not the first time that the British had made the mistake of underestimating the Irish intelligence services. Clearly embarrassed, Maffey could do little more than complain to Machtig that the 'most deplorable feature of the whole business is the humiliating exposure of an escape organisation apparently officially sponsored by us and incredibly *naïf* in its methods and contacts'.

Wilson had been found guilty by the time that Maffey had his next regular meeting with de Valera at the end of the month. He was given a year's suspended sentence, fined £200, and banned from using his car. He was released after he had provided bail of £500 to keep the peace for two years. Maffey found de Valera in no mood to compromise. He was clearly determined to take the sternest action against any Irish citizen who wilfully chose to embarrass his government. Unfortunately, a Polish pilot, Jan Zimek, was forced to land his Spitfire near Wexford that same day. He would be the only Allied airman to be interned in 1942. Walshe told Maffey that de Valera had taken the decision himself and asked him to let it lie. A point had been made. Three weeks later, a Catalina flying boat, which had been forced to land on Lough Gill in Sligo after running short of fuel on a flight from Bermuda to Scotland, was allowed to refuel and resume its journey, and at the end of November, a pilot who landed in Donegal was released and sent back across the border to rejoin his unit.

I have found no evidence that Eric was involved in any escape from the Curragh and have been unable to tie in the dates of any escape with times when Peter was at home from school. Although he was a Protestant and a former British Army officer, Eric was never part of the racing set and none of those who were identified as sympathisers by the airmen ever appear in Morristown's visitors' book. Eric owed it to his family as well as to his fellow directors and the Irish government not to jeopardise the future of Irish Ropes. He did, however, meet at least two of the internees. The visitors' book shows that in October 1941, he and Dorothy entertained a flying officer and Mrs Ward from Vancouver. They were perhaps invited out of courtesy as Leslie Ward was the senior Allied officer at K-Lines. A Canadian, he had been interned at the start of the year after baling out from his Whitley bomber on an operational flight from Limavady in Northern Ireland and had subsequently been joined by his wife. He too had taken part in the Derby Day escape only to be recaptured the following morning while eating breakfast in a bar. However, there is a second and more intriguing entry in the visitors' book a few months earlier. Dorothy wrote it herself in pencil, as she sometimes did. It simply said: 'June 1941: Mr and Mrs Proctor, RAF' without providing any specific date.

Pilot Officers William Proctor and Aubrey Covington had been the first Allied airmen to join Mayhew at K-Lines after they had been forced to land their Miles Master just south of the border four days before Christmas in 1940. They had got lost while flying back to their base in the Isle of Man after picking up some spare parts in Manchester. Although William was knocked unconscious, they were lucky to escape without serious injury as their propeller had struck the ground on landing and flipped the plane over. The plane itself was quickly repaired and, rather than being confiscated, was purchased by the Irish government. Proctor, who had only been married for six months, would be the first of the internees to be joined by his wife. Isobel arrived in Newbridge early in the new year. Meanwhile, nineteen-year-old Covington, the epitome of the dashing and moustachioed RAF officer, would become a constant thorn in the side of the camp's guards with his spectacular attempts to escape. He never succeeded and was eventually repatriated in 1943. The two of them made their first attempt within a month of arriving at the camp and were two of the three 'unofficial' escapers on Derby Day in June. It was the month that Dorothy wrote the Proctors' names in the visitors' book. Covington was recaptured within ten minutes of leaving the camp, but Proctor made good his escape to Northern Ireland and so became one of the first to make a successful getaway.

For a long time, I was unable to find out anything about William's escape and what, if any, part Eric and Dorothy may have played in it. Then a final trawl of the internet showed that in 2014, the Alyth Voice, a monthly newsletter produced in the small Scottish town of Alyth, some 5 miles from the Proctors' home in Blairgowrie, had begun a series of articles about their wartime experiences in Ireland. Called *Escape from the Curragh*, they were based on Isobel's memories and had been written up by a family friend, Arthur Tebbit. Unfortunately, the series stopped suddenly and without explanation after only a few episodes and

Allied internees after a Church of Ireland service at the Curragh Camp, early 1941. The photograph was probably taken by Isobel Proctor. Aubrey Covington is on the right, Bill Proctor third from right, and Leslie Ward and his wife seventh and eighth from right (given to the author by Alistair Proctor, 2018).

before getting to an account of William's escape. However, Irene Robertson at the Alyth Family History Project agreed to put me in touch with their two sons, Gillean and Alistair, and Alistair provided me with a copy of the full story when we met a few weeks later. Sadly, I was just too late to meet Isobel herself. She had died a few months earlier at the age of 100.

Isobel's story revealed that, after getting hold of a passport and all the necessary travel documents, she had crossed over to Ireland early in 1941. She took the ferry from Stranraer to Belfast and then the train on to Dublin. She booked into a hotel in Newbridge but was later offered rooms in the home of two sisters who ran a hairdressing business in the town. Although she and William could spend much of their time together, he had to return to the camp each night. When he told her about the preliminary plans for the Derby Day escape, she agreed to smuggle in some wire cutters and was later approached at her lodgings by a man from British intelligence whom she described as being very obviously English. He asked her to sneak in a letter containing MI9's detailed plans. Her story confirms not only that this was an MI9-led operation to spring six pilots who were desperately needed back home, but also that she, albeit unwittingly, was the MI9 agent later identified by Irish intelligence. According to her story, William and Aubrey were not part of the official plan but chose to ignore the firm warning that the MI9 agent had asked her to pass on to them that they should not jeopardise the success of the operation by making their own private attempt at the same time.[21]

Isobel Proctor, whom Irish intelligence described as an MI9 agent (given to the author by Alistair Proctor, 2018).

William and Isobel had agreed that, rather than trying to get away immediately, it would be better if he hid out locally until the hue and cry died down. He would then make his way to Dublin and catch the train to Belfast, having disguised himself in her clothes and make-up. Once outside the camp, William made his way quickly across country to a vicarage where Isobel had once played tennis and which she remembered as having a long drive and a large garden. It was almost certainly the rectory at Morristownbiller, just a few hundred yards south of Morristown. William's plan was to hide out there among the rhododendrons without the vicar knowing.

Meanwhile, Isobel was unable to leave Newbridge. She had daily visits from an officer and two soldiers at the camp who searched her rooms and tried to find out what she knew. With no chance of contacting William herself, an English jockey named Bert volunteered to take him food and drink. After a week, William felt that it was safe to move and hid under the bed in Isobel's lodgings. Two days later, she shaved off his moustache, made him up, hid his hair in a fashionable turban, and dressed him in the tweed suit that she had made sure that she had been seen wearing around the town earlier in the day. Bert drove him to Dublin, apparently passing through five roadblocks on the way, and one of the hairdressing sisters then accompanied him on the train as far as the border. There he was finally able to reveal his identity to a somewhat surprised British customs official. A few days later, Isobel was summoned to the commandant's office at the Curragh and told that William had made it safely to Belfast. She was then allowed to collect his belongings and leave for home.

It is perhaps a relief that Eric, Dorothy, and Morristown are never mentioned in her story and that there is no evidence that they played any part in William's escape.

11

Pulling Through, 1943–1945

We have all thoroughly enjoyed this adventure.[1]

The thaw in trading relations between Britain and Ireland, or at least the realisation that a more pragmatic approach might benefit both sides, can be traced back in part at least to a private visit to Ireland in the autumn of 1941 by the prominent anti-war and pro-Ireland Labour MP, Richard Stokes. On his return, he wrote a memorandum on food supplies from Ireland in which he suggested that it was 'perfectly crazy not to use Eire to their maximum capacity having regard to the ease of shipping and comparative safety'.[2] Although he sent the memorandum to both the British Ministry of Food and the Irish Department of Agriculture, his intervention was not welcomed by all. Machtig told Maffey that his attempt to become an unofficial intermediary in Ireland's interests was both undesirable and improper.

However, the following spring, in the aftermath of the Japanese attack on Pearl Harbor, Churchill agreed that the previously informal committee on economic policy towards Ireland, which had been chaired by the chancellor of the Exchequer, should be reconstituted as a War Cabinet committee under Clement Attlee. Attlee, who had been leader of the Labour party since 1935 and had previously served in the coalition government as lord privy seal, had been appointed secretary of state for dominion affairs and deputy prime minister a fortnight earlier in a cabinet reshuffle. It was recognition of the steady hand and growing influence of a man who had already proved himself to be a capable understudy to Churchill. The change did much to improve Anglo-Irish relations. From now on, Attlee would have a direct line of communication with John Dulanty, the Irish high commissioner in London.

When the committee met for the first time on 5 March, the first item on its agenda was a proposal from Dulanty for the utilisation of Ireland's spare industrial capacity. It was a logical progression from Stokes's report on agriculture in the autumn. Dulanty's essential argument was that, if Ireland was provided with the necessary raw materials, it would be prepared to use its spare capacity to manufacture those items, excluding munitions and military supplies, that Britain needed most. The committee's acceptance of it would mean a radical change to the current British policy of maintaining economic pressure on its neighbour by withholding supplies. Dulanty was asked to revert with more details of past and potential co-operation. Before the next meeting, he produced a list of fourteen companies and products.[3] It included Irish Dunlop in Cork, which, before Pearl Harbor, had been getting 38 tons of rubber a week to manufacture tyres and other products for Britain, 12 tons of which it was allowed to retain for its own use; two engineering companies in Wexford, which had been supplied with sufficient steel to make forty potato diggers for Northern Ireland and had then been sent another 25 per cent for their own use; and Irish Ropes, which had been provided with enough fuel oil by British Hemp Control in 1941 to salvage 165 tons of damaged sisal and had then been allowed to keep 25 per cent of what it had salvaged.[4] Newbridge Cutlery also appeared on the list. However, the proposal that it should be sent blanks for the manufacture of knives, 25 per cent of which it could then keep for the domestic market, had fallen through when it was realised that there was no shortage of cutlery in Britain. All these examples followed a similar template with Irish manufacturers being allowed to retain for their own use between a quarter and a third of the raw materials that Britain supplied.

At its second meeting in May, Attlee's committee approved in principle the use of Ireland's spare industrial capacity when there was both a clear advantage to Britain and no need to provide Ireland with more coal. In the meantime, the British government would continue to review and, where necessary, reduce its exports to Ireland whenever a commodity was in short supply. At the committee's third meeting a fortnight later, Attlee summarised this new and pragmatic approach:

> Any policy of putting economic pressure on Eire with a view to securing political concessions was most unlikely to prove successful. Our policy in this matter should be dictated solely by consideration of our economic interests.[5]

By then, the committee had already had to address an urgent issue. After the previous year's poor wheat harvest, the Irish government had banned the malting of barley early in 1942 and restricted the export of beer until after the harvest so that the brewers' 20,000 tons of barley stocks could be diverted to make bread for the domestic market. Although the million barrels of beer that Ireland had exported to the UK in 1941 accounted for less than four out of every hundred pints drunk on the mainland, they accounted for four out of every five pints drunk in Northern Ireland. As a result, the ban was felt most keenly in the factories and shipyards of Belfast that were vital to the British war effort. After urgent negotiations, the British agreed to the release of 20,000 tons of North American wheat to Ireland if the Irish released the same amount of barley back to the brewers to enable beer exports to be resumed. They tried without success to hide the deal from the Americans who would probably not appreciate this perceived misuse of precious resources. However, de Valera told Maffey that it was just the sort of co-operation that he was keen to encourage. When Dulanty was informed that the arrangement would not be repeated in 1943, the Irish government continued to allow the export of beer for the time being before finally banning it again in October. Within a month, Guinness had been advised by the British Ministry of Food that it would releasing 24,000 tons of barley in the coming year.

And so was established the principle of barter. Ireland's ability to negotiate a good deal depended on it being able to identify and exploit those items which it could produce and which Britain desperately needed. At the top of the list were cattle, Guinness, spirits, and flax. Nevertheless, Lemass felt it necessary to remind the Dáil in his major speech on supplies in June 1942 that 'in present circumstances our bargaining power is practically nil'.[6]

Figures provided by de Valera to Guinness's managing director, C. J. Newbold, in the spring of 1943 for onward transmission to the British authorities were evidence of the dramatic shift in the balance of trade between the two countries in the first four years of the war. The surplus of Ireland's exports to the UK over its imports had grown from £1.0 million in 1939 to £12.4 million in 1942, and on to £4.9 million in the final quarter of 1942 alone. There needed to be a rebalancing, and if Ireland was to increase its agricultural and industrial exports to the UK, it needed the raw materials and other supplies to support their production. For Irish farmers, that meant access to machinery, fertilisers, and twine.

Throughout 1942 and thereafter, Attlee's Committee on Economic Policy Towards Eire continued to review specific proposals for the release of raw materials to Ireland in return for Ireland's supply of agricultural produce and industrial goods to the UK. In time, it would also receive detailed quarterly analyses of Irish imports from the Ministry of Economic Warfare. One example of its work was its agreement in August 1942 to supply 5,000 tons of coal a month to the Drogheda Cement Works in return for the Irish government's release of 12,500 tons of cement to Northern Ireland. It was a trade that had previously been suspended to preserve coal supplies. At the same meeting, approval was given in principle for Irish shipyards to build British merchant ships. It is clear that both sides were learning how best to play the game.

At the beginning of 1942, when the Department of Agriculture had again challenged him about the feasibility of using home-grown flax to make binder twine, Eric had suggested that it might instead be bartered for British sisal. However, with Attlee's committee not yet established, it was made clear to him that such reciprocal arrangements did not 'come off'. In June, with his own flax-growing scheme now under way, he tried again. He asked Wigglesworths to approach John Ferrier at Flax Control with a proposal that he should release 400 to 500 tons of sisal to Irish Ropes in exchange for the 200 tons of green flax that Irish Ropes was now expecting to produce that year. Ferrier took the proposal to Landauer at Hemp Control but found him very much against it. As Landauer pointed out sisal was in desperately short supply and there was no guarantee of the quality of Irish Ropes's unretted flax. Recent experience in Britain meant that its cultivation was no longer being encouraged. In spite of the British agreement to buy all of Ireland's flax harvest, he was happy to make an exception in this instance and allow Irish Ropes to keep all of its flax to make binder twine.

LIRA's optimistic research reports, combined with the lack of local retting skills, had prompted the British authorities at the start of the war to grow only green flax at home. It had not been a success. In the spring of 1943, the Select Committee on National Expenditure published an extremely critical report on domestic flax production, which highlighted the inexperience of both the farmers growing it and the civil servants directing them. It claimed that there was nobody at the time with any technical knowledge in the department for Home Flax Production. It recommended a reorganisation of the department and the appointment of a new director, the reintroduction of retting, and the release from military service of flax experts, or 'fieldsmen', to provide the necessary advice and instruction to farmers. In July, Charles Peat, the Joint Parliamentary Secretary for the Ministry of Supply, advised parliament that no further increase in domestic flax cultivation was being contemplated.[7]

This lack of success, combined with poor weather in the autumn of 1942, which had often made it impossible to harvest the flax crop, only increased Britain's reliance on Irish flax. By the time that Wigglesworth approached Ferrier on Eric's behalf in June, there had already been discussions within the British Ministry of Supply about asking Ireland to increase its flax production to 35,000 acres in 1943. When Dulanty was advised of this in July, he was already aware that Ireland would fall short of that year's target of 25,000 acres because only 19,500 acres had been planted, including the 1,000 acres in Eric's Tullow Flax Scheme. Just two months after this, the British minister of supply, Sir Andrew Duncan, submitted a proposal to Attlee's committee that British sisal and binder twine should be bartered for Irish flax. It would seem that the Irish had made the most of British desperation by arguing that, if they did not receive sufficient supplies of sisal and twine, they might have to divert all of their own flax production to the manufacture of binder twine for the domestic market. The essence of Duncan's proposal was that Ireland should be given all the sisal and twine that it needed in 1943 in return for it increasing its cultivation of flax to 30,000 acres and agreeing to export it all to Britain. The only problem that still had to be resolved was securing the agreement of the Combined Raw Materials Board in Washington to release the sisal.

Although Attlee's committee did not meet between August and December 1942—he was away in Canada and Newfoundland for the second half of September—he had been able to review and approve a draft of Duncan's proposal before he left. When he circulated it to the rest of the committee, he suggested that their approval should be assumed if no one raised any objections within a week of receiving it. It was this fast-tracking of the scheme that almost certainly allowed Ryan to be optimistic about the following year's supply of twine when he addressed the Dáil in October. However, Atlee's approval of Duncan's memorandum marked the start rather than the end of the process. Negotiations between the two governments continued into 1943. In October, Dulanty passed on the Irish Department of Agriculture's formal response to the British Ministry of Supply. It included a number of detailed proposals: on the length of the agreement which, in line with British policy, it suggested should be for the duration of the war and for one year thereafter; on price, where it suggested that an increase of £56 a ton, or 25 to 30 per cent depending on grade, was required to stimulate the desired increase in acreage; on the provision of adequate supplies of flax seed and fertiliser; and on the British government's agreement to the release of the additional scutching and pulling equipment that would be needed to cope with so significant an increase in production. It also proposed the establishment of a Flax Development Board to provide the same financial assistance to Irish farmers and mill-owners that was already being given to those in Britain and Northern Ireland. This would mainly be in the form of grants for training and technical assistance and for investment in equipment and facilities. The funds would be provided by the British Ministry of Supply but controlled by the Irish Department of Agriculture. In return, the Irish government agreed to do all that it could to encourage the increase in acreage and ensure, through its control of export licences, that it was all sold to Britain. It could not, however, guarantee that the target of 30,000 acres would be met.

Although the question of Irish Ropes's green flax was raised at an early stage of the negotiations it was not immediately resolved. At the end of October, Adams's deputy at the Department of Agriculture had to write to remind John Shillidy at the Raw Materials Department of the British Ministry of Supply:

> I am still awaiting word as regards the question of sisal for Messrs Irish Ropes Limited. The company is about to begin scutching operations and therefore we should require to know at once if the Ministry of Supply desire to have the offer of that flax so that scutching can be done to the standards required by the Ministry, which are higher than those necessary if the flax were to be used for making binder twine. It is understood that Messrs Irish Ropes would be prepared to let the Ministry have the whole of their output of green flax fibre (estimated at 200 tons) against an equivalent quantity of sisal.[8]

On 12 November, Shillidy responded formally with the British counter-proposals. He wanted a deal for one year only and suggested an increase of only £28 a ton, or half that which the Irish had requested. As a sweetener, he was prepared to offer a retrospective increase of £12 a ton for the 1942 harvest as well as a bonus for achieving the targeted acreage in 1943. He also agreed to the establishment of the Flax Development Board and the purchase of Irish Ropes's first crop of green flax (which had now been harvested) for between £90 and £160 a ton, depending on grade, and its following year's crop for between £115 and £175. However, no decision had yet be taken, he said, on whether the 200 tons of sisal that Irish

Ropes received in return was to be included in or in addition to the 1,800 tons of sisal and binder twine that the Irish government had already requested.

Although further progress was made over the next two months on the release of equipment and the establishment of the Flax Development Board, a final agreement was held up by the need to get the approval of the Combined Raw Materials Board for the release of the sisal. Dulanty finally received written confirmation from the British Ministry of Supply on 12 February that 1,000 tons of sisal would be delivered to Irish Ropes in equal instalments over the next four months and that another 1,000 tons of binder twine would be released by June. It meant that Irish farmers would not go short of twine in 1943. Only the day before, Ryan had reminded the Seanad that 'flax is one of the most important crops we have from the point of view of barter, because it is the only crop we grow here with a fibre content.... If we did not grow flax I am afraid we would have very little bargaining power for these things.'[9] He must have been pleased with the outcome of the negotiations. That summer, an Irish civil servant would be bold enough to comment in a draft report that 'there is some reason to believe that this is possibly the only country in the world which has obtained its full requirements of binder twine in the current year'.[10]

Dulanty responded promptly to the final note by confirming that 30,000 acres would now be planted with flax and that orders would be placed with Mackies for ten turbine scutchers to be delivered in time for the harvest. A few days later, a delegation from the British Ministry of Supply went over to Dublin to sort out the final administrative details with the Irish Department of Agriculture and to meet the prospective managers of the Flax Development Board. While there, they approved the board's poster encouraging Irish farmers to grow more flax and assuring them of a ready market and attractive prices for all that they could produce. The deal was announced in the Irish papers in March. In April, Lemass told the Dáil that 2,000 tons of sisal and twine would now be released that year and that they would provide farmers with 'a bare sufficiency, but a sufficiency nevertheless, of binder twine'.[11] They would be made available to distributors in proportion to their previous years' purchases.

The Flax Development Board was incorporated as a company at the end of March. Over the next two years, it received £105,000 from the British Ministry of Supply. Most of this, some £100,000, was spent on grants to build, equip, and repair scutch mills. In order to retain parity with Northern Ireland, the grants were limited to 50 per cent of the overall cost. Another £8,000 was spent on building and repairing retting dams and £4,000 on training apprentices and buying seed-sowers. After staff costs and overheads of £10,000 were taken into account, expenditure exceeded income by £17,000. By early summer, the Irish Department of Agriculture could confirm that 27,500 acres had been planted with flax. Although this was still short of target, it was an increase of 40 per cent over the previous year.

The success of the arrangement meant that all parties were happy to renew it on similar terms in 1944. In November, Dulanty wrote to Shillidy to confirm the

'Farmers! Grow More Flax'—Flax Development Board poster, 1943. (*The National Archives, SUPP 14/570*)

Irish government's agreement in principle and to provide details of what stocks of seed, fertiliser, and other supplies were still held in Ireland and what it would require for the coming year. He was confident that the target of 30,000 acres would be met in 1944 and would be proved right. He also said that Ireland would now require 2,500 tons of sisal and twine to take account of its increased acreage under tillage.

When the final terms of the agreement were circulated to Attlee's committee in January, they incorporated Dulanty's proposals in full. In return for growing 30,000 acres of flax for exclusive sale to the UK, Ireland would receive a provisional 2,500 tons of sisal and other fibres; in addition, it would get 1,000 tons of flax seed, 1,300 tons of fertiliser, and 190 tons of batching oil, which Irish Ropes needed to make binder twine; and, because the country was keeping no flax back for its own use, it would also receive 29 tons of linen yarn for stitching shoes and harnesses and another half a ton for making ecclesiastical vestments and altar cloths. Once again, the only outstanding issue was securing the agreement of the Combined Raw Materials Board, which had yet to finalise its sisal allocation for the year. It was thought that Ireland would probably get less than it wanted. The delay made it difficult for Eric to plan. Two months earlier, Dulanty had asked for deliveries of sisal to be increased to 200 tons a month from the start of the year so that there would be time to make enough twine for the harvest.

A deal on jute was agreed at the same time. As this was less scarce than sisal, Goodbody's had already been getting 1,000 tons a year. Although most of this was for domestic use, some was needed to make the sacks and bags used to export foodstuffs to Britain. Now it would get another 1,000 tons specifically to make the yarn that British manufacturers used to make bags and cordage. What, if any, part Eric may have played in this is not known. However, he already had a close relationship with Goodbody's, and that autumn, he was invited to join its board to take the seat vacated on the death of its former chairman, eighty-nine-year-old Jonathan Goodbody.

However, things had changed by the time that negotiations came round for the extension of the deal to a third year. Britain was no longer in such desperate need of Irish flax. The opening of the Mediterranean after the invasion of Sicily meant that Egyptian flax was becoming available again while Allied successes in Europe in autumn 1944 meant that imports from Belgium and Russia were likely to resume the following year. On the day after D-Day, a meeting at the British Ministry of Supply decided that, although Ireland was on target to reach its 30,000 acres in 1944, this should be reduced to 25,000 acres in 1945. The ministry was also no longer inclined to agree high prices or to buy any green flax. It already had enough of its own and was struggling to find a use for it. In 1944, Eric was already being required to keep all his green tow—the shorter, coarser fibres that were removed during the combing process—which he could then either sell or struggle to spin into binder twine.

Dulanty was told of this new tougher approach when he wrote to Shillidy in September to open negotiations for 1945. Shillidy told him that his department was no longer prepared either to subsidise the Flax Development Board or to pay bonuses for increased acreage. He also suggested that, as it probably no longer wanted any green flax, Ireland's allocation of sisal should be reduced proportionately. The Irish Department of Agriculture passed the news on to Eric as soon as it heard. As a result, he went over to see John Ferrier at Flax Control's headquarters in Surrey at the end of October to try to get a definitive answer on whether his flax would be needed or not. The news came at a difficult time for him and his family. His parents had been over to Morristown the week before for a short holiday, both to celebrate Alice's seventy-third birthday and, more importantly, to make some final decisions about Harry's retirement and the future of H. and J. Jones. Their celebrations were muted by worries about Guy. In September, he, like all the airborne medical staff, had been left behind at Arnhem to look after the wounded after the failure of Operation Market Garden. When his parents visited Ireland three weeks later, they almost certainly did not yet know whether he was still alive. Four days after Eric's meeting with Ferrier, the *British Medical Journal* published a list of casualties in which Guy and three of his colleagues were still reported as missing.[12]

Eric told Ferrier that, while he was happy to accept a decision either way, he needed a definitive answer by Christmas. This would give him time to decide whether to extend his contracts with farmers for another year or just to scrap the scheme and sell off his plant. He had already decided that, if the British Ministry of Supply no longer wanted to buy it, there was no reason for him continuing to grow flax when it was clearly useless for making twine. For the past three years, he had subsidised farmers by paying them up front for their outlay on seeds and fertiliser. He did not want to pay them unnecessarily and, if the scheme was to be abandoned, he wanted to give them as much time as possible to revise their sowing plans. With compulsory tillage now up to 37.5 per cent of available land, or three times the level that had been set at the start of the Emergency, they might find it difficult to set about growing a new and less remunerative crop. Eric also told Ferrier that he was proud to have paid his own way. He had started the Tullow Flax Scheme before the Flax Development Board came into being and had never received any financial support from it, and although he had not made much profit, he had at least been able to recover the cost of his investment over three years. He had even considered retting his flax and had made some experiments with dew retting the previous winter. However, it was not a realistic option. Kildare and Carlow had no tradition of retting, and none of his farmers had been prepared to try it.

Ferrier told Eric that he could not yet give him a definitive answer as he had to get a better understanding of the situation in Northern Ireland. However, he promised to get back to him by the end of November. Afterwards, he sent a report of his meeting to Shillidy in which he praised Eric's contribution to the war effort:

> This morning I had Rigby-Jones down here, and he is the extremely able and efficient manager and driving force responsible for the astonishing success of

Irish Ropes's Mick 'Pinch' Burke operating a mechanical puller to assist a farmer with his flax harvest (given to the author by Benny Maxwell, 2014).

> Irish Ropes in flax production.... He is, I think, without doubt one of the best, if not the best, producer of green flax at the present time in the British Isles.[13]

However, Eric also managed to see Shillidy that day, who later reported back to a colleague that he was 'on the level'. Eric explained to him why green flax was unsuitable as a substitute for sisal for making binder twine and undertook to provide him with a more detailed written explanation as well as a summary of his scheme's financial performance. Remarkably, at a time when there were no computers or real-time financial reporting systems, he was able to send these off within a few days of returning to Newbridge. It shows the detailed grasp that he always had of his business. His reasons for the unsuitability of flax, which Dulanty later reiterated in his formal response to the British proposals, were simple. Spinning even barely serviceable yarn from soft fibres on machines that were designed for hard meant that the process to be repeated several times and so the machines were no longer available for their proper purpose; the resulting twine was too soft to work well on mechanical binders and reapers; and, because the fibre had not been retted to remove any gum that still adhered to it, it tended to rot even after it had been treated with copper sulphate.

Eric's four pages of detailed financial analyses showed that the Tullow Flax Scheme had generated revenue of £56,133 in 1943. Most of this, £35,613, came from the sale of 257 tons of green flax to the British Ministry of Supply at an average price of £139 a ton. Another £7,631 came from the sale of 243 tons of tow at £31 a ton—the fact that there was almost as much tow as fibre, and that it was worth much less, was one of the problems with mechanically-pulled green flax—while £11,651 came from the sale of 236 tons of flax seed. Most of the remaining £1,238 came from the sale of waste products for fuel. On the cost side, farmers were paid £26,560, or £11 a ton, for the 2,350 tons of flax straw that they harvested from their 1,115 acres, £8,284 was spent on providing Irish Ropes's staff to help them at harvest-time and on transporting their straw to Newbridge, and £13,309 on processing it at Irish Ropes's scutch mill. It left a gross profit of £7,980, most of which went towards recovering the cost of Eric's overall investment in equipment and facilities of £18,714. His plan was to write this off over three years in equal annual instalments of £6,238. It left him with an annual profit of £1,742, or 3 per cent of scheme's revenues, before taking any account of interest costs and tax.

Eric already knew that there was no future for flax after the war, whether retted or not. Back in February, in his return to the minister of industry and commerce

The flax store at Irish Ropes prior to scutching (given to the author by Benny Maxwell, 2014).

on the post-war planning of Irish industry, he had confirmed that he would close down the Tullow Flax Scheme at the end of the Emergency. In his view the Irish flax industry would be dead within ten years, just as it was after the First World War. Unless the government told him otherwise or the British asked him to continue for another year, he was planning to 'turn the key in the door and close down the plant'.

Eric started selling off his equipment as soon as Ferrier confirmed the British decision to stop buying his flax. The first items to go were a tractor and flax puller in January. They were bought by the Louth and Meath Flax Company in Drogheda, whose mill Eric had visited in the spring of 1942 when he was first thinking of growing flax. In May, a few days after de Valera had controversially called on the German ambassador to offer his formal condolences on the death of Hitler, Patrick Dawson placed notices in the local papers advertising the sale of the depot at Tullow and the scutching equipment at Newbridge. The war in Europe was over by the time that the first two scutchers were sold. Eric was eventually able to recover £4,200 of his original investment. He was still trying to sell the last of the equipment the following spring when the British Ministry of Supply enquired whether Irish Ropes or Goodbody's might be interested in buying any of its remaining stocks of green flax. They cannot have been surprised by their answer.

Although the British no longer wanted to buy Irish Ropes's green flax, they did eventually agree to release all of the sisal and jute that Ireland had requested. Irish Ropes would receive 1,500 tons of sisal and 480 tons of jute for making binder twine and another 500 tons of sisal for other ropes and cordage. At the beginning of January, when the negotiations were almost over, Ferrier wrote privately to Eric to express his regret at the decision to stop buying Irish Ropes's green flax and to thank him for both his contribution and the excellent quality of his fibre. The decision, he said, had been due to circumstances beyond his control. Eric forwarded the letter to his father who in turn sent it on to Peter. Although it has not survived, Eric sent an equally complimentary reply the following week:

Dear Mr Ferrier

I wish to thank you very much for your exceedingly kind letter of 8 January, to hand. We do not deserve any particular commendation for our effort to serve your Department especially when so much has been given in return. You and your colleagues have brought into the business an element of personal contact which has been wholly delightful to us and which would have provided a further incentive, had one been needed, to do our best. Mr Robertson has been enormously helpful and painstaking throughout his contact with us. It is largely due to him that all our men engaged in flax production came to know what they were aiming at. This seems to me to be the foundation of any good teamwork.

Our Department of Agriculture kindly advised us privately the moment they learnt that you would not be prepared to purchase green flax from the

1945 crop. We have sought a direction from our Minister in the matter of the disbanding of our equipment. Since our efforts to encourage farmers in Co. Carlow and adjacent counties to dam-ret their flax have been quite unsuccessful there is really no alternative before us as a private firm other than to close down.

If you should express a wish that the plant and equipment be kept intact, and without committing yourself officially in the slightest degree, we should be inclined to hold it together. Otherwise we propose to dispose of the equipment as it becomes redundant if, as we expect, our Government give their approval over the next week or two. We have had a number of enquiries for parts of this equipment and they might as well be put to useful service elsewhere.

We have all thoroughly enjoyed this adventure: it was really tough going in the first year and has demanded constant care and attention. We feel we have proved to our satisfaction at least that there is no one golden rule that makes for success in flax production. Indeed it is necessary to give the utmost care and attention to every single detail from start to finish. Few people outside Belgium seem to have realised this even now.

With renewed thanks and with the hope of seeing you many times in the future.

I am yours sincerely, Eric Rigby-Jones[14]

Ferrier forwarded Eric's letter to Shillidy with a note saying that he had been heartened by the spirit in which he had accepted their decision. Shillidy felt the same, writing back that 'it was with regret that we took the decision in regard to green flax from Eire, and that regret has been deepened after reading Rigby-Jones's letter'.[15] However, when he proposed writing a similar letter of thanks to John Dulanty after the deal was finalised in February, he was warned off by the Dominions Office:

We are glad to note that your negotiations with the Irish seem to be working out so satisfactorily. We appreciate that in the circumstances you would wish to make some civil remark to Mr Dulanty. The United Kingdom Representative in Dublin [Maffey] feels however that it is in general not advisable to go too far in putting in writing expressions of appreciation for the co-operation and assistance of the Eire Government in trade matters. He feels that this kind of expression may well be quoted by the Eire Government in the post-war period when they are trying to justify their policy of neutrality during the war.

May we therefore suggest that should any future occasion arise for making a civil remark to Mr Dulanty, it would be better not to refer to the Eire Government in this connection and to confine what is said to thanks to Mr Dulanty personally.[16]

It was a considerable achievement, and an example of how the British and Irish governments could co-operate to their mutual advantage, that in the last three years of the war Irish farmers never ran out of binder twine. Indeed, some must have earned windfall profits from their cultivation of flax. In 1944, 99 per cent of Ireland's exports of £29.5 million were still going to the UK. Its traditional agricultural products—live cattle, tinned beef, eggs, poultry, and beer—accounted for £21.8 million, or almost 75 per cent of them. Flax, at £1.1 million, was the next item on the list.

Meanwhile, the sisal growers in East Africa had also benefited in the second half of the war from their cultivation of a scarce but valuable commodity for which they had an assured market. Although production fell back from 172,000 to 123,000 tons in 1943, it was also the year when serious thought was given for the first time to how the industry might best be structured after the war. It would lead to another bitter struggle for control between merchants and growers and London and local interests. Meanwhile, growers saw the price of sisal increase by almost 50 per cent in the last three years of the war, from less than £19 a ton in 1942 to more than £27 a ton in 1945.

In September 1943, the Colonial Office produced an excellent and widely distributed five-page paper, 'Sisal Production in British East Africa', which sought to explain how the industry came to be where it was.[17] A month earlier, the governor of Tanganyika, Sir Wilfred Jackson, had sent Secretary of State for the Colonies Oliver Stanley a detailed memorandum explaining how the future of the industry had been under discussion for some time in both London and East Africa. Stanley would hold off replying until he returned from a visit to the region as part of his African tour that autumn. Before leaving, however, he had made an important statement in the House of Commons on the government's long-term colonial policy. Under its 'doctrine of trusteeship', the Colonial Office's goal, he said, was to make the colonies self-governing within the framework of the British Empire and, for this to be accomplished, they would first have to be made self-sufficient economically. Any other option was humbug. 'Political responsibility,' as he put it, 'goes ill with financial dependence.'[18]

In 1943, it was also suggested that a longer-term sisal contract, for the now standard period of the duration of the war and one year thereafter, might benefit all parties. The growers would have the confidence to invest in infrastructure and find it easier to secure the necessary funding for it while the government would be assured of a continued supply of hard fibre and control of a vital world market. It would also do away with the need for protracted annual negotiations. Any price increases would be based on increased costs of production, the figures for which would be produced and audited in East Africa. On this basis, an increase of £4 a ton was quickly agreed for 1943. However, the final contract was held up until after the end of the year in order to resolve disagreements on a number of important but annoying details such as who should be liable for any claims when sisal shipments were held up at the ports in East Africa due to the lack of shipping. The Colonial Office also suggested that there might be some mileage in the industry setting up its own co-operative marketing structure, which would effectively assume the role of the sisal controller after the war.

Too many parties now had an interest in the success and stability of the sisal industry. Although the original negotiations in 1939 and 1940 had been handled smoothly in London by the Sisal Growers Association and the Colonial Office they had both effectively been representing other parties, namely the growers in East Africa and the Ministry of Supply. Now there were many more parties to be kept happy, including the British government, the governments of Kenya and Tanganyika (who did not always speak with one voice), the hemp and sisal controllers, and, from 1942 onwards, the Combined Raw Materials Board and the Americans. It was a classic recipe for disaster where the many who demanded a final say in the approval of a contract had played no part in its negotiation and were either unaware of, or chose to ignore, the battles that had already been fought and the compromises and concessions that had already been exchanged by those charged with the negotiations.

What also became clear that year was the widening rift between the Sisal Growers Association in London, whose council members were closer to the imperial government and could claim a greater understanding of global commodity markets, and the growers in East Africa, whom it was supposed to represent. Many of the owners of the smaller non-British estates, which represented a majority in number if not in acreage, felt increasingly disenfranchised. It was a rift that had been exposed at the end of 1942 by Nicholas Bosanquet, the chairman of Consolidated Sisal Estates who was now also acting chairman of the Sisal Growers Association, when he sent a seven-page memorandum to the local growers associations in Kenya and Tanganyika that the Colonial Office then copied to the colonial governments. Although Bosanquet sought to address the longer-term competitiveness and efficiency of the industry, he did so from the standpoint of the major estate owners and tried to justify the role of the London association. He must have known that it would antagonise the smaller growers. Some of them he described as 'neither credit-worthy nor desirable members of the sisal-producing community' and others as men who 'through misfortune or for other good reasons have been unable to carry out their perfectly genuine intentions of building up a good estate which would rank as a worthy contributor to the supply of fibre from East Africa'.[19] Some in the Colonial Office agreed with him. However, Gerard Clauson, the assistant under-secretary of state, would comment in a file note that he was 'sadly unimpressed both by the literary style and by the intellectual content of this document'.

It was this rift between the smaller and larger growers that Eldred Hitchcock would in time be able to exploit. Meanwhile, he and his supporters were encouraged by the support of Oliver Stanley who wrote in his dispatch after his return from Africa that the London fibre merchants should not be allowed to recover the dominance that they had enjoyed before the war:

> It is common knowledge that before the war the price level of sisal was habitually lower than it should have been because, while the purchasers of sisal were few in number, well-organised and financially powerful, the sellers were wholly

unorganised and so weak financially that there were nearly always 'distressed' parcels of sisal on the market, which the owners were anxious to sell quickly at almost any price. During the war the arrangements for bulk marketing at fixed prices have overcome this difficulty, but it is obvious that if all organised selling disappears after the war, and individual producers are left to make their own arrangements again, the constant presence of weak sellers on the market will soon create a state of affairs no better than that which prevailed before the war. The question of marketing is of course primarily one for the industry itself, but I venture to suggest that it is one to which the [Sisal Growers'] Association should direct its early and earnest attention.[20]

12

A Family at War, 1944–1945

And all Britain will say to you—'You did your best; you all did your duty; and we are proud of you'.[1]

Eric's son, Peter, had wanted to join a destroyer on completion of his officer training in the autumn of 1943. He thought of it as 'the most dashing option'. Instead, he would join Coastal Forces as second-in-command of a motor torpedo boat, or MTB, which had a crew of two officers and eight men. After ten weeks at Coastal Forces' training base at Fort William in Scotland, he joined HMS *Mantis* at Lowestoft, one of the land bases for the MTB flotillas that operated in the North Sea. Their main role was to carry out night sorties against German convoys off the Dutch coast.

It was an exciting but dangerous life. The MTBs could reach speeds of up to 40 knots, or 45 mph. Given their risk of capture when they went in close to shore their crews had to attend regular lectures from MI9 and were issued with concealed compasses, silk escape maps, and strychnine capsules in case of interrogation. At sea, they wore 'goon suits', all-in-one kapok-filled outfits with a waterproof outer shell, along with heavy sea-boots, flak jackets, and tin hats. If they fell overboard, it would be difficult to stay afloat. They also carried commando knives. Peter and his crew were given theirs by Malden and Coombe Council in Surrey, which had adopted them. Each of the MTB's three screws was powered by a Spitfire engine. On a hot summer's day on a calm sea, it was exhilarating to plane across the water at high speed. At all other times, it was an extremely uncomfortable, wet, and cold experience in cramped and noisy conditions.

The officers were nearly all young men who had signed up for the duration of the war and their life was not unlike that of fighter pilots. They were determined to live it to the full and had little or no thought for tomorrow, let alone for their careers after the war. Many of the MTB commanders were highly decorated and had been awarded the DSC more than once. Peter wrote in his retirement that their life comprised brief moments of excitement punctuated by long periods of waiting. They were billeted at the Royal Hotel on Lowestoft's seafront and, once back in harbour after a sortie, never found any shortage of parties to attend or Wrens to dance with. With officers entitled to six bottles of spirits a month, the parties usually went with a bang. Like his father in the previous war, Peter was not allowed to say much about where he was or what he was doing. 'It's no use guessing where I am,' he told his grandparents a few weeks before D-Day in 1944, 'because you have nothing to go on.' As a result, his letters home often read like a constant round of parties. His parents and teetotal grandparents might easily have got the wrong impression. Peter probably did not mind.

Peter was now second-in-command to twenty-three-year-old Lieutenant Albert 'Harry' Harrington, DSC, on *MTB 88* in 22nd MTB flotilla. In April 1944, in the run-up to D-Day, they moved from HMS *Mantis* at Lowestoft to HMS *Beehive* at Felixstowe. As the day approached, life became more hectic, movements were restricted, and letters, especially those from Ireland, were delayed. Peter wrote home at the end of May that 'the tension gets one down and at the best of times coastal forces is not good for the nerves'. He was one of the few that went on all of the flotilla's thirteen sorties to lay mines in the Scheldt estuary. It was an unpleasant and dangerous task. Carrying mines not only increased the chances of being blown up but also slowed the boats to a snail's pace. Peter's friend, Douglas 'Dougie' Hunt, who commanded *MTB 245* and was awarded the DSC twice in 1944, compared it to having to drive a racing car at the speed of a bicycle.

D-Day was by chance Peter's twentieth birthday. Although his flotilla was confined to barracks all day, he managed to sneak out in the evening for dinner at a local hotel with a Wren friend. He told the waiter that his name was Mr Chance.[2] In August, after the lifting of the travel ban that had been imposed in the run up to the invasion, Peter was finally able to get home to Morristown for ten days' leave. It was the first time in two years that the family was all together. Michael, who would be eighteen in October, had just finished his final term at Rossall and was about to join the Fleet Air Arm after being accepted as a trainee pilot. Once he completed his basic training he was expecting to be sent to Canada or the US to be taught how to fly. The family was unlikely to be together again for some time. As one of the last to join up, Michael would probably be one of the last to be demobilised. For Eric and Harry, it meant that there was no immediate prospect of either Peter or Michael helping them out at Irish Ropes and H. and J. Jones.

Guy also managed to get home to see his parents at the Ruff in August. Since its return from Italy at the start of the year, the 181st Airlanding Field Ambulance had settled back into a routine of intensive training at its new base in Lincolnshire. The officers tried out new formations and methods of working, tested new equipment, and caught up with their surgical skills. In March, they had a visit from King George VI who was given a demonstration of the evacuation of casualties to a

The crew of *MTB 497*, April 1944, with Peter and Harry Harrington at the back. The masts and the flotilla's number on the shield have been blanked out to avoid identification.

MTB 496 in action.

dressing station. In May, Graeme Warrack, the ambulance's commanding officer, was promoted to assistant director of medical services, or senior medical officer, of the 1st Airborne Division and his place taken by Arthur Marrable from the 16th Parachute Field Ambulance. By autumn, Guy was the longest-serving officer in the ambulance. Within a month of leaving the Ruff, he would be taking part in Operation Market Garden.

The Allies' breakout from Normandy after D-Day had led to the liberation of Paris at the end of August and of Brussels at the beginning of September. Their senior commander on the ground, Field Marshal Montgomery, was now desperate to press on to complete the enemy's collapse and ensure that British and American forces reached Germany before their Russian allies. Somehow he was able to persuade General Eisenhower, the supreme Allied commander, to

The king's visit to the 181st Airlanding Field Ambulance, 16 March 1944. Standing behind the king are Colonel Warrack and Brigadier Hicks, who commanded the 1st Airlanding Brigade. Guy is thought to be the surgeon in the mask. (© *Imperial War Museum, H 36729*)

agree to his hastily conceived plan for Operation Market Garden. It called for the massed armour and infantry of General Horrocks's XXX Corps to make a rapid 60-mile push north from the Belgian border to the Rhine at Arnhem, the last major natural barrier before the German border. Horrocks's path would be cleared by British and American airborne troops who would be dropped behind enemy lines to secure a series of three critical river and canal crossings. The American 101st Airborne would secure the first bridges north of Eindhoven; the American 82nd Airborne would secure the bridges over the Meuse and Waal at Grave and Nijmegen; and the British 1st Airborne, with the help of the Polish 1st Independent Parachute Brigade, would capture the final bridge over the Rhine at Arnhem and then hold it until Horrocks arrived. It was expected to take him two days, or three days at most.

The date set for the start of the operation was Sunday 17 September. However, instead of setting off at first light, XXX Corps waited to watch the planes and gliders carrying the airborne troops into action. They did not move until the afternoon. Their late start and slow progress, after they were held up by clogged roads and enemy resistance, meant that they never reached Arnhem. It would indeed be a bridge too far. By the end of the first day, they had got only halfway to Eindhoven, their planned stop for the first night. In hindsight, Mongomery's plan was deeply flawed and should have been scrutinised more critically. It ignored the signs of the Allies' slowing advance due to exhaustion and logistical difficulties and underestimated the growing resilience of the Germany army. Some of the detailed planning was also faulty. The landing zones chosen for the 1st Airborne were on open heathland 6 miles to the west of Arnhem bridge. They were too far away for any surprise attack, especially as the Germans would almost certainly have guessed their destination as soon they picked up their massed planes and gliders crossing the Dutch coast. Furthermore, the plan called for only two of the division's three brigades to arrive on the first day. The 1st Airlanding Brigade, to which the 181st was attached, was to go in first by glider to secure the landing zones and take in all the heavy equipment, transport, and jeeps. The 1st Parachute Brigade, to which the 16th Parachute Field Ambulance was attached, would then follow on with its three battalions and make directly for the bridge while the 1st Airlanding Brigade remained behind to hold the landing zones until the arrival of the 4th Parachute Brigade with the 133rd Parachute Field Ambulance. They were due to arrive the following morning but would be delayed by fog in England until the afternoon. Finally, the 1st Polish Parachute Brigade would be dropped south of the river and close to the bridge on the third day. In total, the force comprised almost 12,000 men. However, only half of them reached Arnhem on the first day, and half of those then had to remain where they landed rather than make directly for the bridge. The opportunity to land in full strength nearer the bridge was missed. Fewer than 4,000 men would eventually get away: 1,500 were killed or died from their wounds and the remaining 6,500 were taken prisoner.

Lieutenant-Colonel John Frost's 2nd Battalion was the only one of the 1st Parachute Brigade's three battalions to reach the bridge. The other two battalions, which took different routes, were held up almost immediately by fierce enemy resistance and never managed to get through. Frost's first company reached the bridge in the evening. In time, it would be joined by men from other units, bringing its total strength to around 700. Over the next three days, their numbers would be whittled down as they came under increasing pressure from the enemy and help was unable to get through. On Tuesday, a short truce enabled 250 of the wounded to be evacuated behind German lines, and on Wednesday evening, the last 100 men, who were now out of ammunition and desperately in need of medical attention, finally had to surrender. They had held out for three days but had been let down by XXX Corps' failure to arrive on time. By then, Horrocks's men had only just secured the bridge at Nijmegen and were still 10 miles short of Arnhem. It was now clear that Operation Market Garden had been a failure. However, the endgame had still to be played out by the men of the 1st Airborne pinned down north of the river.

Although an airborne operation of this sort had been planned since D-Day Guy would claim later that he had been given only three days' notice of his involvement.[3] After a brief mishap with a broken tow rope, the Dakota towing his Horsa glider was one of the first to take off from Down Ampney airfield in Gloucestershire shortly after 10 a.m. on Sunday morning. He and his team had a good landing and by 4.30 p.m. had opened up a dressing station in two nearby houses. They performed their first operation there an hour later. Guy and his fellow surgeon, Captain Michael James, then worked in shifts through the night, performing eight operations and treating sixty casualties. By morning, they had 180 patients and were forced to move to larger premises in the nearby mental hospital. As they had no access to water or light, they could not perform much surgery and for the most part limited themselves to making the casualties comfortable for evacuation.

At this stage, everything was going to plan for them. Major Cedric 'Shorty' Longland and Captain Alexander 'Lippy' Lipmann Kessel, the two surgeons with the 16th Field Ambulance, were not so lucky. They followed the 1st Parachute Brigade into Arnhem and by evening had established themselves at the St Elizabeth Hospital a mile west of the bridge. The hospital was captured by the Germans the following morning, and although it then changed hands several times, it was firmly in German hands from Tuesday onwards. Although most of the men in the ambulance were taken back into captivity the two surgeons were allowed to remain at the hospital and continue working. Warrack even managed to speak to them by telephone on Tuesday morning before the town's telephone system was cut off.

As soon as the 4th Parachute Brigade arrived on Monday afternoon the forces held back at the landing zones were ordered forward to Oosterbeek, a leafy residential suburb midway between the landing zones and the bridge. There they commandeered a number of hotels. General Urquhart set up his divisional headquarters at the Hartenstein (now the Airborne Museum) while Warrack and Marrable established their main dressing station 250 yards further on at the Schoonoord. However, the mounting casualties led to Guy being ordered to set up the 181st's main surgical base 200 yards south of the Schoonoord at the Tafelberg. Until the previous day, it had been the headquarters of the local German commander, Field Marshal Model, who was having his lunch there when he was first told of the airborne operation. Since then, Arnhem's municipal medical officer, Dr Gerrit van Maanen, had quickly converted it into an emergency hospital. He would continue working there alongside the airborne medics with a number of Dutch nurses and his two children, seventeen-year-old Anje and medical student Paul. Guy was one of many to pay tribute to them afterwards, saying that they risked their lives to help the wounded only to suffer terrible retribution over the winter after the Germans forcibly evacuated the local population.[4]

Once they were established at the Tafelberg, Guy and Michael James operated in shifts for the next two days. James started immediately on Monday night with Guy taking over from him early the following morning. Unlike the two other ambulances, they were still at full strength and largely unaffected by the fighting around them.[5] However, the mounting casualties forced them to commandeer several other buildings. They also set up a second operating theatre and worked side by side during the day after it became impossible to continue operating around the clock. By then, most of the hotel's windows had been blown out and, as there was no way of blacking them out, they could no longer use lights to operate at night.

By Wednesday evening, when Frost's men at the bridge were finally forced to surrender, supplies of medicine, food, and ammunition were running low and new supply drops were failing to get through. When supplies of water and electricity to the Tafelberg were cut off Guy and James had to operate by paraffin lamp. As a precaution, they had already filled all the hotel's baths with water and, as a last resort, they could drain the radiators. That evening, a direct hit brought down the ceiling of the room that Guy had been using as a theatre and damaged his equipment and instruments. For the time being, he had to operate on a billiard table in the billiard room.

By then, with the bridge lost, the remaining forces cooped up in Oosterbeek were coming under increasing pressure from all sides. As airborne troops their weapons were no match for the tanks and self-propelled guns that the Germans were bringing up. Unless XXX Corps managed to get through, their situation would only get worse. They were now forced back within the 'Oosterbeek perimeter', a tight horseshoe-shaped defensive cordon half a mile wide that ran north for a mile and a half from the banks of the Rhine. The Germans called it the *Hexenkessel* or Witches' Cauldron. The Tafelberg was in the middle of its eastern side and thus in the front line of any German assault from the direction of Arnhem. It was now being subjected to continuous shell and mortar fire as the buildings around it fell in and out of enemy hands.

On Thursday morning, when he reckoned that he already had more than 2,000 casualties, Warrack decided to reorganise his medical units. He left Marrable in charge at the Schoonoord and established himself as the Tafelberg. With skilled

Drawing of the Tafelberg Hotel during the battle with Guy operating in the room at the back and Warrack standing by the stairs. The artist, Reg Curtis, was one of the paratroopers on whom Guy operated at the Tafelberg. (*Reproduced from The Memory Endures Facebook page with the kind permission of Reg Curtis' nephew, Geoffrey Holland*)

help at a premium he reckoned that he would be of more use there than at divisional headquarters at the Hartenstein. With Guy no longer able to operate Warrack seconded him as his assistant. Meanwhile, James, who was looking after around seventy or eighty patients, continued to operate until the ceiling of his theatre also came down on Friday morning. After that, no further surgery was possible. The medics could only do their best to make sure that their patients were fed and watered and kept as comfortable and pain-free as possible until either relief arrived or the battle was lost. The hotel and its annexes were now effectively in no-man's-land. Their floors were covered with dust and debris and the few remaining windowpanes had to be removed to prevent injuries from flying glass. The wounded, who now covered all the floor space and included a growing number of German casualties, behaved with a quiet and unyielding stoicism. They realised that the airborne medics and the Dutch doctors and nurses were doing all that they could to help them. As many as half of them were either wounded again or killed as they lay there helplessly. John Waddy was one of them. Once, when he sat up to look out of the window, he saw Warrack standing outside and screaming at the top of his voice, 'You bloody bastards! Can't anybody recognise a Red Cross?'

A still from the film, *Theirs is the Glory,* showing the wounded being carried into the Tafelberg Hotel when it was under German control. (*By courtesy of the Allan Esler Smith Collection and from the book, Theirs is the Glory: Arnhem, Hurst and Conflict on Film, by David Truesdale and Allan Esler Smith*)

Guy claimed afterwards that his new role as Warrack's assistant was effectively that of a quartermaster. His job was to go round the dozen or so buildings now occupied by the wounded to tell them what was going on and to provide them with food, water, morphine, and other medical supplies. He clearly relished the excitement. Warrack later described him as a cool customer who was without a nerve in his body and appeared to be totally oblivious to noise and gunfire.[6] Michael James thought that he was in his element and having the time of his life.[7] His jeep seemed to have picked up more bullet holes every time that he got back to the Tafelberg. At first, he had hooked it up to a half-ton trailer, which he then towed to a nearby pond and filled with water using a bucket. The trailer was now too riddled with bullets to be of any use.

As Guy's surgical team could no longer work, it took over the hotel's kitchens and cooked most of the food for the wounded. They had some unexpected luck when the ambulance's dentist-cum-anaesthetist, Captain Peter Griffin, spotted two stray sheep wandering near the Tafelberg and borrowed a Sten gun to shoot them. However, when Guy tried to drop one of them off at the Schoonoord later in the day, he was intercepted at the back door by Regimental Sergeant-Major Len 'Lofty' Bryson, who told him to scarper as the hotel was now in German hands. From then on, whenever he delivered food there, he had to push it through the kitchen windows.

By Sunday, when they had been holding out for a week, the situation had got so bad that Warrack decided to seek a truce so that the worst casualties could be evacuated behind the German lines. After getting Urquhart's agreement, he went off to the Schoonoord with Dr van Maanen and Lieutenant-Commander Wolters of the Dutch navy, who was acting as the Airborne's liaison officer, and made contact with one of the German medical officers. They were then taken into Arnhem by jeep for an interview with the German commander. Warrack was made welcome and treated well. He was given sandwiches and a bottle of brandy and allowed to load up with captured British supplies of morphine before being taken to visit the surgical teams still operating at the St Elizabeth Hospital. An armistice was duly granted, and during a two-hour ceasefire that afternoon, 300 of the wounded were moved to safety. It was an extraordinary incident in the middle of a fierce and bloody battle. Warrack later described it as a fairy-tale. By the time that he got back to the Tafelberg, it was in German hands. That evening, Father Dijker, a local priest who was helping to minister to the wounded, organised a service. Among the hymns, which were sung in English, Dutch, and German, was 'O God, Our Help in Ages Past'. It would be the inspiration for one of the most memorable scenes in the 1977 film of Cornelius Ryan's *A Bridge Too Far*, when the wounded who have been left behind sing *Abide With Me* as they wait for the Germans to arrive and take them prisoner. Thirty years earlier, Father Dijker, Dr van Maanen, and Warrack himself had all appeared in Brian Desmond Hurst's film, *Theirs is the Glory*, which was filmed on location a year after the battle with a cast of those who had fought there. Given the lack of contemporary photographs, it is probably the closest that we can now get to understanding what the battle was really like. It would be the most successful British war film for a decade.[8]

The following morning, Urquhart told Warrack that the remaining men were to be withdrawn across the Rhine that night but that the medical teams and padres would have to stay behind to look after the wounded. Guy described it as a bitter pill to swallow when he was told that evening. He had heard the British bombardment from the other side of the river and had thought that they were finally to be rescued. 'It never entered my head,' he said, 'that they weren't coming.'

The evacuation was completed in secret under cover of darkness. There was an eerie silence when dawn broke over the Oosterbeek perimeter the following morning and the Germans moved forward cautiously to tend to the wounded and to see what was left after nine days of fighting. With the help of two captured British medical officers, Lieutenant-Colonel Martin Herford and Captain Theo Redman, they had already started making plans for how to deal with the Allied casualties. Herford, who commanded the 163rd Field Ambulance, which was attached to XXX Corps, was not an airborne officer but had been taken prisoner on Sunday after crossing the Rhine to deliver much needed medical supplies under the protection of a Red Cross flag. He was not allowed to return. The following day, the Germans took him around the hospitals in Apeldoorn, 16 miles to the north of Arnhem, where he bumped into Redman, a surgeon with the 133rd Parachute Field Ambulance who had been taken prisoner after he was wounded when landing on the second day. Herford suggested that it might be possible to convert three of the blocks at the town's Koning Willem III barracks, which the Germans had already earmarked as a possible collection post for the walking wounded, into a temporary hospital and that, rather than being a drain on German resources, the British wounded could then be left under the care of their own medical staff to await the arrival of the advancing Allied forces. It led to the establishment of what the Germans officially recognised as the Airborne Hospital. It was perhaps a unique creation of the war. By Monday night, more than 800 casualties had arrived there, most of whom would leave the following morning for prisoner of war camps in Germany.

The Germans had laid on forty vehicles to transport the wounded who had been left behind after the British evacuation. The last of them would arrive at the barracks at 7 p.m. With them were 148 men from the airborne ambulances—100 from the 181st, thirty from the 16th, and eighteen from the 133rd—and more than 400 medics and stretcher bearers from the fighting battalions. The

The three blocks at Apeldoorn's Koning Willem III barracks that were converted into the Airborne Hospital in 1944 (author, 2019).

arrangements at the barracks were rudimentary at first. There was a shortage of food and blankets and the wounded had to sleep on straw on the floor. Some of the worst wounded did not make it; others had a very uncomfortable journey. Nevertheless, morale was still high and at last they were safe and able to rest. In total, there were about 2,000 of them distributed across a number of hospitals as well as 1,500 German wounded. Redman reckoned that at the start the barracks accommodated 1,800. By Friday, when he had assumed command and the first of the wounded had been evacuated back to Germany, Warrack was able to provide a precise headcount of 796 patients, of whom 526 were lying and 270 sitting. By Sunday, Red Cross parcels had started to arrive with cigarettes, soap, books, sheets, night shirts, and medical supplies.

Once there, Warrack appointed Herford as his second-in-command and set up separate medical and administrative sections under Marrable and Alford, the commanders of the 181st and 133rd ambulances. He reckoned that within a week the hospital was close to working properly. Given the number of casualties and lack of resources, it was an extraordinary achievement. The buildings were now clean and had proper kitchens, the food was better, the showers and baths were working, and the Germans had provided a quartermaster to assist Warrack's. Each of the three blocks now had its own clean and dirty ward as well as a recreation room. Guy was based in one of the two operating theatres while Michael James, who had been wounded in the heavy shelling of the Tafelberg on the final day, was running a small rehabilitation unit. Although they could hear the artillery of the advancing Allies, it would be six months before they were free again.

The Germans began transferring the wounded back to prisoner of war camps in Germany as soon as they were considered fit to move. Warrack and his team did what they could to delay and disrupt the process, protesting vehemently once when cattle trucks were provided as transport. Nevertheless, 750 men were moved within the first fortnight, 500 of them on a special hospital train where they were accompanied by seventy-four of the medical staff. Although other casualties had continued to arrive in dribs and drabs, there would soon be only 107 of the sickest men left at the barracks where they were now outnumbered by the medical staff. By the middle of October, there were eighty-seven patients and 125 staff. Warrack reckoned that the next train would probably be the last and that the Airborne Hospital would then be closed.

By then, many of the men had tried to escape from either the barracks or the trains taking them to Germany. Redman was among them. He jumped his train and was on the run for three months before he finally reached the Allied lines in February. Security at the barracks was lax. Most of the guards were old and had been issued with obsolete weapons. They were given the nickname of the Bismarck Youth. Warrack had originally ordered his medical teams not to escape as he needed them to look after the wounded. Now, as the number of their patients fell, he summoned a meeting of the 'entertainments committee' where it was agreed that they could now also try to escape. However, the men of the 181st, who formed the largest medical unit and so had been held back from accompanying the hospital trains, were told that they still had to stay behind to look after the dwindling number of patients.

On 16 October, Herford, Longland, and Lipmann Kessel were among the first of the medical officers to escape. Warrack, Marrable, and Guy helped them through the window of the operating theatre while they were meant to be performing an operation. As soon as their escape was discovered, the Germans moved the remaining patients and staff into a single block and announced that the medical staff would now be reduced to a team of just three officers, two padres, and twenty orderlies. Everybody else had to be ready to move at half an hour's notice. In addition to the two padres, Bill Harlow and Alan Buchanan, the three officers that the Germans had chosen were Warrack's second-in-command, Major Jimmy Miller, Marrable's second-in-command, Major Simon Frazer, and either one of the two dentists-cum-anaesthetists, Peter Griffin or Sandy Flockhart. However, when Warrack was told, he insisted that at least one of those who stayed behind had to be a specialist surgeon. And so Guy took Miller's place and had to give his parole that he would not try to escape.

Warrack had already asked Alford to accompany one of the trains taking the wounded back to prisoner of war camps in Germany. Now Marrable and James followed him. Both thought it their duty to stay with their patients rather than escape. Warrack, with his task almost completed, now made his own plans to escape. He had already found what he thought was a good hiding place in a cramped space above the ceiling in a cupboard in his office which he had then proceeded to provision and equip. His plan was to hide there until the Allies arrived. He went into hiding a week before the Airborne Hospital was closed, coming down only when the coast was clear, and then had to spend a second week there after the Germans did not immediately evacuate the barracks. Eventually, he felt that he could wait no longer. Before leaving he hid the minute book that he had found in his office when he arrived and that he had used to write up a detailed account of his experiences at Arnhem and the Airborne Hospital. It was recovered from his hiding place and returned to him when the barracks were liberated in April 1945. He used it as the basis for his 1963 book *Travel by Dark*, before presenting it to the Liddell Hart Centre for Military Archives at King's College, London.

The Airborne Hospital was finally closed at the end of October after the last men had been either moved back to Germany or, if they were too ill to move, transferred to another local hospital. It had been open for exactly a month. Simon Frazer assumed command after Warrack's sudden disappearance. With him now were four officers from the 181st (Guy, Peter Griffin, and the two padres) and five orderlies (Lance Corporals Budd, Mawditt, and Owen and Privates Jackson and Parker). From now on, they would be living and working together at St Joseph's Hospital in Apeldoorn, which the Germans had already commandeered as a military hospital. If the arrangements at the Airborne Hospital had been unusual then those at St Joseph's were even more so. Frazer and his team were given an upper floor to themselves to run as a POW hospital for all the Allied wounded in Northern Holland. They had space for around eighty patients who would be moved back to Germany as soon as they were considered fit to travel. They had the use of the hospital's operating theatres and x-ray facilities; they usually could get hold of enough medical supplies except for penicillin and plaster of Paris, which made it difficult for them to treat fractures; when they ran out of blood they gave their own, seven of them giving forty pints between them over the next four months; and, while they found most of the hospital staff obstructive, the German doctors were usually courteous and co-operative and showed a professional interest in their work. However, although they were prisoners of war, they were not held in a prisoner of war camp and so were not considered eligible to receive Red Cross parcels and letters from home.

It is not clear when exactly Guy's wife and family heard that he was safe. A week before the closure of the Airborne Hospital, Peggy had placed a notice in the paper asking for anyone with any information about her husband to get in touch with her. Personal notices remembering those who had died at Arnhem had started to appear in the papers the week before alongside requests for information on those who were missing. News that Guy was safe must have come through shortly after the *British Medical Journal* listed him as missing at the end of October. At the end of November, Eric and Dorothy received an airgraph from her nephew, Captain John Lloyd Davies, who was serving with the Royal Army Medical Corps in India. They had obviously passed the news on to him as he wrote back to say that he was 'very glad to hear that Guy is safe and presume from the way things are going that he will be away for a short time only'.

At first, Frazer and his team had only sixty-eight patients to look after, including seventeen amputees. Another 140 would arrive between November and April, 143 were taken back to Germany, and eighteen died.[9] There was a limit to what they could do. Frazer, who, like Warrack, had ordered them not to escape, set up two surgical teams under Guy and himself. Each was allocated two orderlies with the fifth on night duty. Between them, they would perform 178 operations. Having seen the quality of some of the German surgery, they insisted on retaining complete control over their patients' care from the moment of their arrival so that they could not be used as guinea pigs by any young German doctor keen to practise his surgical skills. At the end of November, Peter Griffin, Bill Harlow, and Private Parker were sent back to Germany with some of the patients. At the end of March, as the Allies closed in, Guy, Alan Buchanan, and Private Jackson were moved back to Haarlem with thirty-five patients. Frazer was left behind with his three remaining orderlies. They would all still be there when Canadian troops reached the hospital in the middle of April. As the Germans had not had time to arrange a proper evacuation, Frazer agreed to take charge of the whole hospital as long as he was left with enough staff. There were 800 German patients and eighty-five medical staff still with him when the Canadians arrived. His only regret was that Guy and his team were not there to help them celebrate. It would be another three weeks before they too were liberated. Like Frazer, Guy had been given a car by the Germans before they pulled out and told that he was now responsible for five hospitals.

Meanwhile, back in England, Peter's MTB flotilla had returned to Lowestoft after D-Day. In December, they were given new and faster boats from the British Power Boat Company. Their role now was mainly defensive. Most of their time would be spent patrolling the 'Z Line', an imaginary line some 30 miles off the coast of East Anglia that provided convoys with their first line of defence against E-boats. Once in position on the line, they cut their engines and lowered a hydrophone into the water to listen for the enemy's approach.

After a quiet few months, Peter was involved in what was possibly the final naval action of the war in home waters. On the night of 6 April, three MTBs—Alec Foster's *MTB 493*, with John Lake as first lieutenant; Jack May's *MTB 494*; and Harry Harrington's *MTB 497*, with Peter as first lieutenant—were on Z Line patrol when they found themselves up against six E-boats, which had been laying mines in the Humber estuary and were now returning at full speed to their base at Den Helder in Holland.[10] The two flotillas intercepted each other about 15 miles off the Norfolk coast north-west of Great Yarmouth. Their engagement was reported in *The Times* a few days later under the headline, 'E-Boats Routed in Fierce Actions: Night Attacks on Convoy Routes':[11]

> The Admiralty and the Air Ministry report that increased E-boat activity in the North Sea during the weekend resulted in one of the fiercest and closest fought battles yet carried out by light coastal forces of the Royal Navy against the enemy. The official announcement says that on two successive nights the enemy sent out strong forces of E-boats in an attempt to approach the Allied convoy routes between the East Coast and the liberated ports in Belgium and Holland. On both occasions they were intercepted, hotly engaged, and driven off. At least three E-boats were sunk and five others were severely damaged. Two British MTBs were lost.
>
> Aircraft of RAF Coastal Command shadowed the E-boats and reported their movement to warships patrolling in the North Sea. In one action our MTBs pressed home their attack to such close range that one of them was rammed by the leading E-boat and sank. Another MTB rammed the second enemy vessel in line, which was raked from stem to stern with gunfire and sank, a number of survivors being picked up. The remaining MTBs were fiercely engaging other E-boats at a range of about ten yards, scoring repeated hits with all guns.

Jack May's *MTB 494* sank after she was rammed by an E-boat and almost cut in two. He and all but two of his crew were killed or drowned. Alec Foster's *MTB 493* and another E-boat then collided with the wreckage. *MTB 493* lost her bows and, having tried unsuccessfully to return to port stern-first under her own power, had to be towed back when her engines overheated. Harry Harrington's *MTB 497* was lucky to be playing tail-end Charlie at the rear. She went to the rescue of E-boat *S176*, which was lying still in the water after sending up distress flares. Peter was told to lead the boarding party but suddenly realised that, after practising at the shooting range earlier in the day, he had never found time to reload and so was armed with only an empty revolver. Luckily, as Harrington approached the E-boat, he surprised her captain, Lieutenant Friedrich 'Stocki' Stockfleth, by speaking in German. When he got the worryingly precise answer, 'I have seriously wounded men: take us off—we shall sink in seven minutes', he thought that Stockfleth might have set charges to blow his boat and refused to take them off. Instead, he tried to tow her back to port stern-first but had to give up when his engines also over-heated. Another MTB, newly arrived on the scene, eventually took her in tow. *MTB 497* then spent two hours searching for survivors before returning to Yarmouth at dawn with three British and seven German sailors that they had rescued.

Peter later wrote in his retirement that 'it all happened in a matter of seconds and to this day, and after several amicable meetings with our former prisoners of war over fifty years later, nobody can be quite sure what exactly happened'. At one stage, he had to leave his empty revolver on deck when he went overboard to rescue men in the water. It was no longer there when he returned. Harry Harrington had to write to the War Office to exonerate him and prevent his appearance before a court-martial.

Throughout his life, my father had a firm sense of right and wrong. On this occasion, however, and to his lasting regret, he decided to go in for some souvenir hunting and relieved one of his prisoners of his Luger and Iron Cross. My brother and I remember coming across them in his naval suitcase in the attic when we were children. Although he later handed the Luger in to the police during a gun amnesty, it was not until after he had retired that he was able to track down the family of the sailor from whom he had taken the medal. He formally returned it to them when he visited Germany with the Coastal Forces Veterans Association. It had been a great relief, he told me shortly before his death, to have atoned for an action that had haunted him for most of his life.

Afterwards, Alec Foster was awarded the DSC and Able Seaman Frank Ibbotson of *MTB 497* the DSM. Harry Harrington, Peter, and ten others were mentioned in dispatches for their 'courage, determination, and devotion to duty in a successful engagement with a force of E-boats'.[12] The notice of the awards was published in the *London Gazette* on 26 June, three days after a belated twenty-first birthday party that Eric and Dorothy had organised for their son at Morristown. They must have been proud if perhaps somewhat surprised. All Peter had told his mother in a letter on the day after the encounter was that 'I am still quite busy and have had my share of excitement. There is very little else to report. I have been to a dance or two and am going to two more on Monday and Wednesday'. However, a few days later, he wrote in a letter to his sister that 'we are still kept pretty busy and I will have some good stories to tell you when I next see you. Also I have some interesting souvenirs.'

After the war, Peter found it easier to forgive the Germans than the Irish. He joined the Coastal Forces Veterans' Association after he retired and in 1991 made

MTB and *Schnellboot* reunion, Germany 1993. *From left to right*: John Lake, Peter, Alec Foster, Stocki Stockfleth, and Harry Harrington.

the first of several trips to Germany with Harry Harrington, Frank Ibbotson, Alec Foster, and John Lake. They had been invited as special guests to attend the biennial E-boat reunion in Cuxhaven and were met on arrival by Stocki Stockfleth and members of the crew of *S176*. They had all been prisoners of war in the North of England until 1947 and so spoke English with Yorkshire accents. They became friends and later visited Poland together for an armistice service as an act of reconciliation. Ireland on the other hand was a country that Peter could never forgive and which he did his best to avoid. He made his home in England after the war. His last visit to Ireland, thirty-five years before he died, was to attend his brother's funeral in Newbridge in 1972.

13

A Problem of Succession

It seems almost inevitable that I will end up in business, and more than likely I will have to rely on Irish Ropes, as much as I disagree with family businesses.[1]

Eric and his father must have started to think about the future of H. and J. Jones even before the outbreak of war. Harry turned sixty-five in 1937, and after very busy lives, he and Alice must have made some preliminary plans for their retirement. However, Eric was the only obvious candidate to take over the family business from his father, and he was now firmly established in Ireland and had little time to spare away from Irish Ropes. The pressures on him would only grow during the war. His sons, Peter and Michael, were fifteen and twelve when war broke out and still at school. It would be some time before they were able to make a contribution to either business, assuming that was what they wanted as a career. The war would only make it more difficult for Eric and Harry to come up with a final plan.

Harry made the decision to sell the ropeworks in Ormskirk as soon as war was declared. He must have known from his experience in the earlier war that it would be too much of a challenge to continue to run it on his own even if there was still the work to keep it going. He would now be left with just the wholesale cordage business and its warehouse and offices in Liverpool. Unless he and Eric came up with some arrangement with Irish Ropes, H. and J. Jones's future as a family business was likely to be short-lived.

Making fundamental decisions on the future of both businesses only became more urgent as the war progressed. Peter's letters home from 1942 onwards show that he was coming under increasing pressure from his father and grandfather to think seriously about his future after the war. However, they are by their nature one-sided and can only hint at what Eric and Harry may have been discussing between themselves. In any case, Peter was not inclined to think seriously about such things, however important they may have been to his family. Like most of his naval friends, he preferred to leave any decisions until after the war. Faced with the ever-present risk of death or injury, they wanted to live life to the full while they could.

Peter was clearly quizzed about his future every time that he went home on leave to Ormskirk or Newbridge. He usually put his thoughts on paper sometime after he got back. The first such letter was in April 1943 after he had spent a week at the Ruff before starting his officer training at HMS *King Alfred*. He was still only eighteen, and although the Germans had surrendered at Stalingrad and Montgomery's forces were making good progress in North Africa, there were no signs as yet of an early end to the war. The problem of his sending letters direct to Ireland from a British naval base meant that he usually addressed them to 'everybody' and then sent them to Ormskirk where his grandfather typed them up and distributed them. This time, however, he wrote directly to his father and began by hoping that he had recovered from his recent bout of depression. Although Peter makes no further reference to this, Eric had just come through what must have been the worst period of the war for him. It was still only a couple of months since the British government had confirmed that Ireland would getting enough supplies of sisal and twine that year in exchange for its flax:

> On my last leave Grandpa suggested that I take over the H. and J. Jones business after some years with him. I would very much like to relieve him but I think it is either a dying business or one that will need a lot of reviving. As far as I can see it is just merchanting and rather a rut. It seems inevitable, not that I mind, that I will have to go into Irish Ropes.
>
> I would hate to be condemned to a chair for the rest of my life. I am very slow at figures and don't find them very interesting. On the other hand I would be far more interested in the practical development of the new branches. At the moment I know a little about several things but don't know any subject well. Also I know little about rope-making which I should by now know a lot about. I think this is another reason for getting practical experience first. It is hard to make any definite decisions at the moment.

Peter never explained what he meant by the development of the new branches or where they might be. Perhaps H. and J. Jones was one of them. His opinion of its prospects was probably no more welcome for its being accurate. Although he had more respect for his grandparents than for anyone else, there cannot have been much appeal in having to work for several years with his seventy-year-old grandfather before he was deemed capable of running the business on his own, and if he wanted a career in business, which he almost certainly did not, Irish Ropes looked a much better prospect. He would have been very angry if he thought that his father and grandfather had contrived to offer him the short straw.

Peter had been thinking of a career in chemistry during his last year at school. However, his poor grades—a 'scraped' Higher School Certificate as he described them—were unlikely to lead to the first-class degree that was needed to stand any chance of getting a good job in industry. That said, he was keen to follow his uncles to university. Proximity meant that Guy and John Forshaw became more prominent influences during the war and their professional careers, as doctor and architect, offered an attractive alternative to the *fait accompli* of joining the family business.

He tried his hardest to knuckle down. He told his grandparents after his return from leave in Ireland in August 1944 that, with the prospects looking brighter after D-Day, he had started an accountancy course and was trying to keep his own accounts. 'Most people are taking something,' he told them, 'and I think it is a good opportunity to learn what it's all about, although I hope I shall never need it.' He had also dug out his old school science notes. He was trying to keep his family happy, but the war made him restless and he was less conciliatory when he wrote to his parents a fortnight later:

> Grandpa seems to be getting very anxious about my future and has sent me copies of interviews with Levers and a primer of book-keeping. I have given it very little serious thought and it will be hard to decide anything definite just yet. Apart from getting out of the navy and earning a living I have little ambition, I'm afraid, but I hope to get some ideas, especially if I go to university. It seems almost inevitable that I will end up in business, and more than likely I will have to rely on Irish Ropes, as much as I disagree with family businesses.
>
> At the moment I am almost reconciled to the fact that I will have to turn to business but you must admit the lives you and Grandpa lead do not encourage one. Very few people in our game have any definite ideas and we will all probably find it very difficult to settle down after such a life as we lead. I even find at the end of a week's leave that I want to get moving again and yet, when I get back, I think I could settle down quite happily.

Peter was also more interested now in spending time with his girlfriend. However, he promised to think more seriously about his future and to write again if he had any more ideas.

Although Eric told Ferrier early in 1945 that he had thoroughly enjoyed the adventure of the Tullow Flax Scheme, he was clearly now exhausted and depressed. Although he managed to keep Irish Ropes profitable throughout the war, he was finding it increasingly difficult to carry on, and with his focus limited to making sure that farmers never ran out of twine, he had had no time for five years to pursue his own plans for the expansion and diversification of the business. It was perhaps around now that he began to think seriously about his own future and that of Irish Ropes and his family in Ireland.

Peter was still sticking to his guns when he wrote to his parents in October 1944:

I am very well and, as you have no doubt heard, have been kept quite busy.... On the whole life is very much the same but we expect to have some changes very shortly. As regards the Liverpool business, I suggest you sell it unconditionally while you can. As a business on its own I can see little future in it but, as a branch of a larger firm, it may prove useful. Grandpa always seems to have put a great deal more into it than he ever got out. And, as for me, I think it will be a long time before I will be in a position to accept the responsibility. I think the Australian idea has possibilities but I can't see myself out of the navy for well over a year.

His timing could not have been worse. His letter almost certainly arrived while Harry and Alice were staying at Morristown to celebrate Alice's birthday and discuss the future of H. and J. Jones. They were still waiting for definitive news about Guy and the future of the Tullow Flax Scheme. At least Alice remained positive. She wrote in the visitors' book at the end of their stay that 'Granny and Grandpa crossed in big Douglas with windows clear under the hour, enjoyed every minute; enjoyed our meals like hungry children; had lovely presents on my 73rd birthday'. Some final decisions about Harry's retirement were almost certainly made while they were there. A month later, when Peter wrote to his grandfather for his seventy-second birthday, he hoped that 'by your next one you will be the retired gentleman.' Any ideas that Harry might have had about staying on to work with Peter had clearly been scrapped.

However, Peter's letter contained another bombshell. Like many of his fellow officers, he had quickly found a special girl among the Wrens who maintained their MTBs and shared their parties on shore. He had gone out first with Joanna, a leading torpedo operator from Wrexham. However, when she did not move to Folkestone with them in the run-up to D-Day, the girl that he asked out on his twentieth birthday was Muriel, an 'electrical' Wren whose parents lived nearby. It was their first date and Peter had to be back by midnight for his four-hour turn on watch. Now, four months later, Peter told his parents: 'I am afraid things seem a lot more serious than I thought. I hope you will trust in my good judgement to do nothing rash, so don't worry. But, on the other hand, I don't want you to be too shocked all at once'. They would soon be left in no doubt about how he was thinking. In November, when he heard that his friend, Dick Bailey, whom he had met during their basic training in 1942, had got engaged, he wrote home to say that 'he's beaten me to it'.[2]

Peter was even more set in his views when he wrote to his parents the following March shortly after his return from leave in Ireland. They had clearly had a falling-out:

I was glad of the spell of leave and enjoyed it very much in spite of disappointments. I hope you will get over the disappointment of my not being ambitious to enter Irish Ropes. It will mean a break in a long line (too long) of eldest sons, but I hope Michael will be able to relieve you of your load. But still

I am no further forward, yet I am seriously considering architecture. It will be on my conscience if you can't get rid of Irish Ropes as Grandpa is tied to H. and J. Jones but I can't muster the interest for business. It is not that I am afraid of work but I want to enjoy life while I am working. But nevertheless I cannot think seriously yet, apart from the fact that I would very much appreciate a university course. This should be very much easier if the government lives up to its word— yet don't forget I am not qualified for Oxford or Cambridge.

He wrote again along the same lines in April, a few days after his encounter with the E-boats: '... it will be a great relief to get Liverpool wound up and I only hope you will be more fortunate when the time comes'. They are probably the only references to Eric ever having considered getting rid of Irish Ropes. Unfortunately, they are too brief for us to know precisely what he was thinking. However, the Industrial Credit Corporation was almost certainly already planning to sell its shares in the company as soon as the war was over and it could find a buyer. It had now held its 50 per cent stake for nine years and had probably never expected to hold it for more than ten. Peter was also wrong to imagine that in previous generations the control of the family business had always passed smoothly from eldest son to eldest son. Nothing could have been further from the truth. The only time that it happened was when Eric became a director on his twenty-first birthday in 1918. Then there had been three other directors—his father, grandfather, and uncle—to help him and to provide proper continuity and succession planning. In the two generations before then, Harry and John had both had difficulties when they joined the family business. Harry had been asked to leave the firm temporarily after falling out with his uncle, Robert, and John had had to join forces with his older brother, Henry, to push their father into an early retirement so that they could develop the business in the way that they wanted.[3]

Shortly after VE Day, *MTB 497* was taken round the coast to Poole Harbour and 'paid off'. However, it would not be the end of Peter's naval service. He and his friends expected to be posted to the Far East where the war was still being fought. Before then, he was entitled to two months' leave, which meant that he was able to get back to Morristown for a belated twenty-first birthday party. Nearly all the guests that his parents had invited came from Irish Ropes, including Bernard and Monica Roche, Horace and Enid Davies, Alec Nisbet and Dorothy Baxter, and Jim Cosgrove, the company doctor. Perhaps Eric thought that they might be able to persuade his son to join the company. Michael was still in Canada and Ann at school in Liverpool. However, Guy and Peggy made it over in the brief gap between his release from captivity in May and his return to active service in July. At least, they could provide Peter with some moral support. Although the Forshaws could not make it, John had sent his godson Sacheverell Sitwell's *British Architects and Craftsmen* as a birthday present. Inside he wrote a note supporting his recent choice of architecture as a career: '... when Inigo Jones, our first architect of the English Renaissance, was more than eighty but still working hard, Christopher Wren was only twenty-one and not until Wren was over thirty did he forsake Science for the Mistress Art'. Eric and Dorothy may not have appreciated the sentiment.

The following month, Guy rejoined the 181st Airlanding Field Ambulance in Norway as its second-in-command. Arthur Marrable, now also released from prisoner of war camp, had arrived three weeks before him to resume command. The ambulance had been sent there with the 1st Airborne after VE Day to help in the aftermath of the German evacuation of the country. Its main role was to run a 250-bed hospital in a school near Oslo and to look after the Russian prisoners of war who had been left behind by the Germans and were in an appalling condition. It eventually returned in September and was told in the middle of October that it would be disbanded at the end of the month. When Marrable was transferred immediately, Guy was left as its acting commanding officer for the last few days of its existence. The following year, he became the first honorary secretary of the Airborne Medical Society. When the Territorial Army was reformed in 1947, he was promoted to lieutenant-colonel and given command of the 4th (Parachute) Field Ambulance based at the duke of York's HQ in the King's Road, Chelsea. It was one of three field ambulances in the Territorial Army's 16th Airborne Division. It was eventually disbanded in 1956, Guy having served as its assistant director of medical services, or senior medical officer, for five years to 1955.

Peter moved on from Morristown in July to spend some time with his grandparents at the Ruff. Muriel joined him there for a few days—it was probably the first time that she met any of his family—but had to return early for an interview. Peter then went down to spend the weekend with her in London. They announced their engagement in *The Times* three days later. 'I think it is about time I got back now,' Peter wrote to his parents the following weekend, 'as I seem to be always arguing with Grandpa. Naturally, he has been planning everything so I tend to be very carefree and secretive. Two months is a lot too long, but I have enjoyed the rest very much.' Two days later, he was on his way to Australia.

Peter was one of 2,400 sailors on board the troopship RMS *Orion* when she left Liverpool on 8 August. With them were several hundred Anzac servicemen who were returning home after their release from prisoner of war camps in Germany. The first atomic bomb had been dropped on Hiroshima two days before their departure; the second was dropped on Nagasaki just a few hours after they left. Japan surrendered a week later when *Orion* was four days away from the Panama Canal. Although a magnificent dinner was held on board to celebrate the final end of the war, she was now too far into her voyage to turn back without risking a mutiny by the Australians and New Zealanders. They would receive a hero's welcome when they arrived home. Flotillas of small boats, massive crowds, military bands, and members of the government all turned out to greet them when they docked in Wellington on 4 September and Sydney five days later.

Peter found a stack of letters waiting for him in Sydney from Muriel, Michael, Guy, and his parents. It would be a while before he received any more. Once he reached the naval barracks on shore, he was put on indefinite leave. With the war over, he was now on the other side of the world with nothing to do and no

Right: Guy on exercises with the Territorial
Army, 1952. (*Given to the author by Tim
Rigby-Jones, 2018*)

Below: Peter and Muriel's engagement
photograph, 1945.

immediate prospect of getting home. He felt homesick without any of his friends from Coastal Forces to keep him company. 'I look at my pictures of Lowestoft and MTBs nearly every night,' he told his parents a fortnight after his arrival, 'and wish I was still with the old crowd.' Luckily, he had already got in touch with Alice's cousins, the Shorters, who lived only 6 miles away in Paramatta. They quickly took him under their wing and invited him to move into their home. 'They are giving me a wonderful time here,' Peter reported home, 'and I am very thankful to have somewhere to go.' They arranged trips to the theatre, taught him to surf on Manly Beach, introduced him to friends, and encouraged him to see as much of the country as he could. However, Peter was loath to go too far in case he missed the chance of a passage home. Then, three weeks after his arrival and just as he was setting off to spend the weekend with the Shorters at Newport Beach, he heard that he had been given a job. He wrote home immediately:

> I have got a job taking a motor fishing vessel to Hong Kong. It will be my first command and should be a very thrilling adventure. I have never been aboard one but have seen them often enough round the country. I will know more about it tomorrow when I go aboard. They will be brand new crews so they will have to be worked up, not least myself. It will be a bit of a change, stooging along at seven knots, eight with a pinch. In an MTB you had three engines to play about with: these will be single screw—Stand by to ram! Fender! I am looking forward to it and hope we call in at some interesting places.

The Royal Navy had only just returned to Hong Kong after the Japanese surrender. Admiral Harcourt would stay in charge there until Sir Mark Young, the governor who had surrendered the colony to the Japanese on Christmas Day 1941, returned in April. He was desperate for as many vessels as he could lay his hands on so that he could get the harbour working again. Peter's was one of a small flotilla of seven motor fishing vessels (or MFVs) and three tugs, which, on arrival in Hong Kong, would be used for general duties such as carrying stores and acting as tenders.

The 5,500-mile voyage was expected to take them two months. Peter would have the opportunity to see places that he might otherwise never have seen and that he might never get the chance to see again. As he told his parents, 'this trip is going to be quite an adventure. I only hope we miss the typhoons and don't get lost. It may be a little while before you hear from me.' Although he expected any letters from home to be held for him in Hong Kong, it did not stop him writing regularly to his family and daily to Muriel. He also kept a detailed illustrated log of the voyage.

Peter's first impressions of *MFV 1101* were disappointing. He thought her the dirtiest ship that he had ever seen. It would be quite a change from an MTB. Although she was slightly longer, she was slow and top-heavy. She would be difficult to steer and would roll in the slightest swell even when her sails were hoisted to stabilise her. At least her crew would not be pounded as they were on an MTB. The official view was that she was uncomfortable but quite seaworthy. However, one member of the crew told a local journalist that she would roll on wet grass; he was not looking forward to Christmas.[4]

Peter and his crew spent the next few weeks sprucing her up and getting ready for departure. Their small flotilla finally slipped out of Black Wattle Bay in Sydney Harbour on the morning of 25 October. By then, Peter's brother, Michael, had arrived home from Canada. He had been discharged from the FAA after only a year's service and was back at Morristown in time for a belated nineteenth birthday party. Peter expected him to start at university almost immediately. It would give him a three-year head start on his older brother.

The flotilla took its time sailing up the east coast of Australia. Four-day tramps were interspersed with longer stopovers in port to re-provision, carry out running repairs, and strengthen the boats for the open sea. The MFVs were quickly found to be unreliable and in poor repair. They often fell behind when the flotilla was on the move or had to be taken in tow by one of the tugs. The crews also found provisions hard to come by. They had to scrounge whatever they could from American and Australian bases. At one base, where there had been previous reports of thieving, the Royal Australian Navy refused to provide any supplies or allow them ashore except to take showers. While at sea, fresh water was rationed

MFV 1101 under sail.

for drinking only. They had to use sea water to wash themselves and their kit. They had little in the way of fresh fruit and vegetables and lived out of tins when they could not catch any fish. In time, they would become dehydrated and short of vitamins.

Peter's time in Coastal Forces had made him a good navigator and naval signaller. When they were under way, he sat on a box by the wheel and steered with his feet while keeping a lookout for dolphins, whales, sharks, and flying fish. On their way up the coast, he bought a wedding ring for Muriel on a stopover in Brisbane. They finally reached Townsville, halfway up the Great Barrier Reef, in the middle of November and stayed there for a week before setting off on the 800-mile journey across the open sea to New Guinea. 'I don't know what gives you the idea that this is going to be a joy ride,' Peter wrote home, 'remember we aren't very big and the weather is pretty bad at this time of the year.' 'I am very fit,' he added, 'disgustingly brown and my beard is the envy of the flotilla.' Things would get tougher as they sailed on towards the equator and into the typhoon zone.

Once out on the Coral Sea, the MFVs began to roll alarmingly. The instruments that recorded their sway hit their limit of 45 degrees from the vertical and then could go no further. After five days, they finally reached Discovery Bay at the southern tip of New Guinea where they were met by natives in canoes. They were now in what had until recently been a war zone. Like his father before him, Peter was able to experience for himself what life was like in the immediate aftermath of a great war. The US Navy had already evacuated their nearby base at Gili Gili, but only after destroying all that they could not take with them. It was also unbearably hot and they were plagued by mosquitoes. Peter thought it 'one of the most god forsaken plots on this earth. I pity anyone who had to fight in this area. It must have been absolute hell; the smell is enough to put anyone off. I never want to hear about the spicy breezes wafting over Pacific Islands again.' There was no mail waiting for them.

With food still difficult to come by, it was impossible not to notice the rubbish that the Americans had been left behind. Peter wrote home in the middle of December:

> The beaches are littered with landing craft and there are signs everywhere of Yankee extravagance. They are gradually going and what annoys us is the wilful destruction of anything useful. They burnt bottles and bottles of beer and fresh and tinned food when we are so hard up. We managed to get some beer for the troops from the Dutch and the Javanese have been kind. There are large numbers of Jap prisoners working for them and they salute you everywhere.

After a week, they moved off around the north coast of the island and on across the equator towards the Philippines. Foul weather and blinding rain meant that they did not finally reach the Indonesian island of Morotai, midway between New Guinea and the Philippines, until three days before Christmas. It was still only four months since the Japanese 2nd Army had surrendered there to the commander-in-chief of the Australian military forces, General Sir Thomas Blamey. At least Peter found that there were forty-four letters waiting for him, his first news from home in almost two months.

The MFVs were now all in a bad shape. It would take some time to fix them before they could move on. It did not prevent them celebrating Christmas as best they could. 'We haven't done too badly at all,' Peter told his parents, 'with a good helping of turkey, pork, Christmas pudding and oranges and apples. It is the first fruit we have had since Australia. As I told you I haven't been too grand so I went to see the doctor in our escorting frigate. He puts it down to lack of salt and vitamin C.' He opened the bottle of Australian burgundy that he had bought in Sydney and shared the fruit cake that the Shorters had given him before he left. It was his fourth Christmas away from home. He would miss the large crowd that had gathered at Morristown to celebrate the first peacetime Christmas in seven years. As well as their immediate family, Eric and Dorothy had invited ten guests including Horace Davies and his family and Peter's fiancée, Muriel, whom they would all be meeting for the first time. It must have been a daunting experience for her. Peter hoped that she would make the right impression and that his parents would make her feel at home.

Meanwhile, the flotilla was expecting to stay at Morotai for several days to complete its repairs before moving on to the Philippines and the American base at Subic Bay on the island of Luzon. As yet, no decision had been made on whether the MFVs would then be seaworthy enough to cross the South China Sea to Hong King or whether they would have to be loaded on to a larger ship. 'There are all sorts of typhoons and tornadoes which suddenly get up in these waters,' Peter wrote home on Christmas Day, 'we can take the normal sort of sea fairly well but these have a habit of breaking on the top of the wave. Then you are likely to get a hundred tons of water coming on deck. As we only weigh a hundred tons it would be unfortunate.'

They finally left Morotai on 30 December. After crossing the open sea under the escort of HMS *Woodcock*, they sighted the Philippine island of Mindanao at first light on 1 January.[5] After two days struggling around its western coast against a strong current that almost brought them to a standstill, they put in at the small anchorage of Santa Maria. It was a beautiful spot with coral reefs and jungle that came down to the shore but without any no fresh water. After three days, they sailed on through the archipelago to Subic Bay. There they were told that they would be sailing the final 700 miles to Hong Kong under their own power. In good weather, it was a voyage of only four days. Even so, the MFVs would have to be strengthened once more, and their slow progress to date meant that they were now in the stormy season and there was no guarantee that the weather would hold. They ended up staying in Subic Bay for two months.

It was an extremely tedious interlude, not least because they were not allowed ashore at first because of what Peter described as 'trouble between blacks and whites'. With sharks making it dangerous to swim in the sea, they had little to keep themselves occupied except alcohol and visits to the cinema on shore or on one of the larger navy vessels. After four weeks, Peter was fed up:

> We are all in a terrible state of lethargy and depression in which we cannot concentrate and are unable to muster any enthusiasm. Half the day we have nothing to do and the rest there is no need to do anything. Two have been carted off as insane, one with rheumatic fever and all are suffering from a disease of 'I couldn't care less.' Last night we wandered aimlessly about thinking of something to do. We tried liar dice and cards for about five minutes but gave up as we just couldn't concentrate.

Drinking was the only alternative; it was terrible, he admitted, but better than going mad. At least they were now getting regular mail. Peter felt better the next day when he received twenty-one letters, including eleven from Muriel.

At least their extended stay at Subic Bay gave him time to think about his future and to try to patch up his relationships with his parents and grandparents. It was not something that he had been able to avoid even while he was away. Alice's cousin, Elaine Shorter, had written to him shortly before he left Sydney to tell him that 'we received a letter from your grandfather yesterday which has left us in a very delicate situation and will require some diplomacy to deal with satisfactorily.

Peter and his crew in tropical uniform at Subic Bay. Peter is leaning out of the wheelhouse on which his drawing of Popeye is just visible.

It will not be necessary to report this in triplicate to all parties concerned! I think it will be a battle of the Obstinates but you may hear more of this anon'. She never made it clear what the problem was. However, Peter wrote at length to his father early in the new year to pour oil on troubled waters:

> Thank you very much for your interesting letters and all you are doing to help my release. I hope you are well and have now got more help. I often wished I had wanted to follow the business and you must feel very disappointed. I am determined to be a credit to you all and want to repay everything. That will be a big job but probably best expended on the next generation.
>
> I hope you enjoyed having Mu for Christmas and feel happier about the whole thing. If I had been in your place I would have been much more doubtful. I can't see any barriers which cannot be removed and, while we are young, nothing should be impossible. I am very relieved that she has got such a good job and one that I know she will be crazy about. She is a determined young woman but has a sensible outlook as well. If there hadn't been a war I would never have dreamt of such a thing but I have no regrets.
>
> As to funds I don't want you to have any obligations. I think the university grant is £250 a year which is quite reasonable. My bank balance is pretty healthy and I have a lot of back pay to come. I haven't been paid since June and then there is tropical allowance, Japanese campaign money, and hard lying money.[6] As long as I get out by October I am not fussy about how. But I long to come home now that everything is turning over to peace. We get no news at all so feel even further away. I am sure Britain has more opportunities ahead of her if we only advertise. Few people abroad realise how many war inventions and discoveries have been due to us. I only realised the other day that Liberty ships were a British design.[7] I get very jingoistic these days but am very proud of our war record. The British Council have been doing good work and have published several reports of achievements.

He signed off as 'your loving and grateful son'. Muriel was now keen for them to marry as soon as he returned, while he was still in uniform and before he started at university. His parents clearly thought otherwise. Peter found himself caught in the middle, writing home at the end of January that Muriel 'seems to think it will come as a shock so I hope she is wrong'. Although there was still a lot to decide, including where and how they would live while Peter was a student, his family were not slow to offer advice or make decisions on their behalf. He was now expecting to start at London University in the autumn where John Forshaw's collaborator, Patrick Abercrombie, who had received a knighthood in the New Year Honours list, was still professor of town planning. He would be kept busy during term time and spend most of his holidays travelling. If Muriel continued to live in Horsham, as she wanted, Peter would be able to get down to see her at weekends. Otherwise, she would have to find a job in London. Peter wrote to his parents again in the middle of February:

Mu still seems very worried as to our future, mainly because plans being made at home seem to take no account of her. Apparently Grandpa has written to her telling her how I am to live at Cheam [with the Forshaws]. This is the first I have heard of it so I hope it is only an idea. Michael, who is, I am glad to say, on our side, tells me Mother is very dubious about the financial situation. I quite realise our marriage will not be easy at the beginning but it is the only reasonable solution under the circumstances. If Mother put herself in Mu's place I am sure she would be batty by the time I had qualified. From students I have gathered a pretty fair idea of what the life will be like. I have explained it all to Mu and she's determined to be an asset rather than a liability. I can understand a type who do fail at university because of their being married but I think I have proved that I am not that sort. It is very difficult to plan out here when I know so little of what is going on at home. So I am saying nothing definite and will wait until I see you all again. But I am sure Mu would appreciate a letter with your ideas upon the subject.

With letters taking at least two months to arrive from Ireland, there was, as Peter realised, little point in discussing things further until he got home. But first he had to get to Hong Kong, and there seemed to be no immediate prospect of that. Larger ships that had attempted the crossing had already been forced to turn back. However, matters were not allowed to lie. At the beginning of March, just before leaving Subic Bay, Peter felt compelled to write to his parents to say that their last letters to him 'were quite as much a shock to me as mine seemed to you. Anyhow I refuse to talk about it until I come back which I hope will be about June.' Two weeks later, when he had finally reached Hong Kong, he wrote again in a more conciliatory mood:

> Your letters were very helpful and I realise that you have the advantage of experience. For the moment I am not making up my mind either way and will drop the matter till I get home. However bad it is at home I want to square off all our troubles and worries. I can yet see my coming to you for a job. It is so hard to foresee the future and after all one has only the one life to live.

A decision had finally been made to load the MFVs on to a larger ship for the final stage of their voyage to Hong Kong. Their masts and superstructures had to be dismantled, and at the end of February, *MFV 1101* was the first to be hoisted aboard MV *Empire Charmian*, a 5,700-ton cargo ship that had been specially designed to carry heavy loads. It took a fortnight for them all to be loaded. They eventually left Subic Bay on 14 March and arrived in Hong Kong two days later. It was almost five months since they had left Sydney. Peter found sixteen letters from Muriel waiting for him.

It would be another fortnight before *MFV 1101* was unloaded and her crew finally paid off. Peter hoped to have some time for sight-seeing and souvenir-hunting but otherwise wanted to get home as quickly as possible. After a week, he reckoned that he had seen all that there was to see and had spent almost all his money on souvenirs. He blamed the American sailors who were unused to bartering and so willingly paid the first price that they were offered. Meanwhile, he was given a job as signals officer on a frigate that was being used as overflow accommodation. Apart from taking his turn as duty officer every five days, he had little to do, he said, except drink gin and play liar dice.

It was not until the end of April that Peter received his demobilisation notice and then another three weeks before his relief arrived to take over as signals officer. By 1 June, when he embarked on HMS *Suffolk* for the voyage home, he had been in Hong Kong for eleven weeks. Before sailing, he sent off a telegram to the Ruff saying that, as he would soon be home, there was no point in their sending him any more letters.

HMS *Suffolk* reached Colombo after a week at sea and left again two days later for Aden, the Red Sea, and the Mediterranean. She finally docked at Portsmouth on a damp evening at the end of the month. In the eleven months that he had been away, Peter had sailed around the world at the Royal Navy's expense and had passed through both the Panama and Suez Canals. In stark contrast to the rapturous reception that RMS *Orion* had received on its arrival in Wellington and Sydney, there was nobody there to greet HMS *Suffolk*. It was a dismal and dispiriting end to Peter's four years of naval service. When he left the ship on 1 July, he was given a fortnight's foreign service leave and eight weeks' resettlement leave. At the end of it, on 7 September, he would cease to be a naval officer. However, he was allowed to wear civilian clothes and start a new job immediately. It was only later that he found out that he had been promoted to lieutenant for the last three weeks of his active service. It had taken effect automatically on his twenty-second birthday, which he had celebrated on board HMS *Suffolk* two days before she reached Colombo.

Instead of going straight home to Ireland, Peter went first to Felixstowe to try to patch things up with Muriel. Their relationship had come under increasing strain while he was away and at some point they had broken off and then renewed their engagement. It was not something that Peter ever mentioned in his surviving letters home. In fact, he did not speak of it until he wrote his memoirs in his retirement. However, it is noticeable that Muriel features less frequently in his letters after he got to Hong Kong. He had kept in touch with his first girlfriend, Joanna, whom he described as still being 'a very bright flame' even though she was now engaged, and, as he now had more opportunities to meet WAAFs and Wrens, he started going out with a former Irish fencing champion from Dublin.

Although he and Muriel then went back to Morristown for a fortnight's holiday, their reconciliation would be short-lived. By all accounts, she was never able to win over Peter's family. His sister, Ann, disliked her from the start and to this day believes that she was only after his money. Muriel, on the other hand, had had to put up with his family trying to plan her life. After some last-minute cramming from an Irish priest so that he could pass the necessary Latin examination, Peter started at London University's Bartlett School of Architecture in the autumn. Just as his grandfather had planned, he stayed at first with the Forshaws in Cheam. Any ideas of a quick wedding were now past. Peter wanted to hold off until he got his degree in 1951. Piqued, Muriel left her job in Horsham and enrolled as a student at an agricultural college in Essex. Although she went to Peter's first Christmas party at the Bartlett, she was not prepared to wait that long. Their engagement was called off once more. This time, it was not renewed. Not long afterwards, Muriel started going out with another farming student. They were married in the summer.

There had been more surprises waiting for Peter when he returned to Morristown in July. He was probably already feeling fragile. His relationship with Muriel was on the rocks, demobilisation had brought a sudden and dispiriting end to four years of adventure and excitement, and he was about to start a new life as a student in London. Now he heard of everything that had happened while he was away. H. and J. Jones had finally been sold the previous autumn and Harry and Alice were now preparing to leave the Ruff after more than forty years.[8] It was where Peter had been born and where he had spent much of his childhood. Now he might never see it again. He told his grandparents that he was going to miss it almost as much as them. By the time that they celebrated their golden wedding in September, they would be settled in a new home in the Lake District. Meanwhile, Eric had recovered his appetite for work and Michael had been persuaded to give up any chance of going to university and, like his

Alice and Harry in retirement in the Lake District with Alice's sister, Lucy.

father and grandfather before him, had embarked on a round of apprenticeships and external work placements before joining Irish Ropes. He would shortly be finishing a three-month stint at Goodbody's jute works in Waterford. However, the biggest shock for Peter was almost certainly to discover that Irish Ropes was now a public company and that trading in its shares had commenced on the Dublin stock exchange a week before he arrived back in Portsmouth.

The reasoning behind the company's flotation was almost certainly a combination of the ICC's wish to realise its controlling interest after ten years and the company's need of funds for its post-war recovery and development. In his return to the Ministry of Industry and Commerce on the Post War Planning of Industry in 1944, Eric had made it clear that 'further capital will need to be introduced into the company as soon as it is clear that expansion can proceed and that plant will be available. The crucial question is whether the present increased tillage with its correspondingly heavy demands for binder twine will continue and to what extent'. According to the papers, Irish Ropes was planning to use the proceeds of the float to invest in new machinery so that it could extend its range of products, develop the fine spinning of sisal, and manufacture fabrics and floor coverings.

The preliminary legal and administrative work had started in April, soon after Peter's arrival in Hong Kong, when shareholders passed the first formal resolutions to amend the company's capital structure. Harry and Alice then went over to stay at Morristown for the first three weeks of May so that Harry could attend board meetings and sign paperwork. They had to return a week early after the Ruff was burgled. Eric signed a new five-year contract on 18 May, Irish Ropes was registered as a public company on 28 May, and the prospectus for its share offer was published in the press on 14 June.

The offer enabled the ICC to make a profit on its original £20,000 investment, raised £63,000 of new capital, and gave the other shareholders their first returns since the company's incorporation, albeit only on paper. Before the offer, all the existing shareholders were given a bonus issue of one new share for every two shares that they held, thus increasing the company's ordinary share capital from £40,000 to £60,000. The funds for this were taken from the company's undistributed profits to date. At the same time, a new class of 60,000 preference shares of £1 each was created, owners of which would be entitled to a fixed dividend of 5 per cent a year but have no rights to vote at shareholders' meetings. The ICC bought all of these before the public offer at £1.05 a share, thereby raising £63,000 of new capital for the company.

The shares offered to the public comprised the ICC's total stake of 30,000 ordinary shares and 60,000 preference shares. Although the ordinary shares were offered for sale at their nominal value of £1 each, the ICC realised a profit of £10,000 as a result of the recent bonus issue. It represented a compound rate of return over ten years of just over 4 per cent a year. The 60,000 preference shares were offered to the public at £1.125 a share. Although this gave it a further gross profit of £4,500, or £0.075 per share, it had also undertaken to settle all the legal and other costs associated with the offer out of the proceeds.

	End of 1936	Changes 1937-45	Start of 1946	Bonus issue	Public offer	End of 1946	% of total
Rigby-Jones	8,575	1,429	10,004	5,002	2,248	17,254	29
Doyle	2,061	(921)	1,140	570	435	2,145	4
Cox	4,509	(509)	4,000	2,000	1,000	7,000	12
Roche	2,500	-	2,500	1,250	695	4,445	7
Others	2,350	1	2,351	1,176	88	3,615	6
	19,995	-	19,995	9,998	4,466	34,459	57
ICC	20,005	-	20,005	10,002	(30,007)	-	-
New investors	-	-	-	-	25,541	25,541	43
	40,000	-	40,000	20,000	-	60,000	100

Share issues and changes in ownership of Irish Ropes's ordinary shares, 1937–1946, showing the effects of the bonus issue and public offer in 1946.

Under the terms of the offer prospective, investors could apply for either or both classes of share in multiples of 100 shares up to a maximum of 500 shares in each class. Any applications for more than 500 shares in either class would be rejected. The only exception was that existing shareholders could buy as many shares as they wanted. Most of them did. At some point in the previous ten years, Eric and his father had bought another 1,429 shares from Patrick Doyle and Arthur Cox, bringing their total stake up to 10,004 shares, or just over 25 per cent of the shares in issue. Eric now bought another 2,248 shares. When their 5,002 bonus shares were taken into account, he and his family now owned 29 per cent of the voting shares against 21 per cent back in 1936. Arthur Cox was the next biggest buyer, his purchase of 1,000 shares bringing his total stake up to 12 per cent, and with Bernard Roche and Patrick Doyle also increasing their stakes to 7 per cent and 4 per cent respectively, the four executive directors between them now controlled over 50 per cent of the voting shares. As long as they worked together and did not fall out, they would once more be in control of Irish Ropes's destiny.

The offer, which was one of the first in Ireland after the war, was heavily oversubscribed. Applications for both ordinary and preferences shares had to be subjected to a draw and then scaled down. Those who had applied for 100, 200, or 300 shares would now get fifty shares and those who had applied for 400 or 500 shares would get seventy shares. When trading in the shares commenced on Monday 24 June, they performed briskly on an otherwise quiet day on Dublin's stock exchange. The price of the ordinary shares leapt by 40 per cent to £1.40 before falling back slightly to end the day at £1.39, and the price of the preference shares increased by 4 per cent to £1.175. Both continued to perform strongly throughout the summer. After a late surge, the ordinary shares ended the year at £2.75, thus coming close to tripling their value in their first six months of trading. For Eric and his family, it meant a paper profit of some £30,000.

By November, when the company sent in its first annual register of shareholders to the Companies Registration Office in Dublin, many investors had managed to build up portfolios of more than 500 shares. University College Cork held 1,000 preference shares as did four spinsters, presumably nuns, from St Patrick's Infant Hospital in Blackrock. However, small investors were still in the majority. In addition to its original investors, Irish Ropes now had more than 200 ordinary shareholders and 350 preference shareholders. They came from all over Ireland and Northern Ireland and from all walks of life, including farmers, doctors, teachers, housewives, widows, business colleagues at Mackies and Goodbody's, and a surprisingly large number of clerics, as well as one bishop. Michael Rigby-Jones had also bought 100 shares and was listed in the share register as a textile student.[9]

The success of the share offer was a significant milestone in the history of Irish Ropes. In just thirteen years, during six of which the world had been at war, the company had grown from its challenging birth in a derelict building in a depressed town in a young state during a worldwide recession to become a listed company and Ireland's leading manufacturer of rope and twine. It was a vindication of Lemass's industrial policy. The funds raised from the offer would mark the start of a major new phase in its development.

The prospectus had provided investors with some brief details of Irish Ropes's financial performance since incorporation. It showed that it had made a profit in all but one of its first twelve years of trading, its only loss in 1938 having been the result of a fall in the value of its stocks after the worldwide collapse in sisal prices. However, Eric's policy of keeping large stocks of raw materials, and his decision to stockpile sisal at the start of the war without receiving any financial support from the government, had also contributed to the high profits earned in 1940. Thereafter, profits had fallen in four of the next five years. For the last four years of the war, when demand for agricultural twine had increased significantly but fibre had become expensive and difficult to source, annual profits were on average only 7 per cent higher than they had been in 1937. This was almost certainly due in part to the emergency powers given to the department of supplies to control prices and profits. However, while Eric was the first to recognise that businesses had to make a profit to survive, he was never motivated primarily by money and certainly not during the Emergency. He felt a deep responsibility for ensuring that Irish famers never ran out of twine and, as the Tullow Flax Scheme demonstrated, he was prepared to take significant commercial and financial risks to achieve his goal. However, although he faced and overcame considerable challenges, his mental and physical health suffered and on more than one occasion he was close to throwing in the towel.

And yet I suspect that he and Irish Ropes never fully escaped the charge of profiteering. The period immediately after the war was a difficult one. Peace brought its own problems, not least for a country that had stood aside from the fighting and experienced neither victory nor defeat. The thousands of Irish men and women who were returning home after serving in Britain's armed forces

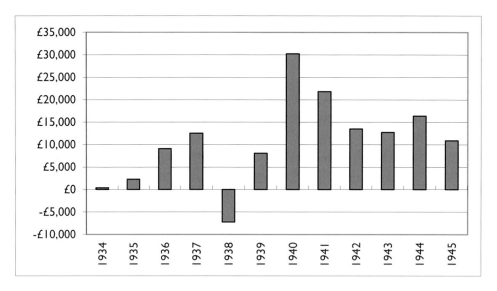

Irish Ropes's annual profits (before interest and income tax) for its first twelve years to 31 August 1945 (from the share prospectus published in the *Irish Independent*, 14 June 1946).

or working in its war industries would find it difficult to get a job. Many were blacklisted as deserters and banned from working in the public sector. They would not receive a formal pardon until 2013, by which time it was too late for many of them. The government's wage freeze in 1941 had also prevented workers striking for higher wages. Its repeal in 1946 led to an avalanche of industrial disputes. Peter's letters home from the Far East suggest that there may even have been some unrest in Irish Ropes's workforce. The 500 farmers who had grown flax for Eric might also have felt aggrieved by the sudden demise of the Tullow Flax Scheme. It had enabled them to make good profits and they may never have fully understood or accepted the reasons why the plug was pulled so suddenly. Irish farmers would have a tough time in 1946. It was one of the wettest summers on record. According to Liam Wylie's 1997 film, *Harvest Emergency*, the country was facing hunger for the first time on the same scale as the great famines of the nineteenth century. Crops were left to rot in the fields, those that could be salvaged were of poor quality, and the sodden fields made it impossible to build haystacks. Soldiers, civil servants, office workers, and schoolchildren were all enlisted to help with the harvest. Kildare was one of the regions worst hit. All Gaelic football matches in the county were suspended for six weeks between August and October. As part of a 'Save the Harvest' campaign, 4,600 local volunteers were recruited in September to help the farmers. Irish Ropes provided 250 of its men on full pay along with two lorries and two cars, Newbridge Cutlery forty men, and Bord na Mona 100 men and three lorries.[10] However, Eric was certain that he could contribute the most by increasing production and employment at the factory.

14

The Lifting of the Clouds, 1945–1948

Quality is a product of human endeavour which thrives best when the spirit is free.[1]

Even before the end of the war, Morristown's doors had been thrown open once more to family, friends, and business acquaintances. Henry Hitchcock arrived from New Zealand in the spring of 1945 to seek Eric's advice. His company, New Zealand Woolpack and Textiles, would diversify into floor coverings before the end of the year. Representatives from Donaghy's Rope and Twine in Dunedin came in the autumn. John Gailey and his colleagues from Mackies continued to visit regularly as they had done throughout the Emergency. In the spring of 1946, as Irish Ropes was preparing to go public, visitors included Alec Le Maitre, later the secretary and chairman of the Tanganyika Sisal Growers' Association; R. H. Pullen-Burry, who ran Kenya's high-level sisal research station at Thika; and Hugo Tanner, the Swiss manager of Amboni Estates, who was described by Alfred Wigglesworth as the doyen of African sisal.[2] He arrived with his wife and Sandy Neish, a director and later chairman of Wigglesworths. Over the next few years, they would be followed by ropemakers from Scotland, Argentina, Switzerland, and Sweden and other guests from South Africa, Mozambique, Rhodesia, Denmark, Iceland, and Holland. All were assured of a warm welcome and generous hospitality, as well as an opportunity to talk shop. In the autumn of 1945, when Dorothy's sisters, Lottie and Gwen, visited with their husbands, the Reverends Evan Thomas Jones and Evan Rees Jones, Britain still had rationing. 'Best holiday of my life—what a table!' Lottie wrote in the visitors' book at the end of their stay.

However, the most significant visitors were almost certainly a party of five who arrived in July 1945, a month after Peter's twenty-first birthday celebrations.

They were led by Dr Paul Wilson from the sisal division at Leeds University's Department of Textile Industries, which had taken over responsibility for sisal research from LIRA during the war, and included George Lock, who was in charge of Tanganyika's sisal research station at Ngomeni and had been appointed deputy sisal controller in 1943; Sydney Tranter, Wigglesworths's senior man in East Africa, who was also chairman of the Tanganyika Sisal Growers Association and a member of Tanganyika's executive council; and Andrew Fraser and Eric Pope, Wigglesworths's representatives in Belfast and London.

Their visit was the result of a letter that Eric had sent to the Sisal Growers Association in London a few days after VE Day in which he shared his thoughts on the future of the sisal industry. The SGA circulated it to all its members. Like the majority of manufacturers, Eric believed that manila, once it became available again, would quickly recover the ground that it had lost to sisal during the war. It was still the preferred raw material for ropemakers and users of marine cordage as it was less prone to sudden breaking, did not swell when wet, and was not harmed by immersion in saltwater. As a result, Eric was convinced that sisal's future depended on diversification into fine spinning and the development of new products and markets. It meant that growers and manufacturers would have to work together for their mutual benefit. The first step, he argued, was to improve the quality, consistency, and grading of East African sisal as it was

Dorothy entertaining visitors at Morristown, and possibly Paul Wilson's party in 1945. Eric Pope has been identified second left and possibly Sydney Tranter fourth left.

currently inferior to Javanese sisal in every respect. There was still too much leaf tissue left on the fibre after processing, and it needed to be straighter and of more uniform length. The certainty of an assured wartime market for all that they could produce, and the restriction of its use to rope and twine, had meant that growers had become lackadaisical about quality. For manufacturers, that meant more machine breakdowns and lower-quality end products.

The party's four-day visit to Irish Ropes, which Wigglesworth had helped to arrange as chairman of the SGA's technical research committee, was the first stop on a fortnight's fact-finding mission. They moved on from Newbridge to LIRA and the Belfast Ropeworks in Northern Ireland before returning to visit ropemakers in England. Eric had planned their visit carefully to ensure that his message was clearly received. When he and Dorothy entertained them at Morristown on the evening of their arrival, Wilson was impressed by the quality of the Tintawn carpets that Eric had laid in his own home. The next day, when he showed them round the factory with Horace Davies and Alec Nisbet, Eric was able to prove, just by opening a few bales, that Javanese sisal was of demonstrably higher quality and that East African grades and estate marks were no guarantee of either quality or consistency. Machine-dried fibre from Tanganyika's Rudewa Estate was probably the best that East Africa could offer—and the minimum that he required for fine spinning and carpet production—but even this fell short of Java. He also introduced the party to John Gailey, who was paying one of his regular visits to Newbridge, and arranged for them to visit Goodbody's jute factory in Clara. Finally, he showed them a film that he had made to illustrate how poor-quality fibre could damage machinery and disrupt production. Wilson, who was planning to visit East Africa before the end of the year, suggested that he send copies of it out to the growers along with samples of Irish Ropes's products and especially its carpets.

Although the English ropemakers that the party visited agreed with Eric that manila would recover its market and that the quality and grading of East African sisal needed to be improved, they did not have the same interest in fine spinning and the development of new products. They all served larger domestic markets, which allowed them to focus almost exclusively on the manufacture of rope and twine. Eric's goal, on the other hand, as he told the Imperial Institute the following year, was 'to exploit the potentialities of the fibre to its economic limits'.[3]

George Lock was as impressed as Wilson by his visit to Irish Ropes. Five years younger than Eric, he had studied at the Agricultural Economics Research Institute in Oxford before joining the Colonial Service as an agronomist in 1930. He was appointed the first director of Tanganyika's sisal research station four years later, a position that he held for the next twenty-five years. Two years after his visit to Irish Ropes, he was awarded the OBE for his services to the sisal industry, and in 1962, he was persuaded out of retirement by the Tanganyika Sisal Growers Association to write a book on sisal for Longman's Tropical Science series. The result, *Sisal: Twenty-Five Years' Sisal Research*, remains the standard work on the commercial cultivation of sisal and is the source of many of the statistics in this book. According to his daughter, Eric had little time for most of the 'sisal men' that he and Dorothy entertained at Morristown. George Lock was the exception. They became good friends, and George and his wife often visited Newbridge when they were home on leave from Africa. Eric admired his hard work and enthusiasm, which are apparent in the letter that he wrote after this first visit:

Dear Mr Rigby-Jones

I wish to thank you personally for the most interesting and enjoyable time afforded to me by you and your staff during our visit to Irish Ropes. Nothing was too much trouble for you all in showing me the processes of manufacturing sisal and the quiet and enlightened efficiency seen on all sides was certainly most impressive. The visit has been of inestimable balm to me and at long last I feel I have a better comprehension of what a spinner looks for in the quality of sisal.

Prior to this visit I think those of us in East Africa were rather prone to be content with the advances already made in improving the quality of our fibre but I can now see that we have still a long way to go before the ideal is reached. There is no doubt that the miscellany of marks with which you are supplied in these days of shortage is accentuating the variability of East African sisal as a whole and, as we are dealing with a natural product, it seems likely that it will never prove possible to depart from the marks system. The uniformity of Java sisal however does demonstrate that, if our estates were to employ similar methods in field and factory, it would not be impossible for East African sisal to approach Java quality. That is a far cry I am afraid but at least we ought to be able to achieve great strides in improving the quality of specific marks.

It was most refreshing to meet somebody like yourself who has such faith in the possibilities of our fibre and I also found it gratifying to have my opinions on our fibre texture qualified and confirmed by all we met. This carries us right back to the plant and in future much higher planting and cutting standards will be needed. Present methods are too slip-shod and primitive and, with very little extra expenditure and care to detail, I am confident that considerable strides towards uniformity both in length and texture could be made.

Next comes cleanliness of decortication. Our machines need to be better tuned and the load lightened. More machines will be required to cope with our output but it is hard to see who is going to manufacture them although much could be done by using correctly machined concaves and beaters of stainless steel which are now available. The importance of using washing water efficiently is also stressed.

The foregoing would contribute considerably to overcoming the difficulties now experienced in the brushing and packing of sisal fibre. Here the unreliability of the African worker can be intelligently anticipated by removing blemished leaves, checking cuts or growths, and mechanising grading for length. I think it may be foreshadowed that more artificially dried fibre will be forthcoming from East Africa in the future.

In short I am sure that a big improvement could be made in a relatively short time by modifying our present imperfect technique without great capital expenditure and I shall strive to put across all the valuable lessons learnt in your ropeworks. Dr Wilson's projected visit to East Africa comes at an opportune moment. His work will doubtless prove many of our ideas and so lend valuable aid in showing how we can make good our shortcomings. As long as sisal is in great demand I am afraid progress may tend to be slow as dictated by economic considerations but progress will be made—of that I am confident.

As time goes on the immense value and instructiveness of my visit to Irish Ropes will become more and more apparent and I am greatly indebted to you for all the facilities afforded to me. I shall keep in close touch with all the developments arising out of our visit and, if need be, I know you would not mind if we referred any perplexities to you for your opinions. This question of quality has become of absorbing interest and I certainly intend to examine some of our Agave hybrids more closely. It might easily be the case that some of them would provide fibre of the right texture as well as giving a more economic return per acre through their superior leaf number. Any of Wigglesworths' estates would be only too keen to grow them on a commercial scale.

I apologise for writing at such length but you have opened up new vistas and one can picture all sorts of possibilities in the future.

With kindest regards. Yours sincerely, George W. Lock.

When his committee met in September to consider Wilson's final report, Wigglesworth was equally complimentary about Irish Ropes, suggesting that 'of all the places in the country in which was sisal was used, Ireland was perhaps the most up-to-date'. He claimed that it was already weaving dyed carpets that 'could not be distinguished at sight from wool carpets'.[4]

Lock's letter must have given Eric the reassurance that he was on the right track. However, improving the quality of his raw materials was only a means to an end. He would spend the first three years after the war developing and implementing a wide-ranging plan to prepare Irish Ropes for the next stage of its growth. By 1948, he was ready to enter the export market and to sell Irish Ropes's products around the world.

When asked by the Minister for Industry and Commerce in 1944 what products Irish Ropes might manufacture after the war, Eric had listed three key areas for development: the extension of current rope production to supply the full range of ropes and twine, from 6-inch ropes down to the lightest fishing lines; the perfecting of the techniques of fine-spinning so that sisal could compete as a cheaper substitute for cotton and soft hemp; and the development of weaving to make sisal carpets and floor coverings. To achieve these goals, he now set out some key objectives—a reorganisation of his workforce, the strengthening of his management team, the procurement of new equipment, the investigation of more efficient methods of production, and the rebuilding of relationships with both customers and suppliers after almost six years of isolation. Underlying everything else, however—and seen by Eric as the key building blocks in his plan—were the creation of a happy and motivated workforce and the vigorous pursuit of quality in everything that they used and did.

In 1944, when the Tullow Flax Scheme was still in operation, a quarter of the factory's 280 staff had been employed in the scutch mill. Eric would now have to find them other jobs or make them redundant, something that he was desperate to avoid. In addition, those who had worked on Tintawn before the war would have to relearn their skills before they could start making carpets again. In October 1945, when he was asked to address the Dublin Chamber of Commerce, Eric chose as his subject 'Manpower as a National Asset'. He used his speech to make a strong case for treating the workforce of any enterprise as a capital asset rather than simply as a source of consumable energy. 'Without a moment's hesitation I place first the human factor in business,' he had told the Dublin Rotary Club back in 1940, 'those whose work is under our guidance are unquestionably the first charge upon our intellect as they are upon our conscience.... The employer under any social system must be the architect of his industry and not merely a decorator with a careful eye for camouflage.' His idea had always been 'to build upon the genius of the worker, to equip him with the very best machinery, and to rely upon him to make a success of it', and he also made sure that the working environment was light, airy, and brightly painted because, as he said, 'quality is a product of human endeavour which thrives best when the spirit is free.'

He was also keen to improve the health and welfare of Irish workers generally. He thought that all employers should be required to provide proper holiday entitlements so that their workers could enjoy a good break and return to work refreshed in mind and body. He even suggested that the government set up holiday camps where married workers might take their families at a reasonable cost.[5] It was an idea that he had been developing for some time and one which he had probably discussed with John Forshaw who, in the autumn of 1945, was asked by the Workers' Travel Association to judge a national competition with Patrick Abercrombie for the design of affordable holiday camps.[6] In his return on the post-war planning of industry in 1944, Eric had also allowed himself what he called a final but 'altogether too brief reference to a wide subject':

> No question has been asked about industry's share in contributing to better health and social conditions nor has any reference been made to wages, etc. These are matters which concern us deeply and our plans include the improvement of working conditions, canteen facilities, etc. Even at the moment we are contemplating the employment of a doctor (full time, if possible), being so much disturbed by the lack of adequate facilities in the town. We should like to include x-ray examination for latent tuberculosis and take up the study of industrial psychology.

Once again, Eric was prepared to take the lead and invest his company's money when others preferred to wait for government assistance. After Dorothy's experience during her first pregnancy, tuberculosis was a subject close to his heart, as well as being of national concern in Ireland. Widespread poverty meant that it carried a terrible stigma. After the war, it became politicised as a symbol of the failure of de Valera's government to address social deprivation. At the time, 1,190 people per million were dying annually from the disease. It was the highest rate of incidence in Europe, and although it was less than half what it had been at the start of the century, it would not finally be brought under control until the 1950s. By the end of the decade, it would be down to 160 people per million.[7] Much of the credit was due to thirty-two-year-old Noel Browne who was appointed minister for health after Fianna Fáil lost the general election in 1948. He made elimination of the disease a priority and introduced a free national screening programme. Like Eric, he had personal experience of the disease. Both his parents had died of it, and he himself had been diagnosed with it while studying at Trinity College Dublin in 1940. He was treated successfully at King Edward VII Hospital in Sussex where his fees were paid for by the same benevolent family that funded his university education.[8]

Throughout the war, Eric had been supported by a loyal and stable management team that included his original partner, Patrick Doyle; Horace Davies and Dorothy Baxter who had come over with him from Liverpool; Bernard Roche, who had taken charge of sales after joining the company in 1937; Alec Nisbet, the works chemist who had transferred from LIRA at the outbreak of war; and, last but not least, Arthur Cox, who as chairman continued to offer invaluable advice and counsel on every aspect of running the business. Now, with Peter showing no interest in joining the company and Michael still learning the ropes, he set about strengthening his team for the challenges to come. He had completed the changes by the summer of 1947 when he invited them all to Morristown for a party to celebrate his and Dorothy's silver wedding.

Bernard Roche would now be responsible for distribution as well as sales. When Irish Ropes started trading in 1933, the government had encouraged Eric to use existing channels of distribution. However, these were more suited to servicing markets in imported goods and Eric had often found himself in conflict with the ingrained conservatism of the distributors and their representative bodies. Now he proposed cutting them out altogether. Creating his own distribution network would also reduce costs to the farmer. Patrick Doyle, who was now part of Roche's five-man sales team, kept his seat on the board. Alec Nisbet was promoted to works manager. He had recently married Dorothy Baxter, whose role as company secretary was more important now that Irish Ropes was a listed company. They would be joined by four new recruits: Arthur Shiel as company accountant, Jim Cosgrove as company doctor, and Tom Murphy and Paul Quigley, two young engineering graduates from University College Dublin, who had also spent time in the Irish army. Horace Davies was invited to join the board that summer after the death of Colonel Henry but was a director for only a few months. He died two days before Christmas after a long illness. He was only forty-nine. Tom Murphy was asked to take his place as chief engineer.

The Irish Ropemakers' Union scroll in Irish Ropes's canteen (from Irish Ropes's brochure, 1954).

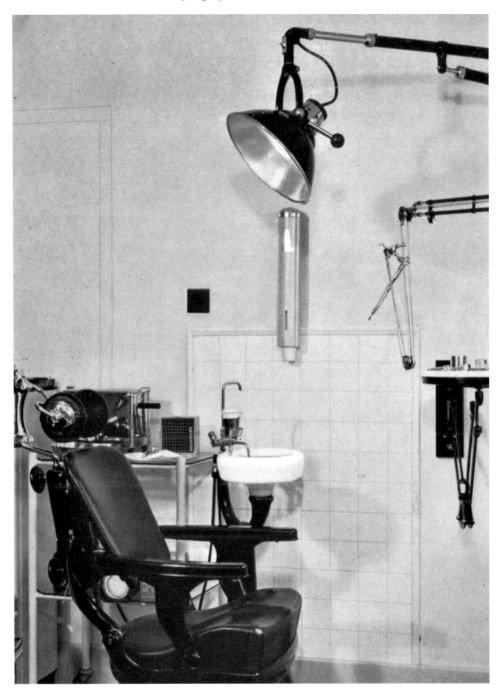

Dental facilities at the factory (from Irish Ropes's brochure, 1954).

Eric's decision to continue investing in new buildings at the start of the war, together with the demise of the Tullow Flax Scheme, meant that he already had enough space in which to expand and diversify production. The building that was now earmarked for the development of fine spinning was one of those completed in 1940. Renewed access to the heavy machinery markets and the £63,000 raised from the share offer meant that he was now able to invest heavily to replace his worn out and obsolete machinery and to start the manufacture of new products. He spent all of it and more. The company's accounts show that £67,000 was spent on plant and machinery and £8,000 on land and buildings in the four years to 1949.

With his new team in place and the first tranche of equipment installed, Eric turned to the reorganisation of his workforce and a review of the factory's working practices. He spoke about it to the Dublin Society of Chartered Accountants in 1951 in a talk entitled 'Factory Organisation and Efficiency Schemes'. At the beginning of 1947, six months after the flotation and 'as soon as the clouds were lifting from our raw material horizon and when machinery ordered eight years previously was about, at long last, to be delivered', he appointed a leading firm of British consultants to help with what he described as a major redeployment of labour and the introduction of a production incentive scheme. He saw the eighteen-month project as an essential prerequisite to entering the export market. Realising that it might be controversial, he recruited a senior union official to the project team so that the process was seen to be fair and that the workforce was involved at every step. As he said, 'the worker is the first to become conscious of muddle and inefficiency, whether real or apparent, but is usually the last to be afforded an opportunity of helping to put things right'. However, he could not head off all resistance. That September, 300 workers—who presumably represented all or nearly all his workforce—gave notice of their intention to strike after the breakdown of wage negotiations. They were asking for another £1.50 an hour on top of a recent increase of £0.80. The dispute appears to have been resolved by the end of the year. Early in the new year, William Mullen, the president of the Irish Transport and General Workers Union, presented the workforce with a large wooden scroll from an old sign for the Irish Ropemakers' Union. From then on, it would hang in Irish Ropes's canteen as a reminder of the shared heritage of workers and management.[9]

Eric also realised that the project required the support and commitment of senior management. As he no longer had the time to get involved in every detail himself, he delegated this to his second new recruit, Paul Quigley. The experience that he gained contributed to his being appointed the first director of the Irish Management Institute in 1953. However, Eric acknowledged: 'I had to understand the principles and be ready on occasion to say "thus far and no further". I never had to say this but people got to feel that I might and there was just this necessary amount of restraint in what was to us at the time a daring experiment'. Irish Ropes was the first company in Ireland to introduce such a scheme. Although it was an expensive and risky exercise, it paid immediate dividends. Eric described

Inside the sisal store (this and subsequent photographs of the factory are taken from an album given to me by Benny Maxwell in 2014 and were probably taken for the company's 1949 brochure, *The Story of Irish Ropes*).

The hard fibre mill (formerly the indoor riding school).

its effects as 'stupendous'. Within a year, output, wages, and productivity had all increased by more than 25 per cent.

Paul Wilson's report for the Sisal Growers Association, which had suggested that there might be some mileage in exploring whether other fibres might be better suited to bridge the gap between sisal and soft fibres, prompted the Imperial Institute to get in touch with Eric in 1946. In August, it asked for his opinion on some samples of sansevieria, or mother-in-law's tongue, and Mauritius hemp, a member of the aloe family. The small size of the samples meant that Eric could do no more than examine them closely. In any case, as he told the institute, he was already committed to the development of sisal. Nevertheless, he did send Alec Nisbet over to talk to them and called in himself both on his way to East Africa in September and on his return at the end of November. The institute's notes of these meetings, together with brief newspaper reports of the talks that he later gave to the Rotary Club and Textile Institute, now provide the only details of his trip.[10]

Eric's aim was to get to know the growers and find out more about how sisal was grown and processed. On arrival, they told him that he was almost certainly the first manufacturer to make such a visit. He was accompanied by Wigglesworth's Sandy Neish, whom he had entertained at Morristown in May in the run-up to the flotation. They left from Heathrow, which had only just begun commercial operations and was still using tents as passenger lounges, and then endured an uncomfortable three-day journey in a converted Halifax bomber. It was one of the fastest commercial aircraft available and could fly at 200 mph with 10 tons of fuel, a crew of six, and room for ten passengers. On their first day, they got as far as Cairo, having stopped to refuel in Libya. Leaving at dawn the next day, they followed the White Nile down to Malakal, 400 miles west of Addis Ababa, where they had to refuel again before moving on to Laropi in Uganda, which Eric described as 'a poisonous spot in a beautiful swamp'. That night, they had to make do with the most basic accommodation in a remote village as one of their engines had failed and a replacement had to be summoned by wireless. The following day, they finally made it to the small port of Beira in Mozambique where they saw ships being loaded with sisal for Newbridge and copra for Drogheda, which Irish Oil and Cake Mills used to make animal feed.

Eric's trip took him to Mozambique, Kenya, and Tanganyika. Although he saw for himself the growers' main problems—a shortage of equipment and labour and what he called their continuous struggle against nature—he remained convinced that improvements in planting, harvesting, and processing could produce the finer fibre that he needed. He must also have become aware of the increasingly acrimonious dispute over the future direction and representation of the industry. It resurrected the same issues that had set growers against merchants in the 1930s but which had lapsed during the war when the market was controlled by the British government and the London merchants were effectively side-lined. Unsurprisingly Eldred Hitchcock could be found at its forefront. According to Tanganyika's governor, Sir Wilfred Jackson, the 'Hitchcockites' had been lining up against the 'anti-Hitchcockites' since 1945.

The role of the Combined Raw Materials Board in Washington had quickly fallen away at the end of the war. It met for the last time in July 1945 and was formally dissolved before the end of the year. However, the British government would eventually extend its contract to buy all of Kenya and Tanganyika's sisal for another three years until the end of 1948. In the spring of 1944, John Shillidy at the British Ministry of Supply, who would be involved that autumn in the decision to stop buying Irish Ropes's green flax, had acceded to the growers' request for a further increase in price. However, he turned down their suggestion of a five-year contract that they claimed would allow them to invest in the machinery and ground clearance needed to maximise production. As well as setting an unwelcome precedent, Shillidy was afraid that the government might be left with excessive stocks of overpriced and unsaleable sisal when fibre production recovered in the rest of the world. It was agreed at first to extend the contract until two years after the end of the war in the Far East, but this was subsequently extended for a third year when it became clear that manila production in the Philippines would take longer than expected to recover and that its availability in the sterling area would in any case be limited by currency controls. The government also had to accept further significant price increases to protect its continued access to fibre supplies. By 1946 and 1947, the price had increased to £78 a ton from the £30 set in 1944, albeit against an open market rate of £96. Along with a further increase of £10 a ton, the growers then asked for an extension of the contract for a final six months until the end of 1948 to give them time to finalise their plans for a new marketing organisation. This would give them the opportunity to control their own destiny and to make substantial profits at the expense of the London fibre merchants, who had by now been side-lined for nine years.

It had quickly become clear after the death of Sir William Lead in 1942, when Hitchcock failed to be appointed sisal controller but chose to stay on in East Africa, that, whatever he might say to deny it, he was determined not only to foul relations between the sisal associations in London and East Africa, indeed to eliminate the former altogether, but also to create for himself a leading role in the future direction of the industry. In 1944, he reportedly stormed out of a private meeting with Samuel Hogg, the new chairman of the Sisal Growers Association who was visiting East Africa to try to pour oil on troubled waters, shouting that 'if anybody is going to jockey me out of a position I am going to fight.'[11] Although it was not a welcome prospect for the British and colonial governments, there was little that they could do to stop it.

It was only after he had arrived in Africa in 1941 that people became aware that Hitchcock had left London in what Charles Carstairs at the Colonial Office described as 'somewhat dubious circumstances'.[12] Indeed, when Gerard Clauson, the assistant under-secretary of state, reviewed Carsons's note, his only comment was to question his use of the word 'somewhat'. The precise details are no longer clear. In 1944, when Hogg reported the outcome of his meeting with Hitchcock back to the SGA in London, he said only that he had referred to 'certain misunderstandings and unfortunate incidents of which Mr

Hitchcock would be abundantly aware and for which blame must be accepted both by London and by Tanganyika', which he was keen to put behind them. The closest that we get to any details is when Wigglesworths's Sydney Tranter stood against Hitchcock that year for election as vice-chairman of the Tanganyika Sisal Growers Association. It was an important election because whoever was elected traditionally took over as chairman the following year. At some point in the course of a vitriolic but victorious campaign, Tranter threatened to publish 'correspondence showing Mr Hitchcock's not too honest dealings with the funds of the London Association'.[13]

Hitchcock and Tranter were very different characters. Elspeth Huxley, who had no particular liking for the sisal industry or the men who ran it, met them both. In her 1948 book *The Sorcerer's Apprentice*, an account of her travels through East Africa in the immediate aftermath of the war, she described sisal as 'an impersonal, industrial, brave-new-world sort of crop' when she was taken round some estates near Tanga by an unnamed sisal baron.[14] From the nature of his comments on the industry and her description of him as 'bearded, forceful, and pocket-sized', it can only have been Eldred Hitchcock. She later found herself sharing a carriage with Sydney Tranter on the train inland from Dar es Salaam to Kongwa—'another sisal baron,' she said, 'but a mild and genial one, with a benevolent curiosity about the lives of his labourers.'[15]

Although abrasive and ambitious, Hitchcock had as many friends as enemies, and even his enemies had to concede that, while he often seemed to put self-interest before the common good, he was probably the ablest man in the industry. Once he had made the decision to stay on in Tanganyika, he lived frugally, setting up home and entertaining visitors in a flat above his company's offices in the port of Tanga. He developed a keen interest in local history and built up a valuable collection of early Islamic pottery, as well as inviting the famous archaeologist, Sir Mortimer Wheeler, out to excavate.[16] He would be knighted in 1955, thus adding to the CBE that he had been awarded in 1920 for his wartime service as assistant director of raw materials and deputy director of wool textile production. When he died in 1959 his friend, Dr Greville Freeman-Grenville, the colony's former education officer, wrote a glowing appreciation of him as a man who combined business acumen with an acute artistic sensibility and the humility of the scholar. It was a picture that many of his enemies might not have recognised.[17]

Discussion of the future structure and organisation of the East African sisal industry had begun during the war. However, it was only after it ended that the industry grasped that it had just two years to get its house in order before the British government's contract came to an end and it was again faced with a free market and renewed competition from the Far East. For sisal to compete effectively against other fibres, it was essential not only to improve its quality and consistency but also to establish an effective marketing structure. The prevailing view within government was that the industry should be left so far as was possible to manage its own affairs. However, it was beyond the capacity of the growers to organise the industry entirely by their own efforts, and given its importance to the local economies, the colonial governments could not afford to abdicate all responsibility.

Wigglesworth and Hitchcock had been among many who responded to Oliver Stanley's dispatch in 1943 by sharing their thoughts on the future marketing of sisal. It led to Tanganyika's director of agriculture, R. W. R. Millar, who had succeeded Lead as sisal controller, being asked to work with the Tanganyika Sisal Growers Association on a new sisal ordinance for the colony. This would seek to clarify the roles of the three main players—the colonial government; the Sisal Board, which comprised members chosen by both government and growers and whose role was to advise the governor on all matters relating to the industry; and the TSGA itself, which represented the growers. It was expected that Kenya, as the junior partner in the sisal industry, would follow Tanganyika's lead and that, once the ordinance was passed, the role of the Sisal Growers Association in London would fall away.

The war was over by the time that the new ordinance was passed by Tanganyika's Legislative Council and given the governor's assent in December 1945.[18] Although the delay was caused in part by a change of governor, with Sir William Battershill taking over from Sir Wilfred Jackson in April 1945, the main reason was because the TSGA had withdrawn its earlier drafts after failing to get agreement on a number of key terms. Jackson also believed that Hitchcock's personality was a stumbling block that prevented co-operation between the Kenyan and Tanganyikan growers. Some way had to be found to rein him in. However, as one senior Colonial Office official wrote in 1944: 'Mr Hitchcock is well entrenched in Tanganyika and is going to be the leader of the industry there whether we like it or not'.[19]

The growers were not nearly so homogeneous a group as the colonial government would have liked. By 1943, British estates accounted for only a third of Tanganyika's sisal production. Indian interests, most notably those of the Karimjee family, accounted for 19 per cent, Greek for 18 per cent, and Swiss for 9 per cent (although this probably included Wigglesworths's Anglo-Swiss joint venture, Amboni Estates). Most of the remaining 21 per cent was made up of the former German estates, which the Custodian of Enemy Property had confiscated and leased out for the duration of the war, mostly to Indian and Greek growers.[20] Furthermore, British interests were usually concentrated into a few major enterprises that tended to operate the larger estates. It meant that, when the confiscated estates were taken into account, Indians and Greeks owned a majority of the estates between them.[21]

These differences in the size and ownership of the estates not only affected the economics of production but also led to the emergence of rival interest groups. The prices agreed with the British government were based on average costs of production and so made no allowance for the higher operating costs of the smaller estates. It meant that, while the larger, more mechanised estates could make reasonable profits, the smaller, less efficient ones often struggled to break even. Hitchcock saw the opportunity to build a power base by setting himself up as the

champion of the smaller, non-British estates. As many of these were producing
sisal of lower quality, they stood to gain the most from any centralised collective
marketing scheme.

The three main areas of disagreement in the drafting of the new sisal ordinance
had been over who would be responsible for grading once the role of the Sisal
Controller fell away; how and by whom the chairman of the Sisal Board should
be appointed; and the respective roles of the TSGA and Sisal Board in any future
marketing arrangements. The colonial government was determined to keep
control of grading and prevent it passing to the TSGA, whose members would
stand to gain the most from the application of lower standards. The growers
argued somewhat disingenuously, as the merchants had done before them, that
they were best placed to know what their customers wanted. The government was
also adamant that the governor should appoint the chairman of the Sisal Board,
especially as only four of its sixteen members would be government appointees.
Millar was the obvious candidate. His name had already been put forward
informally by some of the anti-Hitchcockites in the TSGA who were later dubbed
'the Tranter group'. He was clearly qualified for the role and, as Charles Carstairs
had warned in a Colonial Office file note in 1944, if he was not appointed then
'the frightful possibility looms that their choice might light on Mr E. F. Hitchcock,
now in EA [East Africa] and "in" with some sections at least of the industry....
He could not be counted on to pursue the sound policy which Mr Millar would,
nor would it be prudent for any administration to repose full confidence in him.'[22]

However, Hitchcock's main goal was to secure for the TSGA a monopoly on
the marketing and selling of East African sisal when the British government's
contract finally ended. If he was successful, it would not only limit the role of
the merchants generally but also damage the interests of men like Eric and Alfred
Wigglesworth who were convinced that sisal's future depended on improving its
quality and consistency. The Colonial Office was only prepared to sanction such a
move, which would allow the TSGA to interfere in the private business affairs of
every grower, if it was seen to have clear and overwhelming support.

Wigglesworth, who was now eighty, made his own views clear after the ordinance
had been passed. In August 1946, a month before Eric left on his ten-week trip to
Africa with Sandy Neish, he restated the case for the fibre merchants in a pamphlet
entitled *The Future of the Sisal Industry in East Africa and Sisal Marketing*. Once
again, he refuted the accusation that they had been responsible for the collapse
in prices in the 1930s, claiming that 'it is quite a delusion to assert, on superficial
evidence, that merchants were to blame for the unavoidable troubles of sisal in a
world economic cataclysm'. He made another strong defence of what he believed
was the merchants' crucial role in maintaining the fibre's competitiveness and
price stability, in understanding the needs of consumers and matching supply to
demand, and in securing improvements in quality and consistency; he repeated
his criticisms of the Mexican henequen co-operative, citing it as an example of
how controlled economies could maximise prices when times were good but were
a blunt and cumbersome weapon when they turned bad; and he was remarkably

prescient about the potential impact of any sudden increase in the price of raw materials:

> There is nothing more dangerous than to allow a substantial rise in price to hamstring consumption for it inevitably induces consumers to search for a substitute fibre. Frequently markets have been permanently lost by excessively high prices charged by the producer. Jute is a notable example when twenty years ago it reached a price of £60 a ton and the large demand from the cement trade was permanently lost by the adoption of paper bags. Any scheme purporting to guarantee price stabilisation at a high level is founded on entirely false assumptions and should not be relied upon. The true facts are that nothing short of a monopoly of the world's hard fibre production and an insatiable demand could guarantee the stability of high prices and these are advantages we do not enjoy.[23]

He also predicted a decline in demand for binder twine in developed countries as combine harvesters replaced mechanical binders. In the US, the number of combine harvesters had increased from 61,000 in 1931 to 375,000 in 1945 and would reach almost 1 million by 1956.[24] Although their impact would be offset in the short term by greater demand for baler twine, which was three times as thick as binder twine and was still needed to tie hay and straw, Wigglesworth was more convinced than ever that any growth in demand for sisal would come from the development of new products for which fine-spun fibre was essential and which in turn required the development of new plant hybrids and improved methods of processing.[25]

The Tanganyika government ended up winning the battle of the sisal ordinance. The governor would be responsible for grading and for appointing the chairman of the Sisal Board and, after proper consultation with the board, would make the rules for 'regulating and controlling the cultivation, treatment, keeping, storage, marketing, and export of sisal'. Furthermore, any change to the TSGA's rules would now require the support of not just a simple majority of its members but also a majority that accounted for two-thirds of the colony's fibre production in the previous calendar year.

The TSGA finally voted on Hitchcock's proposal to establish a monopolistic marketing co-operative in May 1948, shortly before the final six-month extension of the British contract to the end of the year. Although Hitchcock was now chairman of the TSGA and had the backing of seventy-six of the ninety-eight growers who voted, their estates accounted for only 59 per cent of production and so fell short of the required two-thirds majority. By themselves, Wigglesworths's estates would not have been able to reach the 33 per cent needed to defeat Hitchcock's scheme. However, they had the support of a number of growers who were motivated as much by their hostility to Hitchcock as by any fundamental opposition to his scheme. Although many growers would choose to join Hitchcock's Tanganyika Sisal Marketing Association (TASMA) when it was established in 1949, the others could now once more make their own arrangements for the sale of their fibre.

Inside the hard fibre mill.

Drawing slivers of sisal for the spinning of fine yarn (from Irish Ropes's brochure, 1954).

Back in Ireland, 1948 also saw the completion of Eric's post-war restructuring. Irish Ropes was now ready to expand, diversify, and, most importantly, enter the export market. At some point, almost certainly in 1949, it produced its first corporate brochure. Although it is not dated, it refers to both the ending of the British government's sisal contract and Ireland's winning of the Triple Crown, something that its rugby team achieved in 1948 and 1949 for the first time since 1899 and then did not achieve again until 1982. Richly illustrated and subtitled *The Story of Irish Ropes*, it described all the stages that were involved in growing and processing sisal and included pictures of the company's trademarks and new management team. It also explained:

> Since the passing of Controls we have reverted to selective buying, pin-pointing and visiting the estates which turn out fibre best suited for our requirements. This great African industry is on the march, especially for those growers who believe that diligence in all aspects of production is the only guarantee of their continued success. The whole system is changing. Carefully planned planting programmes are being followed, meticulous attention given to decortication and controlled drying of the fibre in place of haphazard sun drying; better baling methods to ensure, so far as ever possible, that the fibre will reach its final destination in the same perfect condition as when packed. Selection of fibre, according to its spinning properties is another part of this policy of progressive estates and we intend that our products shall benefit through close contact with all that is best in this development.

These improvements had allowed Irish Ropes to move forward with its fine spinning of yarn, which, according to the brochure, had 'not long emerged from the experimental'. It was already the first factory in the world capable of spinning fine 3-lea sisal yarn. At 2,700 feet per pound, it was more than four times lighter than standard binder twine. Further developments were in the pipeline. Quality was at the heart of everything that the company did. It demanded the highest quality raw materials and it was confident that its finished goods were of the same high standard. A photograph of Eric appeared on the brochure's first page beside an opening message:

> Greetings
>   To friends at home and abroad!
>   To those whom we serve—in our own green countries and in industrial cities across the sea; in the icy North, on warm Mediterranean shores, across the grey waters of the Atlantic and beyond the Prairies.
>   To those who serve us—sisal planters in East Africa, growers of fibre in many lands, engineers, research workers, merchants, seamen, and all adventurers.
>   To our fellow craftsmen—competing for pride of place in this age-old industry.
>   And to all who spin and enjoy a good yarn—we send good wishes

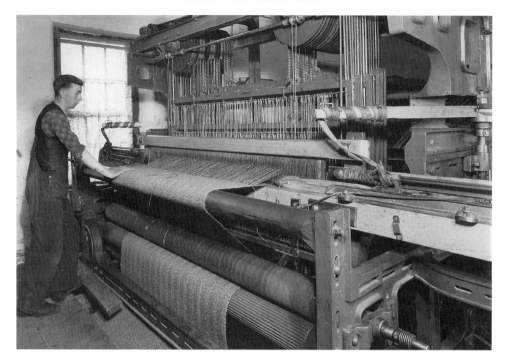

Weaving Tintawn.

Detecting and repairing flaws and making Seal shopping bags and Red Setter cricket mats.

Eric's decision to enter the export market was another example of his pioneering spirit and his willingness to risk his own capital rather than wait for government grants and encouragement. Not long afterwards, in May 1949, the Irish government established the Industrial Development Authority to 'stimulate, support and develop export-led business and enterprise in Ireland'.[26] When he had been asked by the Department of Industry and Commerce back in 1944 whether he would be able to develop an export trade after the war, Eric's reply had been that he could not yet be certain. It depended on when he might regain full access to imported raw materials and whether foreign tariffs would then permit him to compete fairly in international markets. The one thing of which he had no doubt was that 'as far as quality goes we can fully hold our own and this is the first pre-requisite'. By the time Irish Ropes celebrated its twenty-first anniversary in 1954, it was employing more than 400 staff and exporting to more than forty regions around the world from Canada to New Zealand. Sadly, Eric would not live long enough to see it.

15

A Triumph of Brain and Effort,
1949–1952

We don't think we are being over optimistic but, as coals are to Newcastle or as china is to Dresden, so shall cordage be to Newbridge. It is to that end we strive.[1]

The reorganisation of Irish Ropes in the three years after the war was sandwiched between general elections in the UK and Ireland that saw both Churchill and de Valera fall from power. Like Lloyd George in 1918, Churchill had called the first British election for a decade immediately after the end of the war in Europe. Unlike Lloyd George, he suffered a humiliating defeat. Clement Attlee, his deputy in the wartime coalition, won 61 per cent of the seats, albeit on only 48 per cent of the votes. It was the Labour party's first overall majority. Three years later, in 1948, de Valera lost his first election in sixteen years. His Fianna Fáil party lost eight seats, and although it remained the largest party in the Dáil, it was now six seats short of an overall majority. The other parties managed to form an unlikely coalition under John Costello, who took over from Richard Mulcahy as leader of Fine Gael. It was Eric's first change of political master since the foundation of Irish Ropes. Churchill and de Valera would both return to power in 1951.

It is unlikely that Eric was able to vote in any of these elections. We do not know how he felt about the results and we have few clues now, beyond his family's long-standing liberalism and his own actions and attitudes, as to his true political persuasion and how it might have changed during his life. Although he would almost certainly have admired Churchill's wartime leadership, there is also much that he would have applauded in Attlee's practical and pragmatic socialism, and not least his efforts to improve equality and the lot of the working man. And yet, in spite of his own predominant concern for his workers, he would have believed that democracy was for the polling booths and not for the workplace. He was always determined to be the master of his own destiny and rarely welcomed interference except from his closest friends and colleagues. Business leaders, unlike politicians, owed their success to their own efforts; they were not elected by their workforce.

Eric probably held similar, but less radical, views to his brother-in-law, John Forshaw. Shortly after Attlee's victory John stepped down as architect to the London County Council to become chief architect and housing consultant at the Ministry of Health, which was responsible at the time for housing as well as health. He moved on to the Ministry of Housing and Local Government when it was created in 1951 and would stay there until his retirement in 1959. He would play an important role in the post-war reconstruction of Britain. Labour's 1945 manifesto, *Let Us Face the Future*, had put food, work, and housing at the top of its agenda. In six years, the Attlee government built more than a million new homes, 80 per cent of which were council houses. John was made a Companion of the Order of the Bath in 1954 and was given a glowing obituary in *The Times* when he died in 1973:

> Mr J. H. Forshaw, CB, MC, FRIBA, who died on September 16 at the age of 78, was an early and distinguished example of the type of socially responsible official architect who now plays a major professional role but in Forshaw's day rarely made a contribution of much note or set standards for the rest of the profession to follow. This Forshaw emphatically did when he was chief architect from 1926 to the Miners' Welfare Committee. The pithead baths and other surface buildings at collieries all over the country, designed in the office of which he was the head, not only represented an advance in social welfare but, because of their appropriate use of materials and direct expression of their function, were among the pioneer modern buildings in this country....
>
> Although his building activities at the LCC were restricted by wartime conditions, and at the Ministries of Health and Housing he was more of an administrator than a designer, he left his mark on public authority architecture through his sense of the social responsibility architects ought to show and his understanding of the proper role of the official architect.[2]

Although Eric chose not to play any formal role in either national politics or local municipal affairs, he was always keen to promote Irish business and to improve the general lot of the people of Newbridge. During the war, he had provided them with turf when fuel was in short supply, and in the appalling weather of 1946, he had provided men and equipment from Irish Ropes to help with the harvest. Early in the new year, he was asked to chair a public meeting in the town to discuss the fuel shortage that had arisen after the bad weather had made it impossible to dig enough turf the previous autumn. He arranged for Irish Ropes to find the £200 that was needed immediately to buy timber as an alternative fuel and, a few weeks later, as chairman of the finance committee for the town's fuel drive, arranged for the factory to release and distribute fifty tons of turf to those most in need. At the same time, he was chosen as one of Dublin's ten representatives on the executive council of Ireland's Chambers of Commerce, and at the end of the year, he and Vincent Crowley were co-opted to the Council of the Federation of Irish Manufacturers.

In 1949, a Gaelic football match between Irish Ropes and Goodbody's led to the creation of Irish Ropes's Sports and Social Club. The company later provided land for the club, and although it has now been renamed Ryston Sports and Social Club, it has kept the company's red setter as its emblem and still has its original stone signs at its entrance. When the Taoiseach, Bertie Ahern, opened its new clubhouse in 2007, he paid tribute to the club's history and the role that it played in the local community. In 1952, Eric also tried to buy and give to the town a strip of land beside the Liffey known as the Strand on which the town council wanted to build a municipal swimming pool. Unfortunately, he could not complete its purchase before he died. Although the pool was never built, the land is now part of the town's Liffeyside Park.

Eric claimed that the main reasons for his decision to enter the export market were to secure and increase employment at the factory and to enable Irish Ropes to compete effectively against foreign manufacturers in the domestic market once import tariffs were removed. The eighteen-month work study may have significantly improved productivity and efficiency, but it meant that the factory was now producing more than the domestic market alone could absorb. It would have to find new outlets for its products if output was to be maintained. With the demand for binder twine likely to fall with the decline in acreage under tillage and the increased use of combine harvesters, and wire and manmade fibres set at some point to take over from vegetable fibres as the preferred material for cordage production, Tintawn always looked like being the product with the brightest future. It was cheap and hard-wearing and so appealed to two markets—the middle classes who had previously been unable to afford expensive fitted carpets and the working classes who could perhaps now afford floor coverings for the first time. Its method of promotion changed as it gained acceptance, it being described in the company's advertisements first as matting, then as a floor covering, and finally as carpet.

Although the UK was the obvious first foreign market to test due to its proximity and shared currency, it proved impossible to break when Eric tried for the first time in 1948. In February, he had to tell the Department of Industry and Commerce that 'the British market on which we firmly expected to sell after the war is utterly and completely closed against us'.[3] After he had been told by his British customers that all their applications to import Irish Ropes's products were being turned down by the British Board of Trade, he wrote to the UK's trade commissioner in Dublin to demand an explanation. He was told that the board's current policy was to refuse import licenses for both sisal matting and cordage made from vegetable fibres and that this was unlikely to change in the foreseeable future. He immediately went over to London to talk things through with Alfred Wigglesworth and to meet Alfred Landauer, who would remain in post as hemp controller for another year. Landauer told him that, because of the continuing

'A floor that started … in East Africa'—an Irish Ropes's advertisement, 18 March 1948. (*With thanks to Irish Newspaper Archives and the Irish Press*)

shortage of hard fibres, he was not permitting British manufacturers to make sisal matting and so could hardly allow it to be imported. Although Eric argued that Landauer was quite happy to let those same manufacturers export their rope and twine to Ireland, it was not an argument that he could win. With the government's sisal contract remaining in place until the end of the year, he left the meeting worried that his current allocation of fibre might be reduced. Meanwhile, as he reported back to Arthur Cox, stocks of finished goods were piling up at the factory and, unless he found a buyer, he would have to cut back production and perhaps even lay off staff.[4]

The situation eased in 1949 after Wigglesworths finally recovered control of how and where it sold its sisal. Although we now have only limited statistics, they paint a coherent picture of Irish Ropes's progress over the next few years. By 1950, it was selling almost 4,200 tons of cordage a year against 1,800 tons before the war. After falling to less than 1,500 tons in 1942 and 1943 sales had risen every year since then and had increased by more than 30 per cent in the last two years.[5] It was now buying enough sisal for it to be shipped directly to Dublin rather than having to have it trans-shipped via Britain. In 1951, Eric gave the Industrial Development Agency a detailed and well-reasoned review of Irish Ropes's scope to expand. Although he was afraid that it might sound like an absurd boast, the company was now leading the world in the fine spinning of hard fibres even though its output of fine yarns was still insignificant.[6] The company's exports grew from £107,000 in 1949 to £173,000 in 1950 and on to £277,000 in 1951. By then, it was exporting more than 1,100 tons a year. Although 80 per cent of these went to the UK, its next largest customer, with 13 per cent, was Iceland where there was steady demand for its fishing lines, nets, and maritime rope. By 1952, exports were accounting for a third of the company's sales.

There was also growing interest in Tintawn from Canada and the US where it was promoted as a cheap, hard-wearing, and easy-to-maintain alternative to traditional floor coverings. One American agent was so keen to get himself an exclusive marketing deal that he jumped the gun by putting inaccurate and premature advertisements in the American trade press under the headline, 'Irish Sisal Carpet Debuts in New York Market'. It prompted an angry response from the company's existing agents. Donal Scully, Ireland's trade consul in New York, also did all that he could to promote the company. However, when he asked to be sent some samples and price lists in the first half of 1951, Eric had to decline because the sisal industry was going through a period of extreme volatility where, as he put it, its price was going up almost daily.[7] Not only did this come at the worst possible time for a company trying to develop its international markets, but it also threatened its very survival.

It would be another busy and difficult year for Eric. Ann's twenty-first birthday in April was quickly followed by the weddings of both Peter and Michael. Michael had finally joined Irish Ropes as purchasing manager in 1949 after completion of his four-year apprenticeship. After his brief stint at Goodbody's, he had moved on to work first as a machine operator at a textile factory in Switzerland and then as

Sisal being unloaded at Dublin docks (from Irish Ropes's brochure, 1954).

a sales representative for Mackies in Belfast before joining Irish Ropes's agents in Leeds. While at Mackies, he met Nancy McGookin who worked in John Gailey's office. They were married in Belfast on 20 June 1951. A fortnight later, and only shortly after getting his BA in architecture from London University, Peter married Pamela Whitehead in Shelton, the small village in Bedfordshire where her family had farmed and bred horses for many generations. Pam had served in the Wrens during the war and, when she met my father, was acting as housekeeper for her brother, Bill, who, after serving in the British Army in India, had been offered the job of managing the Maharajah of Baroda's stud farm near Newbridge. They knew no one in Ireland when they arrived. However, their aunt, Helen Whitehead, who had spent most of her working life as a midwife in Ormskirk and had attended the births of both Eric and Peter, suggested introducing themselves to the Rigby-Jones family. Peter, who was away at university at the time, would be the last member of his family to meet his future wife.

Meanwhile, Eric and Dorothy continued to play host to a hectic round of visitors at Morristown. They put up members of the family before and after Michael's wedding in Belfast and in the first half of July, as well as travelling over to England for Peter's wedding, they entertained guests from Australia, Tanganyika, and New Zealand. Then, three weeks after Peter's wedding and five years after his first visit, Eric set off again for East Africa. This time he went with Wigglesworths's Eric Pope. He kept a diary of his trip, the first sixteen pages of which survive and give a detailed account of his first fortnight there.

The trip came at a worrying time for ropemakers and users of sisal products. The price of the fibre had rocketed since the start of the Korean War in June 1950. Fears of another world war had led to a desperate race to rearm and re-equip. In the US, both the government, which had provided an extra $3.8 billion for strategic stockpiling under the Defence Production Act of 1950, and cordage manufacturers were buying sisal in quantities previously unheard of by their European counterparts.[8] The resulting shortage of fibre was exacerbated by one of the worst droughts in East Africa, which restricted production of the higher grades of sisal. A report by the Commonwealth Economic Committee in February 1951 quantified the steep rise in the price of industrial fibres. Using a pre-war index of 100 as its base, it showed that jute had reached 612 by November 1950, cotton 709, and sisal 845.

Eric's trip came as the price of sisal reached its peak. Questions had been asked about it in the House of Commons three weeks before he left.[9] In his answer, Hervey Rhodes, the parliamentary secretary to the Board of Trade, confirmed that the price of binder twine, which had doubled from £42 a ton in 1939 to £83 in 1945, was now standing at £269. He claimed that this was almost entirely due to the increased cost of raw materials, which had risen from £17 in 1939 to £45 in 1945 and was now £243 a ton. It meant that British manufacturers were being severely squeezed. Although their prices had more than tripled in six years their gross profits had fallen from £38 to £26 a ton and their gross margins, before taking any account of manufacturing and distribution costs, from 45 per cent to 10 per cent. They would be exposed to substantial stock losses as and when prices

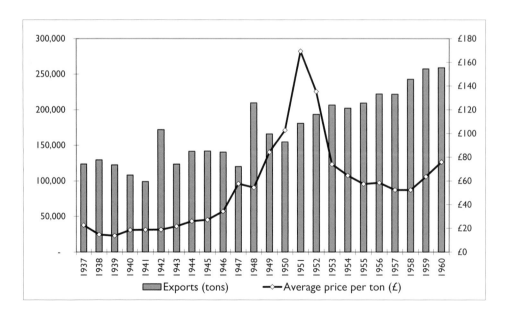

Quantity and average price of annual sisal exports from Kenya and Tanganyika, 1937–60 (from figures in Lock, *Sisal,* Appendix I). The annual prices do not fully reflect the short-term volatility in price in 1951.

fell. The price of sisal reached almost £250 during Eric's time in Africa and would peak at £256 later in the year. At one point, he said, Irish Ropes was paying £30 a ton more for its raw fibre than it was charging for its finished twine.

The company had already placed notices in the press at the beginning of June advising farmers to place their orders for twine immediately. Since the end of the war, they had become complacent about its availability and so had felt safe to improve their cash-flow by delaying their orders until the last minute. Now they risked missing out if they delayed any further. The company made it clear that the whole system for the distribution of binder twine was in danger of collapse.[10] Manufacturers themselves were facing a major dilemma. They had to decide whether to continue to buy sisal in anticipation of further price increases or to hold off in the belief that the current prices were unsustainable and would eventually collapse. If they continued to buy, then farmers would continue to have access to binder twine as long as they could still afford to buy it. However, if they did not find a ready market for all that they made, then any fall in the price of sisal would make it impossible for them to get rid of their stocks without incurring significant losses.

For Eric, the cost of making a wrong decision was potentially disastrous. The future of his business was jeopardised by a volatility in price that was completely outside his control. Irish Ropes's stocks, which comprised raw materials awaiting manufacture, products in the process of manufacture, and finished goods awaiting sale, were and, for many years, would remain the most valuable asset on its balance sheet. In 1948, when sisal prices were less than a third of what they would be in 1951, its year-end stocks had been valued at £154,000 against a cumulative gross investment in its land, buildings, and equipment of only £127,000.[11] The company had been similarly exposed before. In 1938, it had suffered its only loss in its first twelve years of trading as a result of a collapse in sisal prices. It was a risk that, as a listed company, it could no longer afford. A fall in the value of its stocks of between 10 and 20 per cent, which was insignificant when compared to the scale of the recent price movements, would wipe out its profits for the year and prevent the payment of the dividends on which its investors now relied.

Eric's flight was not only more comfortable but also three times faster than it had been five years earlier. He and Eric Pope left London on the morning of Friday 27 July on a South African Airways Constellation and, after stops in Italy and Israel and breakfast over Ethiopia, touched down in Nairobi shortly before noon the following day. It had taken them just twenty-five and a half hours. After checking in at the Norfolk Hotel, where Wigglesworth had stayed in 1913, they went to register their arrival at Government House before rushing off to a nearby game reserve in an unsuccessful attempt to beat the record of seeing lions within thirty hours of leaving London.

After three days spent visiting sisal estates near Nairobi, Eric moved on to Tanganyika on Wednesday. He had to get up at 5 a.m. for a five-hour flight to the coast and then on across the border to Tanga. On arrival, he was surprised to find

Above left: Eric in tropical gear, Morristown.

Above right: Eric in tropical gear, East Africa.

that Hugo Tanner and his wife had invited him to a lunch party for 150 people at Amboni Estates to celebrate Switzerland's 650th National Day. That night, he stayed with the Locks at the nearby Ngomeni sisal research station where he helped them late into the night with their final preparations for the annual Planters' Day celebrations, which were due to take place there the following day. It was only when they gave him a copy of the programme that he saw that he had been listed as one of the two guest speakers, 'co-starring in gold letters on the programme,' as he said, 'with the Member for Agriculture.' He had to get up early the following morning to hammer out his speech on a typewriter.

His speech—to 180 people in the sisal industry—brought him into direct conflict with Eldred Hitchcock who also spoke in his capacity as chairman of the TSGA and subsequently tried to engineer a very public row in the papers. Hitchcock's star was now in the ascendant in East Africa and he was determined to make the most of it. Sisal was already Tanganyika's biggest export as well as providing employment to a third of its workers; the British government had finally withdrawn its support for the disastrous Tanganyika Groundnut Scheme, which had for a time threatened sisal's dominance; and the US Department of Agriculture's latest statistics on hard fibres, which were published shortly after Eric's arrival, showed that global production had finally recovered to its pre-war level and that British East Africa was now leading the world in sisal production.[12]

Its 70 per cent share of the sisal market meant that it was now producing almost a third of the world's hard fibres.

The anti-Hitchcockites had also just lost their champion after the death of Alfred Wigglesworth in May at the age of eighty-six. He had continued writing to *The Times* to the end, his final letters on the stability of the pound appearing on 28 April and 16 May. Just before his death, he presented a set of wooden doors for the entrance to the William Lead Memorial Hall in Tanga, which the TSGA was now using as its headquarters. Perhaps they were his parting shot. They were carved with sisal plants and had a brass plaque with the words, 'Doors donated by Alfred Wigglesworth, May 1951'. Hitchcock would be reminded of him every time that he entered.[13]

In addition to his chairmanship of the TSGA, Hitchcock was also chairman of both Sisal Estates and the Tanganyika Sisal Marketing Association (TASMA).[14] According to his own figures, TASMA, which he had set up in 1948 after his failure to secure the necessary majority for a compulsory marketing co-operative, now represented 70 per cent of growers and 50 per cent of production. The composition of its board showed that its support came largely from non-British interests. The fifteen directors whose names and nationalities were listed on its letterhead included two members of the Karimjee family, one of whom was Hitchcock's vice-chairman, and five directors who were specifically identified as Greek or Syrian. Apart from Hitchcock, only two of the remaining seven had obviously British names, one of whom was C. A. Bartlett, Hitchcock's deputy at Sisal Estates. Hitchcock had chaired TASMA's annual general meeting only a fortnight before Eric's arrival and had used it to announce his securing of a $10 million deal with American buyers. It would, he claimed, earn the colony more dollars than every other industry combined.

He had only recently taken over as chairman of Sisal Estates. This listed British company had been created in 1936 to take over two existing East African sisal businesses, the Usambara Sisal Company and Bird and Co., in which Hitchcock had been an investor since its incorporation in 1920. The amalgamation was part of a consolidation of the struggling sisal industry in the mid-1930s that had already seen the flotation of two other companies that year, Consolidated Sisal Estates and Central Line Sisal Estates. At the beginning of 1951, the control and domicile of Sisal Estates was transferred from London to Tanganyika for tax reasons and Hitchcock replaced Colonel Charles Ponsonby, the Conservative MP for Sevenoaks, who had been its chairman since its incorporation. The company's accounts for the year to June 1950, which included Hitchcock's first annual report as chairman, were published a few weeks later ahead of the shareholders' annual general meeting in March, which would now be held in Tanga rather than London. Although Hitchcock conceded in his report that the price of sisal had more than doubled in seven months, from an average of £91 a ton for the year to June 1950 to more than £200 by the end of January 1951, he was confident that his members faced no immediate threat of competition. Sisal was still relatively cheap compared to other fibres; it would be some time before any new estates

Sir Eldred Hitchcock showing a sisal plant to Princess Margaret, 1956 (still from the newsreel, *Royal Visit to Tanga*, provided by British Pathé).

were in a position to harvest their first leaves; East Africa was the only producer of hard fibres in the British Commonwealth and the sterling area; and manila was still far from recovering its pre-war levels of production in the Far East. In short, it was a sellers' market. There was, as Hitchcock knew, no substitute for sisal that could be secured in sufficient quantities at a reasonable price. However, while he was confident of a rosy future in the short-term, he did recognise that the priority now was for sellers and buyers to work out how best to cushion the expected fall in price over the longer term.[15]

Hitchcock was also keen to point out, with some justification, that the growers' standard practice of selling their crop forward at an agreed price at the start of each season meant that they rarely received the high prices that were currently being bandied about in the press. That said, many growers saw the current high prices as some compensation for the lean years before the war when they had struggled to make any money at all. At that time, many had been forced to give up prematurely for lack of capital, and those that had survived had rarely, if ever, been able to pay themselves or their investors a dividend. It had been, according to Hitchcock, a period of struggle, disappointment, and frustration with prices falling as low as an unsustainable £15 a ton. Even after the consolidation of the industry Sisal Estates was unable to pay a dividend until 1943. Now the story was very different. After paying dividends of 20 per cent in 1948, 30 per cent in 1949, and 45 per cent in 1950 the *Tanganyika Standard* reported on the day of Eric's arrival that the company had just declared a dividend of 100 per cent for the year to June 1951. It was not alone. Consolidated Sisal Estates, which had also not paid a dividend until 1943, increased its dividend from 25 per cent to 60 per cent while Central Line Sisal Estates, which paid its first dividend in 1948, paid a 30 per cent dividend in 1952. However, Hitchcock did face some criticism from shareholders at the annual general meeting for the size of his remuneration package. As well as an attractive salary of £2,000, he was entitled to a bonus based on a percentage of the company's profits.

Given that he had little time to prepare his speech, Eric chose to focus on two of his favourite themes—the long-term prospects for sisal and the need to produce fibre of higher quality. While he agreed that the latter could not be achieved 'at the expense of uneconomical production at your end', he was convinced that the future of the industry depended more than ever on close co-operation between growers and manufacturers. For his own part, he said, he had decided to focus on exploring the opportunities for fine spinning, which required the fine fibre that came from first-cut sisal. Although this currently accounted for only 250 tons, or 6 per cent, of Irish Ropes's annual output, he was able to report that progress was encouraging and that production was being stepped up. However, as most growers in East Africa seemed reluctant to improve the quality of their fibre, he warned that 'the odds are that Indonesia will be giving us the well-prepared fibre we need and not British East Africa'.

Given the current crisis, he could not ignore the 'elephant in the room'. In what he hastened to assure his audience was a friendly warning rather than a complaint, he said that the recent high prices were a threat to everyone in the industry. All he asked of the growers was a little more consideration for the manufacturers' current difficulties. Otherwise they might lose their customers to manila and other fibres when they became available again in sufficient quantities. Although other fibres had experienced the same volatility as sisal, their prices had now begun to fall—so much so, he claimed, that he had recently been able to purchase 100 tons of manila for a £100 less per ton than the current price of sisal. All that stopped him from moving more strongly towards manila were the difficulties of finding the dollars to buy it and getting the necessary currency approvals from the Irish Department of Finance.

Eric's speech made the headlines. It was, as he put it, 'duly misreported' the following day on the front page of the *Tanganyika Standard* under the headline, 'End of Sisal Boom in Sight?'[16] Hitchcock had already tried to put him in his place by suggesting in his own speech that, while he welcomed any co-operation with manufacturers, this was probably best handled through the Cordage Federation of Great Britain. It was a crude attempt to side-line Irish manufacturers and those who were keen to develop new uses for the fibre. He followed this up in a letter to the *Tanganyika Standard*, an 'outburst' according to Eric, which he then copied to all the members of the TSGA. It was published on the inside pages of the paper the following week alongside an interview with him and a more detailed report of Planters' Day. Hitchcock suggested that Eric, whom he described simply as 'an Irish spinner', had exaggerated both the price differential and the threat from Indonesia. He accused him of painting 'an entirely erroneous picture' by failing to compare like with like. Although he was prepared to concede that the occasional parcel of low-grade manila might be sold at a heavy discount, Indonesia was currently exporting less than 5,000 tons of sisal a year and so could not be seen to be competing seriously with East Africa's 174,000 tons.

By the time that he saw Hitchcock's letter, Eric had moved on from Tanga to spend the weekend at Kikwetu, another major sisal growing area close to the Mozambique border. However, he felt that he could not let Hitchcock's challenge go unanswered. He also wrote to the *Tanganyika Standard*. His letter was published the following Friday. In the meantime, he made a 160-mile round trip to visit the Karimjee estates at Mikindani before flying back to Dar es Salaam with Eric Pope on Wednesday. He then had two days at the Rudewa estate before moving on to spend the weekend on the Ruvu estate. The owners and managers of all three estates had previously been Eric's guests at Morristown and so were returning his hospitality.

Unlike Hitchcock's letter, Eric's response again made the front page, this time under the headline, 'Expert Notes "Gigantic Strides" Made by Sisal Industry in Tanganyika':

In his letter to you of 3 August Mr Hitchcock has rightly drawn attention to the wrong inference which might have been drawn from your first brief report of the proceedings at Ngomeni on Planters' Day. However the more detailed report in your issue of today (6 August) makes it quite clear that my only reference to Indonesia, made in Mr Hitchcock's close proximity, was to the effect that in the matter of an exacting quality standard (my specific reference being to fine fibre only) the Indonesian producers are probably still on top, despite their setback of the war years.

My real intent was to impress upon the sisal industry in East Africa that the time available to them in which to gain a lasting ascendancy is growing short. It is very apparent to me that the majority of growers are doing their utmost to place their industry upon a scientific basis comparable to that achieved by the Indonesian growers twenty years ago. The gigantic strides which the African industry has taken since equipment became available after the war appear particularly impressive to one like myself visiting the territory after an interval of five years.

As to manila prices I must protest that the statement attributed to Mr Hitchcock in the same issue of your paper is indeed misleading. The grades of manila hemp quoted are unquestionably superior to sisal and have always commanded a higher price. Sisal is generally equated with grades J2 or K and any price comparison of recent date will go to prove my assertion that sisal at £245 today is not competitive. Time will show who is right.

I have no axe to grind save this. If the price of sisal is maintained at too high a level the pendulum will eventually swing back too far to the serious discomfiture of the spinner. A little compromise and restraint are all that are needed to carry the producing and consuming sides of the sisal industry completely through a period of crisis which does not end until prices assume a sensible, profitable, and stable level.

As it is not my habit to appear (much less to re-appear) in print I would be most grateful if I might through you express my appreciation of the extreme kindness and lively interest which it has been my pleasure to encounter from everybody in this veritable League of Nations which comprises the sisal industry of Tanganyika.[17]

Although Eric was keen to pour oil on troubled waters by offering some gracious remarks, he felt that the row summed up the amateurish approach and blinkered attitudes of many of the growers that he met during his trip. Most seemed to be interested only in making their fortunes. One of the Empire Marketing Board's first posters had claimed that 'Jungles Today are Gold Mines Tomorrow'. Now East Africa was experiencing a Klondike-like rush for the white gold of sisal. New farmers had already arrived in droves to purchase poor land in the hope of making a quick return. They had little, if any, experience. The greatest risk that they faced, as Wigglesworth had warned in 1946, was that any sustained increase in price would make sisal uncompetitive against other hard fibres, which were of demonstrably higher quality and consistency, and that, once they lost their customers, they would probably never be able to recover them. Eric was glad to have made his position clear but, as he wrote in his diary, he was determined not to be drawn into a public slanging match:

I shall not continue the argument further and am determined not to be annoyed by the quite obvious antipathy of Mr Hitchcock towards myself. By contrast everybody else with whom I talk seems to support my point of view. The impression that Mr Hitchcock possesses very few friends in Africa grows daily but, of course, I am moving mainly among people who have long opposed his point of view.

Eric had kept up a busy schedule during his first fortnight in Africa. As well as visiting many estates, he met formally with Hugo Tanner, the TSGA's president, and members of its board and, before staying with the Locks at Ngomeni, he was shown round Kenya's sisal research station at Thika. He was impressed by what he saw and by its new director who had taken over from Pullen-Burry, who had been a guest at Morristown five years earlier:

I liked Nicholls: his work appears to be essentially practical and he knows what he is up against—primarily soil conservation and the prevention of wasting diseases; also the lack of intelligent appreciation on the part of many growers....

However, although he seems to be co-operating with Lock, doubtless to the advantage of both, there is no official liaison between Kenya research, which is government, and Tanganyika, which is now the Tanganyika Sisal Growers Association.

He also spent some time with the sisal inspectors at Dar es Salaam, whose job was to certify and grade the bales of sisal before they were exported. He was not convinced by what they were doing, not least because they used two easily changeable grades for rejected fibre—'R1' for what was supposedly acceptable and 'R' for what was not. He decided not be tempted to buy 'even the first-class rubbish.... The great trouble is that "fit for export" may mean anything or nothing. One cannot have any confidence at all in the integrity of these rather ignorant but clever processors of native sisal'.

Most of all, he was unimpressed by those he met on the estates. His diary includes some scathing pen portraits of men like Hertzfeld, a young South African who had just taken over Mrefu Farm north of Nairobi. Eric's visit on the day after his arrival set the tone for what was to come:

> He came here recently with his wife and with intent, as I would suppose, to profit by the boom in sisal prices. The farm comprises 450 acres of previously abandoned sisal, now in a shocking condition. The man knows nothing of sisal or ramie [a fibre-producing member of the nettle family] or engineering but he has a very fine car and a good house. Some of his fibre may be excellent but much is abominable. Much of it is discoloured and Hertzfeld has been playing around with bleaching when washing. His wife, he said, 'got something from the chemist' but it was too dear but he now has some chloride of lime coming forward. Wigglesworths have obtained the selling of this sisal but it may not prove a wise move. Hertzfeld will be off as soon as the price breaks and, if his engineer leaves him, he will be sunk.

A manager from the Anglo-French Sisal Company shocked him with the assertion that 'we growers now have more money in our pocket and can afford to call the tune'. He was happy to admit that they could get by if prices fell by £100 a ton or more. When Eric tried to explain to one grower the potentially ruinous stock losses that manufacturers faced, he got the glib response: '… well, I suppose it is the banks which will really stand the loss'. Although he was impressed by the Kenya Chemical Company's new factory in Thika, which, after years of delay, was about to start making pectates out of waste sisal leaf, he found it hard to warm to its director, Mr Ambler:[18]

> He was a pale and pansy gentleman, not more than thirty, with 'co-respondent' shoes and faultless attire but a bit bloodshot about the eyes. I felt that if we interrupted his patter he would lose his place and need the prompt book. He has many other interests—I wonder who they are—but is still not producing and is

already a joke in the locality. What is the true story? I cannot do justice to this: it needs a Hollywood scriptwriter but Mr Ambler could do it. It sounds all too good to be true! He would not give me an answer to my questions. We should have taken tea in his private office but it was not quite laid on and we had had quite enough of being impressed so we expressed our wonder and admiration, bowed politely and departed.

Eric's visits to other estates were similarly stage-managed. He wrote of one that there was no baling in progress when they arrived and so little fibre in the brush-room that it was quite obvious that they were trying to impress their visitors by showing them only what could not be criticised too seriously. 'The tragedy about such estates,' he said, 'is that they are being operated by people who lack the fundamental knowledge of sisal and its production and whose interest in the fibre is unlikely to continue beyond the time when easy profits can be earned.' Another owner, who knew of Eric by reputation, was keen to meet him but, as Eric said, 'I would rather talk sisal to him against a background of a first-class Tanganyika factory than at his own—from what little I saw of it from passing in the car. He has sound ideas but is doubtless too much of an individualist like so many of those Kenya farmers. I doubt if these people ever get down to the true economics of production.'

Eric's typed diary, which he may have written up later from letters that he sent home, stops suddenly and without explanation shortly after his arrival at Ruvu for the weekend. His original plan had been to carry on to Rhodesia and South Africa and not to return home until the middle of September. However, he was already behind schedule and one of the people that he had particularly wanted to see was away and would not be back in time. The last entry in his diary on Sunday 12 August states simply that 'I hope to return to London on 5 September or by the first opportunity thereafter.' Although he seems to have kept to this schedule and was definitely back in Ireland by the second week of September, it is a mystery how he spent the next three weeks. Perhaps the latter part of his diary was lost or never written up, or perhaps he just needed a holiday. Although there is nothing to suggest that he was yet ill—indeed his diary suggests that, although he was clearly frustrated by much of what he saw, he was still in good humour and full of energy—he appears distracted and world-weary in some of the photographs taken that summer. At least he was able to tell Donal Scully when he returned that his trip had made Irish Ropes the best-known spinner in East Africa.

Eric found himself as busy as ever when he got back. Visitors to Morristown in the last quarter of the year included the manager of the Rudewa estate in October, Paul Wilson and his wife in November, and Sydney Tranter in December, who turned up the week before Christmas with colleagues from Switzerland and Mozambique. In October, Irish Ropes declared a 10 per cent dividend for the year. However, when Eric met with the Ministry of Industry and Commerce shortly afterwards to update them on the company's prospects, he was still preoccupied by the price of sisal. He already had 1,900 tons of raw fibre in stock and could not afford to buy any more even if he had thought it sensible to do so. With supplies once again exceeding demand, prices had already begun to fall. It meant that, although he no longer needed to investigate other sources of fibre, he faced an imminent risk of stock losses. Like all other businesses, Irish Ropes was also beginning to feel the effects of a general trade recession. For the time being, the company's export programme was still running smoothly, its products were competitively priced, and its workforce was working full-time. That would all change if markets remained depressed for any time. However, Eric was feeling sufficiently optimistic to move ahead with plans to double the factory's carpet-making capacity.[19]

In November, five years after the company's flotation had raised £63,000 of new capital, Irish Ropes completed a rights issue that raised a further £90,000. Holders of the 60,000 ordinary shares could apply to buy three new shares for every four that they held at a price of £2 a share.[20] Eric and his family applied for their full allocation and so retained their 29 per cent stake. However, the issue was more a sign of the company's current difficulties than its rosy prospects. The high price of sisal had left it seriously undercapitalised. As Eric had explained to the ministry the month before the company's latest shipment of fibre had cost it 50 per cent more than the nominal value of its share capital.

Eric would live for less than a year after his return from Africa. His death certificate states that he died from cancer of the bile duct with secondaries in the liver. My father, Peter, said that it was a long and distressing illness. He would die of the same disease more than fifty years later, a year after he was diagnosed and after receiving regular chemotherapy to keep it at bay. How and when Eric was told of his illness is not clear. Dorothy wrote in her house-keeping diary, in which she recorded her weekly household expenditure, that he had to be admitted to hospital at the end of February for removal of his appendix. Perhaps that was when his doctors discovered the tumour. However, he may already have been to see a specialist in London. He spent a night with Peter and Pam in Hampstead shortly after returning from Africa—'London, etc.' Dorothy wrote obliquely in her diary on 17 September—and was back again in the middle of January. Peter and Pam's flat was near where Guy and Peggy lived, and Peggy was still working as a cancer specialist. A few days before he was admitted to hospital, Eric wrote one of his last business letters to Donal Scully in New York. By the end of March, Bernard Roche had taken over his correspondence.

In April, Eric and Dorothy left from Southampton on a three-week holiday to Madeira and the Canary Islands. They had booked a first-class cabin on MS *Venus*—which they nicknamed the Vomiting Venus on account of the bad weather—and would spend nine days at sea and eleven nights on the islands. It was probably their first and only holiday abroad together. On their way back in May, they stayed in London with Peter and Pam for four nights. The following week, Eric had to return to hospital for more x-rays. His mother came over from the Lake District for a few days at the end of the month. She returned a month later with Ann but could not stay for long as Harry was now also unwell. Among the many who wrote to wish Eric a speedy recovery was Father Cussen from Newbridge's Dominican College:

> We are very sorry to hear of your serious illness. You must take great care of yourself now and not return to duty too soon. Please take some of the accompanying 'Buck-U-Uppo'. According to P. G. Wodehouse one tablespoon is the dose for an elephant. It has been known to make bishops frequent race-courses and night-clubs. But the laity need not be apprehensive.

In July, Peter returned from London the week after he celebrated his first wedding anniversary. He was at his father's bedside when he died on Sunday 20 July. At the nurse's request, he read him the 23rd psalm—'The Lord is my shepherd: I shall not want'—as he lapsed in and out of consciousness. Eric was two months short of his fifty-fifth birthday when he died. He was probably already bed-bound when he and Dorothy celebrated their thirtieth wedding anniversary in June. Michael's wife, Nancy, was pregnant with their first grandchild, Gillian, who would be born in October. Dorothy wrote one final entry in her house-keeping diary—'My darling Eric died'—and then drew a line under it. She only ever used it again to record Christmas presents given and cards received.

Eric's funeral took place in Newbridge three days later. Irish Ropes's factory was closed for the day as a mark of respect. The service was taken by Dorothy's brother-in-law, Reverend Evan Thomas Jones, who only a year earlier had taken Peter's and Michael's weddings. Eric was then laid to rest beside Horace Davies in Newbridge cemetery. Peter designed a simple granite headstone for his grave. Three days later, the *Leinster Leader* published an obituary under the headline, 'Leading Industrialist's Demise'. That autumn, Arthur Cox paid his own tribute in his annual chairman's letter to shareholders:

> Irish Ropes has suffered a grievous loss in the death on 20 July of our founder, Mr Eric Rigby-Jones, who from the start was not only the managing director of the company but even more so its mainspring. He came to Ireland from Lancashire, bringing with him an old tradition in the cordage industry. He established this company on 3 July 1933 and, taking over a then derelict portion of the former military barracks in Newbridge, he rapidly converted it into a modern factory second to none.
>
> He worked and planned tirelessly. He worked with his brain but did not disdain to work with his hands also. He instructed local unskilled labour and soon converted it into men skilled in an old but modernised craft. He employed new methods and modern machinery. He was a man of exceptional ability with unlimited energy, a clear foresight, and the single-minded purpose to establish this industry. As a result of his labours there arose a factory which may well claim to be one of the most up-to-date and efficient rope factories in the world.
>
> His life was devoted to the success of the company. It is the fruit of his efforts that today we proudly enjoy a high reputation not only in Ireland but in

many parts of the world. No-one realised better than he how essential modern machinery and the most modern methods are but his thoughts never turned from the men who worked the machinery and carried out the methods. He never ceased to think of our employees. No possible effort was spared to institute every possible scheme for their benefit. He realised the importance of making direct contact with the producers of sisal, the raw material of the factory. Through his visits to East Africa and his friendships with growers and producers he became a leading authority on the fibre.

He created and fulfilled much in his comparatively short life. The years since 1933 have been difficult years and to have achieved so much was a triumph of brain and effort. The place of Mr Rigby-Jones in the history of Irish industry must always be a high one. His loss is mourned by this company and by the cordage industry in many lands. It is mourned also by us who had the honour to be amongst his many friends.[21]

Eric's memorial plaque at the factory (from Irish Ropes's brochure, 1954).

Eric had indeed achieved a lot in his short life. He had built up a world-leading Irish industry from scratch and in the process revitalised a whole community. He had introduced new methods of working and had always placed individuals and personal friendships above the arguments of nations and politicians. He had grown to love his adopted country and the people with whom he lived and worked. However, he never forgot that he was born an Englishman, and a proud Lancastrian at that, and that he had fought with honour as a young man in the King's Liverpool Regiment in the Great War. Before his coffin was closed, Dorothy asked Peter to pin his father's miniature medals on his chest. She also placed a short notice in the British papers. It ended with his regimental motto: 'They win or die who wear the rose of Lancaster'.

16
Michael, 1952–1972

I believe the early stages are the most important time for influencing character.
I remember praying for a leader of men and my prayer was certainly answered.
When Eric was born the doctor said 'my word, you have a long-headed son' and
I know the dear has left his mark on many men which now I feel is going to
be handed on to other generations. I know I am passing on dear Eric's blessing
with my own.[1]

Eric's death was a bitter blow for his mother. She had already lost one son, Jack,
when he was only seven. Now she was also mourning the death of her husband
whose health had slowly deteriorated since their retirement to the Lake District.
Harry died nine days before Eric. Two months later, and just a month before her
eighty-first birthday, Alice climbed Harrison Stickle to perform her own private
act of remembrance. At 2,400 feet, it was the highest of the Langdale Pikes and
dominated the view from Little Garth, the house near Ambleside to which she
and Harry had retired. The only person she told was Peter, to whom she wrote
the following week:

> I did manage to get to the top of Harrison Stickle on Wednesday. Instead of
> having our ashes placed in any particular spot I had an idea that I would like a
> bit of us to be up there as dear Eric always called it the Tabernacle—so that now
> hidden in the cairn on top is a particle of father and I with an old shoe lace that
> your Dad must have fingered often and also a button of dear Jack's slippers so
> that I can always think that, whenever the family looks up to Harrison Stickle,
> our spirits will send blessings down. I have not told this to anyone else although
> I think Tim [Guy's 10-year old son] has some idea. The next thing will be getting
> your mother fixed. It has been a year of changes.

Alice returned to Ireland in December to spend Christmas with Dorothy. It was, as she wrote in the guest book, 'my longest visit to Eire for a final visit to Morristown to spend Christmas with the family including the first great-grandchild, Gillian. I give my best wishes to Irish Ropes and to all the family of my dearly loved Eric'. It would not be her last visit. She became a regular guest of Dorothy's and was there again the following Christmas for the christening of her first great-grandson, my brother, William. Her last entry in the guest book followed an extended visit in the summer of 1959 with Dorothy' sister, Lottie, whose husband, Canon Evan Rees Jones, had died a few months before Eric and Harry:

> Coming here with my dear good friend I too have enjoyed this wonderful month and, going back over the years since my first visit when I saw Irish Ropes start with one machine, to see now its present size and the change in the town and people I feel I can only add my blessing to its future.

By then, Dorothy had settled in at Maesgwyn, the new house that Peter had designed for her beside what would become the pitch-and-putt course at Irish Ropes's Sports and Social Club. He had already designed a row of nine houses for Irish Ropes's managers further down the road in Ryston Avenue. Michael and his family lived in one of them before moving in 1959 to The Gables, the house that

Alice in Ireland, 1953, with Eric's first two grandchildren, Gillian and William.

Peter had designed for them beside the River Liffey. Today, these houses, although much altered, are among the only physical reminders of my family's one-time presence in the town.

Eric's death came at a difficult time for Irish Ropes. On the day of his obituary, the *Leinster Leader* carried a gloomy headline, 'Kildare Industrial Depression', which reported a speech in the Dáil a few days earlier about redundancies at a factory in Newbridge. Although local TD Gerard Sweetman did not mention it by name, he was clearly referring to Irish Ropes:

> All over the country the position is serious, particularly in relation to unemployment. In Newbridge today there are 150 employed in a factory that twelve months ago employed 350 people. Those who are employed are daily in fear of their employment coming to an end. Nobody can suggest that that is due to mismanagement or bad handling of the situation by the owners. The factory in question is controlled by a supporter of the Minister's, and I say without fear of contradiction that he is one of the finest industrialists we have in this country. He takes every advantage of all the opportunities that offer. If the industry is not progressing, it is certainly not his fault. The same situation is causing grave uneasiness all over the county.... Apart from the number unemployed, all over the country there are people working on short time. We can only end the present grave situation by giving the people new hope, by encouraging them in the belief that we will get out of the trade recession and out of the depression.[2]

Although Sweetman's figures were exaggerated, the reality was hardly less painful. Eric had tried to keep redundancies to a minimum but was forced to lay off twenty-three staff in January and another forty in February. The town was afraid that up to half the workforce might lose their jobs. By August, staff numbers had fallen by 40 per cent since the start of the year, from 358 to 207. As Arthur Cox would explain in his annual letter to shareholders that autumn the crisis that had preoccupied Eric for the last year of his life had come to pass. Irish Ropes's sales had collapsed as customers cut back on their stock levels in anticipation of a fall in price. The price of sisal had then halved in six months, and while Arthur welcomed this inasmuch as 'our products are mainly for utilitarian use and were being priced out of use', the company had suffered significant stock losses. Three months before Eric's death, the government had intervened to limit its exposure by reintroducing tariffs on ropes and twine to protect it against dumping by overseas competitors who did not have to carry such large stocks in the national interest and so were better placed to take advantage of any sudden fall in price.

In October, in his address at the TSGA's annual dinner in Tanga, Eldred Hitchcock spoke at length about the recent volatility in price, which he claimed to have predicted two years earlier and for which he put the blame squarely on the Korean War and the rush towards global rearmament. However, while he accepted that the quoted increase in price, from £130 to £250 a ton, had been spectacular he claimed that the subsequent fall, from £250 to £90 a ton, had been even more so.[3] He also believed that the scale of the increase had been exaggerated and that the standard practice of forward selling had meant that growers rarely received the prices for which they were being criticised. His own figures, which were similar to Lock's average annual prices and so masked the impact of extreme short-term volatility, showed prices increasing from £167 a ton in 1951 to £179 in the first half of 1952 before falling back to £126 in the latest available quarter to September.

However, criticism of the growers and their attitudes could not be dismissed so easily. Six years later, the TSGA commissioned Cambridge economist Claude Guillebaud, who had recently chaired the British government's independent enquiry into the costs of running the new National Health Service, to write *An Economic Survey of the Sisal Industry of Tanganyika*. Although Hitchcock claimed in his foreword to the book that the survey was intended to be objective, Guillebaud was clearly expected to argue the growers' case. His statistics, which were provided by ten of the largest growers who between them accounted for a quarter of the colony's sisal production, showed the super profits of £103 a ton that were earned in 1951 falling back to £74 a ton in 1952 and £25 in 1953 before finally settling at a steady £17 for the next three years. By then, the price of sisal was down to £60 a ton.[4]

The fall in price in 1952 coincided with a challenging period in East Africa's history. Ten days before the TSGA's annual dinner, the governor of Kenya had declared a state of emergency. Princess Elizabeth and the duke of Edinburgh had already come close to cancelling their trip there at the start of the year. However, they went ahead and were staying at Treetops Hotel north of Nairobi when the princess was told that her father had died and that she was now queen. Trouble had been brewing in Kenya since the end of the war. The indigenous Kikuyu tribe, whose population had quadrupled in four decades, wanted to recover its tribal lands in the highlands, which in 1939 had been reserved solely for European settlers. They were being denied them at a time when Europeans were being offered grants of land to encourage them to settle. A week after the emergency was declared, Eric Bowyer, a farmer and veteran of both world wars, became the first European victim of the Mau Mau uprising along with two of his Kikuyu servants. It was the start of a brutal and horrifying period that saw atrocities committed by both sides. Although it was largely over by the beginning of 1954, the last Mau Mau leader, Dedan Kimathi, was not caught until October 1956. He was sentenced to death and hanged early the following year. Kenya and Tanganyika would both be independent within seven years of his death.

As well as the sisal crisis and the general trade recession, Irish Ropes was also hit by a series of Irish dock strikes in 1952 that disrupted shipping across the Irish Sea. The confidence of its British customers was dented just at the time when overseas demand for its products was growing. At least Arthur Cox was able to reassure shareholders in the autumn that the first signs of recovery had already appeared and that some of the workers who had been laid off at the beginning of the year had been reemployed. These problems must have added considerably to the strain of Eric's final days. During his illness, he had had no choice but to leave his fellow directors to manage the crisis on their own. After his death, they agreed unanimously that Michael, who had joined the board at the start of the year to take the place of his grandfather, should take over as managing director. He would be one of the youngest men to run a listed company in Ireland and would be in charge of Irish Ropes for the next twenty years. October would be a busy month for him. He celebrated his twenty-sixth birthday on the 11th, his first child, Gillian, was born on the 23rd, and Irish Ropes held its annual general meeting in Dublin on the 31st.

Although there is comparatively little information about Michael's first ten years as managing director, it was a time of significant anniversaries and the brochures that Irish Ropes produced to celebrate them, along with newspaper cuttings, give us some detailed snapshots of the progress that was made in a decade when the company continued to focus on the development of its carpet and export trade.

Gerald Sweetman's speech in the Dáil in July 1952 had referred to a more general malaise in Irish industry. Although Irish Ropes bucked the trend, the 1950s are often seen as Ireland's lost decade. It fell behind as other European countries saw high levels of employment and rapid improvements in standards of living. Ireland's economic growth, at just under 2 per cent a year, was the lowest in Europe and a third of the average achieved by other countries. It still suffered from rural poverty and deprivation, its farming practices were outdated and inefficient, and its industries, which had grown complacent and sluggish under the protection of tariffs, were disinclined to invest or innovate. Emigration reached its highest level since the 1880s, and although this helped to relieve unemployment, it was only at the expense of the country's longer-term prospects. Some half a million people, or 15 per cent of the population, left the country at some point during the decade. The funds that they sent home became a significant contribution to the domestic economy. The population fell overall by 5 per cent, from 2.96 million in 1951 to 2.82 million in 1961. The majority of those leaving were young. Life looked rosier overseas, and not least just across the Irish Sea in Britain. It was a reflection of the limited job opportunities that were available at home that the majority of them were women.

The measures taken by the government included the establishment of a commission on emigration, which sat from 1948 until 1954 under the chairmanship of James Beddy, the creation of the state export agency, Coras Trachtala, in 1952, and the introduction of tax reliefs on exports in 1956. Business made its own contribution with the foundation of the Irish Management Institute. In December 1952, 600 business leaders attended an inaugural meeting at the Gresham Hotel in Dublin. It was chaired by Sean Lemass, who had returned to government in 1951 and was now Tánaiste, or deputy prime minister, as well as minister for industry and commerce. He used the occasion to announce a radical change in Irish industrial policy. The era of protectionism was over—free trade would now be the order of the day. It would be a challenge for Irish industry. Businesses would have to raise their game not only to compete in overseas markets but also to survive in their small domestic markets against renewed competition from larger foreign corporations. Lemass was keen that the new Irish Management Institute should play a key role in developing the skills of Irish managers.

Although Eric had argued publicly for such an organisation at the beginning of 1952, his illness and subsequent death meant that Irish Ropes played no part in early discussions about its establishment and was not represented on its provisional executive committee. However, it was a mark of the company's standing that Michael was invited to sit on its first governing council. He was almost certainly its youngest member and found himself sitting beside his father's old friends, Vincent Crowley and Desmond Goodbody, as well as Aer Lingus's general manager, Jerry Dempsey, representatives from Bord na Mona and other major businesses, and economists and academics from Ireland's leading universities. Thirteen years later, in 1965, he would become the institute's sixth and youngest chairman when he took over from Jerry Dempsey. Meanwhile, he showed his early commitment by agreeing to the immediate release of Paul Quigley, who was selected from 200 applicants to become the institute's first secretary, and providing free Tintawn to carpet its offices in Leeson Park.

Quigley would remain at the institute for eight years before moving on to spend the last twenty-five years of his career as general manager of the Shannon Free Airport Development Company. When he and Michael were interviewed in the *Sunday Express* in 1968, he suggested that it was more important for people at the start of their careers to find the right boss than the right job. Of his own career, he said that he had originally thought that all businessmen were out to make as much money as they could. However, he quickly discovered at Irish Ropes that Eric Rigby-Jones's main purpose was to make the best products and have the best industrial relations. Although he expected a lot of his workers, he always looked after them and tried to help whenever they had any problems.[5]

Irish Ropes recovered quickly under Michael's leadership. Within a year of his taking over, its workforce was back up to 380. In June 1953, it placed an advertisement in the papers advising customers that, as a result of more efficient production and a fall in the price of its raw materials, the price of its branded Red Seal binder twine was being reduced by more than 40 per cent, from £285 to £163 a ton, and that its twines were now cheaper than almost anywhere in the world.[6] Meanwhile in Britain, the Hard Fibre Cordage Federation, which represented most manufacturers and effectively operated a cartel by setting industry-wide prices at the start of each year and allowing its members limited scope to offer discounts, was criticised for not reducing its prices fast enough. In August 1952, when the cost of sisal had more than halved to £98 a ton, it reduced its standard price for 3-inch sisal rope by only 10 per cent, from £245 to £220. Three years earlier, when sisal cost a similar £96 a ton, it had been charging only £133 for the same rope. In 1956, it was referred to the Monopolies Commission and found guilty of operating a number of practices against the public interest.

By 1954, when it celebrated its twenty-first anniversary, Irish Ropes was back to full production. It was now producing 350,000 miles of agricultural twine a year and employing 430 staff. All were members of a trade union and their benefits included free medical and dental attention, accident insurance and sickness allowances, and a non-contributory pension scheme as well as a staff canteen and sports ground. In an article for that year's *Irish Review and Annual*, Michael claimed that Irish Ropes had originally entered the export market because the domestic market was too small to keep the factory's modern plant going around the clock. As this had meant developing new methods of marketing and more complicated sales structures, it had focused initially on the UK. However, it now had customers in fifty regions across all five continents; annual sales had just topped £1 million for the first time and were split almost equally between Ireland, the UK, and the rest of the world; and, in just two years, its sales in the US had grown from £10,000 to £50,000 after a niche market had been found for its lassoos and lariats. It was now selling 70,000 a year. The company's strategy, he said, was to focus on those products to which the 'maximum degree of manufacture' had been added—those with the highest 'added value' in today's jargon—as this would maintain employment and minimise the impact of any sudden increases in the cost of raw materials.

Michael was determined that the company should celebrate its anniversary in style just as it had when Sean Lemass visited the factory in 1934. Guests to a formal lunch in the neighbouring town of Naas in July included prominent industrialists and members of John Costello's new coalition government, which had been returned to power in May's general election. Gerard Sweetman, who was now minister for finance, was there along with another Kildare TD, William Norton, who led the Labour party and had replaced Lemass as Tánaiste and minister for industry and commerce. When Norton addressed the workforce after they had been given a guided tour of the factory, his words echoed those of Lemass twenty years earlier. Irish Ropes, he said, played an important role in the lives of not only local people but also the nation. He only wished that there were more such industries with the same calibre of workforce and management. More controversially, he went on to set the company's achievements in their wider historical context, reminding his audience that, just thirty-two years earlier, the factory's site had still been occupied by a foreign invader that was fully equipped for war against the native population. Now the looms that had replaced the British barracks and its guns offered compelling evidence of the scale and speed of Ireland's transformation.[7]

That autumn, a day trip to the Isle of Man was arranged as a less formal celebration for the workforce. Twenty double-decker buses had been booked to take all the staff and their families—some 1,200 people in all—from Newbridge to Dublin Docks. There, at 8 a.m., they boarded SS *Mona's Queen*, a 2,500-ton steamer that the Isle of Man Steam Packet Company usually operated between Liverpool, Fleetwood, and Douglas. For some of them, it would be their first visit to Dublin; for half of them, it was their first time on board a ship or in a foreign country.

Aerial photograph of the factory, 1955. The first four houses in Ryston Avenue have already been built (top right) and, to their left, work has started on Maesgwyn in the grounds of Irish Ropes's sports and social club. (*Image courtesy of the National Library of Ireland*)

William Norton and Gerard Sweetman's visit to Newbridge for Irish Ropes's twenty-first anniversary, 5 July 1954. *From left to right*: Bernard Roche, William Norton, Michael Rigby-Jones, Gerard Sweetman, and Arthur Cox. (© *Irish Photo Archive*: *http://www.irishphotoarchive.ie*)

Irish Ropes's workers listening to the speeches during Norton and Sweetman's visit.

Michael and Nancy, with the other directors and their wives, had to spend the day in a round of formal receptions. After signing the distinguished visitors' book at the town hall and passing on a goodwill message from Dublin's lord mayor to the mayor of Douglas, they moved on to meet the deputy lieutenant-governor and present him with a copy of Irish Ropes's anniversary brochure. Meanwhile, the staff and their families were left to enjoy themselves. A journalist from the *Irish Times*, who joined the trip, wrote that it had been a long and memorable day when the *Mona's Queen*, proudly flying the Irish tricolour, docked in Dublin at midnight:

> It was plain, as soon as we went on board *Mona's Queen*, that for the excursionists the day was already well-aired. All traces of that edgy irritable sleepiness that normally lingers around the heads of Irishmen until about ten

o'clock had vanished long since, and the excursion was in full swing. A row of empty stout bottles—where they came from at that hour of the morning I don't know because the bar didn't open until after the boat had left the quay, but there they were, as large as life, standing in a row along the rail—set the scene: and the first notes of 'The Rose of Tralee' drifted across the sluggish waters of the Liffey before *Mona's Queen* had passed beyond the shadow of the big gasometer.

The row of empty bottles continued to grow in length and the singing in volume as the day progressed. Sixteen hours later, as *Mona's Queen* slipped up the Liffey again to the same berth, the Irish ropemakers were still singing 'The Rose of Tralee' and I dare say the singing went on all the way back to Newbridge. As a marathon performance it would be hard to beat.[8]

Although the statistics that are available for the 1950s are neither consistent nor comprehensive, they paint a coherent picture of Irish Ropes's continued progress. When the company celebrated its twenty-fifth anniversary in 1958, it claimed that production had increased twenty-fold in a decade. Although it continued to use other fibres, sisal was still its primary raw material. It was now buying 10,000 tons a year, or 4 per cent of East Africa's output, and making enough twine to reach to the moon and halfway back. While domestic sales had remained steady for six years, growing from £576,000 in 1952 to £588,000 in 1958, exports had leapt by 80 per cent, from £255,000 to £462,000, and now accounted for 44 per cent of turnover. Tintawn was proving to be a major international success. Production increased from 84,000 square yards in 1952 to 300,000 square yards in 1955. The four new looms that were installed that year would increase capacity from 350,000 to 500,000 square yards. Almost immediately, they were in use around the clock. By 1958, Irish Ropes was producing four types of Tintawn, the latest of them plastic-backed Tintawn Boucle, and was turning out 20 tons a week, 85 per cent of which were for the export market.

The 1950s also marked a watershed in interior design. New houses were designed to be smaller and more functional with fitted kitchens and wall units, open-plan living areas, and affordable mass-produced furniture. After the drabness of the war, people wanted to experiment with brighter colours and different textures, fluid shapes and abstract designs, and natural woods, as well as manmade materials like PVC, fibreglass, melamine, and plastic. It was the age of Ercol, G-Plan, and Heals and of stereograms, space-age light fittings, and coffee tables in the shape of artist's palettes. Tintawn fitted in with the *zeitgeist*, or spirit of the time. In 1964, Irish Ropes's annual report and accounts included a photograph of the Stormont Hotel in Belfast where Tintawn had been used to cover not only the floor of its public areas but also the walls and ceiling, and in 1967, a TD would complain that the members' restaurant had Tintawn on its ceiling at a time when many of their constituents could not afford it on their floor.[9]

'More Irish Ropes for Export'—loading a lorry at the factory gates (from Irish Ropes's brochure, 1954).

Michael showing samples of Irish Ropes's products and a map of its worldwide exports to William Norton at a trade show.

One of Michael's bravest decisions in 1956 was to commission Louis le Brocquy, who would later be recognised as one of the greatest Irish artists of the twentieth century, to design a new range of colours and weaves for Tintawn. It was the year that he represented Ireland at the Venice Biennale and was awarded the Premio Acquisito Internazionale for his bleak, cubist-influenced monochrome painting, *A Family*.[10] His designs for Irish Ropes, which followed a more traditional Irish theme and were given names like Galway Lichen, Bog Orchid, Connemara Red, and Donegal Tweed, were displayed in its twenty-fifth-anniversary brochure and prompted the English food writer and sometime textile designer, Patience Gray, to write in her weekly column in the *Observer* that what had once been dismissed as matting now deserved to be called carpet.[11] It was the start of a corporate commitment to good design that helped Tintawn become an iconic brand in the 1960s. Le Brocquy's designs were followed by those of Margaret Leischner, a former student at the Bauhaus, and Eileen Ellis, both of whom would be appointed Royal Designers for Industry for their work in textiles. Meanwhile, a young Joan Bergin, who would later win three Emmys as a costume designer, was employed by Irish Ropes to travel the world as a roving ambassador for its products.

However, Tintawn's designs did not meet with universal approval. In 1961, Coras Trachtala, the state export agency that was now also responsible for improving industrial design, commissioned an influential but highly critical report from the Scandinavian Design Group called *Design in Ireland*. As part of their research, the reports' authors visited Newbridge but, although they praised the factory's production standards, they found that its carpets had a casual joviality that was not to their taste.[12] They suggested that the company give more careful consideration to its choice of designer. Michael felt that he had to respond when the report was published the following spring, shortly after he and Bernard Roche had returned from opening Irish Ropes's new offices in New York. He pointed to the growing demand for Tintawn in America and the positive comments of other design professionals such as the Council of Industrial Design (now the Design Council) in London, and while he welcomed the report itself, he suggested that, in this instance, 'our friends from Scandinavia viewed Irish Tintawn in a too restricted way, and mainly in the light of what might be suitable in their own countries. The designers of Tintawn set out to create something which, while typically Irish, would also enjoy the widest possible appeal, based simply on excellence of design and colour.'[13]

By the end of the 1950s, Ireland's economic prospects were looking up. One of the catalysts for this was *Economic Development*, the plan produced by the secretary of the Department of Finance, T. K. Whitaker, which resulted in the government's white paper, *Programme for Economic Expansion*, being laid before the Dáil at the end of 1958. It was in large part a response to the emergence in Europe of free trade areas and common markets. The six founding members of the European Economic Community (or EEC)—West Germany, France, Italy, Holland, Belgium, and Luxembourg—had established a common market and customs union with their signing of the treaty of Rome in 1957. In 1960, seven other countries—Norway, Sweden, Switzerland, Denmark, Portugal, Austria, and the UK—would respond by setting up the European Free Trade Association (or EFTA). Ireland was in danger of being left behind more than ever. To catch up, it would have to resolve its problems of unemployment and emigration, open up its domestic markets to foreign competition, and start to compete effectively overseas. The White Paper called for the stimulation of a massive increase in private investment in industry.

Although de Valera had been returned as Taoiseach for a third time in 1957, he did not see out his term in office. In 1959, he stepped down at the age of seventy-six to stand successfully for the Irish presidency on the retirement of Sean O'Kelly. His place was taken by Sean Lemass, who now set about implementing the policies that he had originally laid out at the launch of the Irish Management Institute six years earlier. As Taoiseach, he would oversee seven years of growing prosperity. After its miserable performance in the 1950s Ireland's economic growth rate rose to 3.4 per cent a year in the five years to 1963. That said, the coming decade would be dominated by the efforts of both the British and Irish governments to join the EEC.

Irish Ropes also saw significant changes as Michael began his second decade in charge. When Arthur Cox retired in 1961, Michael took over the role of chairman as well as managing director. Arthur had been with the company from the start and its chairman for twenty-five years. He had always been Eric's closest confidant and greatest support. As well as running his own law firm, he sat on the boards of a number of prestigious companies, was president of the Incorporated Law Society of Ireland in its centenary year in 1952, was a member of the Seanad from 1954 to 1957 after being nominated by his friend and Taoiseach, John Costello, and oversaw the first comprehensive review of Irish company law since independence. Early in 1961, as he approached his seventieth birthday, he gave up all his business interests after the death of his beloved wife, Brigid. To the bewilderment of his friends and colleagues, he decided to study for the priesthood. He was ordained two years later and joined a Jesuit mission in Northern Rhodesia, which gained independence as Zambia shortly after his arrival. He would be there for less than a year before a Land Rover in which he was travelling crashed after a blow-out. He died three days later and was buried in the grounds of the Jesuit Retreat House at Chikuni.

Kenya and Tanganyika had both gained independence before Arthur arrived in Africa. On 9 December 1961, after forty-two years of British mandate, Tanganyika and Zanzibar were amalgamated as the independent Commonwealth realm of Tanzania under the premiership of Julius Nyerere. The following year, it became a one-party republic with Nyerere as its president. Kenya followed suit two years later, with Jomo Kenyatta likewise becoming first prime minister and then president. Independence would threaten the future of the sisal industry in East Africa at a time when it was facing growing competition from synthetic fibres.

Nevertheless, Michael oversaw a period of growing sales and profits at Irish Ropes throughout most of the 1960s. It is now possible to follow the company's progress in more detail because the Companies Registration Office in Dublin holds its annual accounts from 1964 onwards. These, like the chairman's report that accompanied them, became more comprehensive over time. Furthermore, with five-year financial summaries being published in the accounts for the first time in 1966, it is possible to track the company's performance from 1962 onwards.

By 1964, the company's ordinary share capital had been increased from £105,000 at the time of Eric's death to £315,000 and was now sub-divided into 1,260,000 shares of 25 pence to make them easier to buy and sell. Although no new capital had been raised since 1951, shareholders had been given bonus issues of £105,000 in both 1953 and 1964, which were funded out of the company's undistributed profits. As well as bolstering the company's equity, it was an effective way of rewarding investors without making them liable to dividend taxes. Although the Rigby-Jones family's stake had fallen after the deaths of Eric and Harry, when proper provision had to be made for their widows, they still owned 19 per cent of the ordinary shares, most of which were held through a private investment company, Tygwyn Investments.

Irish Ropes's accounts show that its revenues doubled in the six years to 1968, from £1.53 million to £3.14 million. Although domestic sales grew by a satisfactory 40 per cent, from £0.86 million to £1.20 million, exports almost tripled, from £0.67 million to £1.94 million, and now accounted for 60 per cent of turnover. The workforce grew by 50 per cent, from just under 700 staff in 1962 to an all-time high of over 1,000 in the three years to 1970. And profits before tax more than doubled in the three years to 1965, from £96,000 to £223,000, before growing more steadily to £279,000 in 1968. When the effect of the bonus issues was taken into account, shareholders saw their dividend returns increase from 15 per cent in 1962 to 40 per cent in 1968.

With its focus still on carpet production and exports, the company acquired a warehouse and sales office in Slough in 1960 to replace its previous reliance on agents and to ensure that there was always a ready supply of Tintawn on hand for the British market. By 1964, Irish Ropes was the largest manufacturer of sisal carpets in the British Isles and had its own sales team in Bentall's department store in Kingston-upon-Thames. After it quickly outgrew Slough, it had to move to new premises in Reading, which were four times as large. Tintawn was now being marketed both on television in Ireland, in a series of adverts that featured the dog, Rin-Tintawn, and in the British Sunday papers' new lifestyle-oriented colour supplements.[14] It had been registered as a trademark in the US back in 1953. In 1962, when American sales hit $500,000 and Tintawn was chosen as the floor covering for some of the public areas in Atlanta's iconic new 'jet age' air terminal, the company set up a sales office and American subsidiary, Tintawn Inc., in the Textile Building on New York's 5th Avenue. When John F. Kennedy became the first serving American president to visit Ireland in June 1963, five months before

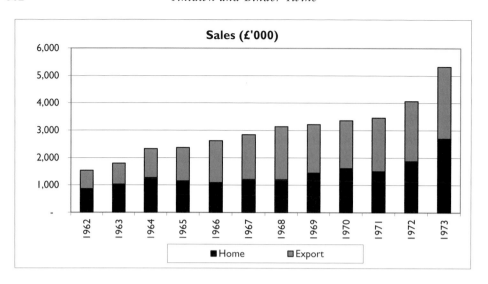

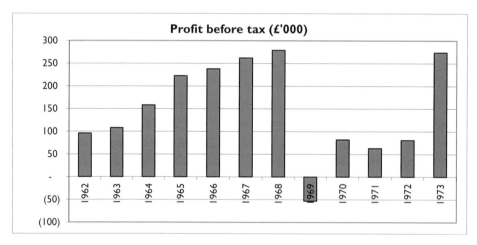

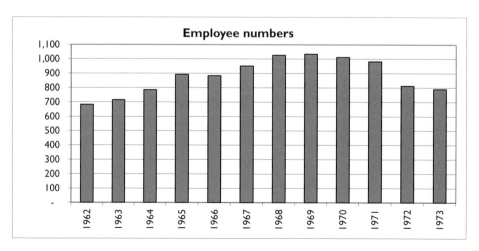

Irish Ropes's sales, profit before tax, and employee numbers, 1962–73 (from its annual audited accounts).

he was assassinated, he stepped down from Marine One at Limerick's Greenpark racecourse on to a runner of Tintawn Boucle.

The company continued to innovate and diversify under Michael's leadership. He became recognised as one of the best risk-takers in Irish business, unafraid either to introduce new products and materials or to withdraw them as and when they proved unsuccessful. Tufted Cushlawn carpets were introduced in 1964 and first exported to the UK in 1967. Although they were made from nylon, the plan was to introduce other natural and synthetic fibres over time. Curragh carpets, made from 80 per cent wool and 20 per cent nylon, appeared in 1968. Plytawn sisal webbing, which was designed to reinforce plastics, was developed in 1962. However, as there were no plastics manufacturers in Ireland at the time, all of it had to be exported. Manufacturers tried using it as a substitute for fibreglass in a range of products from plastic trays and pipes to wheelbarrows and dashboards. However, it was not a success and was eventually discontinued in 1968. After British Ropes became the first company to use polypropylene to make binder twine in 1964, Irish Ropes introduced it the following year to manufacture polythene film before extending its use to cordage, Tintawn Softcord carpets, and, in 1968, Sealstrap strapping for securing bundles of peat briquettes. By the end of the decade, Irish Ropes held the Irish Export Award for its outstanding success in the export market and was the first company to receive the government's award for scientific and technological innovation for its development of polypropylene carpeting. By all accounts, it was a shining example of the country's new economic direction and industrial potential.

But all was not well. Over the course of the decade, events outside its control increasingly jeopardised its ability to compete at home and abroad. It had always been exposed to the volatility in sisal prices, and in his review of the company's otherwise excellent results in 1963, Michael once more had to draw shareholders' attention to the potential impact of recent increases. Prices had risen by 50 per cent in the first half of the year, from £99 to £148 a ton, and had then stayed at that level. He blamed an increase in demand and Tanzania's imposition of a 5 per cent export tax, which it subsequently increased to £14 a ton.

Sisal production reached its peak in Tanzania the following year at 234,000 tons, more than double what it had been at the end of the war. By 1970, it was down to 202,000 tons, and over the next decade, it would fall by almost 60 per cent to 86,000 tons. Thereafter, the decline only accelerated. By 1986, it was only 30,000 tons, or less than had been produced in the middle of the 1920s. It is a level from which it has never recovered. The main reasons for this were increased competition from both synthetic fibres and Central and South America, where the Brazilian government had made concerted efforts since 1945 to promote its cultivation and so reduce its economic dependence on coffee.[15] The directors of Irish Ropes spent much of their time in the 1960s looking at natural and synthetic substitutes to reduce their reliance on sisal. They were always aware that they might not be moving fast enough. Nyerere's government had also begun to flex its muscles after independence. Early in 1964, it announced a £300,000 joint venture with a Dutch and German company to build a sisal-spinning factory in Dar es Salaam. Ten days later, Noorani Plantations, which owned four sisal estates, announced plans to raise £500,000 of local capital to build a similar factory in Tanga. Within a month, there were four such projects. One of them involved British Ropes and another was led by the Karimjee family and would have its equipment provided by Mackies. At the same time, the Tanzanian government created a new sisal authority to determine marketing policy and fix export prices. These first attempts to gain control of the sisal industry and to develop a local manufacturing base would be followed by a general policy of nationalisation, which saw most of the country's sisal estates nationalised in 1967. Among the businesses taken into public ownership were Eldred Hitchcock's former employer, Bird and Co. (Africa), and Wigglesworth's East African import-export house, Wigglesworth and Co. (Africa). In future, they would be run by the Tanzanian Sisal Corporation. Cutbacks in research and investment and poor marketing strategies would prove disastrous to the industry and were made worse by a deterioration in soil quality due to over-cultivation, labour shortages, and, in 1965, the breaking-off of diplomatic relations with the UK after the British government refused to recognise Rhodesia's unilateral declaration of independence.

At home, Irish Ropes was forced to increase its wages by 12 per cent across the board at the end of a ninth round of national wage recommendations that were completed at the beginning of 1964. It would add £50,000 to its annual wage bill, or a third of its previous year's profits before tax, as well as having a knock-on effect on the cost of all the supplies and services that it bought. Worse was to come. Within ten days of coming to power in the autumn, and only two months after Irish Ropes had moved into its new premises in Reading, Harold Wilson's Labour government rushed through a white paper to address the UK's desperate economic position. Among the drastic measures that it introduced to correct a projected balance of payments deficit of £800 million was the immediate imposition of a temporary 15 per cent duty on imports. Although this was later reduced to 10 per cent, it was potentially disastrous for Irish Ropes. To remain competitive, the directors realised that they had little choice but to absorb the cost rather than pass it on to their British customers. They reckoned that at best it would cost the company another £50,000 a year. Its profits were now in danger of being wiped out. The Irish government, having failed to convince the British government that its actions contravened the terms of the 1938 Anglo-Irish trade agreement, then helped cushion the impact on Irish business by subsidising 50 per cent of the cost. Even so, by the time that the duty was finally removed in 1966, the directors reckoned that it had cost Irish Ropes £193,000, £105,000 of which it had been able to recover from the government.

In a remarkable show of support for the company and its management, Irish Ropes's workers volunteered to work three full shifts on Saturday 14 November without pay. According to a report in the *Irish Times*, they had originally offered to work every Saturday without pay but the directors had refused because, with the factory now employing 80 per cent of Newbridge's working population, it would cause 'too great a reduction in the amount of money circulating in the town'.[16] Instead, they called for greater productivity during the working week. The following year, as a thank you, Michael personally presented each of the company's 717 workers with a prize bond that gave them the chance of winning between £100 and £10,000. The first to receive their bonds were James Coogan and Patrick Geraghty, two of the six workers that his father had originally recruited in 1933.

In spite of this gesture, which reflected the historically good relationship between management and workforce, industrial relations deteriorated throughout Ireland and the UK over the course of the decade. Irish Ropes was unable to avoid the fallout. External strikes and deflation led Michael to describe 1966 as a year of frustration. The country's electricity supply was disrupted and the picket of power stations meant that at one point 75 per cent of industrial workers were unable to work; a dock strike in Dublin once more interrupted exports and, when Irish Ropes's own imports of sisal were diverted to ports in France, Belgium, Holland, and Germany, Michael had to fly over to France to negotiate their release once he had settled the local warehousing costs; and a three-month bank strike over the summer made it almost impossible to pay staff and suppliers and to bank receipts from customers. In June, an exasperated Michael was reduced to telling the press that 'we are fed up living on tenterhooks all the time. I think this country is committing suicide.'[17]

Too often, to remain competitive in its export markets, Irish Ropes had to absorb rather than pass on these additional costs. Luckily, with raw materials still accounting for 50 per cent of its costs, their effect was cushioned by a sustained fall in the price of sisal. Prices fell from £148 a ton at the end of 1963 to £110 in 1964 and £82 in 1965. By the end of 1967, they were down to almost £70, their lowest level in twenty years. The growing use of synthetic fibres meant that supply now outstripped demand. Once more, falling prices, although good news for the Irish farmer, triggered stock losses for Irish Ropes and made its margins on twine unattractive against its other products with a higher level of manufacture. In addition, they meant that growers were once more losing money and might not be able to survive. Irish Ropes was exposed. In spite of the directors' attempts to diversify, they could not yet afford to lose their access to the factory's primary raw material.

As early as 1964, Michael had written in his annual report that 'we are all aware in our everyday lives of the growing use of synthetic fibres and it is of great concern to us that your company is not using synthetic fibres to the extent that it should.'[18] The following year, he appointed consultants to advise on the company's plans to move away from sisal and to review its management and organisational structures in a period of continuing growth. It led to the reorganisation of the company into seven divisions, one for each of its five main product lines—cordage, spinning, Tintawn sisal carpets, Cushlawn tufted carpets, and Plytawn—with another two responsible for planning and administration and research and development. Joe McCabe and Vincent Brazil, both of whom would later be managing directors of the company, were put in charge of the Tintawn and cordage divisions respectively. Although they were not that much younger than Michael, their appointment marked the start of a changing of the guard. McCabe, the third of six brothers to get engineering degrees from University College Dublin, had joined the company in 1958 and would be appointed to the board in 1968. Brazil, a native of Newbridge and one of five members of his family to work for Irish Ropes in the 1970s, had joined as a sixteen-year-old in 1947 and would be appointed to the board in 1974.

Yet, in spite of all the problems, Irish Ropes continued to grow. It was now in danger of outgrowing Newbridge even though the town itself had also grown rapidly. The 1966 census revealed that its population had more than doubled in forty years to 5,400 people and had grown by 16 per cent in the last five years alone, making it one of the fastest growing towns in the country. A newspaper article at the end of the year would describe it as Ireland's most prosperous town and a casebook of the country's industrial development.[19] However, Irish Ropes was already employing almost 900 staff. Unless more houses were built and the town's infrastructure and services improved, the company would struggle to find the additional staff that it needed to expand. The factory itself had also run out of space. It now occupied a large part of the former barracks, having taken over the premises used by the last works in 1963, and was operating around the clock at almost full capacity. Speculators were trying to turn a quick profit by asking exorbitant prices for any adjacent land. In 1966, Michael left the Newbridge town commissioners in no doubt that, unless they found a satisfactory solution, Irish Ropes's next big development might be elsewhere, and perhaps even in Northern Ireland where it would not face tariffs on its sales to the UK. It might mean that the whole factory would have to move. 'I intend to make Irish Ropes grow,' Michael told them bluntly, 'I intend to expand; and, if I cannot do it here, I will go somewhere else.... Over £1,000,000 worth of export orders crosses that bridge at the bottom of the town each year and in view of that I think there should be an overall plan for industry. If there is not what is the future of Irish Ropes in Droichead Nua?'[20] In the event, he did not have to carry out his threat. The following year, Irish Ropes was able to acquire 22 acres of adjoining land and start construction of a new 47,500-square-foot carpet factory.

However, overriding every other consideration for a major exporter was the question of European free trade. Although Ireland, Denmark, Norway, and the UK had all applied to join the EEC in 1961, President de Gaulle's veto of British membership had led to the suspension of all four applications. Ireland's continuing economic dependence on its neighbour meant that there was little point in joining the EEC if the UK was not also a member. Although all four countries reapplied in 1967, it was only in 1969, after Georges Pompidou had succeeded de Gaulle as president, that the French veto was finally lifted. Meanwhile, Lemass continued to prepare his country for the era of free trade. His signing of a free trade

Aerial photograph of the factory, 1965. The factory now covers a much larger area and all the original buildings have been demolished with the exception of the indoor riding school. The staff hostel can be seen at the bottom right corner of the site beside the water tower.

agreement with the UK in 1965 was seen an important first step and a trial run for membership of the EEC. Under the agreement, the UK would abolish all duties on Irish goods the following year and Ireland would implement a staged programme of tariff reduction that would see all its tariffs removed within ten years.

In 1966, Michael succeeded Jerry Dempsey as chairman of the Irish Management Institute. At around the same time, he was asked to become a non-executive director of two of the country's largest state enterprises, Cement Ltd in 1966 and Bank of Ireland in 1968. He was now well placed to contribute to national business policy, and in particular to Ireland's prospective membership of the EEC. One of his final duties as IMI chairman was to present Sean Lemass with a specially-bound copy of the institute's recent research report, *The Management of Irish Industry*. It was more than thirty years since Lemass had visited Newbridge to help celebrate Irish Ropes's first anniversary. Now, in two days' time, he would step down as Taoiseach and be replaced by his minister for finance, Jack Lynch. The institute's 420-page report, for which Michael had written the foreword, was a detailed review of the character and quality of Irish management and included a number of recommendations on how a national policy for management training and education could be developed over the longer term. It provided a much-needed reality check. Many medium-sized Irish companies (those which employed between fifty and 500 staff) were clearly ill-equipped and would struggle to survive in an increasingly competitive world. Launching the book at the Shelbourne Hotel in October, Michael described it as 'a searching, factual look by managers at their jobs, their background and training and their standards of practice … the first undertaken anywhere in the world on a national scale'.[21]

In March 1969, the government published its Third Programme for Economic and Social Development. The First Programme, which was the outcome of Whitaker's *Economic Development* and covered the period from 1958 to 1963, had been the government's first statement of its longer-term economic plans after the disastrous 1950s. The Second Programme, which ran from 1964 to 1970, was more ambitious but less successful. The Third Programme, which would cover the three years to 1972, was driven by Ireland's forthcoming membership of the EEC and was described in *The Times* as 'a further programme for industrialisation, particularly through foreign investment, which now stresses even more strongly a diversification of exports to markets other than Britain'.[22] It would depend for its success on a significant growth in exports at a time when industrial relations at home were poor and the trading environment abroad was challenging. Two months after its publication, *The Times* produced an eight-page special report, *Industrial Eire*, which included photographs and brief profiles of seven of the country's leading industrialists under the banner 'a vigorous and expanding economy needs people behind it with vision and energy'.[23] Michael was one of the seven and was described as having played 'a key and profitable role in pioneering Irish exports and in raising them to their present level of over £1m a day'. The others included Donal Carroll, the chairman and managing director of the tobacco company, P. J. Carroll, who had been a non-executive director of Irish Ropes since 1961; Guy Jackson, a senior executive at Guinness and president of the Federation of Irish Industries; and Tony O'Reilly, the British and Irish Lions rugby player, who would celebrate his thirty-third birthday the following day and be recalled to play his final game for Ireland in the spring. He had already had a successful career with the Irish Milk Marketing Board, where he launched Kerrygold butter for the export market in 1962, and the Irish Sugar Company and was about to take up a new appointment as managing director of the British subsidiary of H. J. Heinz. He would later be chairman and chief executive of the whole organisation and the richest man in Ireland before becoming a casualty of the country's banking crisis. In 2015, he was declared bankrupt by a court in the Bahamas.

Sadly, Irish Ropes's own run of success had come to an abrupt end by the time of *The Times* report. When the company published its interim results for the six months to February 1969 they revealed an 84 per cent drop in profits before tax. According to the *Irish Times*, it was the company's first profit reversal since 1960.[24] By then, it had its own labour problems in a period of growing industrial unrest throughout the British Isles. In 1967, the workforce rejected the wage agreement that had been recommended by its union representatives, and although the company then made a revised offer, which included a 10 per cent increase in basic wages and was higher than the directors 'considered prudent for future security', this too was rejected.[25] The dispute had yet to be resolved three months after the end of the financial year when the annual accounts were posted to shareholders. It would eventually be settled at a cost of more than £40,000 a year, but only after five secret ballots and the serving of a formal strike notice. The problem would not go away. High wage settlements in the public and service sectors provided precedents that Irish Ropes would find it almost impossible to match if it was to remain competitive in its overseas markets. It was already paying its workers more than its rivals in Britain. By the end of the decade, wages were rising faster in Ireland than anywhere else in Europe. At the same time, the company's scope for making a satisfactory profit in its domestic markets was limited by the government's introduction of price controls. It was a perfect storm. The company was seeing a substantial and unmanageable rise in costs rise at the same time as it was losing control of what it could charge at home and abroad. Like many Irish businesses, it was finding it increasingly difficult to survive. To make matters worse, sisal prices began to rise again in 1968. By the end of the year, they were back up to £80 a ton. Falling raw material prices could no longer offset the impact of other cost pressures.

Things only got worse in the second half of the financial year. By the end of it, Irish Ropes was losing money. Although revenues improved marginally, from £3.1 to £3.2 million, it had to report a loss before tax for the year of £53,000 against the previous year's record profits of £279,000. At first, it was thought that it might be a temporary blip, but after four years when the company had achieved a steady and respectable pre-tax profit margin of 9 per cent, it would struggle for the next four years just to break even. Even then, the results had to be shored up by some judicious accounting adjustments. The share price, which had risen strongly from £1.15 to £2.50 during 1967 and 1968 and had at one point reached a high of £2.68, crashed to less than £1.00 when the annual results were announced in November 1969. By the end of 1970, it was at a low of £0.45. The directors had to raid the company's reserves to maintain its dividend in 1969. However, only an immediate return to profit would allow them to maintain it again in 1970—and that looked increasingly unlikely.

A number of factors, both internal and external, had contributed to the sudden deterioration in profitability. By 1970 and 1971, the number of days lost to strike action in the UK were at their highest level since the general strike of 1926 and would rise again the following year. However, Ireland had probably the worst strike record in Europe. The number of days lost to strikes in proportion to the size of its workforce was almost two and a half times greater than in the UK. Even before then, a strike by maintenance workers in the spring of 1969 had come close to crippling the country's economy. It only ended when employers acceded to union demands for a 22 per cent pay rise to be phased in over eighteen months. When other workers refused to cross the picket lines Irish Ropes, like many other companies, had to halt production for the five weeks of the strike. It not only damaged its credibility with its overseas customers, who could no longer be sure when, or even if, their orders would be fulfilled, but with the factory already working at close to capacity, there was little chance of making up for lost time afterwards. The strike would cost the Irish economy an estimated £7 million. Michael reckoned that the cost to Irish Ropes was £125,000, or 45 per cent of its previous year's record profits.

Unfortunately, the strike coincided with the company's own round of wage negotiations, which led to another series of secret ballots and strike notices. It eventually had to agree to an immediate increase of 13.5 per cent with a further 6.5 per cent to follow at the end of the year. By the end of 1970, Irish Ropes's wage rates had risen by 50 per cent in five years. However, the settlement would provide only a temporary reprieve. At the next round of wage negotiations at the beginning of 1971, the workers asked for an increase of 25 per cent, which, if accepted, would cost the company £270,000 a year. To make matters worse, the British carpet market was going through a period of intense competition and over-production. As a result, Irish Ropes's Cushlawn carpet division was losing money without there being any immediate prospect of a turnaround.

The crisis marked a turning point in the management of the company. The changing of the guard had already started. Arthur Cox had long since retired and coming men like Joe McCabe and Vincent Brazil were already part of the senior management team. Now two of Eric's lieutenants stepped down. After more than thirty years' service, Bernard Roche retired as deputy managing director, although he would stay on the board as a non-executive for another six years. Joe McCabe was promoted to take his place. Seventy-two-year-old Patrick Doyle, who had been Eric's partner and the only other director and shareholder when Eric founded the company in 1933, also stepped down as an executive and would leave the board the following year. Henry Guinness, who was managing director of the merchant bank, Guinness Mahon, retired after eighteen years as a non-executive. By 1971, the board was down to five men. The three executives were Michael, as chairman and managing director, Joe McCabe, his deputy, and Arthur Shiel, the finance director and company secretary who had been promoted to the board in 1963. Joining Bernard Roche as a non-executive was forty-year-old Con Smith, who replaced Donal Carroll after he had resigned to take up a new appointment in Britain. Smith, whose company, Smith Group, was listed on the Irish stock exchange in 1969, was one of Ireland's most successful young entrepreneurs. If the directors were going to get Irish Ropes out of trouble, they were going to do it as a small and nimble team with limited outside interference or corporate governance.

Life would get no easier in 1970. It was made worse by another bank strike, which this time lasted for more than half the year. At least the company was able to report another increase in turnover and a return to profitability. However, its profit before tax of £82,000 was achieved only with the help of £69,000 of accounting adjustments without which it would have again struggled to break even. After an independent valuation of the company's land and buildings had yielded a profit, on paper at least, of more than £1 million it was decided that it was no longer necessary to write off the cost of its buildings over their expected useful life because inflation would ensure that they increased in value each year. It was also decided that its plant and machinery could be written off over a longer period than had previously been thought prudent, and that stocks could be valued less cautiously. Such changes to accounting policy are nearly always a sign that a company is struggling and employing every device to shore up its profits. However, Irish Ropes had always adopted an exceptionally conservative policy, knowing perhaps that it would then have reserves on which to draw when times turned bad. The changes, albeit made at a time when they were needed most, brought its accounting policies back into line with current standards and practice. It was not a trick that could be repeated. Dividends, which the board had managed with some difficulty to maintain in 1969, now had to be halved to 10 per cent and would remain at that level in 1971 and 1972.

Michael and his fellow directors came up with a three-point plan to return the company to profit. Its central element was a fundamental reorganisation of the factory to streamline production and improve efficiency. It would be the largest project that the company had ever undertaken. Although costly and disruptive, it was something that could no longer be put off. 'If the re-organisation had not been commenced,' Michael wrote in what would turn out to be his last chairman's statement in 1971, 'the results would have been disastrous with the ultimate closure of the factory.'[26] At the same time, the directors began a new marketing drive and became more ruthless in their decisions to exit loss-making product lines. As Michael told shareholders, 'we shall not continue to employ people unprofitably and shall face up to the harsh fact of pricing ourselves out of some of our traditional trade'. Joe McCabe's first job as Michael's deputy would be to supervise the reorganisation.

According to Michael, the first stage, which began in June 1970, required an 'almost a complete re-building of our factory'. Hard fibre production was relocated to a new spinning mill, which, along with two adjoining buildings, created 2½ acres of factory space under a single roof. Around 250 machines had to be moved. It would be followed by a reorganisation of the cordage mill and then the carpet and synthetics factories. However, although they were all completed successfully and led to record levels of production, any gains were wiped out by further damaging wage settlements. A graph in the 1971 accounts showed the stark realities that the directors faced. Basic wages had risen by 83 per cent since 1964, far outstripping a 45 per cent increase in consumer prices. Worse, carpet prices had gone up by only 15 per cent over the same period while cordage prices, after significant falls in 1965 and 1966, had yet to recover their level in 1964. Worst of all, wages were expected to rise by a further 32 per cent in twelve months after the implementation of a third and final phase of the National Wage Agreement at the beginning of 1972. Such increases were clearly unsustainable. No business could survive for long in such an environment. Nevertheless, while he was wary of making any forecasts at such an uncertain time, Michael told shareholders at the end of 1971 that he was feeling more optimistic than at any time in the previous three years.

One of the main reasons for his optimism was Ireland's prospective membership of the EEC, which was now only a year away. After the withdrawal of the French veto, the six original members of the EEC had agreed that Ireland, Denmark, Norway, and the UK should become its first new members on 1 January 1973. As a leading exporter, Michael had always recognised the benefits of Irish membership and, with like-minded business leaders, had worked hard to ensure its achievement. Since joining would require a change to the Irish constitution the decision was put to the people in a referendum on 10 May 1972.[27] Just over 70 per cent of the country's 1.8 million voters turned out, of whom 83 per cent, or 58 per cent of the total electorate, voted to join. It was a decisive popular mandate and one that was reflected in Irish law a month later, on 8 June, with the passing of the Third Amendment of the Constitution Act. It was almost fifty years to the day since the people of Ireland had voted for independence on 16 June 1922.

Ten days after the passing of the act, Michael was in a delegation of fifteen business leaders and representatives of industry who were travelling to Brussels for talks with EEC officials. Three of them had arranged to make their own way there, but the other twelve flew together from Dublin to Heathrow on the afternoon of Sunday 18 June. There, just before 4 p.m., they boarded a BEA Trident for the onward flight to Brussels. They were travelling a day early, and the plane was unusually full, because airline pilots around the world had called a one-day strike the following day to protest against the recent escalation in the hijacking of commercial aircraft. Tragically, the plane went into a deep stall within two minutes of take-off and before it had gained sufficient height for the pilot to take corrective action. One eye-witness described how it just dropped from the sky before crashing on a thin strip of open ground near Staines, two miles from the airport. It was a miracle that it avoided not only the town but also the reservoirs to the west of the airport, a line of overhead power cables, and the busy A30 road. All 118 people on board—112 passengers and six crew—were killed. Although the first to arrive on the scene reported an overwhelming smell of aircraft fuel, the plane did not explode. What they remembered most was the eerie silence punctuated only by the hissing of air lines.

One of them was thirty-one-year-old Frances Castledine, a nursing sister in the accident unit at nearby Ashford Hospital, who had been at home looking after her twelve-week-old baby. She remembers hearing a dull thud before a boy from the paper shop knocked on her door to tell her the news. She rushed to the scene. Although she was warned of the risks of explosion or fire she climbed into the fuselage to see who she could help, giving first aid to the two to three passengers who were still alive, albeit for only a short while, and then checking for signs of life before the bodies were removed. Her detailed witness statement, given three days after the accident, is testimony to both her great courage and the horrors that she saw.[28] She would be awarded the MBE for her gallantry a year later on the day that the report of the public enquiry into the disaster was published.

The Staines air disaster, as it has become known, is still the worst accident in British aviation history. Only the terrorist bombing of Pan-Am flight 103 over

The Staines air crash, 18 June 1972. (*Mirrorpix*)

Lockerbie in 1988 resulted in greater loss of life. The crash was also a devastating blow to Irish industry. Most of the twelve Irish businessmen on board were still in the prime of their lives. *The Times* compared its likely effect on Irish business to that of the 1958 Munich air disaster on British football: '... in one afternoon twelve of the Republic's leading industrialists ... were swept away from their leading positions in the business community.... In the close-knit circle of Irish commercial life, the real loss is far greater than the numbers imply'.[29] The list of those who died, which is given in an appendix, underlines the scale of the loss. Irish Ropes itself lost two of its five directors in Michael Rigby-Jones and Con Smith.

The scale of the tragedy was felt immediately in Ireland. People across the world will always remember where they were when President Kennedy was assassinated in Dallas in 1963 and Princess Diana was killed in Paris in 1997. The Staines air disaster had the same impact on the people of Newbridge and Ireland. Irish Ropes's factory, like businesses throughout the country, was closed the following day as a mark of respect for the victims. Aer Lingus's only flight of the day came after the union representing the striking pilots allowed a Boeing 737 to fly from Dublin to London with the victims' families. That evening, the Newbridge town commissioners called a special meeting to pass a vote of sympathy for Michael's family. The following day, the Dáil stood in silence after tributes had been paid by the Taoiseach and the leaders of the main political parties. On Thursday, they went to Dublin airport to meet the first six coffins when they were flown back from Heathrow.

Michael's funeral was held in Newbridge the next day. Ann remembers that she and Peter were given a police escort from the airport when they arrived from England. It is still thought of as one of the darkest days in the town's history. Everything came to a standstill: every shop and business was shut, their blinds drawn as a mark of respect; the police closed the roads and diverted all traffic away from the town; and more than 2,000 people followed the cortege as it processed slowly down Main Street. Peter walked immediately behind the hearse alongside Joe McCabe; fourteen of the factory's longest-serving staff formed a guard of honour on both sides of it; and six of its union representatives acted as pall bearers. The funeral service was attended by the minister for industry and commerce and representatives from national and local government as well as by business leaders and representatives of many organisations. The sermon was preached by the protestant archbishop of Dublin, Alan Buchanan, who had already conducted a service at Dublin cathedral that morning for another victim. As padre of the 2nd Battalion, South Staffordshire Regiment, he had served with Guy in Sicily and Arnhem. They had spent all their captivity together, from their first days at the Airborne Hospital in Apeldoorn through their transfer to St Joseph's Hospital to their final release at Heemstede in May 1945.

After the service, the cortege stopped for a few moments at the factory before moving on to Newbridge cemetery where Michael was buried near his father and Horace Davies. A few days later, the *Irish Times* published a personal appreciation of his life by Paul Quigley. His words echo those that Arthur Cox had written about his father twenty years earlier:

Michael Rigby-Jones was forty-five when he died so tragically. He died when he still had, to an unusual degree, the vigour and drive of youth. Few men accomplished more in their lifetimes. Fewer still had so much left to give. Ireland has suffered a heavy loss when its need is great and growing.

There is a certain restraint in writing about him because nobody had less use for pretentiousness, humbug, or flattery. If he had a fault it was in under-valuing himself. Not through any false modesty but because of a penetrating honesty which did not allow the self-deception with which most men protect their self-regard.… He worked so hard and had so little use for social distraction that it was almost as if he realised that time was short. His concern for people was expressed as much in quiet ways, known to very few, as in his public offices. Two recent private letters from him deal with ideas related, on the one hand, to alleviating problems of unemployment and, on the other, with developing qualities of leadership and responsibility in youngsters. He saw a need and worked to meet it, without any interest in personal credit. He took office not because he enjoyed its honours but because he knew that it could enable him to contribute to the community.

Michael's funeral cortege passes the Bank of Ireland on its way down Main Street.

Michael's family at his graveside. In the centre of the photograph are (from left to right) Helen, Nancy, and Gillian Rigby-Jones, Joe McCabe, and Peter, Dorothy, and Ann Rigby-Jones.

He gave a great deal, took little. He lived modestly. His pleasure was to be with his family. His only outside relaxation was sailing. He loved the sea, perhaps because its demands were for the qualities he had in such excellent measure—self-discipline, a sense of responsibility, a reality and a clarity of thought. And sailing was a sport he could share with his family.

He built well. In the fullest and best sense of the word he lived nobly. His death at the height of his ability is a bitter loss.[30]

17

The End of the Ropes

The morning hooter called the workers to the factory line
To weave the bales of sisal into rope and binder twine.[1]

On the day of Michael's funeral, Irish Ropes announced that Aer Lingus's former managing director, Jerry Dempsey, had been appointed its new chairman and Joe McCabe its managing director. The company's three remaining directors—Bernard Roche, Arthur Shiel, and Joe McCabe himself—had had to act quickly and decisively. Dempsey, whom Michael had succeeded as chairman of the Irish Management Institute in 1965, later revealed that Michael had already been thinking of separating the roles of chairman and managing director once more and of promoting McCabe to managing director. Perhaps he thought that a fresh outlook was needed or he may simply have been exhausted after four of the most difficult years of his life. Although he was only forty-five when he died, he had been running the company for twenty years, longer indeed than his father.

Although the Rigby-Jones family would remain Irish Ropes's largest shareholders for some time, Michael's death marked the end of their active involvement in the fibre industry after more than two centuries. They had progressed from flax dressers in North Wales in the eighteenth century to twine merchants and rope-makers in Lancashire in the nineteenth, and, finally, to manufacturers of sisal ropes and carpets in Ireland in the twentieth. At the time of Michael's death, his four children—Gillian (nineteen), Helen (eighteen), Robert (sixteen), and Philip (eleven)—were all still teenagers. So too were Eric's other two grandchildren, my brother William and myself. None of us had the age or experience to take his place. There were no obvious heirs as there had been in previous generations, and even if there had been, it would have been wrong to choose them. Irish Ropes was

Michael and Nancy with their three eldest children, Gillian, Robert, and Helen. Their fourth child, Philip, was born in September 1960.

now a major listed company and of a size and complexity that it could no longer be thought of as a family concern. The board's choice of Dempsey and McCabe was both appropriate and astute.

Dorothy, like Alice before her, now had to cope with the loss of a son. She never fully recovered from the shock. She suffered a stroke and sold Maesgwyn within a year of Michael's death, moving to live with her daughter in Devon. Ann gave up work to look after her. Peter designed a self-contained annexe for his mother at his sister's house, Tygwyn, which he had designed for her a few years earlier. However, once it was built, Dorothy preferred to live with Ann in the main part of the house. Perhaps she remembered how lonely she felt at the Ruff when Eric first went to Ireland. She would spend the last ten years of her life in Devon. By the time of her death in 1983, she had been a widow for more than thirty years. Her ashes were flown back to Ireland and buried beside Eric in Newbridge cemetery. A year after Dorothy left Newbridge, Nancy sold The Gables and moved to Dublin with her four children. They are all still living there with the grandchildren and great-grandchildren that Michael never lived to see. Nancy is now well into her nineties and has been a widow for half her life.

Michael's death, like his father's, came at a difficult time for Irish Ropes. The directors had to make almost a fifth of the workforce redundant in 1972, cutting its numbers from 982 to 812. Moreover, as Jerry Dempsey made clear in his first report to shareholders at the end of the year, the country's already difficult commercial life had been made worse by the recent escalation of violence in Northern Ireland. Internment without trial had been introduced the year before and the British Army's shooting of fourteen protesters in Londonderry on Bloody Sunday in January had marked the start of a year that would see the greatest loss of life during the twenty years of the Troubles.

Nevertheless, McCabe and Dempsey oversaw a remarkable recovery in Irish Ropes's fortunes. By 1975, Dempsey, who adopted an attitude of cautious optimism throughout his time as chairman, felt confident enough to write in his annual report that 'our company is in a substantially stronger position than at any time in our history, notwithstanding the continuance of worldwide economic recession/depression coupled with abnormally high rates of inflation.'[2] In 1973, after the reorganisation of the factory, profits recovered to the levels that had been achieved before the crisis in 1967 and 1968. Thereafter, they rose steadily to reach £869,000 in 1979. Sales almost quadrupled in the same period, from £5.3 million to £19.5 million, but margins remained tight at around 5 per cent and would never again reach the 9 per cent of the boom years in the 1960s.

The improvements were not achieved without making some tough decisions. As well as shedding staff, the directors continued to invest heavily in buildings and equipment as they moved away from sisal to focus on specialised high-quality and export-oriented products. Their decision was made easier by Tanzania's imposition of a £50 export levy on sisal, which contributed to its jump in price in 1973 from £108 to £260 a ton. In the three years to 1974, Tintawn's share of the company's sales fell from 30 to 10 per cent. In 1979, Irish Ropes discontinued

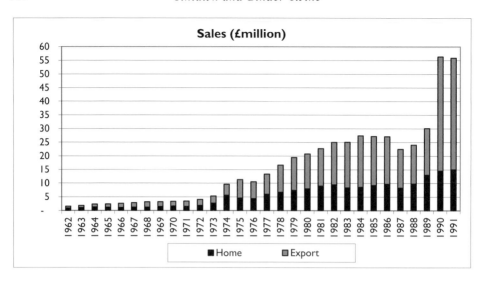

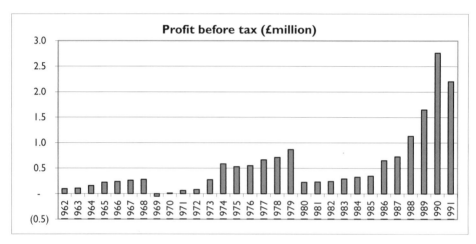

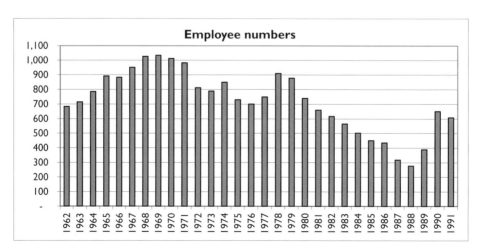

Irish Ropes's sales, profit before tax, and employee numbers, 1962–91 (from its annual audited accounts).

its fine spinning of sisal and the manufacture of sisal carpets. It was a significant moment, for these were the products and processes on which Eric had staked the company's future immediately after the war and which had done most to earn it a worldwide reputation. But sisal, which had still accounted for 95 per cent of the factory's production at the time of Michael's death, would soon account for less than 20 per cent. It no longer had a future as a raw material. There was a certain irony that in 1979, Tanzania's President Nyerere was given a guided tour of the factory during a state visit to Ireland. In part, it was recognition of the company's contribution to the development of the former colony. However, the directors, having realised that they could no longer compete against the low cost of manufacturing in East Africa, had also agreed to provide technical and administrative assistance to the Tanzanian Carpet Company so that it could make its own sisal carpets.

Anticipating that there would be a worldwide decline in demand for cheaper synthetic carpets, the board chose instead to focus on high-quality wool carpets that appealed to the international interior design market. It also developed new polypropylene products like Versatex carpet backing, which both Axminster and Wilton would use for their own carpets. In 1978, after another strategic review that recommended diversifying into non-textile businesses with a wider geographical spread in order to reduce risk, the board made its first significant foray into the acquisitions market by buying businesses in both Ireland and the UK. It had already dipped its toes in the water a year earlier by buying a 30 per cent stake in Anderco, a Cork-based company that supplied ropes and lifting gear to the offshore oil and gas industries. The largest of the latest acquisitions was a successful bid for Alfred Lockhart, a publicly quoted manufacturer of industrial plastic and polypropylene sheeting based in Isleworth in West London. The purchase price of £1.75 million was funded partly by a share issue, one new Irish Ropes share and £1 in cash being offered for every Lockhart share. It would dilute the Rigby-Jones family's stake in the company from 12 to 10 per cent. The other acquisitions were Turners (Cordage and Canvas), a wholesaler based in Bedford, and an 80 per cent stake in Edward Earls Ropes, a family-owned manufacturer of barbed wire and chain-link fencing in Limerick.

In spite of this change in strategic direction, Irish Ropes hit the wall again in 1980 after another good run of seven years. Although inflation helped sales break through the £20 million barrier for the first time, margins fell back to 1 per cent as the company reported a fall in pre-tax profits of almost 75 per cent, from £869,000 to £224,000. Worse, in line with financial reporting standards at that time, this reported 'headline' profit reflected only ordinary trading activities and so excluded £1.2 million of one-off redundancy and restructuring costs, which were booked 'below the line'. These would have plunged the company deep into the red but for the judicious booking of a 'paper' profit of £2.0 million on the revaluation of its land and buildings. Meanwhile, employee numbers, after a brief recovery in 1978 and 1979, fell by 16 per cent, from 880 to 740, and would continue to fall for the next eight years before finally bottoming out at 280 in 1988.

It was another period of strikes and industrial unrest throughout the British Isles. In Britain, the winter of discontent brought down James Callaghan's Labour government in March 1979 after it lost a vote of confidence in the House of Commons by a single vote. The general election five weeks later would see Margaret Thatcher become the country's first female prime minister. That autumn, Dempsey wrote with gloomy lyricism in his annual report to shareholders that 'it would be foolhardy to venture into the future of tomorrow without facing the reality that our take-off pad consists of shifting sand. And yet we dare not stand still—to do so would be to stagnate and die'.[3] The following year, the company was hit by another series of perfect storms. The worst European harvest on record led to a fall in demand for agricultural twine; deep economic depression forced many British carpet manufacturers to close, leading to the distressed selling and dumping of stock; Australia's decision to increase its import duties from 11 to 40 per cent destroyed in a stroke a market that Irish Ropes had carefully built up over a decade; the oil crisis that followed the overthrow of the Shah in Iran saw a threefold increase in hydrocarbon taxes in Ireland, which in turn increased the company's production and transport costs; and, in addition to the problem of persistently high interest rates, the Irish punt's peg to sterling was finally removed after more than fifty years of independence when Ireland joined the European Monetary System. Currency fluctuations would now add another element of uncertainty to Irish Ropes's trade with the UK.

Again, the company reacted in the only way that it knew by implementing another immediate and far-reaching package of measures—a reorganisation of the factory's physical layout and machinery to improve efficiency, a rationalisation of the management structure, the review and closure of loss-making product lines, and a series of cost reduction programmes. But once again there was no easy or instant solution. Although the company's management had shown itself to be nimble in the past it was becoming increasingly difficult to dodge the bullets. Although turnover continued to grow over the next six years, reaching £27 million in 1985, profit margins remained stuck at 1 per cent. Another £933,000 had to be spent on redundancy and reorganisation costs between 1982 and 1984. With such costs incurred in four of the previous five years, it was getting increasingly difficult to argue that they were either unusual or exceptional except in terms of their sheer scale. Altogether, they totalled more than £2 million over a six-year period, and although they were partially offset by a profit of £461,000 on the sale of land in 1984, they exceeded the company's profits on its ordinary trading activities. Whatever positive spin they tried to put on it, the directors could no longer hide the fact that the company was consistently losing money.

In 1983, Jerry Dempsey, who was now seventy-seven, stepped down as chairman after eleven years. Joe McCabe took his place and Vincent Brazil was promoted to group managing director. It was Irish Ropes's fiftieth anniversary. The minister for finance, Alan Dukes, visited the factory to unveil a commemorative plaque and a special 'Irish Collection' rug was woven to celebrate its golden jubilee. However, the celebrations were muted as the company was not yet out of the woods. Joe

McCabe stepped down as chairman only four years later to become chairman of Irish Distillers Group. His place was taken by Conor McCarthy, a former managing director of the Ryan Hotel Group who had taken Con Smith's place on the board back in 1972. He was chairman for only eighteen months before he too resigned over what a company press release called 'a policy disagreement over the long-term strategic development of the group'.[4] Joe McCabe, who had remained on the board as a non-executive, had resigned six weeks before him, finally severing his connection with Irish Ropes after thirty years—longer than either Eric or Michael Rigby-Jones. McCarthy's place was taken by Brendan O'Kelly, the chairman of a firm of management consultants.

In spite of the irreconcilable differences in the boardroom, the company had again been able to recreate and relaunch itself. It finally stopped making sisal baler twine in 1986. Although it continued to make Red Setter twine from polypropylene, the closure of the sisal plant marked the end of Irish Ropes's association with the fibre after more than fifty years. It was, as the *Irish Times* reported, the end of an era.[5] The old sisal warehouses were converted into a cold storage facility, which would reportedly be used to store the Irish 'butter mountain', the surplus agricultural production, which, along with milk and wine lakes, was the unintended consequence of the generous subsidies provided under the EEC's Common Agricultural Policy.

Irish Ropes's profits began to improve again in 1986 and then rose dramatically to reach almost £2.8 million in 1990. Sales more than doubled over the same period, from £27 million to £56 million. However, yet again, the cumulative profits over the five years of £7.1 million were virtually wiped out by exceptional costs of £6.4 million. It meant that the company only just managed to break-even over the course of the decade. A large proportion of the exceptional costs were booked in 1987 when the company sold its carpet division, now known as Curragh-Tintawn Carpets, to a management buy-out. Although the precise terms of the deal were not made public, it had all the signs of a fire sale. Although the division still accounted for almost a third of the company's sales, it had been losing money for some time. In addition to booking £3.2 million of other costs, most of which were the losses incurred by the division after the decision had been taken to sell it, the directors had felt it prudent to assume that the £1.5 million interest-free loan, which it gave to the new owners to sweeten the deal when it was in danger of collapsing would probably never be repaid.

Irish Ropes now bore little relation to the company that Eric Rigby-Jones had founded in 1933. After the sale of Curragh-Tintawn Carpets, it was left with just its cordage plant and cold store in Newbridge and its plastics and wire divisions in Isleworth and Limerick. The plan now was to open a new plant in Newbridge to manufacture polypropylene containers for butter, yoghurt, and other food products. Times change and companies must necessarily change with them. However, Irish Ropes was no longer using sisal or making the iconic products for which it is most remembered even now—Tintawn carpets, which were said to be so rough that they grazed children's knees and encouraged them to stand at an early age, and Red Setter twine, which could be found on every Irish farm and which farmers used for everything from tying gates to holding up their trousers.

The decision to issue shares to fund the acquisition of Alfred Lockhart in 1978 meant that by 1986 Irish Ropes's share capital had more than tripled since Michael's death, from £511,000 to £1.65 million. Now the directors' new strategy of expanding aggressively by acquisition in both the UK and Europe—it was surely this that caused the rift within the boardroom—was funded by a series of increasingly ambitious share issues. These raised £1.8 million in 1986, £3.7 million in 1989, and £8.3 million in January 1990, when the company bought KSH Plastics (Belgium) from ICI for £7.7 million. The acquisitions led to a boom in sales and profits. By the end of the decade, the company was listing its principal activity as the processing of polymers and the production of plastic-based packaging products. Only 30 per cent of its output was now being produced in Ireland, and only 26 per cent of its sales were to Irish customers. In 1989, the company decided to change its name from Irish Ropes plc to the more anodyne and anonymous IRG plc. The company had already lost its original purpose and most of its spirit of place. Now, along with its name, it was losing its identity and perhaps even its soul.

By the end of 1991, it was clear that the revival in IRG's fortunes had made it a potential target for a takeover. By then, the Rigby-Jones family held only a negligible stake in the business. Tygwyn Investments had outlived its purpose by the mid-1980s—1983, the year of Dorothy's death, was the last time that it was disclosed in the accounts as a significant shareholder—and the shares that had then been distributed among the family had mostly been sold after the share price rocketed in the three years to 1989.[6] According to the company's 1991 accounts, ten corporate investors, most of them insurance companies or investment managers, now held almost two-thirds of the company's shares between them. One of them, Barlo Group plc, held a 6 per cent stake which it subsequently increased to 15 per cent before launching a hostile but ultimately successful bid for the company in May 1992. It saw it as a good base on which to build a European plastics business. It marked the end of Irish Ropes (or IRG) as an independent enterprise.

Today, rope and twine are no longer made in Newbridge. Barlo ceased production in 1999 and handed over Irish Ropes's sports and social club to the people of the town. It sold the factory site, which had been left semi-derelict after a fire the previous year, for £6.8 million. Today, it is home to the Whitewater Shopping Centre, which was the country's largest shopping centre outside Dublin when it opened in 2006. For some reason, the only building not to be demolished was the cube-shaped staff hostel, which was built in 1958 and designed by Michael Scott, the architect who had been responsible for Ireland's award-winning pavilion at New York's World Fair in 1939. Like Tintawn, it is a product of its age. It is still there, surrounded by hoarding, an empty and dispiriting eyesore with its peeling paint and broken and boarded up windows. If

Irish Ropes's staff hostel beside the town's water tower and in front of the Whitewater Shopping Centre (author, 2019).

it can no longer be saved, someone should deliver the *coup de grace* and put it out of its misery.

Axminster acquired Curragh-Tintawn Carpets in 1994 after the management buy-out had run into difficulties. A collapse in demand for high-quality carpets had left it unable to pay its creditors. The Revenue Commissioners, who were owed £1.7 million in unpaid sales taxes, tried to close it down but were eventually persuaded to accept a settlement of 65p in the pound while Barlo agreed to write off the outstanding £600,000 of the interest-free loan that Irish Ropes had made at the time of the buy-out. The factory moved to new premises in Newbridge in 2006 and for a time was the only carpet manufacturer left in Ireland. However poor trading conditions finally forced it into liquidation in 2012 with the loss of forty-three jobs. By then, its parent company had its own problems. Axminster went into administration four months later with liabilities of £35 million, most of them owed to its pension fund whose funding deficit had almost doubled in a year. Unlike Curragh-Tintawn, it could be rescued, but only after most of the workforce had been made redundant. Today, after more than 250 years, it is still making carpets. The Tintawn trademark, which was first registered in 1938, was finally removed from the Irish Patents Office's Register of Trade Marks in 2018 when its renewal fee was not paid.

Although IRG plc continued to be the holding company for most of the group's investments, it had itself ceased to trade even before Barlo's acquisition. After the acquisition, it was effectively dormant. Procedures for the voluntary winding up of the company finally began in 2015 and were completed in 2018. The final documents filed by the liquidator were received by the Companies Registration Office on 3 July 2018, eighty-five years to the day after the company's incorporation.[7] In 2004, Barlo was itself taken over by the Quinn Group in an €84 million deal. In 2008, the group's founder, Sean Quinn, would become one of the biggest casualties of the Irish banking crisis. He was at the time, according to the *Sunday Times Rich List*, Ireland's wealthiest man with an estimated fortune of €4.7 billion. Four years later, he was facing bankruptcy proceedings.

Today, Irish Ropes lives on in the memories of the many families whose men and women worked there, in the contribution that it made to the development of Newbridge as a town, and in the names of its few surviving brands. Sealstrap Packaging is now part of the Carlyle Group and still trades in nearby Naas, and while I have been unable to unravel the recent history of Red Setter twine, the Irish Patents Office shows that its trademark, which had been registered by H. and J. Jones in 1922 before the Irish Free State came into being, was acquired by the Italian crop packaging specialist, Novatex Italia SpA, at the beginning of 2019.

Eric and Dorothy's beloved home, Morristownbiller House, has been unoccupied for many years and has fallen into ruin through neglect. I saw it for the first time in 2011 when I spent a day in Newbridge with my aunt, Ann, and members of my family. We were in Dublin for the weekend to celebrate her eightieth birthday with Nancy and her family.[8] The house was already in a sorry state and had no roof or windows. There was no glass left in the greenhouse, the plaster mouldings from its walls and ceilings had fallen down and lay damp and disintegrating on the floor, the wooden staircase had rotted, and saplings had taken root and were growing up through the rooms. An abandoned shopping trolley poked out from the grass on the front lawn. When I returned in 2019, I was shocked by the change in just eight years. Any remaining grass was now gone, trees and brambles made it almost impossible to get close to the house, the drive and the kitchen garden on which Eric and Dorothy worked so hard could no longer be made out in the woods, and the wrought-iron entrance gates, which had been blocked with boulders to prevent anyone getting in, had almost disappeared under a covering of ivy and foliage. It was ghostly experience. Nobody passing in a car would know that there had ever been a house behind the railings. As Christy Moore has said of the old Newbridge generally, it will soon be a place that exists only in the mind.

Morristown in the 1940s.

Morristown now (author, 2019).

The Twelve Irish Business Leaders who died in the Staines Air Crash, 18 June 1972

Edward Coleman, 46

Deputy general manager of Irish Steel and member of the Cork Chamber of Commerce.

Edward Gray, 47

Director-general of the Confederation of Irish Industry. As the negotiator for the Irish Banks Joint Standing Committee, he had been instrumental in settling the bank strike in 1970.

Guy Jackson, 50

Deputy managing director of Guinness and chairman of Cantrell and Cochrane and the Marketing Institute of Ireland. He had been president of the Confederation of Irish Industry immediately before Con Smith and still chaired its international affairs committee. Like Michael, he had been profiled in *The Times* supplement on Irish industry in 1969. A former Davis Cup player, he had represented Ireland in tennis, hockey, and squash.

Hugh Kilfeather, 29

Assistant general manager of Coras Trachtala, the Irish Export Board, with specific responsibility for market research, the European Union, and Ireland's participation in foreign affairs.

Owen Lochrin, early 50s

Managing director of James Lochrin and Co. in Drogheda and vice-president (and president elect) of the Association of Chambers of Commerce of Ireland.

Melville Miller, 55

Managing director of Rowntree Mackintosh (Ireland). He was a former vice-president and deputy chairman of the Federated Union of Employers and a former president of the Marketing Institute of Ireland.

Fergus Mooney, 27

Secretary to the delegation and economics and trade officer of the Confederation of Irish Industry. He was due to marry twenty-one-year-old teacher, Nora Daly, a fortnight later on 1 July.

Michael O'Reilly, 47

Dublin stockbroker and president of the Dublin Chamber of Commerce.

Michael Rigby-Jones, 45

Chairman and managing director of Irish Ropes. He was a non-executive director of Bank of Ireland and Cement Limited and sat on the council of the Confederation of Irish Industry. He had also been the youngest chairman (1965–67) and president (1970–71) of the Irish Management Institute.

Con Smith, 43

President of the Confederation of Irish Industry and managing director and majority shareholder of the Smith Motor Group, which held the Renault franchise in Ireland. He was also a non-executive director of the Central Bank and Irish Ropes. At the time of the crash, he was about to complete a merger with the fertiliser manufacturers, W. and H. M. Goulding. It was announced six days before the crash and would have created Ireland's second largest industrial company after Cement-Roadstone. Smith would have become its executive vice-chairman and the largest shareholder with a 20 per cent stake. Goulding's chairman, Sir Basil Goulding, had been profiled with Michael in *The Times* supplement on Irish industry.

Michael Sweetman, 36

Cousin of former minister for finance, Gerard Sweetman, and director of business policy at the Confederation of Irish Industry. He had been seconded as full-time director of the Irish Council of the European Movement in July 1971 and led its campaign for Ireland's membership of the European Union in the run-up to the referendum.

Ivan Webb, 62

Joint managing director of the building contractors, G. and T. Crampton. He was chairman of the Irish Employers' Confederation and a former president of the Construction Industry Federation.

Endnotes

Chapter 1

1 Unidentified press cutting, 31 December 1925.
2 *Rhos Herald*, January 1938.
3 Talbot House, or Toc H, was established by Reverend Tubby Clayton in the Belgian town of Poperinghe in 1915 as a club and rest house for all soldiers regardless of rank. After the war, it was incorporated by Royal Charter with the aim of creating local branches throughout Britain to replicate the same spirit of comradeship in civilian life and provide opportunities for young people.

Chapter 2

1 Harry Rigby-Jones, A Short History of H. and J. Jones (unpublished).
2 Romans, 12:11.
3 Dáil Éireann, 19 December 1921: Debate on Treaty. The Houses of the Oireachtas is the creator and copyright holder of all Irish legislation and debates in Dáil Éireann and Seanad Éireann, extracts from which are provided here under the Oireachtas (Open Data) PSI Licence.
4 Dáil Éireann, 27 April 1932: Public Business—Constitution (Removal of Oath) Bill 1932, Second Stage.
5 Dáil Éireann, 11 May 1932: in Committee on Finance: Financial Resolutions—Minister's Statement.
6 Hansard, HC Deb. vol. 267 col. 688, 17 June 1932.
7 *Imperial Economic Conference at Ottawa, 1932: Summary of Proceedings and Copies of Trade Agreements* (1932).
8 Dáil Éireann, 11 May 1932: in Committee on Finance: Financial Resolutions—Minister's Statement.

9   Finance Act, 1935: First Schedule.
10   Daly, The Irish Free State and the Great Depression of the 1930s: the interaction of the global and the local, *Irish Economic and Social History*, 38 (2011), pp. 19-36.

Chapter 3

1   Irish Ropes 21, a brochure produced to celebrate the company's twenty-first anniversary in 1954.
2   The company's first minute book, which has a record of all its board meetings up to April 1936, was given to me by Benny Maxwell in 2014. Benny worked for Irish Ropes for thirty-seven years, having joined from school in 1955.
3   Girvin, *Between Two Worlds: Politics and Economy in Independent Ireland* (1989), p. 116.
4   Vincent Crowley founded Kennedy Crowley & Co. with Peter Kennedy in 1919. As Stokes Kennedy Crowley & Co. it was incorporated into the accounting giant, KPMG, in 1987. The firm was Irish Ropes's auditor for as long as it continued to trade.
5   *Irish Times*, 14 June 1965, p. 14.
6   McCague, *Arthur Cox, 1891-1965* (1994), p. 68.
7   *Ibid.*, p. 83.
8   Dáil Éireann, 28 June 1933: In Committee on Finance, Vote 41—Local Government and Public Health.
9   Dáil Éireann, 7 July 1933: Vote 69—Relief Schemes.
10   Eric wrote an account of his arrival and first few days in Ireland, which he headed 'A Chara [dear friend in Gaelic], it happened thus'. It was given to me by Benny Maxwell in 2014.
11   The letter is reproduced in O'Shea, *The Ropes, A History of Irish Ropes Ltd, 1933–1972* (2013), p. 23.
12   There is some inconsistency in the identities of the six local men in the original workforce. The list here is taken from an article on Irish Ropes in the *Leinster Leader* of 17 January 1959. O'Shea (*The Ropes*, p. 40) has William rather than James Luker and William Flood and Charlie Dowling rather than George Halford and Joseph Whitely.
13   Duggan, *The People of Ormskirk Through the Ages, 1500–2000* (2009).
14   I am grateful to Deaglan De Paor, who used to work at Curragh-Tintawn Carpets, for giving me a copy of this.
15   Dáil Éireann, 9 August 1933: Adjournment Debate—Government Policy.
16   *Nationalist and Leinster Times*, 4 August 1934, p. 4.
17   *Ibid.*

Chapter 4

1   The Story of Irish Ropes, a company brochure produced in the late 1940s.
2   Eliot, *The East Africa Protectorate* (1905), p. 256.
3   Huxley, *The Flame Trees of Thika: Memories of an African Childhood* (1959), p. 25.

4 *Transactions of the Third International Congress of Tropical Agriculture: Papers Communicated to the Conference*, Vol. 1 (1915), pp. 503–517 and 560–573.

5 *The Times*, 16 July 1926, p. 13.

6 *The Times*, 8 June 1920, p. 19.

7 Hansard: HC Deb. vol. 163 col. 62W, 23 April 1923.

8 *Empire Grown Sisal and its Importance to the Cordage Manufacturer: Memorandum prepared by the Imperial Institute with the co-operation of its Advisory Committee on Vegetable Fibres* (1928).

9 Wigglesworth, *The Gold Tangle and the Way Out: Meaning and Causes of the Great Industrial Collapse* (1931) p. ix.

10 Wigglesworth, *Wigglesworth & Co. Ltd: A Retrospective, 1895–1935* (1935).

11 Lock, *Sisal: Twenty-Five Years' Sisal Research* (1962), Appendix I: Statistics of Sisal Production and Exports, Tanganyika and Kenya.

12 Wigglesworth, Sisal Growing and Marketing—A Virile Tropical Industry, *Empire Production and Export Magazine*, June 1934.

13 Hitchcock, The Sisal Industry of East Africa, *Tanganyika Notes and Records* (1959), pp. 4-17.

14 TNA, CO 852/517/5: Sisal Production in East Africa, a note prepared by the Colonial Office, 16 September 1943.

Chapter 5

1 *Irish Press*, 17 November 1936, p. 6.

2 Dáil Éireann, 23 May 1935: Financial Resolutions—Report Stage: Financial Resolution No. 9—Customs.

3 *The Times*, 4 January 1934, p. 7.

4 Kennerley, *Frederick William Dwelly, First Dean of Liverpool, 1881–1957* (2004), p. 149.

5 Dáil Éireann, 23 May 1935: Financial Resolutions—Report Stage: Financial Resolution No. 9—Customs.

6 Dáil Éireann, 4 July 1935: Public Business—Finance Bill, 1935: committee stage (resumed).

7 *Irish Independent*, 14 June 1946, p. 7. The figures, which are taken from Irish Ropes's share prospectus, are stated after corporation tax but before interest costs and associated income tax.

8 Dáil Éireann, 16 November 1938: Ceisteanna—Questions: Oral Answers—annual production of twine, rope, etc.; and 30 November 1938: Written Answers—rope, cord and twine imports.

9 The number of seats in the Dáil had by then been reduced from 153 to 138.

10 Maesgwyn, the Welsh for 'white field', was the name of both the Lloyd family's farmhouse on the Welsh borders (John Rigby-Jones's wife, Lillie, was born Sarah Elizabeth Lloyd) and Harry and Alice's first home in Ormskirk.

11 James Rees Jones was later Professor of History at the University of East Anglia.

12 It was Ireland's last opportunity to compete at what are now the Commonwealth Games. The games were cancelled in 1942 and 1946 due to the war and, by the

time that the next games were held in Auckland in 1950, Ireland had left the Commonwealth.

13 Empire Exhibition Scotland 1938, Official Guide, p. 32.

14 *The Times*, 3 May 1938, p. 13.

15 Hodges, J. H. Forshaw: One of Britain's Leading Architects and Author of the County of London Plan, *South African Architectural Review*, June 1946, pp. 140–142.

16 A copy of Wigglesworth's talk on 4 August 1938 was given to me by Vivian Landon.

17 Wigglesworth, The Sisal Situation Today, *The Sisal Review*, March 1938.

18 NAI, INDC/IND/7/73: Eric Rigby-Jones letter to Arthur Cox, 25 March 1948.

19 Johnston, An Outlook on Irish Agriculture, *Studies: An Irish Quarterly Review* (1939), pp. 195–209 and An Outlook on Irish Agriculture: Part II, *Studies: An Irish Quarterly Review* (1939), pp. 375–390.

20 Dáil Éireann, 12 August 1936: Ceisteanna—Questions: Oral Answers—Price of Binder Twine.

21 Dáil Éireann, 28 March 1939: Vote 57—Industry and Commerce.

22 TNA, DO 130/12: Maffey to Parkinson, 22 April 1940.

Chapter 6

1 The Story of Irish Ropes.

2 TNA, DO 35/1109/22: the four events are presumably Hitler's election as chancellor, his re-armament of Germany in violation of the Treaty of Versailles, the Spanish Civil War, and the Munich conference.

3 Dáil Éireann, 23 November 1939: Finance (No. 2) Bill, 1939—Second Stage (resumed).

4 Many of those rescued, including Captain Burfeind, were among 1,200 German and Italian internees to be transported to Canada in July 1940 on board SS *Arandora Star*. On the morning after she left Liverpool, she was torpedoed by a U-boat off the north-west coast of Ireland. She sank in half an hour with the loss of 865 lives. Captain Burfeind helped the passengers to the lifeboats before joining the *Arandora Star*'s captain on the bridge and going down with the ship. More than 200 bodies were washed ashore on the Irish coast the following month, most of whom almost certainly came from the ship. They were buried nearby. A memorial plaque was erected on Liverpool's waterfront in 2008.

5 Dáil Éireann, 7 March, 1940: Vote 71—Office of the Minister for Supplies (resumed).

6 *The Times*, 25 May 1940, p. 6.

Chapter 7

1 Eric's letter to his children, 26 May 1940.

2 TNA, PREM 3/130: minutes of meeting on 23 May 1940.

3 TNA, CAB 66/7: WP (40)168, British Strategy in a Certain Eventuality, report by the Chiefs of Staff Committee, 25 May 1940.

4 TNA, PREM 3/130: Ismay's note to Churchill, 29 May 1940.

5   TNA, WO 106/6043: Major M. H. ap Rhys Pryce—instructions on appointment as military *attaché* to Eire, 3 June 1940.

6   *Ibid.*: Pryce's request was in his report of 28 June.

7   *Ibid.*

8   TNA, DO 35/1008/8: deciphered telegram from prime minister, Pretoria, to high commissioner, London, 14 June 1940.

9   TNA, WO 106/6043: Major Hailey added this comment to his note with the recipes for the Molotov cocktails, 30 June 1940.

10 TNA, DO 130/12: Machtig's letter to Maffey, 4 July 1940.

11 TNA, INF 1/528: Betjeman's memorandum to the director of the Ministry of Information's Empire Division, 21 June 1940.

12 Ryle Dwyer, *Behind the Green Curtain: Ireland's Phoney Neutrality During World War II* (2009), p. 86.

13 A copy of the dossier came up for auction in England in 2012 (Mail Online, 26 September 2012).

14 Hansard, HC Deb. vol. 362 cols. 1043–5, 14 July 1940.

15 TNA, WO 106/6043: W. H. Skrine's note to Pryce, 8 July 1940. When I first examined the file in 2016, the note had been redacted under the Public Records Act 1958, which allows records to be retained beyond the statutory thirty years. The Ministry of Defence subsequently provided me with a copy after I had made an application under the Freedom of Information Act and restored it to the file shortly thereafter.

16 Alice's younger brothers, Colley and Jos Holland, were both farmers. Edfryn Jones farmed near the village of Caersws in Powys. His sister, Mary, was a school friend of Dorothy's and Peter's godmother.

17 Alice's uncle, Arthur Shorter, established the Shorter Pottery in Stoke-on-Trent in 1878 and later also ran the Wilkinson Pottery after his marriage to Henrietta Wilkinson. His son, Colley, is best known for having discovered Clarice Cliff, probably the most famous British pottery designer of the twentieth century, whom he eventually married in 1940 after the death of his wife. Arthur's younger brother, Jack, emigrated to Sydney in 1879 where his ceramics business was the Australian agent for Royal Doulton until 1979. Lucie, the eldest of his five daughters, became a celebrated ceramics designer while Elaine, the youngest, ran the business after graduating in law from Sydney University in 1926.

18 Kennedy and Laing (eds.), *The Irish Defence Forces 1940–1949: The Chief of Staff's Reports* (2011): Chapter 1—General Report on the Expansion, Organisation, Training, Equipment, and Defensive Preparations of the Army during the period commencing 1 May 1940 and ended 30 September 1940, 24 October 1940.

19 TNA, WO 106/6044: Pryce's letter to Lt-Col. Conyers Baker, 15 September 1940.

20 *Ibid.*: Pryce's report no. 16, 9 August 1940.

Chapter 8

1   The Story of Irish Ropes.

2   *Irish Press*, 4 November 1940, p. 3.

3   Eric's reference to a look-out at the factory, which he describes in other letters as a crow's nest with excellent views over the surrounding countryside, is another intriguing

snippet of information. It is tempting to think that it was connected with plans to resist a German invasion.

4   NAI, DT S11846: Observations on the Heads of Proposed Agreement with Great Britain: McElligott's memorandum to Moynihan, 19 September 1940 (retrieved from www.difp.ie/docs/1940/Trade-agreement-with-Britain/3294.htm, 25 April 2018).

5   Hansard, HC Deb. vol. 363 cols. 1130-1, 30 July 1940.

6   Hansard, HC Deb. vol. 365 col. 1243, 5 November 1940.

7   TNA, DO 130/12: Maffey's letter to Machtig with attached memorandum, 19 November 1940.

8   TNA, PREM 3/128: Churchill's personal minute to the chancellor of the Exchequer and dominions secretary, 17 February 1941.

9   NAI, INDC/EMR/7/18: Record of the activities of the Department of Supplies, including an introduction, regional administration, the 'navicert' trade system, and shipping. The document is part of a draft of a brief history of the department during the Emergency, which it was planned at one time to publish as a booklet.

10 Dáil Éireann, 16–17 January 1941: Essential Supplies—Motion.

11 TNA, DO 130/21: Maffey's letter to Machtig, 4 March 1941.

12 TNA, PREM 3/128, Braddock to Edgcumbe, 26 March 1941.

13 On its incorporation in March 1941, 51 per cent of the shares in Irish Shipping Ltd were owned by the Irish government, 44 per cent by Grain Importers (Eire) Ltd, which had itself been established by the Department of Supplies, and the remaining 5 per cent by Ireland's three largest shipping companies.

14 TNA, BT 64/4443: Hard hemps, a history of wartime control. Victor Bool from the Raw Materials Department at the Ministry of Supply wrote this detailed account of the wartime control of hard fibres in 1945 for inclusion in a wider wartime history of the ministry. He provided a copy to Joel Hurstfield, lecturer in modern history at University College London, who later wrote *The Control of Raw Materials*, which was published by HMSO and Longmans in 1953 as part of their series on the history of the Second World War.

15 Alfred joined his father's firm, Landauer & Co., in 1903 and ran its hard fibre division. He would be hemp controller for ten years before returning to the firm in 1949. According to the secretary of the Hard Fibre Cordage Federation, William Tyson, in his *Rope: a History of the Hard Fibre Cordage Industry in the United Kingdom* (1966), there were at the time of his writing four major fibre merchants in London—Hindleys, Landauers, William F. Malcolm, and Wigglesworths. George Malcolm was appointed jute controller at the same time as Landauer. John Ferrier, who also worked for Malcolms and would later be its chairman, took over as flax controller for the latter part of the war from the director of the Imperial Institute, Sir Harry Lindsay.

16 Hemp is often used as a generic term for fibres, and hard fibres in particular, as well as being the name of specific fibre-producing plants such as true hemp (*cannabis sativa*, the cannabis plant) and false hemp (*datisca cannabina*).

17 TNA, CO 852/311/9: letter from Freeston, the governor's deputy in Tanganyika, to Melville at the Colonial Office, 11 February 1940.

18 In 1939, the *Reichskolonialbund* (or Reich Colonial League) published *Deutsche Heimat in Afrika*, a book of photographs by Ilse Steinhoff, which included a section on sisal.

19   Ryle Dwyer, *Behind the Green Curtain* (2009), p. 169, where he refers to Walshe's memo of 15 May 1945 (NAI, DFAA/A2).

20   The Turf Development Board bought and worked more than a thousand peat bogs during the Emergency, including 250 square miles around the Bog of Allen between Enfield, Edenderry and Newbridge under the so-called Kildare Scheme. Cutting began there in 1942 and more than 600,000 tons of turf had been dug by the time that the scheme was closed in 1947. Fourteen camps, each holding 500 men, were built to house the peat cutters. Part of Newbridge barracks was also taken over to house the scheme's administrative staff as well as 600 workers. The Turf Development Board, which was renamed Bord na Mona in 1946, still has its headquarters there and works the Bog of Allen on an industrial scale.

Chapter 9

1   The Story of Irish Ropes.

2   TNA, CO 852/517/5: Sisal Production in East Africa, a note prepared in the Colonial Office, 16 September 1943.

3   TNA, CAB 102/193: History of the Combined Raw Materials Board. H. Duncan Hall, an Australian historian who served on the British Raw Materials Mission in Washington from 1942 to 1945, wrote this detailed but unpublished account for use in Hurstfield's 1953 book, *The Control of Raw Materials*.

4   *The Times*, 21 July 1942, p. 8.

5   TNA, DO 130/17: Telegram from Churchill to de Valera, 8 December 1941 (retrieved from www.difp.ie/docs/1941/-Now-or-Never.-A-Nation-once-again-/3577.htm, 24 July 2019).

6   Éamon de Valera's speech on Irish neutrality, 12 December 1941, as monitored by the BBC (retrieved from www.ibiblio.org/pha/timeline/411212awp.html, 21 March 2017).

7   *Irish Times*, 6 January 1941, p. 1.

8   TNA, CAB 72/25. Figures for the import of 140 major commodities in 1942, including details of from where they were sourced, were provided by the Ministry of Economic Warfare to the War Cabinet's Committee on Economic Policy Towards Eire in March 1943. Equivalent figures for 1943 were provided a year later while interim figures were provided during the course of the year. Britain's ability to collate these figures is evidence of the control that it was able to exercise over Irish imports.

9   Dáil Éireann, March 1942: Adjournment, Standing Order 27—Supply and Distribution of Bread.

10   The first American servicemen to arrive in Northern Ireland were the crews of four destroyers who arrived in Londonderry on 21 January 1942. Londonderry became a US naval base a month later.

11   *Irish Times*, 28 March 1942, p. 4.

12   TNA, SUPP 14/570: letter from Irish Ropes Limited to H. W. Rigby-Jones, 5 March 1942, with attached memorandum, intercepted by Postal and Telegraph Censorship.

13   TNA, CAB 72/25: Navicerts granted since 1 January 1942 and outstanding applications. Sisal is the first item on the list.

14   NAI, INDC/EMR/8/1: memorandum on trading relations with and supplies from Britain, June–July 1943.

15 *The Times*, 5 April 1939, p. 10. Gibson's letter was published on 28 March and Wigglesworth's on 31 March.

16 Ferrier's speech was widely reported in the press, including the *Mercury*, a local newspaper in Hobart, Tasmania, 8 November 1945.

17 *Irish Press*, 17 February 1940.

18 NAI, TSCH/3/S11627 A: this file, on flax growing during the Emergency, includes Ryan and O'Kelly's correspondence on this dispute.

19 TNA, SUPP 14/571: after meetings with Ferrier and the Ministry of Supply in autumn 1944 Eric provided a number of documents about the Tullow Flax Scheme including a detailed memorandum on 'Possible Use of Green Flax for Binder Twine in Eire' and a four-page analysis of its production, sales, and profits in 1943.

20 The best source of information on the early days of the Tullow Flax Scheme is 'Binding the Harvest: Industry from the Fields', *Irish Times*, 21 November 1942, p. 3.

21 These records were given to me by Benny Maxwell in 2014.

22 Dáil Éireann, 1 June 1942: Ceisteanna—Questions: Oral Answers—Binder Twine Supplies.

23 Seanad Éireann, 11 February 1943: Artificial Fertilisers and Exports—Motion (Resumed).

24 Dáil Éireann, 24 June 1942: Committee on Finance, Vote 69—Office of the Minister for Supplies.

25 Dáil Éireann, 14 July 1942: Ceisteanna—Questions: Oral Answers—Supplies of Binder Twine.

26 A standard acre is 4,840 square yards and an Irish acre 7,840 square yards.

27 Dáil Éireann, 14 October 1942: Private Deputies' Business, Supplies of Food and Animal Feeding Stuffs—Motion.

28 Peter no longer kept any letters from his father after leaving school. The last is dated 19 July 1942. As a result, we have a less complete picture of Eric and Dorothy's life in Ireland in the last three years of the war. However, Eric kept all the letters that Peter wrote home from the Navy. They offer a different perspective and, in their occasional references to life and events back home, are some compensation for the loss of Eric's letters.

Chapter 10

1 Churchill's first broadcast as prime minister, 19 May 1940.

2 Monsarrat, *The Cruel Sea* (1951): reissued by Penguin Books (2009), pp. 159–161.

3 There is a statue of Captain Walker, CB, DSO and 3 bars, on Liverpool's waterfront near the plaque commemorating SS *Arandora Star*.

4 London Metropolitan Archives, LCC/AR/WAR/01/029: War History of the Architect's Department, including London Heavy Rescue Service and War Debris Disposal Service, 1939–1945, final draft.

5 Forshaw and Abercrombie, *County of London Plan* (1943): foreword by Lord Latham.

6 *Plan London Now for Him*: Exhibition of the County of London Plan, County Hall.

7 A film, *The Proud City—A Plan for London*, was produced by the Ministry of Information after the war and featured Forshaw and Abercrombie explaining their proposals.

8   TNA, WO 169/8666: Appendix C to 1st Airborne Division's report on Operation Husky (the codename for the overall plan for the invasion of Sicily).

9   The figures in the sources are inconsistent. The figures here are taken from the Airborne Division's report on Operation Husky (TNA, WO 169/8666). Although it has the advantage of having been prepared shortly after the event, it would not have been updated as and when more details became known.

10 Walter Naismith gave an interview in 2011 in which he talked about the landing. Unfortunately, it is no longer available online.

11 *Sydney Morning Herald*, 16 July 1943, p. 5.

12 Guy kept notes of all his cases in a small leather-bound notebook given to me by his son, Tim, in 2018. Among the twenty-four patients that he lists is Under Officer Hans Maear of the Luftwaffe who broke an ankle after bailing out from his plane.

13 TNA, WO 373/3/322: citation for Military Cross for Captain Guy Rigby-Jones, 181st Airlanding Field Ambulance, Sicily.

14 Dennis Burke's invaluable website, Foreign Aircraft Landings in Ireland—WW2 (www.ww2irishaviation.com), has details of all the foreign aircraft that landed or crashed in Ireland during the war.

15 The wartime experiences of the Mayhew family, including Paul's own account of his escape from the Curragh, are told in Mayhew, ed., *One Family's War* (1985).

16 IWM 9939: Conrad Wood's interview of Verity for the Imperial War Museum's Sound Archive, 17 August 1987.

17 The race was won by the favourite, Sol Oriens. Two English horses, Easy Chair and Lynch Tor, also ran, having made the trip over from Newmarket in spite of the dangers of crossing the Irish Sea and the recent outbreak of foot and mouth disease.

18 TNA, WO 208/3347: debriefing reports for airmen repatriated from Ireland.

19 *Irish Times*, 28 October 1942, p. 1.

20 TNA, DO 35/1109/17: although this file is mainly concerned with the internment of British airmen it includes a section on Wilson's trial and Maffey's correspondence relating to it.

21 Tebbit, *Escape from the Curragh* (unpublished). Isobel suggests that the three 'unofficial' escapers were Proctor, Covington, and Mayhew. However, Mayhew (*One Family's War*, p. 149) says that he was asked to lead the official escape and had to choose the six men, including himself, that he thought would be of most use back home.

Chapter 11

1   TNA, SUPP 14/571: Eric Rigby-Jones's letter to John Ferrier, 16 January 1945.

2   TNA, DO 130/21: Stokes's report.

3   TNA, CAB 72/25: Memorandum of 20 April 1942.

4   NAI, INDC/EMR/8/1: Memorandum on trading relations with Britain and supplies from thence, June–July 1943. The memorandum says that Dunlop received 29 tons of rubber a week from the end of 1942 and sent back 24 tons of tyres, keeping the remaining 5 tons for its own use. The purpose of the memorandum was to highlight, firstly, those areas where rationing was harsher in Ireland than in Britain and, secondly, those arrangements that had been made for the manufacture of goods in Ireland where

a proportion of the raw materials supplied by Britain were retained for domestic use.

5   TNA, CAB 72/25: Minutes of meeting, 29 May 1942.

6   Dáil Éireann, 24 June 1942: Committee on Finance, Vote 69—Office of the Minister for Supplies.

7   Hansard: HC Deb., vol. 391 col. 1228W, 23 July 1943.

8   TNA, SUPP 14/570: D'Arcy's letter to Shillidy, 28 October 1942.

9   Seanad Éireann, 11 February 1943: Artificial Fertilisers and Exports—Motion (Resumed).

10 NAI, INDC/EMR/8/1. The comment was made in the draft section on sisal for inclusion in the Department of Supplies' memorandum on supplies from Britain. It was excluded from the final version as the purpose of the memorandum was to highlight only those commodities where Ireland was worse off than Britain.

11 Dáil Éireann, 14 April 1943: Committee on Finance, Vote 69—Supplies.

12 *British Medical Journal*, 28 October 1944, p. 581.

13 TNA, SUPP 14/571: Ferrier's letter to Shillidy, 24 October 1944.

14 *Ibid.*: Eric Rigby-Jones's letter to Ferrier, 16 January 1945.

15 *Ibid.*: Shillidy's letter to Ferrier, 22 January 1945.

16 *Ibid.*: Costar's letter to Shillidy, 22 February 1945.

17 TNA, CO 852/517/5: Sisal Production in East Africa, note prepared in the Colonial Office, 16 September 1943.

18 Hansard: HC Deb., vol. 391 col. 64, 13 July 1943.

19 TNA, CO 852/432/8: Bosanquet memorandum, 11 December 1942.

20 TNA, CO 852/517/88: Stanley dispatch, December 1943.

Chapter 12

1   Montgomery's message to Major-General Urquhart, 28 September 1944, three days after the evacuation of Arnhem.

2   Peter kept the bill, made out to Mr Chance, from the Ordnance Hotel in Felixstowe. Their two dinners cost *3s 6d* each and their coffees *6d* each, bringing the total bill to 8 shillings, or 40 pence.

3   Mahn Center for Archives and Special Collections at Ohio University Libraries, Cornelius Ryan Collection of World War II Papers: A Bridge Too Far series, Box 109, Folder 20—Major Guy Rigby-Jones, questionnaire and interview. Although Guy never wrote his own account, his story can be pieced together in some detail from the various sources quoted in this chapter.

4   Waddy, *A Tour of the Arnhem Battlefields* (1999), p. 157. Waddy, then a major, commanded 'B' Company of the 156th Battalion, 4th Parachute Brigade. Guy operated on him in the billiard room at the Tafelberg after he had been shot in the stomach by a sniper.

5   Liddell Hart Centre for Military Archives, King's College, London, GB 0099 KCLMA Warrack: Diary of Colonel Graeme Matthew Warrack, 17 September–16 October 1944. Warrack heard on Wednesday afternoon that Guy and Michael James were still all right at the Tafelberg and that the battle had left them alone.

6   Warrack, *Travel by Dark After Arnhem* (1963), p. 37 and Warrack diary.

7   Cherry, *Arnhem Surgeon: the story of Captain Michael James of 181 Airlanding Field Ambulance RAMC, September 1944* (2010), pp. 11–12.

8   The story of the film and its director, Brian Desmond Hurst, is told in Truesdale and Esler Smith, *Theirs is the Glory: Arnhem, Hurst, and Conflict on Film* (2016). Although Guy did not take part in the film the 181st Airlanding Field Ambulance, the Tafelberg Hotel, and the St Elizabeth Hospital all feature in several scenes. One scene inside the Tafelberg features an unnamed doctor telling Warrack that the ceiling of his theatre had just fallen in but that nobody was injured.

9   The main source for Guy's time at St Joseph's is Frazer's report on Operation Market Garden and its aftermath which covers the period from September 1944 to April 1945. It was presented to the Pegasus Archive by Stuart Jebbit (http://www.pegasusarchive. org/arnhem/sm_frazer.htm, accessed 16 May 2018).

10 The E-boats at Den Helder were the first enemy surface vessels to surrender. On 13 May, five days after VE Day, they crossed the channel and entered Felixstowe harbour in line ahead, flying white flags and with their guns pointed upwards, where their formal surrender was received by the captain of HMS *Beehive*.

11 *The Times*, 10 April 1945, p. 2.

12 *Supplement to the London Gazette*, 26 June 1945, p. 3329.

Chapter 13

1   Peter's letter to his parents, 27 August 1944.

2   Richard Bailey was later managing director and chairman of Royal Doulton Group. It was while he was in charge of the company that the Shorters lost their Australian agency for Royal Doulton. He was knighted in 1984.

3   The stories are told in more detail in my book, *Best Love to All* (2017).

4   *Townsville Daily Bulletin*, 25 October 1945, p. 2.

5   HMS *Woodcock* was a sister ship of HMS *Woodpecker* on which Peter had served in the Atlantic.

6   Hard-lying money was a naval allowance paid to crews of small ships when they had to live in sub-standard accommodation.

7   Liberty ships were cargo ships that were mass-produced in the US during the war. They were based on an original British idea for a cheap and simple solution for the replacement of the ships sunk by U-boats.

8   H. and J. Jones's premises in Victoria Street were sold in October 1945. Shortly afterwards, a notice was placed in the Liverpool press—'Cordage business for sale— century-old Liverpool company, engaged in distribution of twines and cordage, to be sold by family interests owing to retirement of principal. Assets comprise stock, book-debts, and goodwill but premises have been sold to a non-competing concern'. On 30 November, three weeks after Harry's seventy-third birthday, the company was wound up at an extraordinary general meeting of the company's shareholders (*London Gazette*, 7 December 1945, issue 37379, p. 5961).

9   Peter did not own shares in Irish Ropes until 1951 when his father gave him 1,000 shares as a wedding present. He was always grateful for them and frequently reminded my brother and me that the income from them paid for our education. My father's

lack of interest in business, and his different perspective on the value of things, is reflected in his purchase of a painting by the twenty-eight-year-old Daniel O'Neill from the Waddington Galleries in Dublin for fifty guineas in 1948. O'Neill would later be recognised as the greatest Irish romantic painter of the twentieth century. When the painting was auctioned in Dublin after Peter's death it fetched a hammer price of €13,000.

10   *Leinster Leader*, 28 September 1946, p. 5.

Chapter 14

1   The Story of Irish Ropes.
2   Tanner helped Wigglesworth acquire Amboni Estates in the 1920s and was appointed honorary Swiss consul for East Africa in 1927.
3   TNA, AY 4/592: Eric Rigby-Jones's letter to Dr J. R. Furlong, Plant and Animal Products Department, Imperial Institute, 21 August 1946.
4   TNA, CO 852/600/9: minutes of meeting of technical research committee of the Sisal Growers' Association, 18 September 1945.
5   *Irish Times*, 1 November 1945, p. 5.
6   *The Times*, 17 October 1945, p. 7.
7   Jones, *Captain of All These Men of Death: The History of Tuberculosis in 19th and 20th century Ireland* (2001).
8   Browne, *Against the Tide* (1986).
9   The scroll now hangs in Ryston Sports and Social Club in Newbridge.
10   TNA, AY 4/592, for the notes of these meetings. Eric's talk to the Dublin Rotary Club was reported in the *Dublin Evening Mail* of 13 January 1947 and to the Annual General Meeting of the Textile Institute in the *Irish Times* of 29 March 1947. Although Eric kept a diary of his first visit to Africa, I have been unable to trace a copy. Local teacher Brigid Larkin remembers seeing one and has told me that Eric's description of flying down the Nile valley was like reading a travel guide.
11   TNA, CO 852/609/4: minutes of a conversation between Hogg and Hitchcock at the Dar es Salaam Club, 13 October 1944, based on Hogg's notes.
12   *Ibid.*, file note of 31 May 1944.
13   *Ibid.*, file note by Leslie Monson, Colonial Office, 31 August 1944.
14   Huxley, *The Sorcerer's Apprentice: A Journey through East Africa* (1948), pp. 101–106 (reproduced by permission of The Random House Group Ltd ©1949).
15   *Ibid.*, p. 133.
16   Lane, *Islamic Pottery from the Ninth to the Fourteenth Centuries AD in the Collection of Sir Eldred Hitchcock* (1956).
17   Freeman-Grenville, Obituary of Sir Eldred Hitchcock, *Tanganyika Notes and Records: the Journal of the Tanganyika Society*, no. 52 (1959).
18   Tanganyika Territory, An Ordinance to Consolidate and Amend the Existing Law Relating to the Sisal Industry, 21 December 1945.
19   TNA, CO 852/609/4: file note of 21 November 1944 quoting the views of Sir Julian Foley.
20   By 1934, a year after Hitler became chancellor, Germans were once again the largest

owners of sisal estates in Tanganyika. They owned forty of the 131 registered estates while Greeks owned twenty-nine, the British twenty-four, and British Indians twenty-two. The German growers were encouraged by their home government to deal exclusively with German banks, traders, and fibre merchants, leading to British fears that Nazi Germany was attempting to recover control of not only the sisal industry but also the colony itself.

21   TNA, CO 852/609/4: the figures are taken from the TSGA's formal response to Stanley's dispatch, 5 May 1944. It was almost certainly written by Hitchcock.

22   *Ibid.*, file note of 31 May 1944.

23   Wigglesworth, *The Future of the Sisal Industry in East Africa and Sisal Marketing* (1946).

24   Guillebaud, *An Economic Survey of the Sisal Industry of Tanganyika* (1958), p. 33.

25   Binder twine was used on mechanical reapers and binders to bind the sheaves of corn when they were cut. Baler twine was used on balers to bind the hay after the corn had been threshed.

26   Retrieved from the IDA Ireland website (www.idaireland.com/about-ida/history/), 26 July 2017. The IDA's first chairman was James Beddy, who had previously been in charge of the Industrial Credit Corporation.

Chapter 15

1   The Story of Irish Ropes.

2   *The Times*, 19 September 1973, p. 21.

3   NAI, INDC/IND/7/73: Eric Rigby-Jones's letter to Haughey, 26 February 1948.

4   *Ibid.*, copy of Eric Rigby-Jones's letter to Arthur Cox, 25 March 1948, giving a detailed account of his two-day trip to London.

5   *Irish Times Pictorial*, 13 January 1951, p. 9, featuring an Irish Ropes advertisement which graphed its annual cordage production from 1938 to 1950 under the headline, 'Let figures speak'.

6   NAI, INDC/IND/7/73: Eric Rigby-Jones's letter to the Industrial Development Authority, 23 February 1951.

7   NAI, DFA/5/348/7/198: Markets in the USA for products of Irish Ropes.

8   In time, the strategy led to extravagant overstocking. In 1962, President Kennedy was told that the government's strategic stocks were 80 per cent above its wartime requirements. At the time, it held 68,000 tons of manila and 144,000 tons of sisal, or roughly half of East Africa's annual production. Four years later, it threatened to send the world's commodity markets into turmoil when it announced plans to reduce its sisal holdings by a third.

9   Hansard, HC Deb. vol. 489 cc. 2486-7, 5 July 1951.

10   *Irish Independent*, 5 June 1951, p. 7.

11   Irish Ropes's stock levels at the end of its financial year in August were probably always relatively low. By then, it would have sold most of that year's agricultural twine and would not yet have built up the raw materials needed for the following year.

12   The Tanganyika Groundnut Scheme was a grandiose and disastrous post-war British project to clear 5,000 square miles of East African bush to grow peanuts for making

oil and margarine. At the time, there were less than 650 square miles under sisal in Tanganyika. When the plug was finally pulled on the scheme in 1951 less than 300 square miles had been cleared and the British government was forced to write off the £36 million that it had already invested.

13   The doors are still there at the entrance to what is now the Mkonge Hotel.

14   In 1950, Hitchcock also chaired the Ex-Enemy Sisal Estates Lessees' Committee. With the wartime leases of the confiscated German estates due to expire at the end of the year applications for new long-term leases had to be submitted to a government committee in the autumn. There were eighty-seven applicants for the twenty-four estates. All but three of them appeared before the committee to make their case as did Hitchcock as their spokesman.

15   *The Times*, 13 February 1951, p. 9.

16   *Tanganyika Standard*, weekly edition, Saturday 4 August 1951, p. 1.

17   *Ibid.*, weekly edition, Saturday 11 August 1951, p. 1. Eric included a copy of his letter in his diary.

18   The factory was the brainchild of Major Conrad Walsh, an early pioneer of East African sisal and deputy chairman of Bird and Co. before its amalgamation in 1936. After the war, he secured a number of patents to manufacture pectins and other by-products from sisal waste. His factory, which opened in May 1951, quickly ran into difficulties and closed within a year. The project was surrounded with such secrecy that even local officials were unable to find out the reasons why.

19   NAI, INDC/IND/7/73: Report of meeting between Eric Rigby-Jones and Haughey and Gray, 27 October 1951.

20   *Irish Times*, 10 November 1951, p. 8.

21   Irish Ropes Limited: Chairman's letter to shareholders, 1952.

Chapter 16

1   Alice's letter to Peter's wife, Pam, on the birth of her first great-grandson, William, in October 1953.

2   Dáil Éireann, 16 July 1952: Committee on Finance—Vote 50: Industry and Commerce (resumed).

3   *The Times*, 6 November 1952, p. 10.

4   Guillebaud, *An Economic Survey of the Sisal Industry of Tanganyika* (1958), Table 10, p. 49.

5   *Sunday Express*, 3 November 1968, pp. 6–7.

6   *Irish Examiner*, 6 June 1953 p. 5.

7   *Irish Independent*, 6 July 1954, p. 8.

8   *Irish Times*, 6 September 1954, p. 5, Pro-Quidnunc writing in An Irishman's Diary.

9   Dáil Éireann, 13 December 1967: Adjournment (Christmas Recess) (Resumed).

10   The painting was rejected when le Brocquy offered it to the Municipal Gallery in Dublin in 1952, a year after it had been shown in London to some acclaim. It was finally returned to Ireland in 2001 and was presented to the National Gallery of Ireland, where it has been on display ever since.

11   *Observer*, 14 December 1958, p. 10.

12 Franck and others, *Design in Ireland: report of the Scandinavian Design Group in Ireland, April 1961* (1962), pp. 17–18.

13 *Irish Times*, 7 March 1962, p. 9, quoting Irish Ropes's press release on the establishment of its American subsidiary, Tintawn Inc.

14 The first Sunday magazine was published by the *Sunday Times* on 4 February 1962.

15 The reasons for the decline are explored in more detail in Kimaro and others, Review of Sisal Production and Research in Tanzania, *African Study Monographs*, 15(4) (December 1994), pp. 227–242.

16 *Irish Times*, 13 November 1964, p. 4.

17 *Ibid.*, 7 June 1966, p. 11. Michael's comments were in a continuation of the main story on the front page that day which had the headline, 'ESB [Electricity Supply Board] Power Crisis Eases After Day of Industrial Chaos'.

18 Irish Ropes Limited, Directors' Report and Statement of Accounts for the year ended 31 August 1964, Chairman's Statement.

19 *Sunday Independent*, 18 December 1966.

20 Unidentified and undated newspaper cutting in my parents' cutting book (possibly the *Leinster Leader*).

21 Cox, *The Making of Managers: a History of the Irish Management Institute, 1952–2002* (2002), p. 125.

22 *The Times*, 6 May 1969, p. 35.

23 *Ibid.*, p. 38.

24 *Irish Times*, 15 March 1969, p. 12.

25 Irish Ropes Limited, Annual Report 1967, Chairman's Statement.

26 Irish Ropes Limited, Annual Report 1971, Chairman's Statement.

27 Referenda were also held in Denmark and Norway. Denmark voted for and Norway against joining. In the UK, Edward Heath's Conservative government decided against holding a referendum, which it would probably have lost, on the grounds that it was unconstitutional. It was only in 1975, when Harold Wilson's Labour government had been returned to power, that the electorate was given its say on Britain's continued membership of the EEC: 67 per cent voted to remain.

28 TNA, DR 11/74: Civil Aviation Authority's file on the BEA Trident crash at Staines, 18 June 1972.

29 *The Times*, 20 June 1972, p. 19.

30 *Irish Times*, 26 June 1972, p. 7.

Chapter 17

1 From the lyrics of *Lily*, the title track of Christy Moore's 2016 album. Christy was born in Newbridge and writes in the sleeve notes to the album that 'I grew up in County Kildare between 1945 and 1963. Early images of Newbridge remain crystal clear in my mind. Since then it has expanded, tenfold, to become a dormitory town to the Nation's Capital. I have tried to write a song about a place that still exists, if only in my mind. It's an old song that was written recently.'

2 Irish Ropes Limited, Annual Report 1975, Chairman's Statement.

3 Irish Ropes Limited, Annual Report 1979, Chairman's Statement.

4   *Irish Times*, 13 August 1988, p. 8.

5   *Ibid.*, 26 August 1986, p. 15.

6   According to the *Irish Times* Irish Ropes's share price increased from £0.56 in March 1986 to £2.25 in July 1989. I used the shares that my father had given me to fund my divorce in 1989.

7   By then, the company had changed its name again, to IRG Holdings Ltd. However, its company number, 8483, is a reminder that it was one of the first companies to be incorporated in Ireland after independence. Today, Ireland has more than 600,000 registered companies.

8   Ann's original party in 2010 had to be postponed when the eruption of the Icelandic volcano, Eyjafjallajökull, caused widespread travel disruption across Europe.

Bibliography

Archives and Data Repositories

The British Library
Companies Registration Office Ireland
Cornelius Ryan Collection, Mahn Center for Archives and Special Collections at Ohio
    University Libraries
Houses of the Oireachtas
Imperial War Museum
JSTOR
Liddell Hart Centre for Military Archives, King's College London
London Metropolitan Archives
The National Archives (TNA)
The National Archives and Records Administration of the United States of America (NARA)
The National Archives of Ireland (NAI)
UK Parliament (www.parliament.uk)
University of Liverpool, Special Collections and Archives

Newspapers and Newspaper Archives

Irish Newspaper Archives
Irish Times
Leinster Leader
Tanganyika Standard
The Times

Books and Other Publications

Beevor, A., *Arnhem: the Battle for the Bridges, 1944* (London: Viking, 2018)

Bew, J., *Citizen Clem: a Biography of Attlee* (London: riverrun, 2016)

Blixen, K., *Out of Africa* (London: Putnam, 1937)

Browne, N., *Against the Tide* (Dublin: Gill & Macmillan, 1986)

Canning, P., *British Policy Towards Ireland, 1921–1941* (Oxford: Clarendon Press, 1985)

Carroll, J. T., *Ireland in the War Years, 1939–1945* (Newton Abbot: David & Charles, 1975)

Cherry, N., *Arnhem Surgeon: the Story of Captain Michael James of 181 Airlanding Field Ambulance RAMC, September 1944* (Warton: Brendon Publishing, 2010)

Cherry, N., *Red Berets and Red Crosses: the Story of the Medical Services in the 1st Airborne Division in World War II* (Renkum: RN Sigmond Publishing, 2014)

Cole, H., *On Wings of Healing: the Story of the Airborne Medical Services, 1940–1960* (Edinburgh and London: William Blackwood & Sons, 1963)

Costello, C., *A Most Delightful Station: the British Army on the Curragh of Kildare, Ireland, 1855–1922* (Cork: The Collins Press, 1996)

Cox, T., *The Making of Managers: a History of the Irish Management Institute, 1952–2002* (Cork: Oak Tree Press, 2002)

Cronin, M., Regan (eds.), *Ireland: the Politics of Independence, 1922–1949* (London: Macmillan Press, 2000)

Crowe, C., Fanning, Kennedy, Keogh, and O'Halpin (eds.), *Documents on Irish Foreign Policy Vol. VI: 1939–1941* (Dublin: Royal Irish Academy, 2008)

Crowe, C., Fanning, Kennedy, Keogh, and O'Halpin (eds.), *Documents on Irish Foreign Policy Vol. VII: 1941–1945* (Dublin: Royal Irish Academy, 2010)

Curtis, R., *Tafelberg: the Hotel Tafelberg and the Battle of Arnhem* (Hove: BN1 Publishing, 2008)

Daly, M. E., An Irish-Ireland for Business?: The Control of Manufactures Acts, 1932 and 1934, *Irish Historical Studies*, 24 (1984), pp. 246–272

Daly, M. E., *Industrial Development and Irish National Identity, 1922–1939* (New York: Syracuse University Press, 1992)

Daly, M. E., the Irish Free State and the Great Depression of the 1930s: the interaction of the global and the local, *Irish Economic and Social History*, 38 (2011), pp. 19–36

Daly, M. E., *Sixties Ireland: Reshaping the Economy, State and Society, 1957–1973* (Cambridge: Cambridge University Press, 2016)

Duggan, M., *The People of Ormskirk Through the Ages, 1500–2000* (Stroud, Amberley Publishing, 2009)

Eliot, C., *The East Africa Protectorate* (London: Edward Arnold, 1905)

Ellis, E. L., *T.J.: A Life of Dr Thomas Jones, CH* (Cardiff: University of Wales Press, 1992)

Empire Exhibition Scotland 1938, Official Guide

Empire Grown Sisal and its Importance to the Cordage Manufacturer: Memorandum prepared by the Imperial Institute with the co-operation of its Advisory Committee on Vegetable Fibres, Empire Marketing Board (London: HMSO, 1928)

Ettighoffer, P., *Sisal: Das Blonde Gold Afrikas* (Gütersloh: Verlag C Bertelsmann, 1943)

Evans, B., *Ireland during the Second World War: Farewell to Plato's Cave* (Manchester: Manchester University Press, 2014)

Fanning, R., *The Irish Department of Finance, 1922–1958* (Dublin: Institute of Public Administration, 1978)

Ferriter, D., *The Transformation of Ireland, 1900–2000* (London: Profile Books, 2004)

Fisk, R., *In Time of War: Ireland, Ulster and the Price of Neutrality, 1939–1945* (London: Andre Deutsch, 1983)

Foot, M. R. D. and Langley, *MI9, the British Secret Service that Fostered Escape and Evasion, 1939–1945, and its American Counterpart* (London: The Bodley Head, 1979)

Forshaw, J. and Abercrombie, *County of London Plan Prepared for the London County Council* (London: Macmillan & Co, 1943)

Fox, J., *White Mischief* (London: Jonathan Cape, 1982)

Franck, K., Herlow, Huldt, Petersen, and Sorensen, *Design in Ireland: Report of the Scandinavian Design Group in Ireland, April 1961* (Dublin: Coras Trachtala/The Irish Export Board, 1962)

Freeman-Grenville, G., Obituary—Sir Eldred Hitchcock CBE, *Tanganyika Notes and Records, the Journal of the Tanganyika Society*, no. 52 (March 1959)

Girvin, B., *Between Two Worlds: Politics and Economy in Independent Ireland* (Dublin: Gill & Macmillan, 1989)

Girvin, B., *The Emergency: Neutral Ireland, 1939–1945* (London, Macmillan, 2006)

Guillebaud, C., *An Economic Survey of the Sisal Industry of Tanganyika* (Welwyn: The Tanganyika Sisal Growers Association and James Nisbet & Co., 1958)

Hindorf, R., *Der Sisalbau in Deutsch-Ostafrika* (Berlin, Reimer, 1925)

Hitchcock, E., The Sisal Industry of East Africa, *Tanganyika Notes and Records, the Journal of the Tanganyika Society*, no. 52 (March 1959)

Hodges, T., J. H. Forshaw: One of Britain's Leading Architects and Author of the County of London Plan, *South African Architectural Review*, June 1946, pp. 140–142

Hurstfield, J., *The Control of Raw Materials* (London: Her Majesty's Stationery Office and Longmans, Green and Co., 1953)

Huxley, E., *White Man's Country: Lord Delamere and the Making of Kenya* (London: Macmillan, 1935)

Huxley, E., *East Africa* (London: William Collins, 1941)

Huxley, E., *The Sorcerer's Apprentice: A Journey through East Africa* (London: Chatto & Windus, 1948)

Huxley, E., *The Flame Trees of Thika: Memories of an African Childhood* (London: Chatto & Windus, 1959)

Imperial Economic Conference at Ottawa, 1932: Summary of Proceedings and Copies of Trade Agreements, Cmd. 4174, Secretary of State for Dominion Affairs (London: HMSO, 1932)

Johnson, D., *The Interwar Economy in Ireland* (The Economic and Social History Society of Ireland, 1985)

Johnston, J., An Outlook on Irish Agriculture, *Studies: An Irish Quarterly Review*, 28(110) (1939)

Johnston, J., An Outlook on Irish Agriculture: Part II, *Studies: An Irish Quarterly Review*, 28(111) (1939)

Jones, G., *Captain of All These Men of Death: the History of Tuberculosis in 19th and 20th Century Ireland* (Amsterdam and New York: Editions Rodopi, 2001)

Jones, T. (Middlemas, K. (ed.)), *Whitehall Dairy, Volume III: Ireland, 1918–1925* (London: Oxford University Press, 1971)

Keefer, R., *Grounded in Eire: the Story of Two RAF Fliers Interned in Ireland during World War II* (Montreal and Kingston: McGill-Queen's University Press, 2001)

Kennedy, M. and Laing (eds.), *The Irish Defence Forces 1940–1949: the Chief of Staff's Reports* (Dublin: Irish Manuscripts Commission, 2011)

Kennerley, P., *Frederick William Dwelly, First Dean of Liverpool, 1881–1957* (Lancaster: Carnegie Publishing, 2004)

Kimaro, D., Msanya, Takamura, Review of Sisal Production and Research in Tanzania, *African Study Monographs*, 15(4) (December 1994)

Lane, A. (intro.), *Islamic Pottery from the Ninth to the Fourteenth Centuries AD in the Collection of Sir Eldred Hitchcock* (London, Faber & Faber, 1956)

Lock, G., *Sisal: Twenty-Five Years' Sisal Research* (London: Longmans, 1962)

Lukacs, J., *Five Days in London, May 1940* (Yale: Yale University Press, 1999)

McCague, E., *Arthur Cox, 1891–1965* (Dublin: Gill & Macmillan, 1994)

McCulloch, J. (under the pseudonym, Michaelhouse, J), *Charming Manners* (London: J.M. Dent & Sons, 1932)

McCulloch, J., *Limping Sway* (London: Michael Joseph, 1936)

Macintyre, B., *Operation Mincemeat* (London: Bloomsbury Publishing PLC, 2010)

McMahon, D., *Republicans and Imperialists: Anglo-Irish Relations in the 1930s* (New Haven and London: Yale University Press, 1984)

McMahon, P., *British Spies & Irish Rebels: British Intelligence and Ireland, 1916–1945* (Woodbridge, The Boydell Press, 2008)

Matheson, J. K. and Bovill (eds.), *East African Agriculture: A Short Survey of the Agriculture of Kenya, Uganda, Tanganyika, and Zanzibar, and of its Principal Products* (London: Oxford University Press, 1950)

Mayhew, P. (ed.), *One Family's War* (London: Hutchinson, 1985)

Miller, C., *The Lunatic Express: an Entertainment in Imperialism* (London: Macdonald & Jane, 1972)

Miller, V., *Nothing is Impossible: a Glider Pilot's Story of Sicily, Arnhem and the Rhine Crossing* (Barnsley: Pen and Sword Books, 2015)

Monsarrat, N., *The Cruel Sea* (London: Cassell, 1951)

Montagu, E., *The Man Who Never Was* (London: Evans Brothers, 1953)

Nicholson, V., *Singled Out: How Two Million Women Survived Without Men After the First World War* (London: Viking, 2007)

Nicolson, J., *The Great Silence, 1918–1920: Living in the Shadow of the Great War* (London: John Murray, 2009)

O Grada, C., *Ireland: A New Economic History, 1780–1939* (Oxford: Clarendon Press, 1994)

O'Halpin, E. (ed. and intro.), *MI5 and Ireland, 1939–1945: the Official History* (Dublin: Irish Academic Press, 2003)

O'Halpin, E., *Spying on Ireland: British Intelligence and Irish Neutrality during the Second World War* (Oxford: Oxford University Press, 2008)

O'Shea, M. R., *The Ropes, A History of Irish Ropes Ltd, 1933–1972* (Newbridge: Naas Printing, 2013)

Pakenham, F., *Peace by Ordeal: an Account from First-Hand Sources of the Negotiation and Signature of the Anglo-Irish Treaty, 1921* (London, Jonathan Cape, 1935)

Peters, M., *Glider Pilots in Sicily* (Barnsley: Pen & Sword Books, 2012)

Regan, J. M., *The Irish Counter-Revolution, 1921–1936* (Dublin: Gill & Macmillan, 1999)

Rigby-Jones, J., *Best Love to All, the Letters and Diaries of Captain Eric Rigby-Jones, MC and Bar and his Experiences as a Young Officer with the Liverpool Pals on the Western Front in 1917 and 1918* (Solihull: Helion & Company, 2017)

Ryan, C., *A Bridge Too Far* (London: Hamish Hamilton, 1974)

Ryle Dwyer, T., *Guests of the State: the Story of Allied and Axis Servicemen Interned in Ireland during World War II* (Dingle: Brandon Book Publishers, 1994)

Ryle Dwyer, T., *Behind the Green Curtain: Ireland's Phoney Neutrality During World War II* (Dublin: Gill and Macmillan, 2009)

Steinhoff, I., *Deutsche Heimat in Afrika* (Berlin, Reichskolonialbund, 1939)

Tebbit, A., *Escape from the Curragh* (unpublished)

Tomlin, B., *The Management of Irish Industry: a Research Report by the Irish Management Institute* (Dublin: Irish Management Institute, 1966)

Transactions of the Third International Congress of Tropical Agriculture: Papers Communicated to the Conference, Vol. 1 (London: John Bales, Sons & Danielsson, 1915)

Truesdale, D. and Esler Smith, *Theirs is the Glory: Arnhem, Hurst, and Conflict on Film* (Solihull: Helion & Company, 2016)

Tyson, W., *Rope: a History of the Hard Fibre Cordage Industry in the United Kingdom* (London: published by Wheatlands Journals Ltd for the Hard Cordage Fibre Institute, 1966)

Van Maanen, A., *Tafelberg Field Hospital Diary, Oosterbeek, 17–25 September 1944* (Oosterbeek: Uitgeverij Kontrast, 2015)

Verity, H., *We Landed by Moonlight* (London: Ian Allan, 1978)

Waddy, J., *A Tour of the Arnhem Battlefields* (Barnsley: Pen & Sword Books, 1999)

Warrack, G., *Travel by Dark After Arnhem* (London: Harvill Press, 1963)

Westcott, N., The East African Sisal Industry, 1929–1949: The Marketing of a Colonial Commodity during Depression and War, *The Journal of African History*, Vol. 25, No. 4 (1984), pp. 445–461

Wigglesworth, A., Sisal Growing and Marketing—A Virile Tropical Industry, *Empire Production and Export Magazine*, June 1934

Wigglesworth, A., *Wigglesworth & Co. Ltd: a Retrospective, 1895–1935* (London: Wigglesworth & Co., 1935)

Wigglesworth, A., The Sisal Situation Today, *The Sisal Review*, March 1938

Wigglesworth, A., *The Future of the Sisal Industry in East Africa and Sisal Marketing*, August 1946

Wigglesworth, F. and A., *The Gold Tangle and the Way Out: Meaning and Causes of the Great Industrial Collapse* (London: John Lane The Bodley Head, 1931)

Wills, C., *That Neutral Island: a Cultural History of Ireland during the Second World War* (London: Faber and Faber, 2007)

Wilson, T., *Victorian Doctor: being the Life of Sir William Wilde* (London: Methuen, 1942)

Wood, A., *The Groundnut Affair* (London: The Bodley Head, 1950)

Wood, I. S., *Britain, Ireland, and the Second World War* (Edinburgh: Edinburgh University Press, 2010)

Websites and Social Media

Feat of Arms—Operation Ladbroke and the glider assault on Syracuse, Sicily (www.
    operation-ladbroke.com/)
Foreign Aircraft Landings in Ireland—WW2 (www.ww2irishaviation.com)
Newbridge Down Memory Lane (Facebook group)
Ormskirk Bygone Times (Facebook group)
ParaData—a Living History of the Parachute Regiment and Airborne Forces (www.paradata.
    org.uk/)
The Pegasus Archive—the British Airborne Forces, 1940-1945 (www.pegasusarchive.org/)